MY STORY

GENERAL
PETER COSGROVE
MY STORY

HarperCollins*Publishers*

HarperCollins*Publishers*

First published in Australia in 2006
by HarperCollins*Publishers* Australia Pty Limited
ABN 36 009 913 517
www.harpercollins.com.au

Copyright © Pelynco Pty Ltd 2006

HarperCollins*Publishers*
25 Ryde Road, Pymble, Sydney, NSW 2073, Australia
31 View Road, Glenfield, Auckland 10, New Zealand
77–85 Fulham Palace Road, London, W6 8JB, United Kingdom
2 Bloor Street East, 20th floor, Toronto, Ontario M4W 1A8, Canada
10 East 53rd Street, New York NY 10022, USA

National Library of Australia Cataloguing-in-Publication data:

Cosgrove, Peter, 1947– .
  My story.
  Includes index.
  ISBN 13: 978 0 7322 8384 1.
  ISBN 10: 0 7322 8384 1.
  1. Cosgrove, Peter, 1947– . 2. Generals – Australia – Biography.
  3. Soldiers – Australia – Biography. I. Title.
355.0092

Cover and internal design by Matt Stanton
Front cover photo: Newspix
Back cover photo and photos on flaps: Australian Government Department of Defence
Typeset in 11.5/18 ACaslon Regular by Kirby Jones
Printed and bound in Australia by Griffin Press on 80gsm Classic

5 4 3 2 1   06 07 08 09

I dedicate this book to the two families I love so much.

First, and more than anything, my own dear wife, Lynne, and sons Stephen, Philip and David, and my sister, Stephanie, all of whom are the greatest source of inspiration and comfort to me.

Secondly, I dedicate this story to that other great family in my life, the men and women of the Australian Defence Force and their own families and loved ones — ordinary people who are extraordinary Australians. To have had their affection and support has always made me the luckiest of men.

Contents

Prologue

FRIDAY, 1 JULY 2005 — my last day in uniform. The moment I had thought about off and on for a few years as I faced the inevitability of retirement had now arrived; the moment I had thought about deeply over the last few months as I watched the calendar march down to my last few hours in the Army. Now it was upon me and I was stuck for words — even though they would be private rather than uttered out loud. I was standing in the Hall of Memory at the Australian War Memorial, at the foot of the Tomb of the Unknown Australian Soldier. I had decided to pay a last visit in uniform to that most symbolic of places — encapsulating beyond any other the ethos of being a soldier. I laid a wreath at the foot of the Tomb, stood back, saluted and groped for some meaningful words. All that I could come up with, after more than forty years in uniform, was 'I did my best, mate'. With that it was out the door into the pale sunshine of a chilly July late morning to farewell my staff and drive home with Lynne — out of the job, out of the Army.

To all intents and purposes, the great adventure was over. While I didn't have a definite idea about the future, I thought it would remain fairly hectic. Equally, I was sure that my participation in public events would be greatly reduced and thus my 'public profile' (a euphemism for mentions in the media!) would similarly diminish. I welcomed this prospect.

You can seek public profile or it can be thrust upon you. You can embrace it or run a mile from it. I am guilty of embracing it, but initially it was an accident of place and time. Back in September 1999, as the prospect of an Australian military commitment to East Timor grew stronger, I was in the job that would impel me to step into the limelight. As part of my confidence that I could do the job in East Timor, I accepted that I would need to be an available and proactive 'performer' in media terms. Still, I had no idea just how intense the public's interest in the campaign would turn out to be. I simply saw it as a fundamental duty and skill for a senior commander to be ready, willing and able to deal with the media in meeting the public's interest in what the military are doing. This translated to the jobs I did after Timor as Chief of Army and then particularly as Chief of the Defence Force.

A number of times after I returned from East Timor, I was asked if I planned to write a book about these hectic times. For six years, my quick response was a firm 'no!'. I was still serving, and I thought for a military officer to be considering writing a book post-retirement might suggest a lack of focus on the present. From time to time though, as the years rolled by, I would hear or read public comments and perceptions on one issue or another that I knew something about, and I'd think, 'Maybe one day I'll say something on the subject.' That grew into the idea of this book, which is no diatribe or manifesto, but simply the story of a young boy from Paddo who many years later found himself like a kangaroo in the headlights, running hard in order not to get flattened.

I hope you enjoy *My Story*.

I

The Early Years

ON THE AFTERNOON OF 28 JULY 1947, Warrant Officer Class 2 John Cosgrove was sitting on a tank turret in the middle of the Puckapunyal firing range in Victoria.

With apologies to the locals, 'Pucka' can be an awful place in the high summer or in the depths of winter, especially if you're sitting on top of a tank during a live firing practice. Round after round goes downrange with an ear-splitting, brain-rattling crack from the gun of the antiquated tank your student gunner is using to vanquish the imaginary foe. The discomfort of the cold and the noise had been heightened for Warrant Officer Cosgrove by the knowledge that, hundreds of miles away in Sydney, his wife, Ellen, and four-year-old daughter, Stephanie, were expecting the imminent arrival of a new addition to their family.

Suddenly, his grim pursuit of professionalism was broken by a radio call to cease fire because a messenger was about to enter the range with a message for the warrant officer. An Austin Champ in

Army khaki bounced across the paddock and came to a halt beside the tank. Out jumped the School of Armour Orderly Room Sergeant, waving a piece of paper and wearing a silly big grin.

A telegram from Cosgrove's father-in-law, Bob Henrys, announced the outcome: 'Born with a spout. Mother and Son both well. 6lb 12oz, born at 1015hrs' (Henrys too was an Army man!). With a roar of joy, Dad called off the gunnery practice then and there, and the race was on to put the tanks to bed and get to the sergeants' mess where (I am told) many beers were had to celebrate my arrival. Dad was a hugely popular and gregarious man, so it would have been quite a party.

Dad was the son of John Cosgrove but not named for him directly. (In fact, Dad was christened Cave John Francis Xavier Cosgrove. As soon as he was old enough he ditched his first moniker, Cave, because at school the other kids used to drive him mad teasing him by calling him 'little Cavey Cosgrove'.) John Senior was a giant of the Australian theatre and film industry in the early part of the twentieth century. A Falstaffian figure, he was a very prominent actor, particularly in repertory and touring companies. Dad was born when his father was forty-nine years old, the fifth child of this larger-than-life character and his first wife, Florence, herself an actress. Almost three years after Dad, his brother Bill was born. When Florence died, John Senior remarried twice, first to Mildred and then to Madeleine.

John Cosgrove Senior had no military background but he did have a great capacity for love and life in the fast lane. When he died in 1925, Dad was nine and little Bill just over six. Madeleine, without a breadwinner and without savings, somehow managed to keep things together, and the boys were both able to attend the prestigious Melbourne school, Xavier College.

When Dad was about fifteen, family finances had reached the end of their tether, so he left school while his younger brother stayed on for a year or two more. Jobs weren't falling off trees in those days, so Dad took whatever work he could get.

At one stage he thought he had fallen upon steady employment as apprentice to a couple of older fellows who were plasterers. Like most apprentices, he had all the drudge work to do, such as setting up in the morning, fetching and carrying during the day and cleaning up when they knocked off. On one particular evening, which happened to be payday, the two older fellows knocked off work but left Dad with instructions to dismantle the scaffolding, move it to another room and set it up for the next morning as they gave him his meagre wages.

He got as far as setting up the scaffolding in the new work area, but without tightening all the nuts and bolts. He had a big date that night, so he decided to head off and come back early in the morning to complete the job.

By now you will have guessed what happened. He was running late the next morning and arrived in time to walk through the door and find that the plasterers — with all their fresh plaster in drums and probably grumbling about their tardy apprentice — had unwittingly got to the top of the scaffolding. As Dad went to warn them, the scaffolding gave way; down came the plasterers, their tools and gallons of sloppy wet plaster. Dad did a smart about-turn and withdrew rapidly with howls of anguish and abuse ringing in his ears. He did not bother to give notice.

Next, he decided he might give the Army a try. Enlisting as a gunner in 1937, he was posted to the Coastal Artillery on Port Phillip Bay.

He had found his niche — an active life with tremendous camaraderie, enough money for a young man of simple tastes and a sense of belonging. He was a devilishly handsome youth, and I know from his old mates that he was an active 'cruiser' of the smart hotels and nightspots around the Bay, wherever glamorous young ladies down from Melbourne might be found.

On a Monday morning after one such weekend, Gunner Cosgrove, in his role as the 'lowest of the low', was out the front of the barracks at Fort Nepean. Dressed in a drab fatigue uniform and a large giggle hat, he was pushing a broom to sweep the roadway when he spied a very flash little red roadster hurtling up the road towards the main gates. Horrified, he dived into the bushes. The car pulled up to the guard room with a flourish and out stepped a sophisticated vision of loveliness, one of the leading lights of the Portsea set. Instantly, the guard commander bustled out to greet this beautiful young woman and enquire as to how he could help her. From his place of concealment, Dad heard her say to the guard commander that she had met a lovely man from the barracks over the weekend. She wanted to say hello to him now, so would the guard commander be a good chap and run off and fetch Lieutenant Cosgrove? Dad said he was not sure what the guard commander replied, because by that stage he was backing ever further into the bushes.

Soon enough World War II crashed over the horizon and Dad's coastal artillery battery had the distinction of firing Australia's first shot of the war, across the bows of a coastal freighter which had ignored the curfew by continuing to steam out of harbour. After much signalling with flags and lamps had brought no response, a shot was fired from one of the very large cannon (to miss, of course!) and that brought the anguished response from the freighter that he *had* heaved to but the Rip was still carrying him forward at a rate of knots. No harm done, in the end.

Dad was posted to Darwin and then into the Australian Imperial Force (AIF) where he had the dubious honour of being with the first Australians to be attacked by the Japanese on Nauru a few days after 7 December 1941. A flight of bombers (originally mistaken for American) came over and bombed his artillery battery and the island's facilities. He and his mates were evacuated off the island a while later in a Free French destroyer.

After that, Dad was posted to Ingleburn near Sydney. While there, he met Ellen Henrys. Mum was a bright, attractive and outgoing redhead who, judging by photos from the time, was an eye-catcher.

She and some girlfriends had gone to the Trocadero, the famous ballroom and nightspot in downtown Sydney. After a dance or two, Dad made a date to meet Mum at the State Theatre on the following Friday night to watch a movie.

On Friday, Mum, dolled up to the nines, was there right on time in the crowded foyer of the theatre, waiting for her escort to turn up. As the bells rang and the crowd drifted into the theatre to take their seats, there was still no sign of Dad. Mum cut a forlorn figure, waiting lonely and sad, a pretty girl stood up. As she went to leave the empty foyer, she took one last look around and spotted a figure lurking in the deep shadows of a pillar in one remote corner. The figure gestured her over and, as she got closer, she saw it was a soldier wearing a greatcoat and a slouch hat pulled down low over his face. It was Dad, a little the worse for wear. He was at that time a dispatch rider for his artillery unit and that very day had come off his BSA bike and skidded down the road face first. Fortunately his tin hat had saved him from anything worse than grazes, but even those were pretty spectacular. He was raw down one side of his face and covered in gentian violet or friar's balsam or some other lotion that made him look like the Phantom of the Opera. He had skulked into town and had hidden in the foyer wanting Mum to have the option of reneging on the date if he should prove too ugly to be seen in public. Mum thought he was a silly goose and they immediately went to a nearby Cahill's restaurant for dinner and the romance was launched.

In wartime the pace of life accelerates. Like many romances, theirs was a lightning courtship, followed by a lifelong, loving and happy marriage.

Dad of course met Ellen's dad, Bob Henrys. Born in country New South Wales late in the nineteenth century, Bob was a fit, strong country boy, hard as nails and ready for anything — perfect for the 1st AIF, which he joined in time for the campaigns in France from 1916 to 1918. He was a machine gunner in a machine gun battalion and was wounded several times. His most vivid memory of battle was the German breakthrough, which was brought to a halt by a mixed bag of Aussies under (then) Lieutenant Colonel Leslie Morshead (in World War II, the outstanding Commander of the Rats of Tobruk, 9th Division, 2nd AIF).

After the war, Bob Henrys married and had two daughters, the first of whom was Ellen. After leaving the Army for a few years, he had signed up again and, like Dad, when World War II broke out was serving as a regular soldier, a warrant officer in the elite Australian Instructional Corps. He was then in his forties and for a year or so helped to train the young men in the AIF heading off to the Middle East.

Bob eventually made it into an infantry battalion, the 2nd/19th, part of the 8th Division destined for the defence of Malaya. He was the regimental quartermaster sergeant, a tough job which involved getting and distributing the myriad of weapons and stores that the battalion needed for its overseas service. The heavy workload continued after the battalion got to Malaya and around September 1941 he sustained a burst ulcer, which made him very ill. He was evacuated to Australia and his operational war was over.

Looking back, I feel that, with his age and that ulcer, he would not have survived if he had gone into captivity with the rest of 8th Division. After recovering, he was back into training and administrative duties at Randwick racecourse, which had been turned into a military bivouac area for the duration. When his daughter Ellen brought Dad home to meet him, the two professional soldiers hit it off straight away.

Dad soon enough moved off to an endless round of training in North Queensland. The Island Campaign was an infantryman's war and, while artillery was used to smashing effect whenever possible, the difficulty of getting the guns across the most hellish terrain into position to engage the Japanese meant that relatively few field artillery units deployed forward. Late in the Pacific War, his frustration led him to transfer to the fledging Armoured Division then being raised in the west (presumably with some thought of a break-out campaign in terrain where armour could be useful in big groups). This too was unrealised, as the Australian land operations reached a high water mark in Borneo: for MacArthur everything after that on land was to have only the Stars and Stripes flying overhead.

When the terrible war finished, Dad had to think of a future for his little family, which now consisted of a wife and infant daughter (my sister, Stephanie, born in 1943). While the Army would be radically reduced in size, the new Australian Regular Army would continue to contain an armoured element of modest size, so Dad stayed on in the rank of warrant officer in the Armoured Corps.

By this time Bob's wife was ailing. When she died, Mum and Dad knew that Bob (Pop to us kids) wasn't in great health himself. They decided that Mum would keep house for us all, including Pop, and that we would stay put in Sydney, while Dad went where the Army required.

There weren't a lot of jobs for an Armoured Corps warrant officer in Sydney so, apart from a couple of years in the 1950s when he had a job at Parramatta, a phase of life of lengthy separations began for Mum and Dad, with Mum running the show in Sydney and Dad getting home about once a month for a few days.

This lasted for years, until I was a teenager. I really missed Dad and I felt sorry for Mum and Dad, who so obviously loved each other so much. Later, Dad managed to get postings closer to home and we saw him just about every night.

This was the family environment into which I was born, a loving, tempestuous Irish/Australian family with khaki uniforms and big boisterous men and a feisty, indomitable woman who gritted her teeth against the separation and played the hand dealt her with courage and enormous good humour. Our house was a place of laughter and debate, not scholarly but impassioned and shrewdly insightful. While I wish I had seen more of my dad while growing up, it was fun being a young Cosgrove.

And where was all this fun being had? Some time during the war, the family had moved into a little single-storey bungalow in Underwood Street, Paddington, exactly across the road from the Grand National Hotel.

In those days, Paddington (or 'Paddo') bore no resemblance to the Paddington of today, which is characterised by very high property prices and high income earners. Back then, it was an avowedly blue-collar suburb with people living in cramped terraces because they couldn't afford a modern designer home with a front and back lawn in the outer, developing suburbs of Sydney.

This did not breed seething discontent; it was just a fact of life. I knew instinctively that what characterised the Paddington of those years was a profound sense of community, of knowing about your neighbours and looking out for them.

When I was just a little fellow, my mum enrolled me in the Peter Pan Kindergarten, not far away in Union Street. Like most kids who have had the undivided attention of their mum, I was pretty dubious about this and needed to be coaxed down there, day after day. It was the usual kindergarten deal, with some activity and early learning lessons, lots of play both inside and outside, then lunch, a sleep, a bit more play and then time to go home.

I took a dislike to a particular carer there whom I shall call Mrs Sassafras (obviously not her real name). About this time I first saw the movie the *Wizard of Oz*, starring Judy Garland. Like most kids in that era, I was terrified of the flying monkeys and equally terrified of the Wicked Witch of the West. Mrs Sassafras was a dead ringer for the witch. To make matters worse, Mrs Sassafras doubled as the chief cook for our lunch. She seemed addicted to fish: fish mornay, fish pie, tinned fish, fishcakes, fish jelly — and even fish shakes for all I knew. I didn't like fish too much and when I inevitably demurred, a confrontation would erupt and drag on to the point where I felt sure that she would bring out the flying monkeys to take me away.

One day before lunch I had had enough, so I assembled a group of like-minded boys and we climbed the high cyclone wire fence and sneaked away up Underwood Street (where I think the plan was to take them to my place to hang out). I deeply suspect that one of the girls at the kindergarten dobbed us in, but we had made a good 800 metres or so before a teacher (breathing fire from her nostrils and flashing panic from her eyes) caught up to us and we were marched back into captivity. I was probably put on a 'no lunch' punishment, which would have suited me fine. I know that Mum was called to a deep and meaningful discussion with the principal of the kindergarten and I was given some stern counselling at home. Reflecting on this, I later figured that my mistake was to be selective in the gang for the breakout — I should have taken the lot, leaving no witnesses to dob us in!

I grew up with a small family of blood relations but an extensive family of 'social' aunties and uncles, close friends of Mum and Dad whom we called 'Aunty' and 'Uncle' and whom we respected and liked as if they were indeed our blood relations. Aunty Dot ran the grocery shop across the road and Uncle Cedric and Aunty Betty ran the barbershop next door to Dot. Just next door to Aunty Dot was Mr Beveridge who ran the fish shop and who was a proud Commo (a member of the Australian Communist Party).

Mr B was a good bloke who sold the very best fried and battered fish and chips and he would always give you heaps of the latter for threepence or sixpence. He was well liked by the grown ups but kindly dismissed as a raving Commo in a suburb and working-class society that was relaxed about, but in no way seduced by, communist notions. The spot in Paddo for political campaigning was the corner of Oxford and Elizabeth Streets, near the Paddington State School. The Commos would regularly set up there on Saturday morning and a couple of intense young men would harangue the passing proletariat and hand out leaflets, while Mr Beveridge (no orator) would stand there in his normal garb of felt hat, collarless white shirt, dark trousers and braces, arms akimbo, giving out an appropriately impassioned revolutionary air. I'm told he suffered moral agonies after the Hungarian Revolution and never had the same zeal again.

In an age before political correctness, local characters were nicknamed more for aptness than for charity. One fellow, who was harmless but simple, was known as 'Chesty Bub' for his penchant for wearing only Bonds athletic singlets above his trousers at all times of the day and night and in all weather. That covered the 'Chesty' part, the 'Bub' part came from his simple innocence. But nobody ever let him come to harm. He was a local, one of our community and a suburb full of ex-diggers and working-class Aussies took care of their own. Another chap was called

'Aeroplane Joe' because some disability had caused him to permanently have his head way off to one side and cocked upwards as if on the lookout for aeroplanes.

From time to time the roving two-up school, Thommo's, would settle in to Paddo down near the tip at the low end of Elizabeth Street. For the genteel urchins who roamed the streets, this was irresistible. Parents would rumble on about two–up schools, police raids and the like, so we all knew that Thommo's game was a big challenge for little, would-be stirrers. On one occasion, in a youthful commando operation, we did a reconnaissance and spotted several layabout youths standing around smoking Capstans and acting as cockatoos for the game. Hiding just around a nearby corner, we shrieked in unison, 'Coppers!' and watched, most gratified, as the cockatoos took up the cry and the gamblers went flying in all directions. We kids had the good sense to, as the cops would say, 'decamp in a northerly direction'. We might have a got a decent clout over the ears if we had been caught.

The SP bookmaker operated about thirty houses up the road from us in Underwood Street. The Book was run inside a lockup garage appended to one of the bigger terrace houses. It had a loudspeaker connected to a radio, extracts from the newspaper form guide tacked on to boards, a chalkboard with the odds on it and a milling crowd of punters studying the form, placing bets and listening to the races.

I knew all this from an early age because Pop would send me out to the SP to put on his bets on those occasions when ill health prevented him from going to the races, the dogs or the trots. (Mum didn't really like me going up there but everybody in our street knew that the likelihood of a raid by the local police was almost zero, although on the odd occasion, for form's sake, an external group of police might put in an appearance.) For a young fellow, going to the SP to put on a bet was initially quite exciting, but after a while I became somewhat blasé about it. The cockatoos, the other patrons and the bookie got used to seeing me intermittently and would always ask after Pop when I was there in his place.

Pop was a superstitious chap and any number of things could put the mozz on his day or night at the races, trots or dogs. But without doubt his biggest phobia on race day was to receive ha'pennies in his change from any source — that was enough to cruel the whole day. He had been known to shout in frustration and rage and storm off the tram when a tram conductor handed over ha'pennies when he bought his ticket. From time to time (not often!) when he had sent us on an errand to go and see Uncle Ced at the barber's to buy a packet of Champion ready-rubbed pipe tobacco, we would sneak ha'pennies into the change which we would then innocently hand over for the glee of watching him have a fit.

He was a flamboyant and melodramatic loser: when he returned from Randwick on a Saturday, Mum would call out, 'How did you get on?' and he would reply, 'Have you got my fare to the Gap?', or sometimes, 'Hide the bread knife!' (phrases we have kept in currency in the family over the years). On the odd occasion when he had made a killing, he would come home with his pockets stuffed with fivers and tenners and we kids would be allowed to discover the money in his jacket pockets. Then it would be presents all round and feasts of poultry and roasts.

On one occasion at Randwick, when somehow he had tickets for the Members' enclosure, he took Mum and Dad to the races as a special treat. In a particular race the red-hot favourite was beaten and the crowd was incensed and staged what the newspapers of the time used to term 'a noisy demonstration'. Noisy, that is, in the St Leger and the Paddock, but decidedly not so and never in the Members — except on this occasion. As the hoops dismounted in the saddling enclosure, the dignified silence of the Members' area was broken by Pop leaning over the upper deck railing and, with a fist-shaking gesture, giving the jockey an absolute spray, rich with the colourful language that soldiers sometimes use. Mum and Dad wanted to shrivel up and die, and I think that was the last time Dad ever went to the races.

Pop was a Labor man through and through, an official in the clerical union of the Commonwealth Public Service. He helped the famous knockabout Federal Labor member Eddie Ward in a few of his campaigns (not that he needed much help in the Eastern Suburbs of Sydney in those days). Like many Labor stalwarts he was caught up in the ideological and religious pressures which caused the great schism in Labor in 1955. The Catholic Church took a deeply anti-communist political role in this turmoil within socialist ranks and for a man of Irish Catholic background like Pop, it was a dilemma creating volcanic pressures. It rose to a head during the election campaign in late 1955 when the family was at Mass at St Francis in Paddington. I must have been there as an eight year old, but I don't remember it. Mum and Dad certainly recalled every painful moment. The young priest celebrating Mass was using his sermon to rail against communism and all its evils. Pop was sitting there quite relaxed because like the vast majority of Aussies and Labor supporters he had no truck with Commos. However, things turned when the priest started to pay out on the Labor Party, leading to the rhetorical flourish that 'A vote for the Labor Party is a vote for communism'. Enraged, Pop shot to his feet from the middle of the congregation and in his parade ground voice bellowed, 'You lying bastard!' He stormed out of the church, never to be seen there again. I think Mum and Dad probably wished they had gone to an earlier Mass.

Now and then, the Little Sisters of the Poor used to wander around Paddo, door-knocking at the homes of the Faithful for cups of tea and, if the hosts were willing, a couple of laps of the rosary. Mum and we kids were very observant Catholics, as was Dad on his visits home. Pop was recalcitrant. The nuns knew precisely the background but were never deterred. When they called, they would always enquire after him to Mum at the front door. If he was home he would twig they were there and he would yell out to Mum, 'Tell them to bugger off!', and similar enjoinments.

My primary school in those days was a little parochial school attached to the church and called by the same name, St Francis Paddington. In the lower grades, it was a co-educational school run by the Sisters of Charity. In the upper primary school grades, we were segregated into separate boys and girls classes, with the nuns teaching the girls and the Christian Brothers teaching the boys. I did really well academically at primary school, principally because I learnt to read very early and was devouring newspapers by the time I was eight. Mum was the prime influence in this regard. I have a vivid memory of talking to her about the Hungarian Revolution in 1956, discussing and debating newspaper articles on the subject.

Our school may not at that time have been multicultural but it sure was multi-ethnic. Our classes were a fair old mixture of Anglo-Celtic, Southern European and Eastern European background kids with the discipline being tough and the learning very much by rote. The nuns were enormously holy and, as I now know, somewhat unworldly. But they were absolutely disciplined and dedicated both to their religion and their responsibility for us kids. My first football coach in the St Francis Paddington under eights rugby league team was a nun who, while training us at Centennial Park in full habit, used to hitch up her ankle-length robes and fly along beside us exhorting us as we manfully tried to catch, kick, run and pass. She was also the woman who taught us a somewhat distorted version of a well-known rugby league adage, her version being, 'they can't run without their heads'.

It was about this time that Dad and the family enjoyed a period when he was posted back to Sydney, to the 1st/15th Royal New South Wales Lancers, a Citizen Military Forces unit based at the Lancer Barracks in Parramatta.

By now Dad was a Warrant Officer Class 1 and the regimental sergeant major of the regiment. This was during that period of the first national service scheme when the Army was awash with soldiers and regiments such as the Lancers were full to overflowing.

Not all of those soldiers were thrilled out of their socks to be in the Army, so a regimental sergeant major had plenty of scope to improve discipline and attentiveness to training in the ranks of his unit. I vividly remember one Sunday as a young fellow, about nine years old, hanging around in one of the laneways of the barracks. The lane was absolutely jam-packed full of junior soldiers in full ceremonial uniform waiting to be called on to parade and not looking 'over the moon' about it. None of them would have noticed me or known who I belonged to if they had.

Around the corner at one end of the laneway came my dad, marching like a large mechanical man. As he moved along the length of the laneway, his head swivelling left and right, his booming voice was issuing rockets and instructions non-stop and soldiers were leaping to their feet, dusting themselves off and generally looking a lot more sharp and interested.

As he disappeared around the corner, that well-known aftermath in such army episodes took place. A ripple of *sotto voce* remarks, universally uncomplimentary, volleyed forth. Some of the remarks were more *voce* than *sotto*! Scandalised, I took off after Dad, caught up to him some distance away from the scene of the crime and tugged on his sleeve. When he asked me what was up, I whispered in his ear the general tenor of what I'd heard and even some of the words that had been used. He surprised me by saying that being a regimental sergeant major was not to be an entrant in a popularity contest.

The pub opposite our house was always very interesting, especially on evenings late in the week when the crowd got a bit rambunctious. There was a public bar, which in those days was men only, and a ladies' parlour, exclusively for women. I suspect that most of the ladies who went there had their menfolk in the public bar. It was not uncommon to see local ladies go in with a paper bag full of unshelled peas or other vegies needing preparation, and the saucepan in which to place the vegetables after they had been prepared.

It seemed that the public bar was crowded most the time and there were a few stalwarts in the ladies' parlour who were often there till closing time. I know all this because my bedroom was at the front of the house and my window overlooked the street. As I got a little older, I would set myself up at the window to watch the excitement across the road. Most nights at closing time there would simply be drunks saying endless farewells to each other and some colourful and ribald language, but occasionally there would be a dingdong, rolled-gold stoush — right there in the street — with an instant crowd shouting either admonishment or encouragement. On one celebrated occasion, two women from the ladies' parlour staged a knock-down, drag-out battle which would have rated highly overall for energy (if not skill) and which left nothing out in the area of colourful language.

It was unusual to see the paddy wagon, known by us as 'the trawler', attend any of these closing time escapades. In fact, it was altogether unusual to see the cops around the streets. I'm sure they would attend a real emergency, but at no stage did they anticipate that this daily rough-and-tumble would ever seriously challenge peace and harmony in Paddington's streets.

However, there was one memorable occasion when a woman, who'd had a great deal to drink, was causing a nuisance at the pub, and the publican apparently called the Paddington police station for assistance.

Whoever was in charge there sent down a very young, baby-faced probationary constable. When he got to the pub he found to his horror that the woman was so drunk, she could not walk and was virtually incoherent, except that she remembered all the bad words she knew and was using them on him. By this stage the crowd had emptied from the pub and gathered to watch the fun. The poor constable had her by one arm as he desperately looked around for a way of getting her away from the crowd and ending his own vast embarrassment. Some unlucky cab driver came along just at that moment and the constable hailed him into the footpath. He opened the back door of the cab to put her in, but at that point she recovered enough to grab both sides of the open doorway with her hands and spread her feet so that she looked like a starfish that was definitely not getting into the cab. By now the crowd was almost hysterical with laughter and offering gratuitous advice. In desperation, the constable stood behind her and put his foot on her rump to push her into the cab. As he did so, her dress rode up and it became obvious that she had forgotten to put on certain underwear! Large, strong men were so weak with laughter that they clung to each other for support. The policeman eventually got her into the cab and back to the station. She had a night in the cells; he immediately transferred to Darlinghurst.

In my last year of primary school, I found myself 'volunteered' to be an altar boy at St Francis. Learning the ropes about how you serve on the altar and the duties you had to perform in the sacristy was pretty straightforward. I even found the Latin easy to memorise. All in all it looked like I would soon be garbed like an angel and looking like a cherub as a fully-fledged altar boy. There were others in the 'training programme' so to speak, but I was the fellow who, by all reports, would be next cab off the rank. One day, presuming on my seniority and preferred status, I was hanging out in the sacristy with the other trainee altar boys, waiting for the priest to arrive. Alas, temptation overcame me and I found myself garbed in the priest's robes, handing out absolution, hearing confessions and generally raving on in Latin, to the vast amusement of my fellow trainees. In walked the parish priest. It was an ugly moment. That was the end of my altar boy career but, in an ironic twist, I was obliged to help all the other boys master the Latin liturgy so that they, in their turn, could become fully fledged.

These carefree days of attending a good, solid and safe school, close to home and reflective of the robustness and the exuberance of the community it served, drew to an end. It was time to go to high school. I suppose that, given the family's modest income and the trend of boys leaving St Francis in those days to attend high schools of pragmatic and limited horizons, I was a little surprised when Mum and Dad suggested that I might go to the most prestigious Catholic boys high school in the Eastern Suburbs, Waverley College.

It's not until you become a parent that you appreciate how careful, concerned and involved parents are in selecting a school and in monitoring their children's progress and development at the school. And it's probably not until you are a parent with a child at a school that you appreciate the huge responsibility of care and emotional and intellectual nurturing that we place on the men and women who teach our kids. It's probably no exaggeration to say that, next to the family, the most important institution or factor in a young man's or woman's life is their school. As I grew older, I came to appreciate the huge advantage that a good education conferred, not just in the academic and intellectual disciplines, but in the core values that guide one's feet through life. I came to appreciate that, after the gift of life itself, one of the greatest gifts my parents gave me was to send me to a really good high school.

At that time, I didn't know much about Waverley except that it was run by the Christian Brothers. I knew a little bit about them from the fact that they had taught me for the last three years at St Francis. I knew also it was a large school, with a number of classes within each year or form. Finally, I knew it was a red-hot sporting school and, while I loved cricket and had played a bit at primary school and in the street in Paddo, that and footy had been somewhat of an afterthought at St Francis.

So, like any kid changing schools anytime, anywhere, I was quite apprehensive when, in my new boater hat and my two-piece dark blue serge uniform, I attended the first day in First Year (these days, Year Seven) as a new boy at Waverley. In no time at all I made great friends who travelled with me throughout those hectic days. Reflecting on those years, I think I gained an instinctive appreciation that I was comfortable belonging to an institution, which certainly great schools, particularly sizeable schools, are. This did not mean that I flourished, that some magnificent butterfly emerged from some unattractive carapace. I was a capable but lazy student and an interested but unfit and somewhat weedy athlete, especially on the rugby field. I was much better at cricket, but that is more a comment on my rugby than my cricket.

I did what was the usual round of subjects in those days — mathematics, English, physics, chemistry, Latin and French. I had a love of English in particular and was good at the other subjects but always too lazy to turn this into high scholastic achievement. For some reason, certainly no part of a master plan, I did debating at school. It was good fun and we won some prizes, but in a muscular school like Waverley it was not the sort of pursuit to attract high admiration. Nonetheless it gave me early experience at that sense of 'dry mouth' which everybody experiences, especially performing in front of strangers.

Of course, like most other young fellows at Waverley College, I joined the school cadets. In those days you would need a clever excuse not to, and thus the Waverley College cadet unit had over 400 boys in it. For my part, I was very much a volunteer, no doubt because of my dad and Pop. I was in the cadets from Second Year and rose up through the cadet ranks to end up as the senior cadet.

This many years away from when I finished at Waverley, my time there has to some degree fragmented into vignettes, such as the May Day Procession, a celebration of the Blessed Virgin at the College: hordes of boys reluctantly at school on a weekend, milling riotously (in what, as a military man, I would now call the Assembly Area) until, harried and chivvied by brothers and lay teachers like stockmen working cattle, we were led piously to the Grotto to invoke Our Lady's blessing on our school. I remember one year the class know-all pointed out a prominent old boy, Johnny O'Keefe, in the crowd. Parents would often attend and, more than once over the years, I felt my dad's laser-like eyes burning into the back of my skull as I quietly played the fool with my mates during the service.

Vignettes such as the annual retreat (a word which I came to dislike in later life!). The secondary school would troop off down to Mary Immaculate Church to be seated on the left-hand side of the church while the girls from St Clare's were on the right, with brothers and nuns patrolling the aisles to ensure it stayed that way.

(I seem to recall that even looking across the aisle would attract a whack.) There, in what could only be described as racy language by the standards of the day, Redemptorist Fathers, obvious specialists in the terrible temptations against which they were warning us, would boom and denunciate until we were all quite purified. This state of purification would often last for several hundred metres as we trooped piously back to school, even though some of the Romeos among us would have used the proximity of the girls in the church to confirm subsequent assignations. At my first retreat, such was the power and passion of the invective from the Redemptorist priest in the pulpit that I wondered if he might shoot lightning bolts from his eyes at some awful guilty boy, or if his head might explode with pious rage!

Vignettes such as the important footy games, the athletics and swimming carnivals: the delirium of seeing our champions prove yet again what we knew and what we desperately wanted them to show — that Waverley was the best school there ever was.

Schoolboys are hugely tribal at great schools such as Waverley College.

After a winter's week spent subverting the school dress and behaviour rules and participating in petty scandals, which made the headmaster puce with rage, a week spent lolling about in class, giving very poor return on Mum and Dad's money for fees, a week spent minutely considering the great contest for the weekend, Saturday would arrive and the school would assemble at Queen's Park where the school had its playing fields. As our gladiators in blue emerged from the sheds, no more fervent cheer ever greeted a Wallaby team. Huddles of prefects on the sidelines, squabbling over the choice of war-cry as the school waited expectantly, a short pause as they pompously dispersed to lead the cheer and then a crash of sound as the first and probably only intelligible word of the selected war-cry, 'HOOLIPOP!', split the afternoon air. HOOLIPOP!? It sounds a little strange when I write it here, perhaps a little funny. But we were dead serious then. We were sending these words as spears of our intent, as the strength and speed of those who were not on the field, to reinforce and uplift our brave knights. As a postscript, though, I am glad that war-cry was largely unintelligible because my imperfect memory tells me that it included reference to a 'slick red gollywog'. There are some strange minds which invent these things!

When we won, as we often did, what a glorious feeling to be a Waverlian. It was at those times that I learnt the enormous power of esprit de corps, when people feel individually and as a group that nothing is beyond them and that they have become part of something great. (I am somewhat unreconstructed when it comes to school sport and competition.)

Then there were the days when the Cadet Corps paraded. Early dismissal from class in order to bustle about putting uniforms to rights and drawing rifles from the Q store, forming up in the street, settling in to a long silence before faintly heard orders and the crashing brilliance of our band. If you were more of Mars than Minerva, you could imagine this long line of boys in uniform, swinging away to fight the savages, albeit conveniently located a stone's throw away at Waverley Park, while the good citizens of Henrietta Street, bordering the school, watched us go with quiet pride and perhaps a tear in the eye for our anticipated gallantry. The return, in the gathering gloom of evening, savages vanquished, for the dismissal. This was always presided over by the teacher who headed up the cadets, the inestimable Brother Farrell, 'Boris' — awesome and immense in his uniform, up on a raised level — who looked down at the massed ranks on the school tennis courts like Caesar surveying his legions. It always has surprised me why all of the boys didn't join the Army, given that experience. More seriously, you can tell from my description that my thoughts were turning to a life in uniform at about this time.

Among the many great teachers there, one stands out — our headmaster Brother M.M. O'Connor, Michael Maximus, better known to all us boys as 'Mad Mick'. We respected him and sometimes feared him, and at times quietly mimicked his eccentricities, but we always saw him as a man of great integrity and principle, and we were fiercely proud of him as our headmaster, the headmaster of the best school in Australia and therefore naturally the world (nothing wishy-washy about a Waverley opinion!).

I found out personally about the tremendous energy and ferocious focus Brother O'Connor brought to all his time at the College. He was capable of kindness, but really didn't want any boy to think he was a soft touch.

One lunchtime when I was in Second Year, I was mucking about with a horde of other kids in the cricket nets when, while running at full speed, I tripped and fell headlong into an iron post. I just got my arm across my head in time to take the impact on my forearm. Result: a bung arm (a compound fracture, as it turned out) and blood. Back in class, the Brother told me to go and see the Head immediately, so off I went with my school bag on one arm and blood dripping off the other.

The secretary noticed that I was a little pale and told Mad Mick that I wanted to see him, but that was all. A few minutes passed and as I stood there feeling very sorry for myself, there was a steady drip, drip, drip of blood off the end of my fingers. Eventually looking up, the secretary noticed this and called out, 'Brother, can you come straight away please?' Brother O'Connor came steaming out, mumbling to himself about idle boys trying to get out of classes, etc.

I was pleased to see his immediate look of concern, but then he exclaimed, 'Good heavens boy — what possesses you? Don't stand there, bleeding on my carpet, get out, get out. In fact, go home and get some Dettol on it!' As I stumbled away, I heard him telling the secretary that he was certain that he would have to have the carpet professionally cleaned. He had that knack of making you feel that you must never knowingly create obstacles to the imparting of a Catholic education.

Humour aside, he was a colossal figure. On one occasion, Cardinal Gilroy made a routine annual visit to the school. As usual, he addressed a school assembly. We patiently (and somewhat knowingly) endured the well-meant but obscure sermonising, waiting for the Cardinal's last few words. The 'knowingly' part was that, by tradition, those last few words were the Cardinal politely inquiring of the headmaster whether, due to the auspiciousness of the day, it might be possible for the school to have a half-holiday from that moment. We were horrified on this occasion to see that, when the Cardinal finished his holy thoughts, he stood back with a vague but final smile, obviously having overlooked the most important part of his whole visit.

Mad Mick went up vastly in our estimation when we saw him step forward and quietly mutter into the Cardinal's ear. In a second the Cardinal's grievous omission was rectified. Only one cynic suggested it was because Mad Mick wanted to get off to the SP bookie that afternoon. The rest of us saw it as an act of true mercy.

As my school years drew to a close in 1964 — in those last few days when the Leaving Certificate class goes slightly mad — pranks and hoaxes abounded, and Brother O'Connor had had enough. He called a school assembly in the quadrangle to read all of us the riot act about this nonsense, finishing with a dire injunction that the next boy found perpetrating a prank or hoax would be expelled, even though he was about to leave.

Just at that moment a giant cement truck full of wet cement tried unsuccessfully to pull into the quadrangle to deliver its load, 'as ordered by Brother O'Connor'! Mad Mick nearly dropped dead with rage. No culprit was found — lucky for him.

All these years later, I think it's safe and proper to reveal to you, Brother, as you watch from up there, that it was me who ordered the concrete.

For me, 1964 had been my second go at the Leaving Certificate. In 1963, my laziness had reached a zenith and my results, while a bare pass overall, were inadequate for any reasonable further academic study. Noticing that I was performing at below periscope depth, my mum and dad and the teachers concluded that I would be looking at repeating Fifth Year in 1964 on both the obvious grounds of crook marks and sadly, equally obviously, my immaturity.

So that year, as well as pulling my socks up academically, I had to give the most serious thought to what to do after leaving school. A number of possibilities crossed my mind in those accelerating months before finishing school. I thought of the law, teaching, journalism, the police force and of course the Army. All involved communicating and all of them were very much occupations involved with dealing with people.

I must say I was quite confused at this time: I didn't see myself as an above-average communicator or leader, but I wanted to be. And I didn't see myself as a particularly active or adventurous person, but I wanted to be.

Dad was keenly interested in whatever career I thought I would like, but when I said that I was thinking of the Army, he exhorted me to have a go at being an officer. Dad had the most abiding affection for all of the enlisted ranks in the Army but he always held that a good Army was run by officers who have the loyalty and respect of the warrant officers and non-commissioned officers (NCOs).

What he said made a great deal of sense to me. At the same time, a few other people I knew through Mum and Dad, through the school and through the parents of one or two of my school friends were lukewarm on some of my other ideas about a career path. For the time being, I discarded none of them and concentrated on knuckling down to my studies in order to keep my options open.

August was the closing date for applications for the Royal Military College, Duntroon. On the basis that it wouldn't hurt to apply, I did so, and soon after was caught up in the procedure of initial medicals, psychological tests, aptitude tests and some rigorous interviews.

I did well enough in these, but was quiet and overshadowed in the outdoor aptitude test, to the point that, when the Selection Board members voted, it took the casting vote of the President of the Board (who happened to be the Commandant at Duntroon) to accept me provisionally into Duntroon, dependent on exam results and a more detailed final medical.

I only found this out years later when, as a reasonably successful and middle-aged officer, I had access to my cadet file at Duntroon. Thinking back, I believe that the Selection Board was right to have its doubts — but I am also profoundly grateful to the President for his casting vote! This has always made me very conscious of the many fine young men and women over the years who would have made top quality officers, but who didn't get the same lucky break as me. Of course, at that stage all I had from Duntroon was the opportunity: much still depended on medical fitness, exam results and, ultimately, on my own decisions.

I did much better in the Leaving Certificate in 1964 than I had done in 1963. In fact, to my great surprise, I gained a Commonwealth scholarship. This would have allowed me to attend University for any number of courses. But the long holidays after the exams had given me the opportunity to reflect on how I thought I would best be able to make my way through life.

Sometime in early January 1965, I decided to go to Duntroon. My marks were well and truly good enough, but now there was the little matter of a final medical. On the due date in January, I attended a medical appointment out in an army barracks in the military reserve at Watsons Bay in Sydney.

There I met a young fellow my age, the son of an old soldier who was a good mate of my dad. Mick McDermott was a Marist Brothers Parramatta boy, a larrikin with a conscience and soon to become my lifelong best mate. Initially we just said hello and went off for our various medical examination activities.

I immediately hit trouble. In what was then a 'buyer's market', the Army had quite stringent medical entry standards. One of these was related to colour perception. A book full of coloured dots was handed to me. The coloured dots made patterns and within the patterns were various numerals. I was invited to nominate which numerals I could see on particular pages. I could see some of the numerals on some of the pages, but decided that some of the pages were designed to trick me by not having any numerals, so I forthrightly declared that there were no numerals on those pages.

Bad move.

Another doctor was summoned to see this fellow who had dodgy colour perception. Fortunately, there was an alternative test, and I was taken into a darkened room and a shown red, green and amber lights, which I easily identified.

The next obstacle was a simple test on the flexibility of various limbs. In one of these a young doctor made me lock my left elbow by my side while I rotated my wrist and hand. I had broken this arm twice over the years, so it hardly rotated very much at all. The doctor became concerned. He ducked out of the surgery and fetched another doctor, an enormous jovial figure whom I recognised as being an old mate of my dad's. On hearing what the problem was, the older man stroked his chin for a moment and came up to apply the test to me again. He asked me to turn my left wrist and hand and then, looking deeply into my eyes, invited me to do a similar manoeuvre with my right elbow locked by my right side. I turned my (normal) right wrist and hand but only to the same limited degree as my left and the older doctor exclaimed triumphantly, 'See! I thought so — they're both the same, no problems!'

After the battery of tests was finished, the remaining holidays went by in a blur, with my trepidation and anticipation growing by the moment. Late in January 1965, Dad and Mum took me to Central Railway Station in Sydney for the train ride to the unknown, to the Army and to the rest of my life. I secretly felt like running off and hiding, but my years in the nest were over — it was time to fly.

2

Duntroon

IT WAS A NERVOUS YOUNG Peter Cosgrove who got onto the train at Central Station in Sydney in late January 1965.

I had a lot of growing up to do, both physically and emotionally. Although I had been away from home from time to time on school cadet camps, each of those absences had been for no more than two weeks or so. Now I was facing at least six months before I would see my home or my family again: the policies of the day were that young men were not permitted to have loved ones or family as visitors for much of the first half of the year. As we steamed south, I noticed that dotted around the carriages were a number of young men who looked pretty much like me, and I deduced they were also on their way to Duntroon.

A few hours later, we were at the main Canberra railway station at Kingston. As we got off the train we encountered a team of very highly polished, stern-faced and businesslike drill instructors from Duntroon. In short order, we were sorted out and put on the buses for the short ride across the new Lake Burley Griffin to the College.

Sitting on the bus beside me was a fellow who seemed about my age (although years more mature!), a powerfully built calm individual, precisely the sort of chap the College would be looking for.

I decided that it was in order to break the ice and strike up a conversation. I started off by asking him what school he had gone to. He replied by mentioning one of Sydney's most famous GPS schools (the most prestigious of the city's private schools). I was impressed, but not surprised — he had that look about him. I asked him whether he had been one of the prefects and he nodded briefly and said that he had been the school captain. Again I was not surprised, but silently noted ruefully that I had not been captain of Waverley. I asked whether he had been in the school cadets and, guess what, he had been the senior cadet! (So had I, but at this stage he was well ahead on points.) Ploughing on, I asked him about sport. I observed that his school had done very well in the GPS rugby competition in 1964, and asked if he played senior football for the school. He replied that he had played for the first XV and had had the honour of being the captain. I remarked that his school had also done very well in the number of players selected for the combined GPS side and, of course, he had done that too. (I think I played in the Waverley Eighths or some other lowly grade.)

Very despondent now, I asked him about cricket and to my joy he admitted that he hadn't played cricket at school. (I had and, although I was no world-beater, I had done better than at rugby.) I decided to press home my advantage, and asked him why he didn't appear to play a summer sport. I should have known better: he explained that he had no time left for cricket because of rowing and that he had been stroke of the eight when his school had won the Head of the River (the ultimate accomplishment for a Sydney GPS school).

We sat in silence for a moment and then he turned to me and said, 'What about you?' I said morosely, 'I'm on the wrong bus!' He turned out to be the most marvellous fellow and we all thought the world of him at Duntroon. However, I wish I'd sat next to somebody a little less accomplished on that short ride to the College.

The induction and orientation process into Duntroon was frenetic and harsh. There was an extremely demanding routine, strict discipline and intense study (which, while not intellectually demanding, was overlayed onto all the other stuff and was like doing mental arithmetic at high altitude — hard because of the environment). I was under the gun from the very first day — untidy, disorganised, unfit and generally late.

A few days after our arrival, we were whisked out of the College to an orientation training camp out on the Murrumbidgee River. Here we received a high pressure version of recruit training, living in tented accommodation and working for about eighteen hours a day. Here also I came to the unfortunate attention of two officers, one who became Chief of Army many years later and one who, a few years later, was my Company Commander in Vietnam.

We had been doing rope climbing training, involving using the correct technique to climb a 20-foot rope. After the triumphant instructor showed us how to do it, he announced that we could now all in turn climb up and down the rope twice each without touching the ground. I had a feeling that I might touch the ground a little sooner than he had ordained. Going up once was no trouble and coming down was a question of resisting gravity. Going up the second time was problematic. Each reach up the rope became shorter and shorter, each moment of progress further apart, each glance up revealing the head of the rope still impossibly remote. About 3 feet from the top, my muscles shut down as my body said, 'Time to go!' I fell in a crumpled heap at the base of the rope, retaining only the breath to loudly proclaim at the moment of impact what we term a 'soldier's expletive'.

As I lay there, working out the extent of the spiflication which would be visited upon me, I saw two sets of army boots. As my glance rose, I saw that the boots were attached (eventually) to two army heads, tut-tutting away about my bad language. I gleaned from this that all would have been well if I had been more stoic, more Spartan, just more jolly decent about the whole thing.

Back at Duntroon, we returned to the College life. This consisted of an academic course run by a teaching staff of dons, concurrent military training under the auspices of a large military training team and the day-to-day life of the College.

College life was loosely supervised by officers but was the particular domain of the senior cadets. Early on in our time back at the College all new cadets participated in the Novice Boxing. This was organised as a round-robin competition in weight divisions. There was nothing voluntary about it — every new cadet not actually harbouring a disabling injury was in. We got some rudimentary training from our physical training staff, and then it was on for young and old. All the cadets from the three more senior classes attended these afternoons of boxing over about a week, for the glee of watching young blokes punch each other's heads in.

In the limited training we had had before the 'knockout' (ha ha!) rounds of the competition, we had naturally been eyeing off people about our own size and weight to get some idea of the opposition we would face. About my only consolation was that I was unlikely to fight the fellow who was rapidly becoming my best mate, Mick McDermott: he was a little lighter than me and I had a shrewd idea that he could fight like a thrashing machine. Apart from that, I saw plenty to worry me, including a young bloke from Caboolture called Trevor Taylor whom the Physical Training Instructors (PTIs) were always calling on to demonstrate boxing moves because he had considerable junior boxing experience back home.

On the day of my first bout, I went from my room in the barracks to the gymnasium like a man trudging to his execution. In the chummy atmosphere of the dressing room my (no doubt equally terrified) opponent and I were gloved up together and then it was out to where the roaring crowd eagerly awaited the next gladiatorial contest.

When the bell rang to start the first round we rushed at each other and disappeared into a mutual world of whirling arms and brown clad fists, with a PTI as referee dancing rapid circles around us and occasionally shrieking unintelligible instructions. The crowd must have got their money's worth because at one stage I noticed that my opponent was lying down and I had been sent to stand in the corner. Mine was a very popular weight division and this was just the first of many fights I had to front up to.

Just before one of these fights (about my third or fourth), the senior PTI came up to me and told me that the cadet I was to fight had just arrived at Duntroon (having been delayed from entering with the rest of us due to some issue concerning his academic qualifications). He had not had the benefit of even the vestigial boxing training we had. The PTI asked me to 'go easy on him'.

As a boy from Paddo, I was instinctively against letting anybody punch me in the head while I was 'going easy'. Anyway, I did my best and we danced around each other for a minute or so until this chap essayed a left hand which hit me in the mush, whereupon I hit him everywhere from the roof of his mouth to the soles of his feet. That was the end of that. The senior PTI hissed at me very bitterly in my corner as they were assisting this chap out of the ring, 'You're a fine one to give instructions to!' I looked suitably chastened but privately reflected that at least I wasn't the one being carried out of the ring.

The final arrived. I was in — and so was Trevor Taylor. I felt sure I was about to get a first-hand boxing lesson but fate intervened in the form of a know-it-all senior classman in Trev's corner who effectively nobbled him with some dud advice, along the lines that he had seen me fight, that I had no real technique and Trevor should just come in and knock me out without resorting to any fancy stuff. When the bell rang, therefore, Trevor joined me doing the 'whirling dervish'. Things having descended to my level, I was mightily relieved to see Trev doing an impression of a back two-and-a-half somersault with tuck late in the first round.

Despite having won my weight division, I became clear in my view that the Novice Boxing should not be compulsory. There is no doubt that army officers should have physical courage. Equally, though, I found it distasteful that mates of mine should be judged on the basis of their cheerful (or otherwise) willingness to be struck in a fairly unscientific punch-up, by more senior people sitting around in chairs and forming opinions. A few years later there were one or two other aspects of life at Duntroon I took for granted and participated in and about which I came to have a different view.

Life now settled into a routine, which you might find comforting in that it might convey an image of me adapting to requirements and responsibilities. Not a bit of it!

My routine was that I would wake up in the morning earlier than just about everybody else. This was because, at dawn or before, I would have to be at the edge of the parade ground with my webbing equipment and my rifle to do a half an hour of intensive drill, preceded by an inspection. This little diversion, known as defaulters' parade, was the daily purging of an ever-accumulating list of indiscretions and shortcomings to do with equipment cleanliness, uniform smartness, room tidiness and punctuality. The insidious thing was that I was not just starting my day about an hour earlier than just about everybody else but I was adding to my chances of receiving more sanctions, for example during the inspection part of the defaulters' parade. Simply, it pretty much ceased to have a corrective effect because I had built up so many of these summary punishments that I just factored them as a constant into my life.

Some may say that I was struggling to keep my head above water. All these years later, I think it was rather that I was swimming underwater quite happily and from time to time popped up for a bit of air. That's somewhat self-serving, but accurately describes how my life was at that time. Some of my mates were on a similar 'under plateau' but I took the cake.

This obviously also affected both my studies and my reputation with the staff. On the study side I was already a lazy student, capable of swotting and squeaking through but never getting my teeth into my studies, even on subjects I liked. The spiral of petty 'crime' and petty 'punishment' made it too easy to vegetate when I should have been studying. This combination of a bloated punishment record and emaciated academic marks indicated to the staff that I was dodgy. Interestingly, a few people sensed that, despite this, I had something to persist with. People like the famous regimental sergeant major of that time, Tom Muggleton, who thought that I might go all right with diggers, if I made it through the College. Some of the highly polished officers of the staff, themselves closet larrikins, harboured the same heretical thoughts.

Tom himself was a thoroughgoing professional whom we all loved even if he occasionally had to contribute to the correction of my chronic recidivism.

Virtually every morning, rain or hail or shine, the cadet body would assemble on the terrace edging the parade ground, march on to the music of the band and form in great ranks ready for an inspection of our dress followed by dismissal to our various classes or perhaps some drill practice for a half an hour or so on one morning a week.

One particular winter morning was very foggy and, from where we stood on the terrace, we couldn't see the line on the parade ground where we would be forming up in ranks. Tom Muggleton was roaming up and down near us on the terrace as he normally did and, being a keen-eyed devil, he obviously noticed something amiss with my dress. He said nothing at the time.

At the appointed moment, we all marched onto the parade ground. Predictably, when we formed up on the inspection line we could not see the terrace from whence we had come. Tom, who had remained on the terrace, came to us as a disembodied voice through the mist. He launched into his usual critique of the sloppiness of our drill in getting onto the parade ground.

Suddenly he stopped and then shouted out, 'Wait a minute, wait a minute. Who is that in the centre rank of Kokoda Company? Is that you, Staff Cadet Cosgrove? It is, and now I look at you, I see that you have a twisted boot lace on your left boot. Not good enough — you've got an extra drill!' A great gale of laughter erupted from the ranks at this demonstration of supernatural eyesight. I chanced a look down at the offending boot and, you know, he was right — it *was* twisted!

Good fun, but yet another extra drill.

I was in my second year at Duntroon when I received the first bit of the type of sad news that we all endure as our lives go on — the death of a beloved relative. One Sunday in the barracks a grave-looking senior classman came up to me, drew me to one side and told me that my grandfather had died overnight.

I was devastated. In my young life to that time I had never lost a loved one, and it hit me very hard. For all those years when my dad was posted away from Sydney and the family home, Pop had been a stand-in father, at least as far as a loving male presence in the house was concerned. I was quite sure he was the greatest grandfather a boy could have, flamboyant and moody though he could be. I couldn't get to his funeral a few days later, which was very sad, but Mum, Dad and my sister, Stephanie, gave him a send-off for me as well.

It is very sad when you first experience the fact that a loved one has passed from being an immediate and anticipated presence to a memory, no matter how vibrant and cherished you strive to keep that memory. The week of ordinary work that followed was tough for me, because even mates who give you a pat on the back move on quickly to the day-to-day needs of life, and you have to as well.

My life of running hard to inch ahead continued. It would be nice to think that, for a dashing officer cadet, the doldrums of discipline would be counterbalanced by the raptures of romance. Sadly, most of the raptures were in my imaginings. At school I had been much too shy to think about a girlfriend, and looked in awe upon those fellows who seemed so relaxed and dynamic with all those delightful young women who would come along to the football and other school functions on their arms.

Nothing about the routine and environment of Duntroon was designed to help a young bloke like me to be more romantic and accomplished. On the other hand, time was passing me by, and fellows like Mick McDermott were already in stable relationships with young women they had met before they came to the College. A significant number of our classmates had also met young women from the Canberra area and were enjoying female company almost from the time when we as the Junior class first started to have leave on weekends. I was definitely behind the eight ball and, in any event, being in so much lower-level strife, there wasn't actually a lot of romancing time.

Nonetheless, an opportunity came when a senior officer working at Army Headquarters thought that it would be fun for his teenage daughter and her friends from school to have a formal dinner party at their home and that partners might be found from the Junior class at Duntroon. One of the staff at Duntroon selected a handful of us young cadets — who were promptly volunteered for the occasion.

Dressed up nicely in the virtual civilian uniform we all wore (tweed jackets, shirts and ties and tailored slacks), we turned up at the appointed time to a nice home somewhere in old Canberra. We were greeted by a tall, imposing man in a long-sleeved shirt, cravat and slacks. You could tell, from his bristling moustache and eagle eye, that this was the doting father and senior army officer.

The young ladies were very nice and we young cadets did our very best, but it was hard to be suave when you had a senior officer hovering over your shoulder to offer you a platter of peas or some more gravy. Despite this, we all had a lovely evening and I was emboldened to ask one of these young ladies to be my partner at the Queen's Birthday ball, which is held at the College in June each year. We cadets would perform a ceremonial parade in the morning, play our hearts out at football in the afternoon and then pick up our partners and go off to dinner somewhere in Canberra before attending the ball from, say, 9 or 9.30 p.m. until late.

As far as the Junior class were concerned, the major temptation was having the opportunity to dine in a nice restaurant and thus access to wine and other alcoholic drinks, prohibited to us on all other occasions.

My mates and I took our partners to the Canberra Rex for dinner. My partner, a lot more sophisticated than me, ordered some form of oysters as an entrée. I had never tried oysters before but thought I would give them a go. These arrived tastefully arranged on what, in the dim light of the restaurant, I took to be a bed of boiled rice. I didn't like the taste of the oysters at all, but would die rather than admit it, so I manfully gulped them down before frantically looking for something to take away the taste. Taking up a tablespoon, I scooped up a large portion of the boiled rice and popped it into my mouth.

It was rock salt! Still trying to be dead cool, I chewed this up as if it was an everyday thing, little realising what its ultimate effect would be.

After the meal, as the ladies strolled off to the powder room, I was having a little whinge in the foyer about the oysters and the rock salt. One of my mates suggested that the best way to settle my stomach was to have a stiff whisky, so we each had a double.

Bad move! A short time later at the ball, as I was dancing away with the nice young lady, a wave of nausea overcame me and I had to turn on my heel with the briefest of muttered excuses and walk very quickly out of the ballroom. In the corridor, jam-packed with cadets and their partners, the walk became a trot which became a sprint until, hands over mouth, I barged into the nearest toilet. Sadly, it was the ladies toilet. All the ladies in the lavatory were hugely impressed and the word spread rapidly about what a remarkable chap I was. If I had walked nude through the ballroom, wearing naught but a clown hat, I could not have done more damage to my romantic potential.

I tried to sublimate the resulting blight on the romantic dimension of my life, by throwing myself into sport and in particular rugby, to which my growing size and new fitness had to some degree provided a key. Playing footy at Duntroon was a lot of fun. At school I enjoyed the game moderately well, but the game did not enjoy me. It was only when I went to the Army in 1965 that I blossomed, as it were. I became much bigger, much stronger, much fitter and discovered the sense of mongrel that helps enormously in a game of rugby. Canberra rugby in those days was somewhat dog eat dog, with no quarter given to young fresh cadets with gazelle-like speed and public school manners. I had neither, and was to some degree a lumbering angel of retribution from the cadets' point of view. I had learned my footy from the Sisters of Charity at my primary school in Paddo in Sydney and I never forgot that nun's observation: 'they can't run without their heads!'

Unfortunately, my playing style had attracted unwelcome attention from the ACT rugby referees' association. As a result, before a particularly tough encounter against Queanbeyan, a little bird told me that the referee had been instructed to keep the closest possible eye on 'Number 6' — me! — who was inclined to be very violent.

What to do? The leopard could not change his spots and the game would certainly descend to those depths in which I was most comfortable. But could I change my spots? I formed a plan. My good friend and classmate, Trevor Taylor, was a loose forward in the same team and, as luck would have it, about the same size and colouring as me. Alas, Trevor was also very gullible. Before the game, I surreptitiously swapped my jersey with Trevor's and he put mine on without noticing. As we ran on and some swine pointed out the error, he mildly accepted my muttered explanation that, 'I must have mixed them up in the sheds — too late to change now, sorry mate!'

It was great fun for the first few minutes of the game to see the ref watching Trevor like a hawk, waiting for an indiscretion (no cleaner player than Trev ever pulled on a boot).

What I didn't know at the time was that a similar little bird had told Queanbeyan that the ref would be looking to jump on 'RMC Number 6'. Consequently they saw a great chance to get square on him (i.e., me) and to let the ref do the rest. Poor Trev got belted in every ruck, maul and lineout, in tackles and behind play, everywhere but in front of the ref. When Trev eventually lashed out at some vicious provocation, the ref blew the pea out of the whistle and gave Trev one of the most vociferous cautions ever heard, to the effect that his reputation had preceded him and the ref was having none of these gutter tactics, that if there was one more transgression, one sharp intake of breath even, perhaps only an impure thought, he — Number 6 — would be sent from the field, his eyes would be plucked out, his family would be sold into slavery, and he would certainly have no supper.

Poor old Trev — 'perplexed' is an inadequate word to describe the look on his face! With the ref's attention irreversibly focussed on him, I was free to play my normal game, which to a great degree redressed Trevor's earlier sufferings, at least from my point of view.

The sharpest irony occurred just before full time when, from the corner of his eye, the ref caught me involved in something unacceptable and called me to account. Indeed he summoned Trevor over as well. The lecture to me went something like this: 'RMC player, what you just did was unnecessary and dangerous, but I will excuse you from other than this caution because I believe you to be basically a fair player, unduly influenced by this thug in the Number 6 jersey.' I could but nod reluctantly in agreement. I have never forgotten Trevor's noble but unwitting sacrifice on that day!

As the final year propelled us inexorably towards the next phase of our lives as the Army's newest commissioned officers, we received our Corps allocations and our postings. In many ways this was to set the scene for the rest of our careers: that routine choice by higher authorities about whether we would serve in the Infantry, Armour, Ordnance or some other part of the Army would to a large degree determine the sort of jobs we would get in the future and our consequent career path.

Our first posting would also be both our first challenge and first opportunity — generally speaking, the greater the opportunity, the greater the challenge.

With Vietnam in full swing, almost half of the sixty-six graduates from the class of 1968 expressed a desire to go to the Royal Australian Infantry Corps, the backbone of the Regular Army, and the group which in the last several decades had borne the burden of the Army's fighting in Korea, Borneo, Malaya and, over the last few years, Vietnam. Nearly thirty of us may have wanted to go to the Infantry Corps, but there appeared to be spots for no more than about twelve to fifteen. In the end the authorities made room for nearly twenty, and I was delighted to be one of them. By this time I had clawed my way up from ignominy to mediocrity, eventually finishing a smidgen better than halfway up the class rankings, which, given the depths of my descent, was a pretty fair effort. Even some of the sceptics on the staff thought that I might be an acceptable junior commander.

A month or so later, we received the postings which gave us the particular jobs we would be doing in our new Corps or branch of the Army. In my case I was posted to 1st Battalion, the Royal Australian Regiment (1 RAR), at that moment engaged in a tremendously active and meritorious tour of duty in Vietnam. Sounds like good news for an aspiring young warrior, doesn't it?

Not for a moment! I would only be joining the battalion after they were due home to Australia in early 1969.

On the bright side, after a very short period of leave, the battalion was due to pack up and go to Malaysia for a two-year tour of duty as part of Australia's ongoing garrison commitments in that country. This meant that, by the time the battalion came home from Malaysia and I was available to join another unit for duty in Vietnam, I would be considerably senior, possibly looking at temporary promotion to captain and thus unlikely to go on operations as a platoon commander (the real operational grounding for an infantry officer). Equally unpleasant to contemplate was the possibility that the war might be over by that time: young men are always acutely aware of what is happening *now* and want to join in *now*, in case they miss out.

All of the other graduates heading off to infantry were posted to various Regular Army infantry units. I noted with great jealousy that one of our colleagues was due to go to Vietnam with 6th Battalion, the Royal Australian Regiment (6 RAR), in mid-1969 and, all other things being equal, he would be the first of our class to go to war. My partner in this anguish was my best mate, the redoubtable Mick McDermott, who had also been posted to 1st Battalion. Still, it was like being picked for the Thirds when you are hoping to be picked for the Firsts: you play as hard as you can for the Thirds and hope that the future takes care of itself.

In our graduation week the realisation finally hit us: we were finished, we were going, we had succeeded, we were about to be commissioned officers in the Australian Army. At our Graduation dinner in December 1968, a nostalgic affair in the cadets' mess, someone spontaneously started up the popular song of the time by

Mary Hopkin, 'Those Were the Days'. The song was picked up by the graduates and the Junior cadets and rolled around the mess, echoing for chorus after chorus as we confronted our future — for many of us, off to war.

Our Graduation Parade on 11 December followed a timeless ritual and by all reports was a good show. Mum and Dad and my sister, Stephanie, were of course among the proud families watching on. For me, and no doubt for my comrades in the Class of '68, the most significant moment came as we left the ranks of the rest of the cadets and formed up in a solid block of young men to march off the Duntroon parade ground as a class for the last time. In that dense mass of uniforms, in that square of comrades, was the future of the Army. They were and are remarkable men. I have always been so proud to be one of them and so grateful for their friendship, which, as much as any other factor, is why I survived to enjoy such a long and happy career in uniform. Our numbers are smaller now, war and the accidents and illnesses of ordinary life having thinned our ranks. Whoever now among us in the future is the last man standing will be remarkable as a member of the Class of '68.

3

Overseas for the First Time

AFTER A VERY BRIEF LEAVE I reported to Holsworthy in Sydney, then Australia's largest military base.

I started work with a group known as the Australian Component of 1 RAR. The battalion was still in Vietnam, and our job was to prepare for their efficient homecoming and also to set in place arrangements for them to go to Malaysia straight after all these veterans had returned from leave. The Australian Component had a lot of officers and NCOs but very few other ranks. The senior ranks would replace those people who would leave the battalion after getting back from the war. As is normal, the vast majority of the junior NCOs and soldiers would stay on for lengthy tours of duty in battalions, so most of our lot would be heading off to Malaysia. The plan was that most of the new young officers in the Australian Component would become platoon commanders in the battalion after it got back from its post-operations leave.

During this period of limbo, we concentrated on getting to know each other as a group of young officers who had not served together before. McDermott and I were inseparable except that he went off and got married, which put the crimp on our Friday night parties. Nonetheless, we still found plenty of opportunities to work hard and play even harder.

One of our number was a young national service second lieutenant, Jeff Kennett. Jeff was irrepressible, exuberant and irreverent. In him I found a fellow who was likely to get into more trouble than me, which was saying something. I vividly recall one evening when he and I were playing a game of squash. Both of us were pretty hopeless, so we were well matched. Our play was characterised more by vigour and rushing around than by skill and tactics. At one decisive point, Jeff fetched a drop volley that I had dollied up to the front wall from where I was standing at the back. Having got to the front wall in time and with me still at the back, he should have popped it gently back on the front wall, leaving me no shot. Instead, he gave it a ferocious whack which came back to me on the fly. Thinking, 'I've got you now sport!', I replied by giving it everything on the forehand, intending the ball to hit the wall close to him, fly to the back and in turn, leave him with no shot.

This was all well and good, but my placement of the shot was faulty and, instead of hitting the wall close to him, it rocketed straight at his head. At the crucial moment he turned to have a peek at what was happening and wore it straight in the eye. For a long moment the ball remained stationary in his eye socket like a large black monocle. For a long moment he remained frozen. Then he gave a mighty shout and flew backwards through the air, crashing onto his back on the squash court floor, as the ball dribbled out and I rushed forward.

He didn't ask for a let, so it was my point, but under the circumstances I thought we should call the game off. Jeff spent nearly two weeks in the Repatriation Hospital at Concord wondering if he would be blind in that eye, but as you all know, there's nothing one-eyed about Jeff Kennett!

The battalion in Vietnam contained a large number of national servicemen, many of whom would finish their prescribed time just after the unit returned home. Taking this into account, the authorities posted groups of soldiers from other battalions in to make up the numbers before 1 RAR headed off to Malaysia.

One such group came from 3rd Battalion, the Royal Australian Regiment (3 RAR), itself not all that long back from Vietnam and now based at Woodside, near Adelaide. This group of twenty-five or so had travelled from Adelaide to Sydney by train and were picked up at Liverpool station by a couple of army trucks. Now this particular group of soldiers could quite emphatically be described as desperados and that's probably why 3 RAR felt they could do without them. Apparently on the train over they had been on the singing syrup for the entire journey, and were the worse for drink when they arrived at Holsworthy, obstreperous and rowdy. In fact, one of the clerks who had been trying to get some sense out of them told me in awestruck tones, 'Sir, they've even drunk their own aftershave!'

The Adjutant of the Australian Component of 1 RAR was a taciturn but very decent man, Eric Pearson, a Duntroon graduate a couple of years ahead of me. When he heard about all these atrocities, he sized up the situation and decided that, rather than locking them all up (the cells weren't big enough!), he would use the discipline of drill to return them to better behaviour.

When he looked around, he noticed that he didn't have any experienced and grizzled senior NCOs with the right background to command obedience from this group of villains. He wasn't confident that the collection of NCO clerks he had available would be able to achieve the right effect. He found me skulking around the headquarters and gave me the job. As the son of a regimental sergeant major and a very frequent defaulter on such drill parades myself over the last few years, I must admit I was an inspired choice. So one of my first jobs as a young officer was in this very basic way to gain the attention of and return to disciplined behaviour a group of drunken diggers. It worked out okay, but it wasn't quite the heroic, understated impression one dreams of creating.

The officers in the Australian Component of 1 RAR were a mixed bag. Most of the young officers were fresh from places like Duntroon, Portsea and Scheyville. Several had been commissioned for a while and these fellows almost all had operational experience in Vietnam.

One of them had been very severely wounded in the Battle of Balmoral, fought between 3 RAR and a numerically superior attacking force of the North Vietnamese Army (NVA) and Vietcong (VC) soldiers in the Tet offensive of 1968. He was a really good bloke and a party animal, but his wounds and his convalescence meant that he couldn't sustain late hours or very much to drink.

Another great character was Major Felix Fazekas. Felix was an extraordinary man. A Hungarian by birth, he had as a teenager been a member of the Hungarian military forces under German control during the last year of World War II. On emigrating to Australia, he joined the Australian Army and was highly regarded and widely admired for his professionalism and courage during his service with the Australian Army Training Team – Vietnam, for which he was awarded the Military Cross. (The Training Team mentored and accompanied South Vietnamese Army units on combat operations.) He was a bit older than the average major, craggy, crewcut and tough as nails, with a thick Hungarian accent to boot. He was the battalion operations officer and part of his additional duties in getting the battalion ready to go to Malaysia was to act as our teacher in the Bahasa language. We are probably the only group of Aussies who speak Bahasa with a guttural Hungarian intonation!

Felix's family was in Adelaide at this time, so he lived in the officers' mess. One Friday night, a group of the younger officers, including me, were partying in one of the rooms when our chum who was convalescing decided to leave the party by dint of falling fast asleep, unable to be woken without at least a bucket of water. It was then that some good-natured fellow decided it would be better for us to carry him to his room down the other end of a long corridor.

This simple plan started to become embellished. It was decided that he couldn't just be carried, but that he must be borne aloft. Somebody remembered that there was a new door not yet fitted to its frame leaning up against the corridor wall, and this would serve as a splendid Spartan shield. The idea of a quasi-military funeral now took hold. In a flash, steel helmets were brought from rooms, candles gathered from the dining room and fixed with wax to the top of the helmets and we were almost ready to go. Another wag said it would be best if the effect of the candles was not spoiled by the lights in the corridor, so somebody dashed off and pulled out the appropriate fuse from the fuse box, killing all lights on that floor. Lacking a band to play appropriately solemn music, we decided that we would chant the words from 'Poor Jud is Dead' from the musical *Oklahoma!*, substituting our mate's name for Jud.

Finally we were ready. We lit our candles, placed our helmets on our heads and raised our mate, now reverently laid supine and asleep on the door, arms folded piously across his chest, and set off slow-marching down the corridor. Even in our befuddled state it was pretty impressive — pitch dark, lit only by the flickering flames of the candles illuminating the shadowed faces of the bearers, and the still and ghostly form of the 'deceased', with an unearthly dirge rolling down the echoing corridor.

Unfortunately, Felix was sound asleep in a room some way down the corridor and was woken by this strange chanting. By his own later admission, he was pretty spooked by this and not comforted when none of his light switches would work. With trepidation, he opened his door and peeked into the corridor, only to get an eyeful of the mock funeral. It all became too much. He gave out a mighty shriek in a thick Hungarian accent, and slammed and locked his door, ready to sell his life dearly if these evil spirits should come after him. No amount of explaining and buying him beers could mollify him for several weeks, but we won him round in the end.

Soon enough the battalion had reconstituted in Holsworthy and we were off to Malaysia for a two-year stint of garrison duty at a base called Terendak, close to the town of Malacca. We were to be part of a British Commonwealth Brigade whose other members included Kiwis and Brits.

I went up with one of the very early drafts of soldiers and their dependants. It was a long and uneventful flight to Kuala Lumpur (albeit for me very exciting because it was my first overseas journey).

When we arrived, we were waiting to board buses when I saw some Malaysian soldiers, who had been participating in a guard of honour for the King elsewhere at the airport, strolling along holding hands! A senior Aussie NCO standing nearby noticed my goggle-eyed look and with a grin explained that it was quite common in Asia for men to hold hands. How much we have to learn in our endless study of even our nearer friends and neighbours.

I was only in Malaysia for about four months, but it was an incredible period of learning, about the Army and my job as a junior commander, about life out of the cocoon and about the richness and depth of another culture.

As soon as the battalion arrived in Malaysia, all of us new officers were slotted into proper jobs instead of the makeshift work we had been doing back in Australia. In my case that meant that I was a platoon commander in Charlie Company.

As it turned out, I was the only officer in the company without operational experience. My canny commander was the legendary Tony Hammett, an Olympian at the Rome Olympics, a pilot, a distinguished infantry commander on combat operations and very much a larger-than-life personality. My two fellow platoon commanders had both quite recently returned from commanding troops on combat operations in Vietnam. One had a Military Cross and the other had been mentioned in dispatches.

After we had been in Malaysia for about six weeks, the whole battalion went off on a major exercise down in the dense jungle area in the state of Johore. At about this time, the Army had scheduled a course of study for officers who needed to do their promotion exams and this affected both my company commander and the company second-in-command. That meant that they would not be joining the exercise, so another officer would need to be nominated to command Charlie Company. When Tony Hammett went through this with us in his office, I nearly fell off my chair when he stated that, as I was the senior lieutenant (I was a full lieutenant and the other two platoon commanders were second lieutenants), I would command the company on the exercise.

I was a little apprehensive about whether I would have the personal qualities to do this big a job at the ripe old age of twenty-one. However, I knew that I would have the support and cooperation of the other platoon commanders, John Salter and Gordon Hurford, and the Company Sergeant Major (CSM), Ken Phipps. In any event, the Army never gives you choices on these issues, and so your job is to get on, do the best you can under the circumstances and hope that it all works out.

At one time during the exercise, the company was moving through the jungle in single file. John Salter's platoon was leading, followed by company headquarters (where I was) and then the remaining two platoons. This jungle was very thick and we were marching on a compass bearing to get to a particular track junction.

We were sneaking along, trying to be as quiet as possible when, from somewhere up in the forward part of the column, I heard loud shouting and exclamations, entirely against the noise discipline we were trying to observe. I grabbed the radio handset from my signaller, angrily called up my brother platoon commander, John Salter, and asked what on earth was happening. He told me that they were passing through a swarm of wasps and they were stinging the living daylights out of his men. I made some remark like telling them not to be sooks and to keep moving, without all the noise.

In keeping with this instruction, my headquarters unit kept moving on the same line — and you can guess what happened next. As the wasps descended on us, one stung me on the backside, through my trousers. It was as if somebody had whacked me with a red hot needle. I was wearing a big pack and a lot of heavy equipment, but still jumped about 4 feet vertically, and came down clutching my behind tightly in two hands.

I realised not only that I had been an idiot in not allowing Salter's platoon to deviate from the given direction of our march, but that if I wanted the company to keep its discipline we had better make a very quick detour. We did this by making a right turn and marching about 50 metres directly to our front before turning left, back into a single file, and back on our course.

Lesson learnt by me: even hardy Australian soldiers can be defeated by highly motivated stinging insects — and even highly motivated young commanders would do well to keep a bit of commonsense about them.

A day or so later, we were in a defensive position astride a major track through the jungle. We were digging in to produce individual fighting trenches, machine-gun bunkers and command posts and doing the other million and one jobs that infantry do when they are constructing a defended position with a few rudimentary tools and a lot of hard work and sweat. I got a radio message to tell me that the Commander of the Far Eastern Land Forces (FARELF), the Commonwealth multinational command under which the brigade and thus our battalion fell, would visit Charlie Company in about half an hour.

The Commander, Lieutenant General Sir Peter Hunt, was a distinguished British officer, making his first visit to 1 RAR. As is normal in such visits, he would be accompanied by our own commanding officer. No sooner had I got the radio message than a soldier came huffing and puffing up to me, as I stood knee deep in a trench I was digging, to say that a 'bunch of trumps' had turned up about 50 metres away on the road in a convoy of Land Rovers. I turned to the CSM and rolled my eyes, but he said, 'You'll be right boss.'

I hurried out to greet the VIP group on the roadway and there met the lieutenant general, the Kiwi who was the brigade commander and my own CO. I briefed them on our layout, our mission, our organisation and the number of soldiers I had. This briefing was a lively affair with me giving information and the lieutenant general chiming in with questions. From my point of view it all went very well. But the amusing part was that my CO, standing directly behind the lieutenant general during this dialogue, kept appearing over the lieutenant general's shoulder or round the side of him after each question or comment, mouthing the reply he thought I should make with a somewhat anxious smile on his face. It was hard for me to keep a straight face and give proper replies while this pantomime was occurring. The CO meant well, of course, but it was off-putting to say the least.

Things were quite 'regimental' in the 1 RAR of the day. We living-in officers all had batmen who were locally employed Malays and who had been doing the job for years. These men kept us spick and span in the extraordinary heat and humidity of tropical monsoonal weather.

On my first morning in the officers' mess, my batman, Saleh, a middle-aged family man, woke me with a cup of tea and vanished. When I moved off to the communal bathroom, I returned to find he had laid out all my kit, gleaming, starched, immaculate. (Oh Saleh, where were you when I was going through the purgatories of Duntroon?) After I got into my underwear, Saleh magically reappeared to dance attendance while I put my uniform on. I thought this was a little overzealous, but realised why a moment or so later. I began to put on my starched green cotton short-sleeved shirt and my green shorts (equally starched to razor creases). I had just done up the various trouser buttons when, quick as a flash, Saleh dropped to his knees in front of me and, to my shock, raced his hand and arm up the leg of my shorts, grabbed my shirt tail and hauled it down with great vigour, until it sat to his satisfaction at my waistband. I was somewhat wide eyed at this but kept my cool and later asked the other blokes how they had fared. They'd all got the same treatment. You needed to be broad-minded.

Garrison life was pleasant enough and we quickly got into a routine of military training, sport, a little bit of internal tourism in Malaysia and great rollicking weekends in Singapore, Kuala Lumpur and even Malacca. Very enjoyable in itself, and I was learning a lot, but I still pined for the opportunity to serve on operations in Vietnam.

Like a bolt from the blue in late June 1969, a message was received by 1 RAR from Army Headquarters in Canberra saying that two junior infantry officers from the battalion were to be dispatched in late July as reinforcements to serve with infantry battalions in Vietnam. What is more, the message from Canberra said that Lieutenants Cosgrove and McDermott should be the officers sent.

Oh joy, oh rapture! It was a bit tough on Mick because he was recently married, but I was absolutely footloose, fancy free and raring to go. My company commander, Tony Hammett, was very happy for me but sat me down and told me in no uncertain terms that there was much that he had planned I should learn before being sent off to Vietnam. He told me that, as of now, he was embarking me on a crash course of study to ensure that I was up to scratch before I left Malaysia.

He was right. My days suddenly became longer, as Tony and all the other experienced men in the company, from my fellow platoon commanders to even junior soldiers with operational experience, in ways direct and subtle filled my waking moments with vital information and handy hints. Even at the time I appreciated their efforts but later came to fervently bless Tony's judgement, care and patience in relation to getting me ready to command troops in combat. Some time in there I phoned Mum and Dad and told them what was happening and they were quietly supportive. Now these many years later, having had one of our sons go off to war, Lynne and I can appreciate how they must have been feeling.

At that time, it was customary for departing officers to present an item of silver to the mess. In this way, the mess hoped to build up over time a handsome collection of silverware to dress the table on formal dinner nights and other mess occasions. Plenty of officers' messes have this tradition but it somewhat galled Mick McDermott and me on this occasion because we had been in the unit for such a short time and we were expected to provide something of substance by the President of the Mess Committee (who was also the battalion second-in-command and, we thought, did not like us very much).

One Saturday not long before we left, Mick and I were sitting in Malacca having a quiet beer and trying to come up with an idea on what silver we might present. After a sarcastic comment about the atmosphere engendered in the mess by the mess president, one of us suggested that a coffin with a silver plate attached would be appropriate.

A masterstroke! We immediately went into a huddle to plan this little rebellious gesture, with neither of us having any idea about how much a coffin would cost. We asked a taxi driver to take us to a coffin shop, which was on the road out of town towards the garrison. I had all the money but not very much, so I would do the bargaining.

When we walked in, the Chinese proprietor asked us how he could help. When I replied that we had come to buy a coffin, he immediately summoned a large number of family members from the inner workings of the shop. They all lined up and commenced weeping loudly, a polite gesture of sympathy for us, the (presumed) bereaved.

We got down to talking prices for some of his more elaborate offerings. As I beat him down, the available selection grew smaller, and various family members were dispatched from the mourning line to other duties. In the end, we were down to a rock bottom, bargain basement, plain and simple product and with one small child left wailing (mainly because she was being kept in the shop crying while all the rest were whooping it up in the back!). Finally, we settled on a price and we were the proud owners of a brand-new coffin.

Triumphant but fairly light in the pocket, we walked out carrying the coffin between us and stood by the side of the road to hail a taxi. We were a little surprised when none of them would stop. We worked out soon enough that the coffin was the problem, so Mick was dispatched, with the coffin, to stand in the doorway recess of a nearby closed shop while I stood at the side of the road and hailed the next taxi. It duly stopped and I hopped in, keeping the door open and engaging the driver in a running commentary while Mick manfully struggled to the vehicle with his burden. The driver was not best pleased, but we mollified him with a handsome tip.

For the sake of secrecy we took the coffin to Mick's place. The look on his wife's face as we two lunatics brought a coffin inside was priceless. She grudgingly allowed us to place it on a trestle in a downstairs room set aside for ironing. Mick's job was to get a little silver plate, have it inscribed and bring the coffin in for presentation at our farewell in the officers' mess the following Friday.

A pretty good plan all in all, except that we hadn't bargained on the fact that on the Monday morning, the McDermotts' *amah*, or housekeeper, turned up bright and early for work, let herself in and walked straight into the ironing room. The McDermotts, who were upstairs, heard a loud scream, the sound of running feet and then a door slamming shut. The *amah* was not seen for several days and had to be coaxed back to work. All the trouble was worth it when we presented our item of silver (a little silver plate with a coffin attached!). The mess president did not want it but he was howled down by the multitudes who thought it was a very fine present. I suspect that he got rid of it as soon as he could!

The days flew by. Suddenly I was saying goodbye to everybody in 1 RAR and flying down to Singapore for an overnight stop before taking an Air France flight into Saigon.

My overnight stay was at the Tanglin Officers' Mess in the city, a multinational mess for the headquarters officers from FARELF, the Commonwealth garrison forces in the region. While there were a number of Kiwis and Aussies, the mess was dominated by British Army officers in one of the few remaining British outposts east of Suez. By the time I got from the airport into the mess it was about five o'clock in the afternoon and, in virtually every State in Australia, the sun was well and truly above the yardarm. In other words, as a young Aussie officer going off into untold dangers, I thought an ice cold beer would be nice.

I wandered around the mess looking for the bar through room after room of unearthly quiet, passing a forest of khaki-clad British legs sticking out from armchairs, all surmounted by newspapers from which only the occasional turning of the page was evidence of life underneath. The very rare glimpse of a British uniform shirt behind these newspapers showed me that I was the junior member present by at least several ranks.

Eventually, I found a firmly-locked hatchway in a wall, which was the nearest the Poms came to a bar. I waylaid a passing Singaporean steward and enquired about getting a cold beer. He looked down his nose at me and told me that it was tea time — that is, time for tea, not beer. I was pretty despondent and then my saviour arrived: an Australian Army Pay Corps captain, an 'old and bold' about my dad's age wandered down the corridor and I explained my predicament. He said, 'I'm your man. What do you think I'm here for. These useless so-and-sos wouldn't shout if a shark bit them!' He promptly knocked on a side door to the bar area and, magically, two ice cold beers were produced and we drank our beer in the corridor. I never got his name, but if he reads these words, mate you're a champion!

That evening, wanting an early night and a clear head for the morrow, I wandered a short distance away from the barracks and found a Chinese picture theatre which was showing the movie *Funny Girl*, albeit with Chinese subtitles. It was quite bizarre — as the comic lines rolled out from the various characters in the movie, I would burst out laughing, the only person in the theatre to do so; a little while later, when the subtitle caught up with the dialogue, the whole theatre would erupt in laughter, if that particular episode appealed to the Chinese sense of humour.

The next day, with a minimum of luggage, I reported to the international airport and boarded an Air France Caravelle jet to Saigon. In December 1968 I had been fretting because I thought I would be held back from going to Vietnam for about two years. Now, here I was, only the second of my class to be sent on operational service, to a war which was being termed 'the platoon commander's war'.

4

Vietnam

THE JOURNEY FROM SINGAPORE to Saigon didn't take long, but it was like passing into another dimension.

An air hostess offered me glass of champagne. Initially I declined the offer, but then called her back to take it on the basis that there would be no champagne for quite a while to come.

Just before descent, as we were flying over the Mekong Delta, I was gazing out at the lush wetlands, marred by shell and bomb craters and the detritus of war. There was a glimpse from the window of the rambling, shambolic city of Saigon and then we rolled into a landing at Ton Son Nhut, at that time the busiest airport in the world.

The aircraft parking area was chaotic and crowded. Every second person was in uniform and armed to the teeth. The noise was stupendous, as military jets and transport aircraft and a goodly number of commercial carriers constantly took off and landed. In among the throng I eventually spotted an Australian Army movements soldier, with a brassard on his arm to prove it. Coming from Malaysia where, as a token of our garrison status, we were immaculately dressed and groomed at all times, I was a little taken aback by his appearance. He was in an unironed field uniform (the old jungle greens that the Army wore for many years), he needed a haircut and his shave that morning had been imperfect. I reminded myself that this was to be no garrison existence. He was cheerful enough and ushered me into a decrepit Army Kombi van for the ride into Saigon proper.

I was to spend the rest of the day and night at an allied barracks facility before going forward to Nui Dat the next day. A few months in Malaysia and visiting Singapore had prepared me for the dense crush of humanity and the exotic sights, sounds and smells of the city streets, but it was necessary to remember that here the teeming throng was possibly harbouring armed Vietcong. The barracks to which I was taken was a multi-storey hotel acquired for the purpose; it was a heavily sandbagged and barbed-wired fortress in the middle of the city.

The surreal nature of the war was gently demonstrated that night at the dinner for the permanent residents (mainly Americans with some Aussies and a couple of 'blow-ins' like me). It was a roof-top barbecue with American beer available in abundance. The entertainment on a mini stage at one end of the roof top was an all girl jazz quartet from Australia and the whole evening was framed by a ceaseless fireworks display of rocket, artillery and machine gun tracer fire and parachute flares from different parts of the Saigon horizon, all to the strains of 'Mood Indigo' and 'Stranger on the Shore'. The 'locals' told me it was like that every night.

The next day, still in my spiffy garrison uniform affected by the sleek men of the 28th Commonwealth Brigade, I retraced my steps to Ton Son Nhut and boarded an RAAF Caribou transport aircraft for the short flight to Nui Dat, the Australian main base in Phuoc Tuy province, east of the capital.

Just as I arrived at this major base carved out of the jungle and rubber plantations around the hill which gave the base its name, the heavens opened and, riding in an open Land Rover to the part of the base where I would report, I became a drowned rat, the first of several hundred soakings in my time in Vietnam. I arrived within minutes at the 1st Australian Reinforcement Unit, a holding and training establishment set up as an adjunct to the fighting organisation based at Nui Dat, the 1st Australian Task Force. The Task Force comprised three infantry battalions, a tank squadron, an armoured personnel carrier squadron, three batteries of field artillery, an engineer squadron and an assortment of support and logistic units. After two weeks at the reinforcement unit, I would be posted to one of the infantry battalions.

The spiffy uniform was consigned to the depths of the kit bag and I put on the jungle greens of my true calling — an infantry officer on operations. On this second night in a war zone, the first night of being among soldiers in a combat area, I was restlessly asleep in a tent when there were the most enormous explosions, which sounded so close as to be virtually on top of us. I rolled straight out of my cot, grabbed my rifle and webbing and hurriedly shoved my feet into unlaced boots. I raced out of the tent, preparing to sell my life dearly. In the dim light from a nearby wooden hut, I saw another figure a few metres away, clad only in a towel and thongs — the officer commanding the reinforcement unit, Major Paddy Hallinan, a grizzled and veteran officer of World War II and Korea vintage. He saw me square-jawed and resolute, oddly clad in shortie pyjamas, webbing, rifle and unlaced boots and asked what on earth I was up to. I told him that, following the massive explosions, I thought I'd better be ready to do whatever was needed. He told me that I was a bloody idiot, that the explosions were our artillery firing directly over our heads and that I'd better get used to it.

I did too. In no time at all, I could sleep soundly as our stuff went out but woke up instantly if there was a rustle in a bush which was out of place. In this regard, I've learned to trust my intuition to a very high degree. After a while, so did my soldiers. On this night, however, I felt like a goose — not for the last time either!

A few days later Mick McDermott turned up for the orientation process alongside me. This programme was designed to provide the most up-to-date insights and skills pertinent to operating in Vietnam. It was open to all ranks and concentrated on those fundamental soldiering skills necessary to survive and operate alongside more experienced soldiers.

One day, straight after the lunch break, I noticed that Mick hadn't turned up for the start of the afternoon's lesson. I remembered that he had been going off to his tent to listen to the Radio Australia news. A short time later, he walked up to the group of soldiers, NCOs and officers attending the lesson and motioned me to join him off to the rear. There he told me that our classmate, Charlie Eiler, had been killed in a training accident in Australia. Charlie was everybody's mate at Duntroon, a wonderfully generous, kind, tough and loyal mate, and a special mate of Mick's. They had been at school together since they were youngsters at Marist Brothers Parramatta and had come into Duntroon together.

Charlie had been posted direct from Duntroon into the Special Air Service Regiment (which happened quite a bit in those days). He had been going through the comprehensive and intensive training the regiment requires of all of its novices. He was involved in a parachute jump from an RAAF Hercules aircraft in Western Australia. Charlie and the other soldiers were doing what is known as 'double door exits' from the aircraft — using both the rear passenger doors for parachutists to leave the aircraft as quickly as possible (necessary when the drop zone is quite small). Charlie and a sergeant came together in the slipstream. Their parachutes became entangled and neither parachute filled with air. They both plummeted to the ground still entangled and Charlie was killed instantly. The sergeant lingered for a short while but he too died of his massive injuries. Totally against our collective expectations, the Class of '68 had lost its first member, not in combat but to a training accident.

I felt very sad for the loss of our mate, but equally for Mick, stuck in Vietnam and unable to be with Charlie's family in Sydney to comfort them and help them mourn. The Eilers were Hungarian Australians and wonderful people. Charlie would have been the most admired and respected combat commander — he was a natural.

When the additional in-country training drew to a close, Mick and I were none the wiser about which of the three infantry battalions we would be sent to. Each was on a twelve month tour of duty but in distinctly different cycles, deliberately so to ensure that there was only one novice battalion at any given time. At this time, in early August 1969, 9th Battalion, the Royal Australian Regiment (9 RAR), had been there the longest and was due to return home in December. Next came 5th Battalion, the Royal Australian Regiment (5 RAR), due back in January 1970 and then 6 RAR, newly arrived. Being so fresh, 6 RAR was unlikely to need reinforcement/replacement officers this early in its tour, but the other two were quite possible.

One night Paddy Hallinan had been out visiting cronies elsewhere in Nui Dat and on his return he said to me, 'Pack your bags, Cosgrove, you're off to B Company, 9 RAR, tomorrow — I was playing cards and I made you the stake!' I politely asked whether, if I was the stake, he had won or lost the bet. He was silent on the issue.

I asked who my company commander would be, and he replied that it was Ted Chitham. Ted had been my company commander at Duntroon. I was a little despondent at this because when Ted had been my boss at Duntroon, I was absolutely in the doldrums — from which I surmised that it had been Ted who had lost the bet!

I was to join 9 RAR in the field, taking over from a Duntroon graduate from the year before me, Ivan Clark. Paddy said that Ivan had been doing a fantastic job but had been pushing his luck, with the result that the powers that be thought that he should take a break from platoon commanding. I knew Ivan pretty well and thought that any group he commanded would be a happy and effective bunch.

All in all, I was content (if nervous): the moment of truth was at hand.

The next afternoon found me getting off a Huey helicopter at a base which B Company had established with engineer help alongside a road looking over paddy fields towards the jungle about a kilometre away.

The base was like an earthen fort of Roman Legionary times. It had been set up to support an engineer operation which was clearing a large swathe of jungle in the vicinity. The engineers would employ giant bulldozers with a huge chain dragged between them to rip down vegetation and to deny the enemy the concealment and sanctuary of the jungle close to the villages and towns in the region. The nearest town was a place called Dat Do, about one and a half kilometres away to the east. The engineers would knock down the jungle by day, protected by the infantry, and retire to the safety of the base by night (again protected by the infantry).

As well as protecting the engineers, the infantry would also operate out of the base on missions to ambush likely routes that the enemy would use. I knew that B Company and the platoon I was going to, 5 Platoon, had been in frequent combat so far during the battalion's tour of duty. Meeting the platoon was pretty intimidating, but I did my best to look focussed and cool.

These were the men who had done it — they had the thousand-yard stare, the quiet demeanour of the seasoned warrior. Imagine my confusion when, shortly after meeting me, a great posse of them went rushing past me, whooping like banshees. It turned out that they were in pursuit of a large poisonous snake. The snake rocketed up a bamboo clump and perched among the higher foliage, metaphorically poking out its tongue at them from on high. Not to be thwarted, one of my inherited warriors promptly produced a 40 mm grenade launcher (commonly known as a 'bomb gun'). This resembled a short but very fat-barrelled shotgun. It would fire a 40 mm grenade up to about 400 metres but was also useful in jungle fighting to fire at bunkers or into the trees near an enemy so that the explosion created shrapnel. On this occasion, it was put to the not very warlike task of shooting the hapless snake out of the bamboo clump with a buckshot round!

Previous sage advice from my legion of instructors and mentors didn't seem to cover this one, so I did the officer-like thing of nodding knowingly and slowly sipping my brew, waiting for Ted Chitham to put me on the mat (again!).

Ted must have been busy because the incident passed without comment. Soldiers are generally respectful of fauna with the exception of poisonous snakes. That's because soldiers on duty occupy the same living space as snakes, and no soldier will let a poisonous snake slither out of sight when he knows that it might return to bite him or a mate. That said, there were only one or two serpents killed in the whole year that I was in Vietnam. (In Australia very few snakes get killed, because the soldiers have the option of moving somewhere else and leaving the snake to mind its own business.)

After this glimpse of less-than-life-and-death behaviour, you might think that I would ease off on the adrenaline rush. Instead, I found myself mentally running hard and I didn't slow down the whole time I was in Vietnam. Despite that, the light-hearted moments just kept rolling.

On the night I arrived, as I crept around inside my platoon perimeter checking on my people and those among them who were acting as our sentries, I passed by the back of a tracked armoured personnel carrier, an M113. These vehicles were dotted around our perimeter to beef up our firepower with their machine guns. As I passed the open hatch at the rear of the vehicle, a hand reached out to grab me. I was hauled inside and in the stygian dark a hot brew was shoved in my hand and a whispered command was given to me to 'shut up and drink'. I did, took a fair swig, and took in about four ounces of OP rum thinly flavoured with hot coffee. The Armoured Corps sergeant who was in charge of the vehicle was an old mate of my dad's who had seen me stumbling around in the gathering gloom and thought he'd better welcome me to Vietnam.

One intriguing aspect of my first day of operations happened when I was called into a conference with Ted Chitham.

As we sat there, near to us was a soldier who was on field punishment. By the military law of the day, a soldier who committed some transgression of a quite serious nature while in the field on operations could be charged and heard on that charge in the field. If found guilty, the sort of punishments he might receive would have to take into account the nature of the operation and, naturally, the safety of the soldier and his comrades.

In this case, the soldier in question had been given a number of days field punishment. This punishment was carried out each day when he had finished the set tasks for his group and would otherwise have been having a breather. He had been set to digging a hole near the company commander's headquarters and when the hole was finished, filling it in again. I have never seen such a hate-filled look as that which he was bestowing on our small group of officers. (I recalled that moment several months later when I put that soldier into custody for the murder of his platoon commander.)

One or two nights after my arrival at the base, some Vietcong attacked the Vietnamese Army posts on our side of the edge of Dat Do. B Company were spectators because of the distance, but we had ringside seats nonetheless. In my platoon area we had a whopping great big night observation telescope, a monster version of the miniaturised night vision equipment every soldier can now wear and use to operate almost as well by night as by day. The thing we had might have gone well at Mount Stromlo but it also gave us a very good look at the battle.

The Americans had adapted some of the old World War II vintage DC3 aircraft by equipping them with an electrically driven multi-barrel machine gun called a Minigun, which fired out the side of the aircraft. Equipped with searchlights and with plenty of flares, they could offer devastating fire support to beleaguered forces under attack. With the military penchant for nicknames, these aircraft were nicknamed 'Spooky'. A 'Spooky' gunship turned up and started to 'hose down' the general area of the VC in an awesome display with its Miniguns blazing. I was able to see several little stick-like figures, which were VC, standing defiantly upright in the open, firing back at the gunship with their puny small arms. They were the enemy in a ruthless war of assassinations, ambushes and sometimes atrocities, but they were capable of great courage.

A few nights later, my platoon had to move a couple of kilometres away from our base to do an ambush on a patch of old paddy deemed to be part of an infiltration route for the VC in and out of the town of Dat Do. Arriving at the designated spot, we set up our ambush with claymores, trip flares and machine guns all laid out, and the platoon settled into firing positions.

About 10.00 p.m., it began raining like the Great Deluge. In less than an hour, we were sitting hip-deep in swiftly flowing water, with the claymores, flares, etc., no doubt miles away downstream. I could feel the diggers' eyes burning into me from up and down the 'aquatic ambush'. The foe would have needed to be able to swim like Ian Thorpe to get near enough for us to tear into.

Maybe a week later, after we had been out for a day protecting the engineers, accompanied by tanks and APCs, one of our tanks broke down miles from home.

We stayed with the APCs and other tanks to protect the broken-down tank until it was fixed. For hours into the night the maintenance experts and tank crew swarmed all over this thing looking for ever bigger spanners to bash it with, in a bizarre form of the 'Phuoc Tuy Open Noise-Making Competition'. Some bright spark had the idea that we should fire off parachute flares to help light their way and speed them along in their work. And so, every minute or two, 'whoosh-pop', up would go another one.

I was sitting on the deck of an APC, envying the diggers having all the fun firing the flares. Eventually, I couldn't resist it any longer. I grabbed one with a flourish, set it up and banged the back end hard with my hand in the accepted manner to fire it. It fired like a beauty, but my aim was off — instead of describing a gentle text-book parabola into the night sky, it screamed at a thousand miles an hour straight into the teeming hordes on the back of the busted tank. You know, you've never truly heard Australian swearing until you've got a few outraged diggers going.

This operation in support of the engineers was not especially wide ranging or demanding and soon came to an end. I was relieved to have performed adequately but still in my mind, and no doubt in the minds of my men, was the fundamental question of how I would perform in combat — none had come our way in the few weeks of our time protecting the engineers.

After a short break back in Nui Dat, we were off on a much more dangerous enterprise, a search and destroy operation against whatever VC activity and base areas we could discover in a notorious enemy sanctuary area, a jungle wilderness called the Hat Dich well northwest of Nui Dat. The nature of the task called for stealth, persistence and patience, as it would be a very long operation of about five weeks.

I could tell from the demeanour of the older hands among my fellow officers and soldiers that it was 'game on!' Patrolling in this sort of environment is enormously wearing and stressful. The VC and the North Vietnamese Army were a skilful and brave enemy who would especially take you on if they could seize the initiative against you. The Australians were without doubt the most accomplished jungle warfare troops in the world at this time, but not one of us underestimated our adversary. The nature of our task — long range patrolling through dense jungle to discover the enemy without him knowing our presence — required us to carry exceptionally heavy loads for day-long marches through exceedingly difficult terrain for day after day, looking for signs of our foe. We had to be constantly vigilant because at any instant we might be in battle.

(I always thought it was sad when some veterans of previous conflicts scoffed at our fellows that the Vietnam War was somehow not as real or deadly as theirs. Only the soldiers who fought in the Pacific campaign would appreciate the moment-to-moment dangers typical of jungle operations in Vietnam; even then, not too many of their patrols away from the support of their main forces would have extended to the four weeks or so which was par for the course in Vietnam.)

There are some prosaic but interesting aspects of such a patrolling regime. For the duration of the patrol you generally do not bathe. You are all well and truly 'on the bugle' after two days or so, but you can't tell because everybody smells the same. You simply pong for five weeks. Sometimes VC captives would opine that the VC could smell us coming!

Secondly, you generally wore the same clothes throughout. The jungle green of the uniform very quickly took on the red/brown colour of the earth and provided a splendid if monochrome natural camouflage that we all prized. If you ripped your shirt or trousers on vines, etc., and had to take on a new uniform at a ration resupply, you couldn't wait for the seemingly brilliant, emerald green, almost glowing, clean uniform to take on its protective patina of dirt.

You slept on the ground with a thin, supposedly waterproof sheet of rubberised fabric between you and the earth. If it rained, you got wet. If you got wet, you stayed that way until you dried out naturally. Nobody wore underwear. Any garment close to sensitive skin and body creases would promote rashes, leading to infections. Half the diggers wore no socks for the same reasons.

In short, you lived a very basic, primitive, almost animalistic life with virtually no creature comforts.

One result of this was that you became extremely attuned to the environment — more so than the VC. They tended to form little jungle bush-camp hideaways, and this is where we would sometimes have the drop on them. Infrastructure needs resources and we would see the pattern of their living: cut saplings for shelters, tracks for access in and out of their camps, dug earth for their trenches and bunkers. Living in a camp with even rudimentary amenities would lull them into ordinary behaviour like moving around, making 'domestic' noises and cooking communal meals with attendant odours (the sense of smell worked both ways!).

A week or so into the operation, we were working well north in the battalion's area of operations, right up near the provincial border. We were ordered to cross the provincial boundary out of Australia's broad area of responsibility, into the southern part of the adjoining province which was the responsibility of the Thai military. Our mission there was to check vague intelligence reports of enemy activity in the border area.

We were patrolling very quietly and carefully up a shallow jungle-clad ridgeline when we came across a substantial track through the jungle. I didn't need the older hands to tell me that this was a significant discovery. It showed signs of recent use so, if anything, we became even more vigilant and cautious as we moved ever so slowly up the line of the track.

After a while, we started to see the tell-tale signs of cut saplings with mud smeared over the cut stumps to obscure the fresh raw colour of the cuts. We were obviously very close to a camp of some sort. Just then, I got a radio message telling me to stop immediately as there had been an enquiry from the Thais about where we were. I told the company commander of our discovery and stopped our cautious advance.

We went to ground astride the track. I put a machine gun facing up the track and a sentry about 10 metres out in front of the gun to spot any enemy before they could see any of us. I got the other two sections of the platoon and looped them back around each flank to join on our back track.

We settled down to wait while our superiors worked it out with the Thais. Because of our obvious proximity to an enemy position there was no relaxation, brewing up or any other refreshment.

Our platoon was deathly quiet and remained so for the best part of an hour. I didn't know it at that moment, but our sentry forward of the machine gun was our newest young soldier, Private Colin Moyle, a Tasmanian who had only just joined us in the field. He was a very slender, frail looking young fellow, of very serious demeanour. Initially I had worried about whether he would be able to handle the high physical demands of carrying extraordinarily heavy loads for day after day in the steaming and dense jungle. Bigger, apparently more robust men had found it too hard to carry the loads and maintain the right level of vigilance and stamina.

Without warning, a booming volley of shots rang out from a few metres away near our machine gun and sentry position. Every man in the platoon took up a fighting position on the ground facing out. I ran immediately the few metres to just behind the machine gun, just in time to see Col Moyle coming back into our perimeter like a racing ferret — about 6 inches off the deck and going like the clappers. As soon as he was back among us, we saturated the area up the track with a great volume of fire from our machine gun, rifles and carbines.

Col reported later that he had been out on sentry about 10 metres in front of the machine gun when, from his position lying down behind the cover of a tree, he had seen an armed VC creeping along the track very carefully and vigilantly. He wisely appreciated that, if he moved, the fellow would see or hear him and we would lose any advantage of surprise, so he aimed his rifle at the man and observed him. As he crept a little closer, Col watched as the VC paused, seemed to hear something, turned in a way which clearly indicated he had somebody with him, and started to gesture. Col realised that they had smelt a rat. Right away, he shot the first man and fired more shots where he guessed the next man might be, before scooting back into the relative safety of where the rest of us were, a few metres behind him.

As the platoon was letting loose with all barrels, I was kneeling alongside the machine gun and firing as hard as I could go. This wasn't exactly wrong, but I was brought to my senses when one of my section commanders, Corporal Bob Carr, called out, 'Hey skip, I've closed up left and I'm in position to do a sweep.'

This jolted my brain into action. I dashed over to Bob's section (in jungle of this nature, all these distances are very short — the whole platoon layout at that moment would have fitted onto half a tennis court). I told him the axis of his advance would be what we call in the trade a left hook — a curving manoeuvre from the left but keeping close to the main direction in which you were originally facing. This sweep was an assault to cover the ground in which our Col Moyle had seen and engaged the enemy.

As we began to advance into this patch of jungle, I moved about two paces behind the line of Bob Carr's troops, but within a couple of steps I realised this wasn't the best place to be. Even that couple of steps back meant I couldn't see as much as the soldiers in the line, so I ran forward and joined them. We quickly encountered two enemy dead lying on the track. It was hard to say who had shot them — Col, the rest of us in our fire after Col had rejoined us or the soldiers in the sweep, but that was less important than the fact that, once again, the men of 5 Platoon had done their job and survived unhurt.

After any action of this nature it is axiomatic that you report as soon as possible to your boss. While I was reporting this small battle, I was standing in the middle of the area where Col had seen the enemy and where we had done the sweep. I made the report, signed off and looked around to ensure that my fellows were laid out on the ground properly, to be ready in case more enemy came along. (We were still standing outside a presumed enemy camp and bunker system. If things turned bad, the nearest help was quite some time away.) Only then did I notice that I had conducted the whole report over the radio standing alongside the bodies of these two poor enemy soldiers we had just killed.

My major feeling was relief that my boys had survived and done their jobs — and so had I. I was extraordinarily impressed with the actions of Col Moyle, a soldier who in his first encounter with a skilful and vigilant enemy had performed like a seasoned veteran. I am pleased to say I had those two thoughts before I also realised that it was my first battle and I had done my job. Apart from that, there was no exultation, no depression, no vicarious thrill, just a moment or two of relief and then the fiercest focus on being vigilant, ready, prepared for whatever came next.

My duties and my training, my wonderful training by all those patient, wise veterans would not allow me the indulgence of feelings. There was an instant coming of military age for me there in that unremarkable patch of Vietnamese jungle. Most of the soldiers probably sensed it. I knew it at a visceral level, even though I was probably not prepared to admit it to myself quite yet.

Soon our orders came through. We were to withdraw a few hundred metres while the company commander moved another of his platoons from some distance away into a blocking position on the other side of what he and I estimated to be the location of the presumed enemy camp.

My own instinct was for us to continue on to have a go at any enemy who might be in the camp while we benefited from whatever confusion and panic we had sown among them. But he was probably right: we had no immediate support available until the other platoon arrived and we were out of range of artillery or mortars (a frequent occurrence for Australian infantry operations in Vietnam).

For quite a few hours we kept a tight and very vigilant perimeter several hundred metres back down the gentle slope leading up to where we'd fought in the morning. This allowed time for 6 Platoon, B Company, to close up towards us and to skirt around to the northeast, behind where we thought the camp was. It also gave a chance for the company commander to bring up 81 mm mortars from the battalion's support company.

The plan was that, when all was in readiness, we in 5 Platoon would go back up the hill and assault the camp, supported by the fire of our mortars and hopefully driving the enemy out of the camp and into the waiting clutches of 6 Platoon.

Late that afternoon, we started back up (too late, I thought, because we had spent so much time preparing that the enemy could have had a sleep before bugging out). As we advanced astride the track, a sergeant from the mortar platoon travelled with us and started to call in mortar fire in front of us. He estimated the range by dint of the loudness of the explosions (you couldn't *see* the explosions of the rounds in the jungle unless they were right on top of you!).

He had brought the mortar fire in pretty close to the leading few soldiers because we anticipated encountering the enemy at close range, given the thick nature of the jungle undergrowth. As the mortar bombs impacted about 120 metres in front of us, we could hear the distinct whistle and whir they were making. During peacetime exercises in Australia, you wouldn't have them that close in a fit.

Suddenly, there was a totally different character to the sound of the next four rounds descending; the whistle became a screech as they impacted directly among us. We all hit the dirt and I have two vivid memories — one of the rounds exploding in a fountain of moist earth and foliage and the other of the sergeant from the mortar platoon remaining standing and yelling into his radio to get the firing stopped. To this day I don't know if he made a blue in his orders adjusting where the rounds fell or whether it was a mistake back at the mortars as they placed the necessary elevation and direction on the mortar tubes. Regardless, there was an immediate deathly hush as we climbed to our feet and found that miraculously no one had been hit. We pressed on up the hill, but we dispensed with the close fire of the mortars!

We soon returned to the vicinity of the previous battle, where we were once again given the order over the radio to stop. I did so, but this time I did not put a sentry out at the front. I felt that we needed to be able to generate maximum firepower along the line of the track towards the perceived camp, and I did not want a sentry out there, possibly exposed and certainly limiting the firepower we could direct into the area until the sentry was safely back with us.

We had been in position for a fairly brief time, perhaps 15 minutes, when the machine gunner covering the track opened up with a long burst at some VC moving down the track very cautiously, much as the characters that morning had been doing.

This time I did the sweep straight up the axis of the track in a rolling series of fire and movement called (again, in trade terms) 'pepper-potting'. In this method individuals make short rushes forward while others cover them, generally by firing directly at the enemy or, in jungle circumstances where the enemy's location is less clear, into areas where you *think* the enemy might be.

The essence of the tactic is a rolling, ceaseless, urgent momentum forward. My experienced platoon did this very well and within about 30 metres we hit the edges of the camp and encountered great pools of blood from the fellows that we had engaged over the last few minutes.

By now it was getting very dark in the jungle. I stopped our progress about 80 metres inside the camp so that we would not be trying to capture more of their fighting pits and bunkers when it was too dark to see.

The company commander's plan worked a treat, because VC fleeing the camp did bump into 6 Platoon who shot several of them but again darkness prevented a more comprehensive follow-up in the area.

That night we slept on the ground in the bunker system. This was a difficult decision — enemy unknowing of the new ownership might wander in and then we would have a stoush by night in unfamiliar terrain. On the other hand, I was not keen to have to possibly fight our way back in on the morrow. The restless and very vigilant night which followed marked the end of a

An ailing soldier and his family, spring 1941: my maternal grandfather, Warrant Officer Bob Henrys, back from Malaya on convalescent leave, with his wife and daughters Ellen, my mum (far left), and Meg (far right).

The RSM and his wife: Mum and Dad at a ball in Tamworth in the 1950s.

Peter the mischievous, about 1952.

My Pop, Bob Henrys, with my sister, Stephanie, and me at the Royal Easter Show in the early 1950s.

The Easter Show again. I have the bull totally under control!

Dad, Mum, Stephanie
and me in Centennial Park
around 1956.

A young warrior,
looking resolute:
Cadet Under Officer
Cosgrove in 1963 at
Waverley College.

Baffled but determined: Staff Cadet Cosgrove as a junior cadet at Duntroon in 1965.

Admiring (but not touching!) a large serpent while on operations in South Vietnam in 1970. Lieutenant Cosgrove is bravely pointing out the non-biting end to some of his nonchalant diggers.

An Army PR shot of the newly decorated Captain Cosgrove in 1971.

One of my favourite photos: Mum, Dad and me at Government House in Sydney, in about May 1971, after the medal ceremony where I received the Military Cross.

Attending the Governor General, Sir Paul Hasluck, at a military parade in 1972. (I'm in the white jacket.)

Lynne and me at our engagement party in early 1976. Note the stylish leisure suit!

Our wedding day, 17 December 1976, at Mary Immaculate Church at Charing Cross in Waverley.

A (very skinny) Peter with Lynne, Stephen (far left) and Philip (far right) at Buckingham Palace in 1985, after receiving the AM from the Queen. Alas, David was too young to come on this occasion.

momentous day for me — I had been in my first and second episodes of combat and been under mortar fire (albeit our own!).

About six days later we had moved from this border area back down into the main part of the Hat Dich area. This consisted of very large tracts of jungle interspersed with areas that had been defoliated or flattened by B-52 air strikes or bulldozing engineers. Towards the end of one afternoon we came to such an open area which was so vast that there was no easy way of going around it. I decided that we would move directly across it and into the jungle on the far side.

About halfway across the clearing, the forward scout sent word for me to come up. When I joined him, he showed me very fresh footprints in the dirt. This seemed to indicate that a lone VC had been standing there for some time.

We followed up the footprints. They headed in the same direction as we were taking towards the jungle, before deviating on a right angle. I surmised that this was a sentry who had seen us emerging from the jungle, had taken off to warn his mates but then had thought better of it and had bolted in a different direction to save himself.

When we got to the light vegetation on the edge of the heavier jungle, we started to see the classic signs of an enemy camp: cut timber and a narrow track. We kept moving forward very slowly, and started to hear domestic noises and even saw shadowy figures moving around in a casual manner. My intent was to get as close as possible silently and then, as soon as the firing started, to attack them with two of my three sections forward.

That's pretty much what happened: within another few metres the firefight started.

I've previously mentioned my first encounter with bomb guns, when one was used to remove a snake at the camp near Dat Do. This time, they were used with more lethal intention. As our diggers were merrily popping off 40 mm grenades towards the VC, I looked up and saw one that had been fired into a clump of bamboo but which had not exploded because it had not travelled far enough for the fuse to be armed. I watched, fascinated, as it tumbled slowly through the bamboo, rattling around as it fell to the ground ... with me praying that it wouldn't go off on its journey to earth, because I was a little close to it!

My prayers were answered. The grenade dropped harmlessly to the ground, so that my men were not distracted from their task by the sudden and explosive departure of their commander.

The battle continued for a short while after that. When it was over, we owned the bunker system. We had also shot a number of the enemy, fortunately without any casualties to my fellows.

We settled in for the remainder of daylight while the rest of B Company gathered around us. Nightfall was so close that we really hadn't had a chance to look the place over, so this was a task left for the next day.

That night, I reflected on the events of the day. After any battle, the thing I noticed about myself was that my voice was hoarse and strained from yelling to be heard above the noises of battle (the jungle canopy tends to confine noise, causing it to rebound and echo). Although the sense of isolation is not as great as in open country, in the jungle when you are on your belly firing or about to get up and run, there is this sense of being the focus of all the attention. Men like me, platoon commanders, actually had an advantage in this regard because we were so busy trying to understand what was happening, shouting orders, running around and giving radio reports that there was not much time to dwell on such feelings.

In the morning we went about the task of exploring the enemy camp while company headquarters and the other two platoons provided security on some of the approaches.

At one point during proceedings a company water resupply task was put on. My platoon sergeant took soldiers from all of the platoons down to the creek inside the jungle, about 150 metres away from the centre of the enemy camp. After he had gone, I discovered that he had taken an entire section of 5 Platoon, which had been guarding a portion of the perimeter, leaving a gap in our defences. I wasn't very happy about this! However, just then I was called to report to company headquarters, so I had to put aside the issue of the missing section.

I walked off the 80 metres or so to join the company commander, Captain Graham Dugdale. As I went past one of my diggers who was resting just behind where the absent section had been occupying the perimeter, I told him to keep a lookout because his mates in front of him had been taken for a job.

I sat down with the company commander and unbuckled the webbing belt which held my ammunition. I had just started to have a chat with my boss when a volley of shots came from the direction of the perimeter where my section was missing. Before I knew it, and without a word to the company commander, I was sprinting back. Passing the soldier I had just spoken to in a flash, I noticed that he was wide-eyed and looking over his rifle barrel.

It turned out that a couple of soldiers from the water resupply party, having filled all the water canteens that they were carrying, decided to wander off back to our position by themselves instead of waiting for the platoon sergeant and the rest of the group. Normally this would be a bad piece of soldiering, but on this occasion it was fortuitous.

As they came up to where the section had been, they spotted a considerable number of VC milling about gazing at the Australian kit, such as backpacks, lying around on the ground. These two Aussies did the right thing by engaging these chaps immediately before themselves going to ground.

I came charging into the middle of this group of enemy and a version of the gunfight at the OK Corral then started. Sadly, I remembered in the middle of this very close range shoot-out that my webbing belt with all of my ammunition was back with the company commander. I yelled out to the digger I had left in my wake to throw me a magazine of ammunition. To his credit, he did this immediately, but unfortunately it turned out to be a magazine of 7.62 mm rounds when what I actually needed was 5.56 mm for my M16 rifle. At one stage I took up an anti-tank rocket in a launcher, to fire at some bloke who was literally about 5 metres away. The rocket this thing fired would not have armed in that short distance but I figured it would be like a very powerful boxing glove if nothing else! Fortunately at that moment I was spared this experiment.

Graham Dugdale quickly arrived on the scene alongside the digger. He was able to throw me a magazine of 5.56 mm so I was able to finish the job. Some of the enemy managed to escape but under the circumstances I wasn't too annoyed because for a minute or so it was a close run thing. I gave myself a pretty big kick in the tail for not immediately putting more soldiers into the gap that I had discovered and for being a goose in not grabbing my webbing belt before dashing into the fray.

Mind you, my personal rocket was nothing on the roasting I got from Dugdale for putting myself in amongst a number of enemy, especially with only the magazine on my rifle. He did have a point, but in combat junior officers must not be shy of taking risks and, given the circumstances, I felt profoundly responsible for the fact that the VC could nearly have walked into our position.

The operation proceeded in this way for several more weeks — every time we turned around, 5 Platoon seemed to be in the thick of it again. Eventually, however, the operation finished, the whole battalion, including B Company, returned to Nui Dat and we were all relieved to be in one piece after all of the action we had seen over the preceding weeks. While I realised that there were still much to learn, I now felt as if I belonged in the job as an infantry platoon commander in combat. The five weeks had been very much a 'post-graduate' course in jungle warfare and in leadership on operations. I knew a great deal more about the men who were my responsibility and no doubt they had been assessing me very keenly as well.

Time flew past and soon it was B Company's last operation: a two or three day search and clear in the jungle north of Nui Dat and south and west of the Binh Ba rubber plantation, around late November.

My platoon was patrolling in this area looking for signs of enemy activity when we discovered a heavily marked, recently used track through light jungle. I put in an immediate ambush on this track and we were rewarded when some chap came along it about 30 minutes after we had settled into the ambush. Unfortunately we engaged him a little early and he fled apparently unscathed, so quickly that I would back him in the Olympic 100 metres over any comers! During the contact, Graham Dugdale rang up on the radio to complain that the 'overs' from the small arms we were firing during contact were cracking in among company headquarters. My radio operator, the unflappable Gary Mayer, converted my unprintable reply into 'Sunray [the commander] suggests you take cover'.

The next morning we were quietly patrolling in quite light jungle when we smelt cooking and heard some human noise. We were closing up on the noise, very likely to be an enemy camp, and were getting ready to cross a small but bush-choked stream when they discovered our presence.

Suddenly it was on for young and old.

My forward section commander, Sepp Sodervik, and his forward scout, Col Moyle, did some very brave things when being engaged point blank by two enemy with AK-47s. Thanks to them, we avoided disaster and captured what turned out to be the bivouac site for about twenty or so enemy. We found out later that they were the Chau Duc District Company — a low-grade local VC unit. While we didn't appear to have killed or wounded any on this occasion, we did capture their breakfast (and their breakfast dishes)!

To add injury to insult, I called a couple of helicopter gunships onto them as they fled, so all in all they had a pretty bad day. I felt particularly sorry for one of them however — during our search of their camp we found where they had fled en masse across the narrow stream. The sides of the stream were heavily scored and muddied by the frantic feet of the fleeing mob. Trodden into the mud there was a pair of now-broken spectacles with the thickest lenses I have ever seen. I had visions of some fellow blundering around introducing himself to trees, like Mr McGoo!

After this bracing couple of days, the company was able to call it quits and the fellows were pretty pleased to be able to return unscathed to Nui Dat. We rendezvoused in the Binh Ba rubber plantation as a company to mount up on a troop of APCs for the journey back to base.

Imagine the scene: all these APCs backing and filling in a small space with engines growling and scores of very happy diggers hooping and hollering at having survived a year of extreme danger. Eventually, we were all mounted on the decks of the APCs and we were ready for the 'off'. My APC was jockeying to get into line when it lifted one side slowly but steeply up a bund. I was sitting on the ammunition boxes on the low side, holding on grimly to one of the long, fibreglass radio antennas bristling from the top deck of the carrier, as the laws of gravity started to apply: more tilt, more downward force, until my anchor point — the antenna, snapped off at its base.

I think I did a forward one-and-half somersault with pike (degree of difficulty 1.4), although all these years later I can't be sure. I do remember lying on my back on the ground, still holding the antenna like a fishing rod, looking up at the APC and at my platoon and the rest of the company who were laughing so hard that I thought there might be the first case in history of mass cardiac arrest. The APC crew commander chose this moment to abuse me, using frightful language, for breaking his radio antenna. I told him where and how hard I would replace the antenna and of course this exchange of pleasantries increased the general merriment, if that was possible.

I know Vietnam was a dreadful place for many of us but there was always humour among the excitement and drama — after all we were Australian soldiers, so what else would you expect?

After this final operation, the battalion joyously started packing to leave Vietnam (I, of course, still had six months of my tour of duty to go). Apart from local security of the battalion base area, the workload now was strictly administrative. The nights were spent by officers, NCOs and diggers alike gossiping on, generally with a beer in hand, about how wonderful it would be to be home in Australia.

The battalion was to be replaced by 8 RAR, who had been training back in Australia. I had last seen many of the 8 RAR fellows in Terendak in Malaysia when 1 RAR took over from them in April of 1969.

Finally the magic day arrived when the advance party from 8 RAR arrived. B Company of 8 RAR would replace B Company 9 RAR. The new company commander and his platoon commanders were greeted by the old hands with open arms. I too was happy to see them but, given that my tour of duty was not over and this new lot had no vacancies, I was a little more restrained in my greeting. The company commander for B Company 8 RAR was Major Michael Jeffery and for us this first casual meeting held no portents for the extraordinarily long association we would have off and on for the next four decades.

In amongst all this euphoria on the part of the outgoing battalion and excited anticipation among the advance party of the new battalion occurred one of the great tragedies of all my years of service.

One night down in the 6 Platoon lines, just after midnight, an explosion occurred.

The digger from that platoon who was on machine gun picket knew that the explosion had come from behind him, from the area where the whole platoon slept. At the same time, about 150 metres away in company headquarters, Ivan Clark heard the explosion and then silence. He realised that this probably meant we weren't under attack. He walked through the dark down into the platoon area and found the picket and one or two other soldiers who had tumbled out of bed.

All were mystified about the cause and source of the explosion, but the sentry was adamant that it had not come from in front of him.

At some stage Ivan asked whether anybody had woken the platoon commander and, when he was told no, he walked into the platoon commander's tent and switched on the light. It was then that he discovered the platoon commander lying in bed, with massive injuries and obviously dead.

Ivan rang me in my tent, waking me, and asked me to come down and take charge while he told the company commander and then the commanding officer. I dashed down there, having told a couple of my boys to get dressed and come down as soon as possible.

I quickly ducked into the tent where the platoon commander lay, just to be absolutely sure that there was nothing that could be done, and then assembled all of his men in the dim light out the front of the tent.

I had one of the NCOs call the roll and then told them all very briefly that their boss was dead, obviously killed by an explosion, and asked if any of them could give me any information relevant to what had occurred. I left them standing there to think about this or a moment or two while I waited off to one side.

First one soldier came up to me, and then another.

The first soldier told me that a group of them had been sitting in a tent drinking, talking 'trash talk' about who they didn't like in the hierarchy. He named those who were sitting in the tent during the discussion.

The second soldier told me that he had been in bed and was woken by the explosion. Straight after that, a soldier had come running in and dived under his mosquito net into bed, fully clothed, and had said something like, 'If you know what's good for you, you'll shut up about this!'

By now, a couple of my soldiers had arrived, so I called this character out of the ranks. It was the same soldier I had seen on field punishment when I had first joined 9 RAR in the field several months earlier. I immediately put him in the custody of my diggers to hold him secure in the company command post. I was anxious that he not have a chance to talk to any other soldiers until the military police had a chance to talk to whomever they wished, including him. Soon thereafter the company commander arrived with the commanding officer, Lieutenant Colonel Alan Morrison — Alby to everybody and much loved in the battalion.

The anguish and sorrow on his face was an awful sight to see. If any military officer was ever the archetypal 'foster parent' to the men under his command, then Alby was it. That one member of his battalion should murder another was incomprehensible to all of us, but most of all to Alby.

It later emerged that the soldier had a hatred for the platoon commander and had decided to lie in wait for him outside his tent. When the officer returned from an outdoor movie show, the soldier waited until he had got into bed and gone to sleep. Then he had reached over the waist high blast wall of filled sandbags, under the mosquito net and placed a hand grenade with the pin out alongside his sleeping victim on his bed. He then ran a few paces and hit the deck. We found this out because he re-enacted it for the military police on film the next day.

In a sad sequel, the company commander asked me to assist the battalion quartermaster to pack up the dead officer's kit as soon as the investigators gave us the all clear to enter the tent. The quartermaster was a really nice fellow, a craggy old soul whom we all liked. It struck me what a terrible blow this had been to the battalion family when, as we worked together to pack up those personal bits and pieces of my colleague's possessions, I noticed that this tough man of many years experience and service had tears rolling down his cheeks.

For 9 RAR, it was an awful way to finish a terrifically dangerous year. For me, instead of reporting for work in my new infantry platoon somewhere, I had to hold myself ready to give evidence at the court martial of the soldier for murder. He was eventually found guilty and given life.

While I was cooling my heels at Vung Tau, which was the Australian logistic base and the location for the court martial, I found out that my next job was to be commander of the 1st Australian Task Force defence and employment platoon. The defence and employment platoon is an adjunct to the task force headquarters. It normally provides close defence to the headquarters itself and other general duties of a housekeeping kind for the headquarters.

My initial reaction was to be devastated that I had been put in charge of a group that had a very mundane and menial role. I quickly cheered up when a colleague told me that this platoon had anything but mundane duties. Its use had evolved over the years from the duties that I feared, to being a form of long-range reconnaissance platoon under the direction of the task force commander himself.

Typically, it was used to reconnoitre large areas of the province not at that time being explored by one of the infantry battalions. It had a spectacular record of successful combat and spent a huge amount of time far away from support in the jungle. It seemed to me to be, therefore, a very good job with lots of the right kind of work and considerable independence.

The people in the platoon tended to be a mixture of soldiers who were there for a full twelve-month tour of duty and others like me who had done part of a tour of duty with another organisation and came to this platoon for the balance of their time. In this regard I was delighted to have a very good sprinkling of 9 RAR men with me: fine NCOs like Corporal Stan Sutherland and diggers like Col Moyle and Jim Muir, both of the latter from my old mob, 5 Platoon. I was also very lucky with my platoon sergeant, Rick Jeffrey, who was a veteran of the first tour of Vietnam by 1 RAR back in 1965. Rick was very professional and popular with the diggers. He had a friendly laid-back style, which complemented my somewhat energetic and robust approach quite well.

In the early part of 1970 while on independent operation in a range of hills west of the task force base at Nui Dat, the platoon had a chance to live up to its reputation. This range of hills was called the Nui Thi Vais, otherwise known far and wide amongst Australians as the Warburtons.

Although the hills themselves arose abruptly from the paddy land which stretched away from the western boundary of the task force base and were only about 7 kilometres from the boundary fence, they were very rugged, steep and clad in thick jungle. These hills (which just missed out on being mountains) also had a strong reputation for enemy activity, being repeatedly used as an operating area for an NVA battalion, D65 Sapper Battalion (in North Vietnamese Army terms, sapper battalions were elite troops that led assaults).

My job on this occasion was to take the platoon up into the southern extremity of the hills for several days. When we got past the first major crest (following a gut-busting climb), the first enemy sign we encountered was a deeply worn foot track showing signs of recent movement.

I decided to place a claymore ambush on the track. In this form of ambush, a series of claymore antipersonnel, command-detonated mines are set in place with overlapping arcs covering a particular feature, such as this track. The mines are typically placed in a line a little way off the track, linked together with detonating cord to enable instantaneous and simultaneous explosion. The whole arrangement is then camouflaged and the system linked back to a firing point by electric wire. We put in the ambush, established the firing point with a good view up and down the track and manned it with an NCO, several soldiers and machine guns covering in each direction. I withdrew the rest of the platoon back into the jungle about 20 metres and settled down to wait.

Every now and then we would relieve the soldiers forward with a new batch from this administrative area we had established. Ambushes require enormous patience and discipline. There must be absolutely no noise to give away the hiding places; there must be no smoking or cooking to provide warning to the enemy by sense of smell; movement to or from the forward position must be extremely careful (on the basis of Murphy's Law, it is while you are moving that the enemy will show up).

A day and a half we waited and two things were heavy on my mind. We were running low on water and, because we were on top of the hill, there was no local water to be found without going right down to the bottom. I didn't want to attempt this because I just had a feeling that we didn't want to be split up if there was to be a fight either in the ambush position or elsewhere on the hill. Secondly, even though we were not far away from Nui Dat, radio communications were very unreliable and I had no confidence that I would be able to call in artillery or air strikes if we got into trouble.

In the late morning/early afternoon of the second full day we had been in the ambush, I gathered the NCOs and told them that if we had not had any action out of the ambush by mid-afternoon, I was going to call it quits and we would move back down off the hill.

Despite this, I still had a really strong feeling about the significance of this track. Later, I was waiting back at the administrative area away from the ambush site when suddenly I felt that I must get ready to fight. I put my webbing on, took up my rifle, checked that it had a round in the chamber and stood up.

Rick, my platoon sergeant, was apparently watching all of this and became thoroughly spooked when he saw the boss making these preparations.

A moment later, the claymores went up with an enormous boom, signifying that our people had sprung the ambush.

I bolted like a rabbit up to the ambush. By the time I got there, the machine gunner was playing merry hell into the eastern part of the track. It transpired that an NVA reconnaissance party of three men had come sneaking down the track and Corporal 'Sludge' Callaghan had opened up on them. These fellows were very heavily armed with two AK-47s and an RPG — the classic composition of an enemy main force reconnaissance party. We got the lot of them.

After conducting the sweep and finding that communications back to base were still unworkable, the same feeling that had alerted me to the imminence of the contact urged me to move off the hill. As soon as we had finished with the aftermath of the battle, we retraced our steps back to the road and I inwardly gave thanks that this platoon was just as professional and brave as the great men of 5 Platoon.

Some time around May 1970, I was given the job of protecting an engineer road maintenance group working on Route 2, the main road directly north from Nui Dat. I was content, because I had my intrepid platoon, a section of armoured personnel carriers (three vehicles), a troop of tanks (again three vehicles) and a troop of engineers (fifty to sixty soldiers plus a lot of earth moving equipment) all under my command — quite the little Napoleon.

In their usual sandcastle way the engineers pushed up a large earthen fortress-style wall for the base and in doing so disturbed every creepy-crawly for miles around. This included the biggest python I had ever laid eyes on, which the aforesaid intrepid platoon captured.

Did I say big? This thing was monstrous! Of course, once you have caught a behemoth like that what do you do with it? You can't cuddle it or teach it to dance, especially if it doesn't like you, as this thing plainly didn't. I wanted the serpent let go, but the diggers cajoled me into letting them keep it (I thought maybe it was the Napoleonic thing to do!). There was a big tea chest-type container inside the base which became the reptile's temporary home and I sort of forgot about it, what with being Napoleon and all.

The next day, the task force commander, my direct boss and he-who-sat-at-the-right-hand-of-God, arrived with an entourage by helicopter to inspect the base. As the brigadier and 'Lieutenant Bonaparte' strolled around the little base, I thought what a nice, kindly old bloke he was. As we chatted he spied a large plywood tea chest in amongst a collection of military kit and casually inquired what was in it. Momentarily my eyes went shifty as I realised it was the snake gaol, and I made the fatal error of saying, 'Nothing really, sir.' Thinking he had caught me out with some contraband, the brigadier gave a loud and menacing 'Well, let's look, shall we?' and, with astonishing speed for one so venerable, darted to the chest and threw open the lid.

His scream reverberated around the base as yards of very angry python erupted from the box, jaws agape. All was bedlam, with the brigadier thrashing around among the boxes and piles of kit as he blundered away from the predator, 'Bonaparte' and the entourage in hot pursuit and diggers going in all directions trying to corral the snake. When he could focus on the job, he called me by some very disgusting nouns and adjectives and left the little temporary base, with his sycophant staff casting reproving glances at me from the ascending helicopter.

The last major operation of my time in Vietnam was again one where we were protecting Australian Army engineers. This time while they were constructing a water pipeline and source for the people of Long Son Island, a small mountainous piece of solid ground in the estuarine waterways and mangrove swamps off the coast of Vung Tau. This was a lengthy project involving weeks of work with backhoes to dig a pipeline trench out from the village of several thousand people and along a major track, which hugged the north-eastern coast of the island, that the locals used to access a small arable area in a northern central valley.

Apart from the village and this little arable area of 300 to 400 acres, the rest of the island was extremely rugged and jungle-clad hill country. This particular protection task was boring and I kept the fellows focussed by frequent patrolling around the island, even to the extent of entering the mangrove swamps from time to time looking for any evidence of local guerrilla activity. It was on Long Son Island that we suffered the only combat casualties among troops I was commanding in my time in Vietnam. In this regard we had been incredibly lucky, but on this day our luck ran out.

On this particular morning I decided to send out a half-platoon fighting patrol under the command of the acting platoon sergeant, one of my corporals. The task I gave them was to follow the general line of the track out towards the arable area and then to explore the jungled foothills on the western side of the paddy fields.

As a casual observation to the corporal before he left, I suggested that, on the way out, he should avoid a particular area on the track where the hill squeezed the track very close to the mangrove swamp, thinking that this would be a good place for an ambush. But it was not a pointed remark and certainly not a clear instruction, more's the pity.

About 20 minutes after they had departed, there was a huge explosion from the direction in which they had gone. Instantly I knew that they had been ambushed. Leaving only a few soldiers to guard our little base, I led the rest in a flat sprint down the track, throwing caution to the wind as we received radio messages from them to say that three soldiers were badly wounded.

When I arrived, I found that the corporal had placed a protective screen with the remaining men around where he and one or two others were treating the three casualties (the forward scout, the section commander and the machine gunner), all of whom had shrapnel wounds from what we assessed to be a claymore-type weapon.

The ambush had occurred at exactly the place that I had been referring to in my casual remark — cold comfort on this occasion to be proved right. We later found the electrical lead from where the claymore was exploded. This led back into the mangrove swamp to where a couple of enemy in a little dugout boat had been lurking and had made good their escape.

All of the soldiers survived their wounds, but all needed to be evacuated to Australia. The war in Vietnam was like that: if you let your guard down for a moment, then you would cop it.

In late July, my time came to relinquish command to another officer and to go home to Australia. The fellow who replaced me,

Second Lieutenant John Burrows, was a good man and I had every confidence that he would do well and take good care of my boys.

On the day after I handed over to him, he took the platoon out on operations in the early morning, his armoured personnel carriers thundering past the tent lines where I was staying. I stood there by the side of the road, waving to the troops who were giving me a good-natured chiacking. Although I was smiling as I waved, I had an incredible sense of loss at seeing my men heading off on operations without me. It was probably only then that I understood the profound sense of responsibility I had come to feel about men put into my care.

Anyway, all things must end, and I packed up and left soon after, boarding a charter flight in Saigon for the long flight home.

As we flew through the night, I reflected on the most intense experiences I'd had in the last sixteen months. I'd had a great apprenticeship under an excellent boss in Malaysia, had the good fortune to inherit a fine group of infantryman in 5 Platoon, been in combat on numerous occasions and had come to be respected and possibly liked by my men. I was what the Army had hoped I would become: a successful junior commander. All that and I was getting home in one piece and so were the vast majority of the troops I had led (even the chaps who had been wounded were making good recoveries)! In addition, somewhere along the track I had discovered that I had a great enthusiasm and affinity for the life of a soldier. In this regard I now saw it, not as some trial or interlude, but as a vocation. I had no set plan or lofty aspirations but I was prepared to bat for a long innings.

The flight was full of American servicemen on their way to Australia for a rip-snorting R&R, with just a sprinkling of

Australians, most of whom, like me, had finished their twelve months. The plane set down in Darwin to refuel in the middle of the night and, as it was on its approach, one of the Aussies aboard circulated quietly among the other Aussies and whispered in each of our ears.

As we all tumbled down the steps of the aircraft to stretch our legs for the 45 minutes or so it would take to refuel, the Aussies surged to the front of the strolling crowd and then sprinted into the terminal, making a beeline for the small bar that was open at that time of night. By the time any of the Americans had twigged to what was going on and crowded in to get a beer, the Aussies were a solid phalanx at the bar with at least one beer in each hand: it's not only on the battlefield that you get some points for local knowledge!

After refuelling and a few more hours in the air, we flew into Sydney. The Americans were getting more and more excited but the Aussies, in contrast, had became very quiet. In the international terminal customs hall, a very large Australian customs officer called the whole planeload of us to order and asked all the Americans to form a long queue at one of the desks. He then turned to our small group of Aussies, said 'Welcome home boys!' and waved us through.

My dad was there inside the customs hall, with pride and relief shining from his face. Mum and my sister, Stephanie, were waiting just outside, together with Mick McDermott, who had got home some time earlier. Australia, family and friends looked pretty good to me.

All these years later, I still reflect on why we were there in Vietnam, what we did and what we achieved. I have enormous admiration for every man and woman who served so wholeheartedly and bravely in Vietnam. When I first started as Chief of the Defence Force, a journalist asked me if I had an opinion about whether Australia's involvement in Vietnam was a mistake. I remember stating clearly and emphatically my admiration for the courage and the exploits and the commitment of the people we had there. I then went on to say that in retrospect we should not have gone. I didn't want to prolong the discussion of that point then, but let me now simply say that all governments face a dilemma in such international challenges, when deciding whether or not to commit their young men and women to danger, in the interests of promoting or securing the national interest. This is a call the government of the day made back in the 1960s in relation to Vietnam and I respect both the pressures of the day and the undoubtedly deep considerations they engaged in before committing Australian troops to that war.

My concern is simple. Regardless of the political and ethical considerations of whether a war should have been fought by foreign troops on the soil of Vietnam (that will always be a matter for endless debate), I remember with sadness that over 500 Australians were killed in that war and many more wounded and maimed; over 50,000 Americans lost their lives.

And we left. And we lost. We mustn't do that with our men and women. Sending troops to war is without doubt the most difficult and agonising decision for any leader. My advice to leaders is never to take the decision lightly and, having done so, never stop until the outcome is worth the cost.

5

Through the Ranks

I HAD TWO MAJOR PREOCCUPATIONS on my return from Vietnam. One was learning about being an officer in that part of the Army not presently on operations — an absorbing task if not a riveting one, but nonetheless necessary. My second preoccupation was going about the business of getting a life outside the Army — which is code for meeting women!

In relation to the former, I landed a pretty good job that allowed me to get about the Army and see how the great institution worked. I was promoted to captain at the grand old age of twenty-three (after all of seventeen months as a lieutenant) and posted as an instructor to Army Headquarters Methods of Instruction team. This unit was responsible for assisting and training the Army's many hundreds of instructors in how to teach — classroom and outdoor training techniques, personal style as an instructor, preparation of lessons and some limited technical assistance in how to make audiovisual aids.

We, or rather the several warrant officers on the team, were really good at all this stuff and it was great fun, travelling the country, visiting bases and working hard — which, in my case, meant learning to be a good teacher so that I could teach others how to teach. I found, somewhat to my surprise, that I had a certain histrionic capability, probably inherited down my dad's side, although my mum could put on an act when she wanted to!

In 1971, I was awarded the Military Cross for service in Vietnam (for the actions of storming the bunker systems during October 1969). Professionally, this was a very significant event. The 'halo effect' is a real and healthy syndrome in the Australian Army. After being a run-of-the-mill platoon commander in Vietnam (albeit quite successful), I suddenly became one of the Army's anointed within that junior officer rank.

More particularly, I instinctively knew I had to lift my game and keep it lifted in terms of professional standards and personal conduct, otherwise I would let the Army and myself down very badly. Throughout the rest of my career, people took it for granted that I had a fundamental understanding of close combat and the command of troops in action. In order not to disappoint them or myself, I became a very assiduous student of tactics and war fighting techniques: if it is preserved, that halo effect can be compounded.

On the romance side, I was starting from a pretty barren field, but I was amazingly zealous and progressively refined my winning approach from the caveman/rugby union forward style to something a little more genteel and courteous.

Without doubt it was the job I landed after the Methods of Instruction team that had the greatest civilising effect. Late in

1971, I was invited to be interviewed as a potential new Army Aide de Camp (ADC) to his Excellency the Governor General, Sir Paul Hasluck. This remarkable possibility rounded out the bafflement of those many people who had observed me either with a wry amusement or with anguish and sorrow at Duntroon.

The 'Sceptics Society' must have received another jolt when the Governor General asked me if I wanted the job. I said yes! I started before Christmas in 1971 and remained on duty over the break as the new bloke.

I thought things might be starting to look up on the romance side when, one quiet day (the Governor General and his family having gone home to Western Australia) I received a phone call from a recent Miss Australia! Alas, it turned out she had a mundane inquiry to place to the Governor General.

After the holidays, Government House swung into its regular work routine. I found myself with the Navy and Air Force ADCs, who became extraordinarily good friends, working very long hours to arrange the Governor General's hectic schedule both at home and travelling. It was the most absorbing year of meeting the Governor General's guests and hosts, who ranged from the most prominent Australians to ordinary community members, especially volunteers. Prime ministers, presidents and princes were a passing kaleidoscope in 1972.

At the Melbourne Cup that year, apart from the money on the horses, the smart money was on the Labor Party for victory on 3 December. Gough Whitlam was at the races that day in the Members' stand. As you would expect of an ADC to the Governor General, I knew him to speak to and nodded to him on several occasions as I moved backwards and forwards putting on small wagers on behalf of the Governor General and slightly larger ones on my own behalf (we were getting some pretty good tips from committee members!).

As I wandered out to put a bet on the Cup, Mr Whitlam ambushed me and asked me what the Governor General was backing in the Cup. I was a bit reticent about this because these two men had 'form' between them (going back to when the Governor General had been a Minister in Parliament), and I wasn't sure if this was bordering on the crime of treason. Reasoning with myself that one ought to be able to trust the next Prime Minister, I revealed that I was carrying a bet on Piping Lane, a six-year-old carrying a light weight. At this point Mr Whitlam handed over a note of currency to me and asked me to put it on Piping Lane for him. Piping Lane duly won and there was much jollity in the vice-regal box. As I marched off to get the winnings, a large Whitlamite hand at the end of a large Whitlamite arm seized me and drew me to the bar where champagne was taken and an ogling group of bystanders wondered what the ADC and the Leader of the Opposition were so chummy about. I did not volunteer this episode to the Governor General.

At the end of this fascinating interlude, it was back into regimental life as a company second-in-command in 5 RAR. This battalion was Sydney based and had been raised specifically to meet our commitments in Vietnam, where it had had two tours of duty, in 1966–1967 and in 1969–1970. It was full of very experienced officers, NCOs and diggers.

By now of course, Australia's involvement in the Vietnam War was over and we were in the piping days of peace. For the Army this meant a comprehensive audit of our likely operating environments and appropriate techniques to deal with those environments, followed by a hectic training programme to get up to speed.

I enjoyed life back in a battalion but, like everybody else in the Defence Force, kept avidly reading the newspapers to divine when and where Australia's next overseas military expedition would be — and to somehow contrive to be part of it. Over these years there were plenty of alarms and excursions of this nature, with the possibilities of UN service in Cyprus, Africa and even the Middle East all being canvassed in whispered tones around the officers' and sergeants' messes. Nothing ever came of these but we were frequently quivering with expectation.

Life was therefore a round of military training in the local area, battalion sport (mostly rugby, which was most enjoyable), major exercises through New South Wales and Queensland and, in the bits in between, attempts to kick-start a social life.

At the end of 1974, I went on leave pretty happy with life. I was by now the adjutant of the battalion and was due to be a company commander in the same unit after we came back from leave in early 1975. I was game to be taking on this job as a captain but this didn't fuss me because by now I was pretty self-confident and the company was the same one in which I had been the second-in-command.

Well, on Christmas Eve a monster cyclone called Tracy hit Darwin and all leave plans were thrown into disarray.

I was staying with Mum and Dad at their married quarters in the military base at Watsons Bay in Sydney. In the hectic couple of days straight after the cyclone, refugees from Darwin were being brought in busloads to be temporarily housed, clothed and fed in places like Watsons Bay. Mum, Dad and all other adults staying in the vicinity became an instant force of volunteers to take care of these homeless, destitute and exhausted people. One day at home the phone rang and it was the duty officer from the battalion at Holsworthy telling me that I had to report in immediately as the battalion was being sent to Darwin to assist in the recovery operation. The next day I was flying in to Darwin in a C130 aircraft as part of a two-man advance party for the battalion's arrival in two days' time. Looking out of the window on the plane, the scene below in Darwin looked like nothing so much as the aftermath of a nuclear explosion: everything was flattened and cast into the street, the next street or several suburbs over. I had never seen such destruction.

The work that the battalion and my company did in Darwin was backbreaking and, after a while, monotonous. Overall, however, it was enormously satisfying, as it was a case of very disciplined, fit and motivated young men and women in uniform helping their fellow Australians who were in desperate circumstances. It was the making of my company (Delta Company) for that year — so high was our morale and our self-esteem after our effort in Darwin that we were virtually unbeatable in sport, in military training and in just about every other aspect of battalion life. As a 27-year-old company commander, I was revelling in this job where somebody entrusted me with a hundred soldiers or more.

There was another great plus in the year of 1975.

In the years after returning from Vietnam, I had had a number of short-term relationships — lovely young women, but nobody who was both just right and prepared to embrace the military life to which I had committed myself. Things were about to change.

Not long after returning from Darwin, the officers' mess had scheduled a mixed dining-in night — a formal dinner where officers wore their finery and we were encouraged to bring wives, partners and girlfriends. I had none of these, but thought that it was about time I brought somebody stunning into the midst of all these doubting Thomases. I annoyed the living daylights out of a pal of mine, who had left the Army a couple of years earlier, to introduce me to some enormously impressive women in his work area.

He was very reluctant, knowing me to be quite possibly a direct descendant of Genghis Khan. Nonetheless, loyalty prevailed and with great trepidation, having prepared the ground previously with a delightful young woman he worked with, he asked her to receive a phone call from me without hanging up or calling the police. I phoned her one afternoon about a week before the big dinner, to ask her out on a 'getting to know you' date. Her name was Lynne Payne. She was a bit younger than me and living in Cronulla. When I phoned her I'd put on my greasiest government house manners and she agreed to come and have dinner with me at Napoleon's, a nice restaurant in South Dowling Street.

At the appointed time, I arrived at the apartment in Cronulla where she lived with her mum and dad (I knew from our phone conversation that she had travelled around the world twice, so I did not think that she was an unreconstructed homebody!). I knocked on the door, not knowing that she had told her mum that, if I was absolutely ghastly, her mum was to say how sad it was that Lynne had been taken ill and wouldn't be able to go out. When her mum answered the door, I saw this beautiful middle-aged lady and said to her, 'Hello, my name is Peter and you must be Lynne's older sister — would you tell her I've arrived?' She stood back, opened the door wide and said, 'Come in, Lynne is nearly ready, I'm her mum — come meet my husband.'

Tactical victories such as these are the stuff of life for Army officers and you cherish every one of them. I was glad that Lynne's mum, Billie, was such a wonderful woman, because going by the instructions that Lynne had provided her for my refusal, it would have been a close run thing: I was dressed in an off-white, rollneck pullover, a brown leather coat and purple flared trousers with modest side stitching. Very spiffy — very gross!

Napoleon's lived up to my expectations. I was absolutely smitten with Lynne from the first time I saw her. We had a wonderful night. I couldn't wait for the formal dinner so that I could see her again and incidentally show her off to all the vultures in the mess.

At the formal dinner, my commanding officer chose her to be his dinner partner across the table from me and so she appeared on the seating plan. This was because I was reputed to be such a hard-nosed so-and-so that he and everybody else were intrigued to find out who would possibly be my partner at such an event. His first question to her, heard by me across the table, was, 'How did you get mixed up with a reprobate like Cosgrove?' I can't remember her exact reply, but for the entire evening she acted with a friendly dignity and charm that captivated every man in the room.

After that, we started to go steady and have never left each other's side since. As the year drew on, I couldn't wait for nights off and free weekends to be with this beautiful girl and to contemplate, if I was very lucky, a lifetime with her. We never spoke of it in the first ten months or so of our relationship, but I thought of nothing else after that first date. I even took her to the end of year Delta Company party, an all ranks affair with a disco, rudimentary snacks, stacks of beer, mixed drinks and good cheer.

This was like an office party — with the sophistication taken out. For example, my wonderful company quartermaster sergeant, Staff Sergeant Colin Cooper, hugely popular with the diggers, was about to leave the company. As a going away present, he was presented with a plastic female breast mounted on a piece of polished wood with a plaque attached which read: 'To Col Cooper, who always kept abreast of the times!' The digger who gave it to him demonstrated that, when you pressed the nipple, it rang a bell inside the breast — the company thought it was a top gift!

Lynne handled the entire evening with great affection and charm, and absolutely captivated the company. Soldier after soldier came up to me, dragged me aside and told me with beery breath, 'You better grab this one boss — don't let her get away!' While one part of me was head over heels in love with her, the other part noted how magnificent she was with people, especially the sort of people I had committed my life to since the days of Vietnam.

As Lynne had already been overseas twice, at the end of 1975 I thought I'd better do a little bit of international touring myself, to give us something to talk about in what I hoped would be the many years ahead.

On my return from a five-week tour to Europe I was just as smitten as I had ever been. Unfortunately for my romantic intentions, I had been posted from Sydney to the Infantry Centre in the country New South Wales town of Singleton.

For a week or two after starting the job there as a tactics instructor on the company commanders course as a newly promoted major, I commuted up and down to Sydney to visit Lynne. One weekend when I couldn't do this because of work commitments, I attended a convivial 'candlelight' dinner in the officers' mess for the married officers and their wives and some of us more mature-age single officers. Looking at all these friends and missing Lynne terribly, I decided to act.

I hadn't worked out how the next fervently desired part of our relationship would be discussed but I marched out to the public phone box just outside the mess (no mobile phones in those days) and phoned her at her place in Cronulla.

I had some small change which I fed into the phone and, in the first few minutes of the time my money entitled me to, I rabbited on about what a nice evening it was and how I wished she was there and how I loved her very much. Getting near the end of the money, I gabbled out a proposal of marriage and, as I fervently hoped, she accepted.

At this point the switchboard operator chimed in to tell me that my time was up and to ask if I was extending. I told her that I had just proposed to my girlfriend and asked if she would give me some more time. She giggled a bit, wished us both luck and departed the line (although there was a suspicious attenuation for the remainder of the long call).

Lynne and I spoke for some time in that dreamy, rhapsodic way of lovers newly espoused. At the end, when decency suggested we should finish the call, we both vowed to keep our news to ourselves until we could discuss the right way to break it to our families and friends.

For my part, I walked back into the mess and immediately encountered my friends Bruce and Jan Osborn who knew Lynne well. They asked me where I had been all this time and I blurted out that I had been proposing to Lynne and that she had accepted! Fortunately we were away from the rest of the crowd and we were able to keep it among the three of us. I felt really guilty about this. I confessed to Lynne the next day and she in turn admitted that, when I had phoned the previous evening, she had been cooking dinner at her parents' home (her parents being out) for herself and her good friend Margaret. She had told Margaret the news the instant she was off the phone. She must therefore have beaten me in breaking our solemn promise by a good measure of time!

The rest of the year sped past and we were married on 17 December 1976 in Mary Immaculate Church at Charing Cross in Waverley — the very same church where the Redemptorist Fathers so passionately exhorted us Waverley schoolboys to modesty and chastity. Our marriage was performed by one of the truly great army chaplains of the era, Father John Tinkler. Lynne was a stunning bride and we both enjoyed the wedding enormously.

At the wedding reception, I muttered a casual remark to my best man, none other than the redoubtable McDermott, to the effect that I didn't want the little car we would be using to drive away from the reception to be generously festooned with tin cans, shaving cream or any of the other usual accoutrements. I thought nothing more of it and, when Lynne and I left the reception to go to a hotel for the evening, nothing more sinister than some lovely flowers scattered over the seats greeted us as we got into the car. It wasn't until months later that I heard that some of our civvy mates had snuck out with one or two others to do the usual to the car. As they approached the vehicle in the darkness, a tall uniformed figure stepped out from behind a tree and said, 'I wouldn't be doing that if I was you!' McDermott had taken me literally and had placed a sentry, rostered from among the military guests, to guard the car! The sentry followed his orders to the letter: all shaving cream, etc., was strictly forbidden, but the sentry's instructions did not include flowers, so some flowers from the local flowerbeds were purloined and put in the car — honour satisfied on both sides.

Lynne and I settled into married bliss in Singleton where, as the newest married couple in a street of married quarters, we were to some degree a centre of attention.

These married quarters were brand new and the army had wasted no money on turfing lawns or establishing gardens and flower beds: that was left to the hard labour and domestic pride of the householders. In the hot summer of 1977, men slaved away before and after work and on weekends, raking, top dressing, seeding, watering, weeding, generally making progress. As a newlywed, I had no garden tools, no expertise, no real interest and very little enthusiasm, but I realised that I would have to strike like a cobra if we weren't to be left with front and back yards full of dirt and weeds.

Here my friend Bruce Osborn played a blinder. His next-door neighbour was the greenkeeper at the local civilian golf club. One day in late summer this chap mentioned to Bruce that he was picking up part of the fairway and verge of the green on one of the golf course holes with a turf cutter. Did Bruce know anyone who might want the turf on the basis of 'where it is, as it is'? Bruce instantly thought of me and we plotted to do the deed to get me back on par with my other more zealous neighbours.

Late in the afternoon, when all the officers-cum-gardeners in the street had called it quits, Bruce and I picked up a number of trailer loads of the rolled turf. By the time we'd got it all back to my place, it was virtually dark, but we rolled it out anyway. The next day, as the other fellows emerged for work, howls of outrage echoed up and down the street when they saw my complete, healthy, lush, emerald green lawns. Our gardening successes weren't entirely due to luck, however: Lynne turned out to have a green thumb on the several flower beds we established, and we won the street gardening prize the following spring.

My preferred recreation was rugby, rather than gardening. I had renewed my enthusiasm for the game in some highly enjoyable seasons with the battalion at Holsworthy and had continued playing when I got to Singleton.

The Army had a team in the local civilian competition, the Hunter Valley Zone, part of the New South Wales country rugby union. Army always had a strong team, limited by the small army population in the region but assisted by our great esprit and generally high levels of fitness. In addition, we always had a handful of genuinely talented players, so Army was one of the stronger teams in the competition.

We used to have epic battles against the Singleton civilian team. While these were frequently bloody and savage encounters, in that quirky way of rugby I made a lot of friends in the town, although many of these friendships only blossomed after I retired from rugby. As a testament to the fact that the zone was not very strong in playing talent, I was often selected to play with the Hunter Valley representative side.

One memorable representative match — against a very strong team, Central North Zone — took place at Murrurundi. As Murrurundi was a small place, the local showground served for many different functions, anything from gymkhanas to football. In the small grandstand a handful of the faithful had gathered to watch the slaughter and with a great arpeggio flourish of the whistle from the ref, we were into it.

Within moments of the start we went into one of our most practised moves — back behind our goalposts, waiting for their conversion attempt. This pretty much established the pattern of the game, and I seem to recall that, after ten minutes or so, we were comfortably behind.

At one of our numerous kick-offs back to them, I thought that I might introduce a novelty into our game by tackling the man who received the ball. I even nominated to our bloke who was kicking off, a particularly large man on the other side as the fellow to receive the kick.

Let me pause for a moment here. For any truly unskilled player who nonetheless has a degree of bulk, this is the ultimate gimme. You have a stationary target, forced by the unwritten rules of the game to stand there looking skywards, arms raised in supplication and expectation, ready to do his duty by his team and catch the ball. If he knew what evil was in your heart, he would forget all about the ball, and instead keep his eye on your onrushing form, so that, as you arrived, he would step to one side and smack you smartly in the mouth. (Of course, the game's lawmakers have now fixed up this little wheeze by protecting those graceful giraffes and gazelles from the hippopotami of the game.)

The opposition forwards gave me one of those 'you must be kidding' looks as we kicked off and the ball described a graceful arc (kick-offs being one the most practised parts of our game!), dropping gently into the arms of the nominated big person.

As he took the ball, I hit him! I hit him from the roof of his mouth to the soles of his feet. I hit him with arms, shoulders, hips, thighs, knees, feet, teeth, eyebrows; I even smashed him with my hair (I had some then). It made a sound like two full coal-trucks colliding. In the grandstand, strong men covered their wives' eyes. In Muswellbrook, locals reported an explosion north along the highway and feared a mine disaster. I drove this bloke backwards several yards as the ball flew from his grasp. In last few feet of the tackle, I was rehearsing what I would say to the coroner.

As we came apart, the man I had now termed 'corpse-still-standing' turned towards me and I noticed two things. Firstly, it was a chap called Brian Mansfield, at that time an incumbent Wallaby second-rower. Secondly his eyes — oh, those eyes! They were dank, deep, fixed and seemingly lifeless. They were looking at me as a shark regards its lunch.

A transformation came over me after that: from a leaden-footed, earth-bound, almost subterranean creature, I became swift, lithe, agile, alert, gazelle-like, one of the most mobile of our forwards, constantly harassing the opposing backs, quick to my feet at the breakdown, not getting bogged down at the rucks and mauls, lurking in deep cover, ever ready to take the pressure off our fullback.

It was during this phase of the game that we Hunter Valley players saw Central North repeat a sequence of the most stunning plays that, in our humble collective view, we had ever seen. It went like this: Central North would clear the ball from the back of the lineout, scrum, ruck or maul and pass it (yes pass it!) from hand to hand along the backline to the winger (yes, I know, unbelievable

— the winger of all people!). The winger would run very fast down the sideline and score a try. We were awestruck.

I was doing a bit of quiet lurking somewhere in fullback territory, when another moment of madness overcame me. I would try the tackling novelty again! I lost a moment as I checked that the smallish figure whizzing down the wing wasn't Mr Mansfield in disguise and then another quick look around to see just exactly where he was, before I went off in full pursuit.

It must have been beautiful to watch — a nuggetty winger, legs working like pistons, hurtling down the sideline; noble, upright, muscular, bronzed, classically-handsome loose forward (me), hair flowing, gliding like a cheetah in that classic winger-killing, corner-flagging run. Strong men in the grandstand would have trembled with envy and anticipation of the death of the troll-like winger.

It was at this point, as prey, predator and corner-flag were about to converge, that one of the opposition (rather too casually, I thought) called out, 'Watch out Nathan, the big bloke's after you!'

Ah, pride! With a sad smile contemplating the death of the troll, I was inwardly debating whether to go for the 'backbone smash' or the 'spider drop' tackle. Then, just as I launched into a mighty dive (8.7 from the Russian judge), the troll nipped inside me. I was still airborne somewhere in the in-goal as he neatly placed the ball under the black dot. Then I landed and slid.

I did mention, didn't I, that they used the showground for gymkhanas? Well, the Pony Club had been there that morning, that's for sure! I did a long, slow, voluptuous slide through an extraordinarily large, fragrantly fresh, pile of horse manure. I was coated from the top of my head to my knees. I was still lying there unmoving, face-down, as the Hunter Valley team assembled for our regular chat under the goalposts. Eventually, I felt compelled to rise like the Creature from the Black Lagoon — wearing camouflage paint somewhat different to that which the Army normally wears and with an odour to add to that of honest sweat. A sort of Al Jolson in mottled greens and browns.

The game came to a standstill.

Children covered the eyes of strong men and their wives in the stand.

The opposition kicker missed his only goal of the game.

After a powerful squirting with the nearest fire-hose and donning the Hunter Valley spare jersey, it was on with the game, although in a way I now felt safer from Mr Mansfield — in fact I was pretty safe from just about everyone. I relaxed.

You should never relax on a rugby field. Bad things can happen. With about twenty minutes to go, I found myself lying quietly in the bottom of a ruck, trying to be inconspicuous, imagining I was a chameleon, blending in with the grass — obviously unsuccessfully. I looked up (as a chameleon, at the bottom of a rugby ruck, you should never do that) and saw a flashing, slashing boot attached to a youthful, blond giant heading towards my looking gear. I averted my eyes from the impending disaster and copped it in the ear instead. Once, twice the villain struck, before the ruck broke up. Now all blokes know the unwritten rule — at this stage you leap to your feet and stack on a blue. I leapt up and hauled off, when my team-mate and Army colleague, Bob Donkin, said in distraught tones, 'Oh God, jeez mate, you're in trouble — go off, get to a hospital!' He was immediately joined by a chorus of other Job's Comforters, including the ref. All thoughts of retaliation vanished. Like a well-trained Shetland pony, I turned for the sideline and trotted off. The spectators in the stand gave me the polite applause one gives a wounded warrior — until I was close enough, when it changed to sickened cries of 'Errgh! Get off, get to a doctor!' By this time I was convinced there was a big problem and I wondered what the blond giant was going to tell the coroner. I also reflected on the fact that it was the third time I had been in the shit that day!

The Hunter Valley team officials met me grim-faced and took me straight into the sheds. There was then much hustling and bustling, staunching of wounds, fumbling with copious head bandages, much urgency in fact.

The calmest person was undoubtedly me, because I appreciated three things: first, I had finished for the day; second, I wasn't going to die; and last, I was safe from the ogre Mansfield and his blond giant assistant. I told the bustling officials that they should stop fussing and simply get me to a quack. One of them, Neil Miles, said dryly, 'I am a quack.'

Before I knew it, with head bandaged into a giant aiming mark, I was rushed back to the sideline and into the game for the last 15 minutes of carnage.

Playing for the Valley was good fun — you got to punch and be punched by strangers; you got to hear the coach John 'Fats' Halter's prematch and half-time rev-ups (the most printable of which was to 'go out there and tear their so-and-so heads off'), and you got to meet some extraordinarily good blokes. I finished playing rugby when we left Singleton, but with a wonderful store of memories.

*

Being married had changed my life immeasurably for the better, but another marvellous event was now in prospect.

One afternoon in the middle of 1977, I had just pulled up at the collection of old huts that served as our office and classroom area when I saw Lynne waiting for me on the verandah of the long wooden hut where we instructors had our individual offices. As I walked towards her, I could tell that it wasn't bad news. She was smiling and I could see that she was holding up the folded cardboard name plate that normally rested on the front of my desk and which read 'Major Peter Cosgrove'. As I got closer, almost up to her, I could read what she had written underneath, in small, neat printing — 'and son'.

We were absolutely overjoyed and had great fun telling the wonderful news to the grandparents-to-be on both sides. The baby was due in March 1978. The time rushed by, and it seemed that every day brought a new and significant 'baby event'. One of the factors we had to consider was that I was getting to the stage of being a candidate to go to Staff College, a year-long military school for majors to give them the requisite skills to be more senior staff officers and commanders. I had done well at the battalion and as an instructor at the Infantry Centre, so I was likely to get an early call. Professionally, this would have been very good news but the college was at Queenscliff in Victoria, which would have made it difficult for the doting grandparents to visit the new grandchild.

On 9 March 1978, Lynne and I duly found ourselves in the labour ward at St George Hospital in Sydney. I was standing around in surgical cap and gown being generally useless while Lynne was getting into the serious business of having contractions followed by a baby. Suddenly, one of the midwives bustled in and inquired whether I was in the Army. When I replied in the affirmative, she said that there was a chap on the telephone in the labour ward office wanting to talk to me.

When I picked up the phone, I found that it was Colonel John Essex-Clark, the Commandant of the Infantry Centre. John told me that it was great news he was passing on: I had been selected to attend Staff College not at Queenscliff in Victoria but at a place called Quantico. My first confused thought was to be aghast at taking my wife and new baby off into the wilds of Pakistan. I had confused Quetta, the Pakistani Staff College, with Quantico, the United States Marine Corps Command and Staff College in northern Virginia.

When John and I had sorted out this little confusion, I was relieved and delighted, albeit still a little disappointed that we would be taking the bub so far away from our extended family. I wandered back into the room where Lynne gave me an old-fashioned look for swanning around taking phone calls while there was a baby to be born, but I soon had her attention with the honeyed words of a beaut overseas posting. Stephen Cosgrove was triumphantly delivered into the world a few hours later. Sadly, by the time I had hugged and kissed his exhausted mum, held the little fellow with extraordinary care (and not a little anxiety), phoned the eager grandparents and said a fond goodnight to mother and son, the pubs were closed!

Our time in the States was marvellous fun.

We lived on the top floor of a three-storey apartment building on the Marine base at Quantico. Summers in that part of

Virginia are extraordinarily humid, virtually tropical in nature. Just about everybody on the base had some form of air-conditioning. In our case we had a thundering great old air-conditioner, a hand-me-down from previous Australian occupants. This sat in our dining-room window, sounding like a jumbo jet doing an engine test but pushing a welcome blast of cold air through the apartment. It went on the blink one day and we got a repair man who took it away with the help of a strong offsider. We sweltered while it was being repaired, but a couple of days later, while I was at work down at the Staff College, the repair men returned it, put it back in the window, started it up and presto, lovely cool air again.

As I was putting my key in the door that afternoon, I could hear it and felt the slight vibration in the door, but I didn't care, because Lynne, Stephen and I would be cool again. I found Lynne in the kitchen, and we started chatting about how nice it was to be cool again.

Suddenly, there was a great silence.

Thinking that the air-conditioner had gone the blink again, I was just groaning, 'Oh no!' when a thunderous boom came from outside the apartment. Rushing into the dining room, I saw a large space where the air-conditioner had been. I was concerned that the immensely heavy air-conditioner might have struck somebody on the ground. Fortunately it had not struck anybody, because it had hit something else. Parked below my window was the pride and joy of one of the ground floor residents, a helicopter pilot with the President's helicopter squadron. He had a classic car which he had been restoring and the air-conditioner had plummeted through the roof of the car, destroying the steering column and driver's seat before exploding sideways through the driver's door. It was now lying alongside the car like some kind of malevolent metal beast.

An awestruck crowd was already gathering as I galloped down the stairs. When I got there, I was somewhat stuck for words (although thinking of dollar signs with some integers and lots of noughts following), but one of my Marine mates, realising that nobody had been hurt, said 'Hey buddy, you can't put a price on a good time!'

I have entered United States Marine Corps folklore, certainly amongst that generation of officers, as the 'air-conditioner man'. This was obviously because of the incident but it was cemented into folklore when, the next day at the college, I said to a colleague (who at that time hadn't heard of the incident), that if he wanted to bring his car around to our apartments, I could drop some air-conditioning into it!

On the professional side, I learnt a great deal from my time with the marines. The USMC operates essentially as a joint army and navy and air force. As the service with the closest relationship with the United States Navy, the Marines have worked together with the USN for hundreds of years. The Marines also have their own infantry, armour, artillery, engineers, logistic troops and, crucially, their own air force, both combat and transport aircraft. I learnt from them not only the characteristics and the individual capabilities of those parts of their force outside my own experience, but the synergies available when these capabilities can be coordinated and harnessed in the same cause. These sorts of insights stood me in very good stead years later when I found myself in command of a major joint force.

We went as a family of three to the United States but we came home as a family of three and a half. Our second child, Philip, was born in October 1979, a few months after our return. It was our good fortune to be posted to Sydney on my return and Lynne was thus able to have the bub with exactly the same doctor and midwives at St George Hospital. By now we were all pretty chatty during Lynne's labour, although she probably didn't appreciate all of this familiar bonhomie while she was busy having contractions.

Having been trained as a staff officer, I was now employed as one for a lengthy posting of a bit over three years at Victoria Barracks in Sydney. In that time we did all the things that young families do, especially spending a lot of time with their extended families, conscious that my next posting might well be far away from Sydney and the kids, their grandparents and aunties and uncles and cousins would all miss each other and would need some time together 'in the bank'.

In the third year of this posting I was promoted to lieutenant colonel and given the news that I would go off to command the battalion to which I had first been posted, 1 RAR, located in Townsville. Professionally this was great news; the battalion was one of two highly ready, fully manned and equipped fighting units available for rapid deployment for any contingency. From a family point of view, it could hardly have been more remote but Lynne was delighted for me, and the grandparents and our other relatives were very understanding. Just to complicate the emotional wrench in the logistics of the move, Lynne was now pregnant with our third child. David was born in late December 1982 and we moved to Townsville in January!

Still, it all went very well, settling into another married quarter, getting to know a new lot of friends and colleagues, catching up with other friends who were also posted there, getting the older kids into school, all while living under the vast moist umbrella of the North Queensland wet season. Life in this battalion environment was very pleasant and exciting. I had become very fit before taking up the job and so, as a very young commanding officer (I was thirty-six at the time, on the young side to be a CO of an infantry battalion in peacetime), I was out there with the troops in just about all aspects of their training, generally watching and assessing but often joining in and certainly getting to know them fairly quickly.

In that first year we went on a major military exercise over in the Pilbara region of Western Australia.

This was one of the *Kangaroo* series of exercises to which we committed a substantial number of troops with heavy support from the Royal Australian Navy and the Royal Australian Air Force. In this exercise, called *Kangaroo 83*, my battalion was designated the exercise enemy; we were the dreaded Kamarians, from a mythical island off the coast of Australia, jealous of Australia's resource riches and ideologically estranged from Australia's democratic form of government and culture. So we had invaded the place and now had to be found and destroyed by the Australian Defence Force.

The major Australian unit tasked with seeking and destroying us was 2nd/4th Battalion, the Royal Australian Regiment (2/4 RAR). This was grist to the mill for my diggers because 2/4 RAR were also stationed in Townsville and we regularly competed in every possible way with them.

As the Kamarians, our job was to carry out a series of predations in the Pilbara, and to conceal ourselves as best we could in between times. We 'raided' mines, small towns, cattle properties and even, on one celebrated occasion, the Millstream pub. We conducted roadblocks where, instead of robbing and murdering as perhaps invaders might do, we politely waved over motorists and spoke to them about the exercise, telling them what notionally an enemy might be doing to them at this moment and encouraging them to report us to the police. After each of these 'atrocities' we would disappear back into the wilderness to hide out before our next expedition. It was remarkable to me how easy it was for the hundreds of us to disappear into the scrub and not be seen even by people on the lookout.

The exercise was taking place at the same time as that wonderful and successful America's Cup challenge in Newport, Rhode Island. While we were on exercise we kept in touch with the gripping progress of the race series. On the night of the final race I was with my headquarters out somewhere in the red dust of the Pilbara. I lay on my back watching the most brilliant natural 'planetarium' of stars, relishing the 'electric blanket' warmth of the red soil and listening to a small transistor radio with an earphone. As many Aussies will recall, we were quite a way behind for much of the race and I drifted off to sleep thinking that another mighty and gallant attempt had failed. Something woke me up a little later on: it was a different note in the voice of the Australian commentator. There was a huge adrenaline charge when he announced joyfully that *Australia II* had taken the lead. Sitting bolt upright, I listened with mounting glee to the final downwind leg as *Australia II* emphatically won the race and thus the Cup. It now was about 4 a.m. and, too excited to sleep, I wandered around the small group who were my tactical headquarters staff and shook each awake with the news, 'We've won the Cup!' That morning we toasted Alan Bond, John Bertrand and the team with the finest ration pack hot coffee.

At that time of my life I would have told you that the three best jobs by far that I had were as a platoon commander, then a company commander and now as commanding officer of a battalion of over 700 men. I knew just about every soldier by name and generally a great deal more about them besides. Each junior officer was required to keep a 'platoon commander's notebook' containing the personal and career details of every soldier under that officer's command. These things didn't take long to become very bulky. There were over twenty platoons in the battalion but I set myself the task of reviewing each one of the notebooks three times a year. I did this both to acquaint myself with all of the many important details concerning the men in the battalion and also to ensure that the junior officers and their company commanders were diligent in record-keeping and following up on matters affecting the soldiers.

The best jobs always seem to fly by. In 1984, we received the news that late that year I would take up the job as the Australian instructor at the British Army Staff College at Camberley in Surrey, UK. This was another plum job with again the only drawback being the further separation of our growing family from our extended family in Sydney. By now our parents were in some cases a little frail and any of these significant separations left you hoping that all would be well while you were away.

We left in September 1984 for a two and a bit year posting with the Poms. Lynne and I had both visited the UK as tourists and I had worked with the Brits in Malaysia, but this would require us to set up a home and settle in for a lengthy stay. We had a great time in Britain, making tremendous friends and enjoying the lifestyle immensely. While Aussies and Poms do chiack each other mercilessly as one proud people to another, major elements of both our populations still share a great cultural and social affinity. While I was with the Brits I travelled extensively through Europe and Africa. I instructed on all segments of their course, even those areas dealing with the tactics and techniques they would use to defend Europe against a Warsaw Pact invasion. This gave me extremely useful insights into modern war fighting techniques on a conventional and a nuclear battlefield. The Australian Army is not organised or equipped to undertake those sort of high intensity operations, but understanding how they might play out was a very significant body of knowledge for me to have when I became much more senior a number of years later.

In early 1985, I was notified by Canberra that I was to become a Member of the Military Division of the Order of Australia. Having been an ADC to the Governor General, I knew the form, so I immediately got in touch with Canberra and asked if it would be all right if I applied for the medal to be presented by the Queen at Buckingham Palace at one of the routine British investitures.

Very quickly, the answer came back in the affirmative, and so in the balmy early summer in London, Lynne, me and the two older boys were off to the Palace. David was a bit too young to sit through an investiture and we had to make a special plea to get both of the older boys in for the occasion. On the day, everybody looked very spiffy, Lynne in a beautiful suit, the boys in blazers, ties and tailored slacks, me in uniform with Sam Browne leather belt. The British Army had given me a car and driver for the day, so we were able to drive into Buckingham Palace and alight at the main entrance.

The boys were very goggle-eyed and, although Lynne and I tried harder to look cool, it was very impressive: a grand sweeping staircase took us from the foyer up to the first floor where the investiture would take place. This staircase was lined every five steps or so by a Guardsman from the Blues and Royals in full ceremonial uniform, silver helmet with horsehair plume, silver breastplate, tall gleaming boots and cavalry sabre drawn and resting on the shoulder.

At the head of the stairs I was taken off into the Queen's picture gallery — a vast room furnished with the most beautiful sofas, chairs and occasional tables and, of course, with the most wonderful artworks on every wall. There, I encountered scores of award recipients waiting to be briefed before proceeding down an external corridor to the ballroom where the investiture itself would take place.

In the meantime, Lynne and the boys had been whisked along another corridor. Lynne thought that the boys should use the bathroom before the investiture got underway, so she took the lads into the ladies powder room. Apparently the fittings in the powder room were very elegant, intricate and fascinating, especially in the water closets and especially for young boys. Lynne was mortified when she discovered that Stephen and Philip had locked themselves in one of the cubicles and were having a great time continually flushing the toilet in order to observe yet again the intricate mechanism in action. I knew nothing of this at the time, but I got an earful about it later!

I was included with those British service people who were getting gongs on the day and, by tradition, servicemen and women are given their awards last. Eventually, we were ushered from the now deserted picture gallery into the corridor leading into the ballroom. When my name was called, I entered the ballroom and moved forward to stand in front of the Queen. I was immediately delighted to spot Lynne and the boys in the audience. The Queen was well briefed on my immediate background and it was a real thrill to be honoured in this way while so far from home. I treated it as a rare privilege, because I didn't think that I would be getting another award from the Queen at any time in the future!

Despite all of the great enjoyment of being at home virtually every night with Lynne and the boys (who were growing like weeds), the death of my dad in 1985 cast a shadow over our time in England. Dad, who had been retired since late 1975, had a turn at his bowls club, was rushed off to hospital and was diagnosed as having had a stroke. Mum phoned me in England and I started for home immediately, but I hadn't even finished packing when a second phone call told me that Dad had died. Of course, I continued on back to Australia to be with Mum and Stephanie and to be at Dad's funeral.

After a couple of days at home in Sydney, I headed back to Camberley and, on the long flight back, I reflected on what a good bloke and a fine Dad he had been. My only regret was that I had not seen enough of him over our lives together, especially when I was young. To some degree that thought influenced Lynne and me when, in years to come, we faced the choice of having the boys in boarding schools or keeping them with us.

We returned to Australia at the end of 1986, back to Canberra where I was to be the military assistant to the Chief of the General Staff — the professional head of the Army. This was another great job, but one which was very time consuming. As the principal personal staff officer to the Chief, his extremely long working hours became mine as well. On the other side of the coin, it was a priceless education in the exercise of high command and every issue and every conversation was a great learning experience. If you had a young family, however, you wouldn't want to do the job for more than one year.

Part of the requirements of the job included accompanying the Chief on his overseas visits, where you acted as a note taker on the important meetings and as an ADC for the rest of the visit. I had some fascinating visits while in the job, none more so than about ten days in India in early 1987. On my return, I raved to Lynne about the exotic beauty and fascinating culture of the place, and we both put it on our list of places we would like to live.

The Canberra posting was a long one — three years in several different jobs, during which the boys all went to the same school and the older two started to play team sports. For my part, I coached the kids' cricket teams and Lynne and I were reunited with some of our old army mates and began to enjoy a growing group of civilian friends.

But advancement beckoned and, for a fellow of my background, a command and training job in charge of one of the Army's training institutions was on the cards.

I had been promoted to colonel in mid-1988 and was now posted back to the Hunter Valley, to command the Infantry Centre, where Lynne and I had spent our first years of marriage. Professionally, this was another great posting, because the work of the centre and the various tasks and responsibilities of command were familiar territory for me. On the home front, the kids were happy, and Lynne and I slotted straight back in to a group of friends which became wider in our two years there.

As the Commandant of the local army base, I was the senior military officer in the Hunter region (excluding some senior RAAF officers at the fighter base at Williamtown). This meant quite a bit of representational contact with the wider community, which Lynne and I much enjoyed. More than once I mused on my perception that the Army gets a wonderful but unpaid ambassador when a spouse or partner throws themselves into this representational role. Lynne is very gregarious, outgoing and charming, and she delighted in this constant, subtle demonstration that army families are normal, friendly people. I learnt a lot from her about relaxing and having fun in public while maintaining any necessary dignity. I also learnt much from her about the usefulness of a phenomenal memory for faces, names and events. Over the years I schooled myself to be much better at this, very much based on Lynne's example.

My next posting was the most significant step in my career up until that stage, even if some earlier jobs had offered more pure enjoyment. I was selected to command 6th Brigade. This entailed promotion to the rank of brigadier and a move to Brisbane where the brigade was based.

Enoggera is a suburb of Brisbane which has for many decades been home to a military base. The brigade had several thousand soldiers, but was going to be the launching platform for the Ready Reserve, an initiative of the Hawke government which linked enlistment in the Army for two years' full-time service with the payment of academic fees to tertiary institutions. The full-time service was linked with a further period of part-time service in the ordinary Reserve.

The scheme proved very popular and, with a brilliantly energetic and talented staff constantly coming up with ways to improve the scheme, in the second year of my command I had the biggest brigade in the Army. One day I put nearly 4000 soldiers on parade, just so that they could look around and observe and absorb what a great and powerful instrument an infantry brigade can be.

There were quite a few naysayers in the wider Army about the scheme because it was felt to be sucking resources from both the Regular Army and the ordinary Reserve. I think that it was worth persisting with, because many of the soldiers who gathered into the Ready Reserve in Enoggera were of extraordinarily high quality, and their ability to germinate energy and talent in the wider Reserve when they finished their full-time service was another big plus.

While I had been soldiering on and having a whale of a time as a brigade commander, Lynne as usual was being the consummate homemaker and mum. We put all the boys into Marist College Ashgrove, a great school just across the back fence from Enoggera, and not far from our home in The Gap.

It was a beaut school with high standards, a good academic reputation and a marvellous tradition of elite sporting teams, notably in rugby union. Although all the boys had played soccer during our few years in Canberra in the late 80s, as soon as we got to Singleton in the Hunter Valley, they had ganged up and insisted on playing rugby. Secretly, I was delighted but I was also glad that I had put no pressure on them. They all turned out to be pretty good, tough team players who each showed more skill than I ever had, certainly at that age. They revelled in the obsessive focus at Marist on the rugby programme.

Marist also had a strong boarding school component, which was about to get some new members. Somewhat out of the blue, I was notified that I had been selected to attend the National Defence College of India in New Delhi.

The one-year course started in January 1994. This was great news in some respects, but created a significant dilemma about the boys' schooling. David, being quite young, would naturally accompany us. His older brothers were problematic because of the more advanced years of their schooling. Reluctantly and in conversation with Stephen and Philip, we came to the conclusion that the older boys would need to board at Marist for the year we would be away. It had wider implications for Steve because this one year would take him to the end of Year 11 and thus well into the Higher School Certificate. It was therefore likely that, when we returned, he would finish off his high school education as a boarder at Marist. Phil, two years behind Steve, would have more options after we returned. The really sad part was breaking up the 'gang of three'. Stephen, Philip and David had hardly spent a night apart since their birth and were very close. We knew that David would miss his older brothers enormously. Mind you, under the generous travel arrangements available to the boys, we were reunited with them in India quite frequently during school holidays.

David's birthday occurred not long before we left for India. We were in Sydney and, to give him a memorable birthday present, we bought him a Wallabies jersey (which became his most prized possession) and even arranged for him to bump into Phil Kearns, the famous Wallaby forward, when David and I dropped in to the Randwick Rugby Club. One of the first things that happened when we checked into a hotel in New Delhi was that somebody knocked off David's Wallaby jersey: he has always been a little sour on India since that moment.

India is the most fascinating of countries. Its culture is enormously complex and exotic. It combines great poverty, racial and caste intolerance, moments of extreme generosity and crushing bureaucratic pettiness, profound spirituality and crass commercialism to rival anything in any cynical western nation. We loved every moment of it, starting as wide-eyed innocents abroad and finishing pretty much the same, except perhaps with a more worldly and cynical veneer and an ability to carve through the worst expressions of 'Babu Raj' — the Rule of the Clerk (petty bureaucracy). We loved the food, but were always on the alert to avoid eating tainted food. We loved our many friends, most of them military families, but knew that we could know them and live within their culture for fifty years without fully understanding what made them tick. We loved the scenery and the presence of history in every roadway, town, fortress and temple.

We even loved our household staff. Tradition and, I suppose, the principle of wealth-sharing required that we have a substantial household staff to support our lives while in India. We had a driver, a *chowkidar* (guard), a *dhobi wallah* (laundry man), a *mali* (gardener), an outside sweeper, an inside sweeper (both women by tradition, but the inside sweeper was infinitely senior!) and, the king of them all, the cook/bearer. Some of the staff lived in a little block of flats attached to our substantial suburban house, so the community to some degree was a 24-hour a day enterprise. When I arrived, a wise man briefed me that Lynne and I would become virtually the mother and father to this community and I must say we scoffed a little at this. Within a few months, however, we were adjudicating family squabbles, forking out money for their personal budgetary shortfalls, helping to celebrate their birthdays, kids starting school, you name it — we were the patriarch and matriarch of this adoptive family. No doubt this sounds terribly paternalistic, but these folk craved our interest and involvement.

One of my most vivid experiences was visiting the Sangam, the confluence of the Ganges and the Jumna, two major rivers of great spiritual significance to Hindus. This confluence occurs at the town of Allahabad in Uttar Pradesh. A giant British-built fort from the colonial era broods over the junction of the rivers from a tall escarpment. From the nearby river's edge, many thousands of people daily take small boats out to the sandbars in the middle of the confluence to bathe in the water and to offer their prayers. Once, while on a tour of Uttar Pradesh, a group of middle-aged men from the NDC, including me, took a small boat out to the Sangam.

The officers with me were urbane, sophisticated and somewhat cynical by objective measure, but to watch them in their profound reverence as they approached the Sangam was quite moving. Many of them stripped down to shorts and bathed in the waters, even inviting me to do so as well but, as a Christian respectful of their beliefs which I could not share, I declined and thanked them for asking me and for the experience of witnessing the simple faith of all who visited there.

There were many experiences of that nature in India, a fascinating place and one for any inquisitive Australian to aspire to visit. India is the world's largest democracy and to observe it for a year was not only a great joy and privilege but a tremendous insight into how democracies survive and thrive. It is, however, necessary to say that the intelligentsia in India feel a certain sense of resentment towards Australia, seeing us as brash Johnnies-come-lately, presumptuous and perhaps most of all unjustifiably dismissive of the deep and ancient cultures and social practices of ancient India. There is also a sense there that Australia, as a wealthy nation, has been dealt an unfairly generous hand. That is the reality as I saw it, but the potential for a mature and productive relationship in the future is undefinably high.

Work at the NDC followed a very academic routine. We had a late morning rendezvous for a pre-lunch lecture from some luminary (and I must say that the quality of the lecturers was outstanding) followed by questions-and-answers and then lunch. After lunch there were some desultory discussions in smaller groups called syndicates and then home around 3 p.m. This seems terribly light-on, but we had an extensive reading list and projects programme including lengthy midcourse papers and a major thesis-level commandant's paper due at the end of the course.

The course itself was a great eye-opener. It took senior military officers who, by definition, were consummately professional at their craft and who knew their own services back to front. The course directed our gaze outwards, forcing us to learn about geostrategic influences, geopolitical realities and the pressures, nuances, limitations and demands of a democratic political structure.

Stephen and Philip visited us on several occasions during the year and each time we sought to incorporate some significant visit to different parts of India. These excursions were always filled with laughter and a sense of adventure. By now the older boys in particular were not afraid of taking the mickey out of their dad.

Even when I was grumping, inwardly I was revelling in having our little family back together, albeit briefly.

I was now keenly awaiting what I would do when I finished in India. The word arrived in the presence of the (then) Australian Chief of the Defence Force (CDF), Admiral Alan Beaumont, who was on an official visit to India. On a visit to the NDC, he whispered in my ear in the corridor that I was off to command the Australian Defence Force Warfare Centre at Williamtown.

Another command, but not one which seemed to illuminate a pathway to more senior rank in the Australian Defence Force. It was a very good job, bringing together the strands of joint doctrine and joint training in the ADF, and there is no doubt that I had strong credentials to do the job. But deep within me I understood that this was a 'marking time' job rather than something on the fast track. Secretly I was a little disappointed, but thought that, having had a marvellous time for almost thirty years, I should not fret, but should enjoy every moment of productive service that awaited me. On the bright side, it was quite close to Sydney and the lifestyle would be relatively sedentary in terms of travel and absences from home. Stephen would remain at Marist, we would see how Philip felt about continuing as a boarder and David would be enrolled locally — all very neat.

As it turned out, we made wonderful friends among the senior Air Force families at Williamtown. In addition, my senior Army colleague at the Warfare Centre was a great friend from years before in both Townsville and Holsworthy, Don Murray. Don, Wendy and their kids were next-door neighbours and we formed a little Army enclave in amongst our Air Force colleagues. It was good fun to be rolling out course after course of younger officers from the Navy, Army and Air Force who had been put through a process of coordination and integration in the study of joint warfare. For a small institution like the Australian Defence Force, 'jointery' was the only way forward, as we sought to maximise the effects we could get by each service supporting and exploiting the others as much as possible.

The only difficult patch in those two years came when, in 1996, a major general who had some pastoral responsibility for my career counselling told me that it was most unlikely that I would ever be a major general, based on the superlative qualities of those with whom I stood in my peer group. I was respectful to him and sanguine when I relayed the news to Lynne. She was very supportive and sunny about the revelation and gently reminded me that, when I was at the Infantry Centre, the same officer had told me that I would not be promoted to brigadier! One thing that this disappointing advice from my superior did do was bring me back to a personal injunction I had always used, which was not to fret and fuss about future jobs but simply to enjoy and perform the present job to the best of my ability.

At the end of my two years at the Warfare Centre I was posted as the Commandant of the Royal Military College, Duntroon. By now I had accepted that, whether I thought it was fair or not, the likelihood was that I would never be promoted to major general and therefore this was probably my last job in the Army before I was tapped on the shoulder for some kind of redundancy.

But what a job! I was over the moon. Again, who would have thought, all those years before, that the cadet who was so chronically in trouble and underachieving would be back as the Commandant? I did not see this as some kind of wry payback, but as an opportunity to exhort and encourage the staff to propel forward the highly talented and capable cadets while always reaching down to give a helping hand to the ones who were floundering.

While I was there, with the assistance of a great regimental officer who was effectively my second-in-command, Colonel Gary Byles, we did our best to nurture and graduate every cadet at the College. I don't know how many young people came down to the College Headquarters expecting to get the sack and walked away with one more chance. I never kept count, but I hope it was more than a few. Quite rightly, Duntroon staff tend to be the best of the best — you wouldn't have other than that as role models and teachers. But equally I wanted these exceptionally talented officers to keep a keen eye out for those who had potential and just needed a bit extra to bring them up to speed. That's not all I did at Duntroon, but it is probably the thing of which I am most proud.

I spent a lot of time watching the cadets in their field and classroom training. I came to know them as people behind the nametags and uniforms. I saw them on the sporting field and in their cadets' mess. I took them on in earnest debate in their tactical training and, very rarely on their social occasions, on less serious subjects. I really felt like some military headmaster and each cadet to me had the potential to be a world beater.

Lynne and the boys settled back into Canberra like a hand into a glove. By now we had so many friends around town that we seemed to be always on the go when there was no College activity to claim our time. Stephen had finished high school and had moved on to university in Canberra, Philip and David were in a local high school and we were living on the 'married patch' at

Duntroon. Life was in a most enjoyable routine, but from time to time there were funny and memorable moments.

One of these came at the graduation parade in December 1997. As is usual, His Excellency the Governor General, in this case Sir William Deane, was reviewing the parade. It had been raining solidly all morning to a point where I thought that, for the first time in the history of the College, I might have to cancel the parade and simply ask the Governor General to hand over the graduation certificates and commissions in the gym.

However, when I walked out to make one last appraisal of the weather, the rain had magically stopped. I called out to the regimental sergeant major standing nearby, 'The parade shall go on!' With this, the die was cast.

Wouldn't you know it — as soon as I had walked back inside, it started teeming again. By the time Sir William had arrived on the parade, the cadets and the rest of us in the official party were soaked. Typically of Sir William, he would not wear a top coat or even accept an umbrella or wear a hat. By the time we were inspecting the troops, very early in the parade, the Viceroy was soaked to the skin.

When people see troops on parade in their finery some distance away, there is this monolithic sense of stillness and silence until orders create movement and noise. Never believe it! On parade, unseen and unheard by the spectators, there is always some lower level of chitchat going on in the ranks, whether it be about the job at hand or some particularly attractive person in the crowd (soldiers are incorrigible in this respect). On this occasion I was the culprit.

As we passed down the ranks with Sir William doing his usual dignified and kindly job, I was conscious that he was soaked to the skin. His ADC was new in the job and was marching along in the small inspection party several steps behind me. I called over my shoulder and said that, when we finished the inspection, he was to leave the parade ground in a very smart and soldierly manner and get in touch with Government House and arrange for a full change of dry clothing to be available for the Governor General in the officers' mess immediately. There was a stunned silence from the young captain. I could tell what was going through his mind — how does a brand-new ADC accomplish such a delicate task? Taking pity on him, I told him to find the Governor General's driver and give him the job.

It all worked out very well. The cadets thought that to do a graduation parade in the rain was marvellous, invoking some legend I had never heard of that, if it rains on your graduation, you will go to war soon thereafter. Long may we have sunny graduations! To a large degree the legend came true because many of that class came under my command a little under two years later in East Timor.

Having reconciled myself most happily to be a sort of military 'Mr Chips' as Commandant of Duntroon, I went on Christmas leave with my family at the end of 1997 with a glad heart, looking forward to the next year and possibly one other after that in charge of one of the world's great officer training institutions.

Lynne, the boys and I were on holidays at Terrigal early in the new year when my mobile phone rang. It was a senior army officer telling me that I was to be promoted to major general and appointed to command the Deployable Joint Force Headquarters (DJFHQ) and Army's 1st Division, without doubt the most exciting senior operational command job in the

Army. This was a bolt from the blue, completely against the run of play. I was ecstatic and couldn't believe my good luck. For her part, Lynne had one of those 'I told you so' smiles but also was enormously pleased for me. 'Mr Chips' now had to become a dashing warrior again.

6

Evacuation Operations in East Timor

LATE IN 1998, LIFE IN COMMAND of the Army's 1st Division was enjoyable and well ordered. Although we in uniform all thirst for the challenge and stimulation of operations in some exotic place, that was not on the cards for an infantry general commanding Australian troops at that time. John Sanderson had performed magnificently a number of years before as the commander of the UN force in Cambodia, but that appeared to be a 'one-off' and although his Australian troop component was an important element, numerically it was only a fraction of the UN force. Before that you had to go back to Vietnam for the last time a senior Australian Army officer had commanded a large number of troops, especially Australians, on operations.

Life looked up markedly though with the arrival of Lynne, the boys and Tilly, the dog, to a brand-new married quarter adjacent to Enoggera, the major Army base in south Queensland and the headquarters of the 1st Division. This was for Lynne and me house number eighteen, and almost as many for the boys, but my heart sang at being with them again.

I'd been busy and professionally very content in the wonderful job of commanding the Army's major fighting force but, on my occasional returns to Canberra, I hated leaving them again. I also hated being no real help during the usual family affairs that confronted Lynne and the boys every day of the week. In this sense, the nine months since I had left Duntroon in Canberra for promotion and command in Brisbane had been long.

With the move, I was delighted for Lynne and the boys, because we had all been in Brisbane in 1992 and 1993 when I was a brigadier commanding 6th Brigade at Enoggera. We had enjoyed our time immensely and still had a great number of friends in the Brisbane community, and so the potentially fraught period of 'fitting in' wasn't a factor. I'd had nine months, with Lynne travelling up from time to time, to get to know 'official' Queensland so that was a pretty easy transition as well. Queenslanders are a mighty part of our society: warm, relaxed, friendly and accepting. They take the services to their hearts naturally and out of a deep and genuine patriotism, without artifice or ulterior motive. People like Peter and Barbara Arnison, who came and stayed, becoming among the most eminent of Queenslanders — he was a magnificent Governor of the State a short time later — and Peter and Helen Gallagher, who'd adopted and, in turn, been adopted by Queensland, took us by the hand and made us into that privileged family, 'honorary Queenslanders'. Our Queensland friends even forgave us Cosgroves when we drew the line at barracking for other than New South Wales in sport.

The only clouds on the horizon were the inevitable disruption to the boys' education and the short time left in my posting — the plum job of commanding the division was rigorously and correctly kept to two years to train, assess and satisfy the aspirations of the maximum number of senior army officers. At the end of 1999, I would be off to what I — and I dare say my peers — confidently expected would be my swansong, probably back to Sydney still as a major general, but in a more senior post as Land Commander.

On 19 December 1998, Prime Minister John Howard corresponded with (then) President B.J. Habibie of Indonesia, urging consideration of a pathway to self-determination for the people of East Timor based on the model the French were using for New Caledonia. Unexpectedly, the Habibie Government announced in early 1999 that Indonesia would contemplate ceding independence to East Timor if an offer of 'special autonomy' was not accepted. In one moment the status quo of this vexed element of the Australian–Indonesian relationship since 1975 was changed dramatically. Australia's previous concerns and contemporary role in the issue meant that our nation would be a high-profile protagonist in East Timor's coming year. During the first months of 1999, international opinion grew that the ballot for self-determination, that was inherent in what Indonesia proposed, should be supervised and conducted by the UN. On 7 May 1999, in Resolution 1236, the UN Security Council sanctioned the introduction of a UN mission, UNAMET — United Nations Assistance Mission in East Timor — for this purpose. From a military viewpoint, East Timor's significance grew from being an area that we monitored as a 'second tier' matter to one of higher importance.

Reflecting on the effect this fundamentally political event had on our broader national security concerns, the government announced on 11 March 1999 that one of my big combat organisations, 1st Brigade, based in Darwin, would be brought to a higher state of readiness by the end of June that year. In keeping with the nation's fairly benign strategic circumstances in the late 1990s, relatively small forces from the three services were kept on a 'ready to go' basis. In Army's case that meant elements of the Special Air Service Regiment, a parachute battalion, 3rd Brigade — two battalions of infantry, an artillery regiment of two batteries, a light armoured personnel carrier squadron, an engineer regiment, some aviation and a grouping of logistics troops — based in Townsville. This 'grab-bag' of capabilities was further supported by some heavier, selected logistic and support capabilities, such as helicopters, from elsewhere in the Army, that were also kept at high readiness.

While naturally all senior military officers (me included!) would want virtually all of their troops to be constantly at high readiness, that's both unreasonable and impractical. Unreasonable because only a select number of units are needed urgently at any one time. It is also unreasonable to keep troops at the highest levels of preparedness because it puts pressure on their families and private life and may limit opportunities for them to attend career development training courses for promotion and skill development. It is impractical because of the huge costs and sustaining it for a very large number of people day in day out takes a tremendous effort.

The government's decision to put 1st Brigade on high readiness gave me different and additional forces now at high readiness, such as an extra infantry battalion that moved in tracked light armoured vehicles. I also had at my disposal wheeled armoured reconnaissance vehicles, tanks, more engineers and heavier calibre artillery. After the announcement, which also advised that funds would follow, there was an eerie silence from the higher military command levels about why the government had decided to direct the ADF to go to the additional expense, time and effort to raise the readiness of 1st Brigade. I had my work cut out directing and supervising this initiative, which involved about a quarter of my overall command, but was left with a blank sheet of paper about the contingencies for which this suite of forces should be prepared. It seemed that having given birth to this fine policy baby, the same effort hadn't been given to its likely adult work.

Still, the work was exciting and took its place within the day-to-day tasks of commanding the 12,000 or so men and women of the division and getting ready for the major Australian–US training activity, Exercise *Crocodile 99* — there was plenty to do.

By early 1999, I couldn't have been happier with the quality of my staff team on the DJFHQ, which doubled as headquarters of Army's 1st Division. They were a happy and extraordinarily professional and talented bunch, under the leadership of Mark Kelly, the most able Chief of Staff. They'd done well on very complex training exercises and had performed brilliantly under the pressure of launching and supporting the relief operation after a tsunami — a huge wave caused by an earthquake on the ocean floor — that hit the north coast of Papua New Guinea. We lost and gained a couple of officers at the Christmas break; one gain was a man I'd worked with before, Colonel Ash Power, a hard driving, well-respected artillery officer, fresh from commanding a regiment in Townsville, now to be my chief of operations, and Lance Collins, who came as the only officer available at short notice to be my chief intelligence officer. I knew very little of Lance, but his reputation was that of being most energetic and diligent.

Basically at this time I was operating on two planes of activity: first — and publicly — I was getting ready for a major exercise and monitoring the preparation of 1st Brigade to achieve its higher degree of readiness; secondly — and discretely — I was watching the preparations for and deployment of the UN mission to East Timor. I wondered whether it would be able to achieve its tasks without some form of strong local backlash against the possibility of East Timor leaving Indonesian control. My higher military headquarters in Sydney and Canberra were silent in response to my informal inquiries about our contingencies if all did not go well in East Timor. In May 1999 there did not appear to be any official contemplation of an Australian military involvement in East Timor.

I decided that it would be prudent for my staff and me to engage in some very discreet contingency planning directed at the possibility of strong violence in East Timor leading to the need to withdraw all UN staff from the country. Of course, there is a danger to this type of activity. In the first place, it might leak. The public would become alarmed about secret military planning that suggested the possible use of Australian forces overseas. My higher headquarters and the government would be embarrassed — something that would be career limiting for me, even terminal.

There was also the problem of raising the expectations of my staff. They could become so enthusiastic about the prospect of overseas service that it might distract them from other important duties and cast them down when — as happens in the majority of these cases — a contingency doesn't eventuate. Nonetheless, I decided that this should be done — with the utmost discretion — as Australia was going to be a major player in any emergency evacuation, not only through the proximity of Darwin to East Timor but also because of Australia's strong involvement both in the politics of establishing the plebiscite and in the day-to-day support of the UN mission. Additionally, my headquarters and the troops and assets under my command would be the logical organisation to conduct an evacuation. I confined planning for contingencies in East Timor to a very few staff officers in the operations, intelligence and logistics sections of my headquarters. In respect to my higher headquarters, I thought it better to apologise if there was a leak than ask permission, and kept it pretty much to myself.

A couple of features of this planning were interesting. We at DJFHQ assumed from the outset that we would conduct any evacuation as a bilateral activity with the Indonesian armed forces. I assumed we would be operating alongside them and relying on them to create a secure environment to enable an air and sea bridge into East Timor to operate unhindered. Secondly, if we were conducting this operation only from Dili and Baucau — the two major north coast towns of the country — where there were airfields and ports, then the Australian 'footprint' could be relatively small: perhaps down to under one hundred troops on the ground. Of course, we would need substantial numbers of vessels and aircraft. There would be potentially thousands of UN personnel, expatriates and East Timorese vulnerable to retribution who would be looking for refuge and possibly escape. The major challenge would be to transport hundreds of UN personnel that might be cut off and isolated at voting stations in remote parts of East Timor. I would need more aircraft to fetch them and additional troops to protect them. This increase in the 'footprint' would lead inevitably to higher risk of friction and misunderstanding with either the militia or Indonesian security forces — or both. The prospect of conflict grew exponentially.

There was a final contingency that we reviewed briefly for the sake of thoroughness. It was the worst of all worlds. The Indonesians might leave suddenly. In the ensuing vacuum, there might need to be a rapid, substantial operation, both to withdraw and protect the innocent and helpless, and to establish an enclave ashore in order to launch a major security operation to re-establish law and order across East Timor. For these last two contingencies, I assessed that we would need substantial forces on the ground — more than one 2500-strong brigade — to succeed.

Needless to say, I was very relieved as time went by, first that there were no leaks from my staff or anybody in the 'loop'. Also around June, I gained some top cover for what we had been doing as a result of a couple of conversations with Major General Mick Keating, who was the head of strategic operations at Defence Headquarters in Canberra, and to a lesser degree Air Vice Marshal Bob Treloar, the Commander Australian Theatre, and Major General John Hartley, my direct boss, the Land Commander. Secondly, around this time, Australia received a discreet approach from the UN official within UNAMET who was responsible for security matters, requesting that Australia give some thought to the possibilities and requirements if the UN needed to evacuate from East Timor. The whole matter remained very sensitive, however, because of the very high stakes involved in the international relationship with Indonesia and because of a series of damaging and debilitating leaks of sensitive information around this time that decreased confidence between our political leadership and senior defence levels. While we were to a great degree insulated from this at my level, nonetheless we were conscious of the tendency for a 'leak paralysis' to permeate the system. The upshot of all of this sensitivity was that I didn't feel I could broadcast even outline elements of our thought processes and plans down to the lower headquarters and troops who would be doing the difficult jobs entailed in these plans. Over time I was emboldened to brief one or two senior commanders within the division, but I couldn't afford the possibility of an inadvertent leak from a dedicated, well-meaning subordinate who could not be expected to realise what was at stake.

At the same time as all this was occurring, I was very satisfied with the way that 1st Brigade had responded to the challenge of taking on new soldiers, some new equipment, a lot more training and a lot of consumable stores and ammunition to bring itself to high readiness, all in one hell of a hurry, under the command of one of the most successful and dynamic officers of his generation, (then) Brigadier David Hurley. This meant I was able to plan using some of the heavier organisations (such as (tracked) armoured personnel carriers and (wheeled) light armoured vehicles) within 1st Brigade in the East Timor contingency plans. The other big matter occupying my time was preparing for Exercise *Crocodile 99*.

This was the next in a series of major Australian–US exercises in Shoalwater Bay, Queensland, that had been going on for many years. The plan was for me to be the senior allied commander of both nations' armed forces on exercise, with my direct deputy being a United States Marine Corps brigadier general. He and I had met on several previous occasions and had been involved in detailed discussions on the numbers of troops, ships and aircraft to be involved, the exercise scenario, the timing and even such things as the VIP visits schedule. In all of this I was in the probably unique situation — certainly in recent years — of conducting all of these negotiations with my US counterpart in good faith, but with the thought in the back of my mind that it may not take place, as we Australians might have something more important to do! When my friend the marine realised that Exercise *Crocodile 99* would be very different to what we had both visualised back in 1998 — he was both cheerful and wistful about this. I am sure he would have loved to have been joining us in East Timor!

As the world and certainly all Australians saw, events in East Timor started to accelerate rapidly in July and August 1999. The pro-integration movement in East Timor, that had started its campaign for East Timor to remain part of Indonesia back in May, became concerned that East Timorese would prefer overwhelmingly to be independent. With this realisation, the militia part of the pro-integration movement became ascendant and there was a significant escalation of violence, particularly in Dili but also throughout population centres in the whole of East Timor. Almost nightly, the media which had re-entered East Timor in force to cover the UN mission in May now broadcast reports and images of violence, intimidation and criminality.

There were significant doubts about the credibility of the ballot: Would the elections be fair? Would the voters turn out? Would there be a clear-cut result?

The scenes from that period are still clearly etched in most adult Australians' minds. Violence continued and got worse leading up to 30 August when the people of East Timor voted in their hundreds of thousands. Although the pundits believed that such a large turnout probably favoured the pro-independence side, the result was unclear until 4 September, when Kofi Annan announced a thumping 78.5 per cent of East Timorese voters had opted for independence. The will of the majority was clear but the vocal and violent minority who preferred to remain with Indonesia erupted in an orgy of violence and retribution against their erstwhile friends and neighbours. The UN mission that planned to remain to prepare East Timor to transition to the next phase became besieged and ineffectual. Plainly, Indonesia would cede control of East Timor to the UN very soon, but the law and order situation would not allow an orderly transition. The situation deteriorated further. There was the spectacle of the protracted 'pseudo-siege' of the UN compound that underscored the inability of the UN mission to continue usefully in East Timor.

Chaos reigned in East Timor as mobs went on a murderous rampage that included attacks on UN personnel. Ian Martin, the head of the UN mission, many of his co-workers and a large number of East Timorese were holed up in the UN compound in Dili. Graphic scenes of the mob rampaging around the compound and of people fleeing, scrambling over the high, barbed-wire topped fence, appalled many Australians. At this time, our military attachés from Jakarta, led by Brigadier Jim Molan, were playing a mighty hand both in assisting our consul general in Dili, Mr James Batley, and Ian Martin, the head of the UN mission, and his senior staff to get Indonesian protection for those in danger and, in an infinitely more risky exercise, even to negotiate with some of the militia leaders to the same end.

The scene was now set for the contingency which I had directed my headquarters to study several months before: that of a Services Assisted Evacuation out of East Timor of up to 2000 people. In our ADF planning doctrine, a Services Assisted Evacuation was one where more benign conditions applied. For instance, it was conducted on the assumption that there would be no violence occasioned towards aircraft or naval vessels moving the evacuees or troops. On this basis it would be normal for troops on the ground to be unarmed, with protection coming from the security forces of the host country. Under these circumstances, well-trained elements of the Army or the Air Force — in the case of an air evacuation — were generally earmarked to perform the administrative duties of marshalling, checking and directing evacuees onto aircraft and ships.

The next level up, a Services Protected Evacuation, envisaged a situation where the host country would be incapable of providing an adequate level of security and therefore our troops on the ground would be armed and ready to protect evacuation points and even assembly and movement of the evacuees to evacuation points. With many thousand Indonesian troops in East Timor, our strong preference was for them to protect the assembly and concentration of evacuees at airfields and for our troops simply to administer processing before ushering evacuees onto aircraft. The prevailing view in Canberra and at various operational headquarters was that while Indonesian security forces would provide protection for all of these activities, there was no guarantee that militia groups wouldn't intrude violently into marshalling areas and airfields.

Plainly, the UN position in East Timor was untenable. In negotiation with the government of Indonesia, the Australian Government decided to launch a military operation to evacuate UN personnel. On 6 September, Air Force C130 Hercules aircraft carrying military personnel to administer evacuees flew out of Tindal Air Base in the Northern Territory and continued a shuttle from Dili to Darwin over the next few days. Although it was very risky and there were some moments of high drama, the operation went without a hitch overall to the great credit of the Air Force and supporting Army elements.

There had been a contest over command and control of this evacuation operation. Most of the supporting Army elements were Special Forces troops under the command of Lieutenant Colonel Tim McOwan, who would normally report to Commander Special Forces, who in turn would report directly to the CDF. This arrangement made eminent sense when the role of the Special Forces was 'special' — for something like a hostage recovery in Australia or offshore. At one stage when the operation was in its infancy these arrangements were being mooted. However, it was unusual for a Special Forces element to be given the role of assisting the evacuation of civilians from a strife-torn area — normally conventional elements of the Army or Air Force would perform that role.

I made a strong bid that I should command the Special Forces on this occasion for a number of reasons. At that stage there was significant pressure on Indonesia to accept an international military presence in East Timor for the transition from Indonesian control to a UN administration. Australia would probably play a major role in such a military presence. In that event, it was my belief that my headquarters, hopefully with me at the head (there was some ferocious lobbying taking place elsewhere to replace me with someone else!) would be the headquarters that would deploy to East Timor to command a multinational force. If all that occurred, it was in my high self-interest to gather people like the Special Forces and the C130s under my wing at that early stage so that whatever their experiences were on the evacuation operation, they could come to me and my staff directly without filters. Secondly, in any subsequent operation I would be relying on them very heavily. Again it was in my interest to start to get to know their capabilities as a group and some of their more senior officers and NCOs as individuals as soon as possible. Over the years I had come to know quite a few of them but I had never commanded them on operations. Thirdly, commanding and monitoring this operation would be an excellent warm-up for my headquarters staff, while it was plain that the static headquarters of our Special Forces would not be required or able to deploy overseas. Consequently, the experience of commanding an operation into East Timor would be wasted on them. Lastly, we on the headquarters staff had been looking at scenarios like this evacuation for months and felt better placed than any other group to do it justice.

Happily the decision fell my way. I was given command of the tactical forces conducting the operation, including the Special

Forces. However, Headquarters Special Forces remained in the loop because of the ability of its staff to use highly technical communications to keep in touch with their people on the ground. Proving that nothing is perfect when last-minute changes are made, it was impractical and undesirable for me to attempt to exercise detailed control of what the SAS did at airfields in Dili and Baucau. I simply gave them some rules of engagement and other guidelines and trusted to the commonsense, maturity and forbearance of the soldiers on the ground.

The actions of our Defence attachés in East Timor, who brokered deal after deal with Indonesian security forces, with the UN — even with the militia — were crucial for success. The shambolic and chaotic nature of what was occurring in East Timor resulted in vehicle transport not showing up or being diverted time after time. People would misunderstand directions, or officials would renege on deals, or the militia would decide to intervene and intimidate. In one famous episode at Baucau, our aircraft was sitting on the ground waiting for a load of evacuees and our Special Forces were arrayed around the aircraft, processing scores of people, including on this occasion Nobel peace laureate Bishop Belo, who was making an undisclosed departure from East Timor, when a notorious militia band under the command of a fierce militia leader, Juanico, decided that the group should not leave. His grounds were that the Australians were attempting to abduct East Timorese nationals off to Australia. He blocked the runway with vehicles and his heavily armed militia.

A major stand-off ensued. Our attaché on the spot, Brigadier Jim Molan, negotiated with the militia leader that the aircraft would not go direct to Australia but would land at Dili where it would offload all East Timorese before proceeding to Australia. On this basis, Juanico was prepared to allow the aircraft to take off and directed his men to clear the runway. A very quick loading of the aircraft was accomplished in case he changed his mind and the C130 made a rapid departure. Needless to say, the aircraft went direct to Darwin where UN staff and East Timorese alike felt safe for the first time in quite a while. Hats off to Jim Molan.

On another occasion in the early stages of the operation, it came to my notice that there were a couple of British junior officers on an official visit to Australia, who had somehow found their way to Tindal. They were proposing to go on what could best be described as a joyride into East Timor with the SAS. On the surface, given the traditional friendship between ourselves and the Brits, this was understandable, and slightly amusing — but not excusable or permissible! I didn't think the British military leadership or the British Government would be delighted if there was some scandal or disaster and their chaps were involved unofficially. I sent a very strongly worded message to Tindal directing that they were not to go into East Timor, but I would be delighted to see them as soon as possible in Brisbane where they could explain to me why they felt their duty in Australia encompassed operational visits to another country. They came to Brisbane with their tails between their legs and were probably surprised to get only a gentle chastisement before being sent on their way — 'A' for effort and initiative and 'D' for judgement. I gave those involved in the SAS a quick kick in the tail as well for contemplating this folly.

During the course of this short but hectic operation, the then Defence Minister, John Moore, decided to visit Tindal. He and some of his staff wanted to have a first-hand look at the mounting base where our C130s and the SAS prepared for their daily missions and also repaired to for rest and maintenance. I accompanied him as the senior officer responsible for the operation. The Minister had one or two journalists from the Press Gallery accompanying him during his short visit. This was a time of intense media interest in the operations and preparations of the ADF. The journalists were agog at the sights and sounds of military activity at Tindal and of course very inquisitive about the potential for further military operations. Catherine McGrath, a seasoned and much respected ABC radio journalist, was with the Minister and at one stage turned to me when I was lurking around in the background and asked, 'Where do you fit in to all this, General?' I gave a nebulous answer along the lines of, 'We always send a senior officer to accompany the Minister when he visits the troops and it was my turn' — a true but selective statement of the facts! About this time I knew that I was a good thing to be the commander of the multinational force and felt a bit sorry that I couldn't provide a more direct answer to her question. I knew it was a bit early to be providing a scoop: I needed to do a lot more work before I would be able to answer consequent media questions comprehensively and with confidence.

Overall, the evacuation operations — called Operation *Spitfire* — was a great success. The joint task force safely evacuated from danger — without any loss of life — scores of very weary and traumatised UN staff, a number of expatriates and a not inconsiderable number of East Timorese. The reputation of the ADF and, crucially, our knowledge of the operational environment were greatly enhanced. As we had all come to expect, the men and women who operated our C130 fleet performed to the highest professional standards, as they had been doing in all forms of disaster relief and the like for many years. Even more importantly, our SAS, who had been diligently training and developing new doctrine and tactics for many years, but who had not had the opportunity to show their wares on operations in their own right, had demonstrated that they were extremely well disciplined, mature and reliable.

For me, it was back to Brisbane — one mission had been accomplished but the situation in East Timor was getting worse and the pressure on the Indonesian Government to invite international intervention was building.

7

Towards Intervention

AFTER RETURNING TO BRISBANE from Tindal, I found that my headquarters staff had continued to refine the plans for a peacemaking intervention operation into East Timor — still a most sensitive contingency plan. At that time, the Indonesian Government did not appear to be preparing to invite a multinational peacekeeping force to assist with restoring law and order in East Timor, despite the worsening situation there and increasing international pressure. The ballot result determined that the international community would become involved sooner or later. The United States and the UN might ask Australia, Indonesia's closest and most capable neighbour, to lead. My staff and I had to 'back this particular horse' if we were to have any chance of being ready if the government ordered the ADF to project forces into East Timor at short notice. We were the only deployable headquarters that could command this type of operation. We had to identify what forces would be needed in order to prepare them to leave their bases and barracks as soon as possible after Cabinet made a decision to take military action. Planning for this contingency was not a very big gamble unless there was a breach of operational security. We were used to an endless cycle of preparing for possible operations. Sometimes these preparations increased readiness and brought ships, units and aircraft onto very short notices to move. As a result of our planning and preparations, the government could keep its options open, that is, put forces on standby, order forces to deploy or cancel the operation altogether.

An Australian-led intervention into East Timor had to be a coalition operation. It would be politically and militarily impossible for Australia to act alone. Politically, East Timor had become a regional and international challenge after President Habibie allowed the agreement on 5 May permitting UN electoral intervention, leading potentially to independence for East Timor. The region and the UN had to be involved. More particularly, the ADF alone did not have enough forces ready or the range of capabilities, such as strategic lift, to intervene on this scale.

So, three factors shaped our planning: first, Australia would lead with the major and earliest military component; secondly, under these circumstances, Australia would have to command and support the entire force; lastly, the operation would have some duration. This would be no short lived 'in and out' operation lasting a few weeks. It would go for several months and possibly longer, depending on the levels and persistence of violence, and how quickly a follow-on force could be sent to replace the initial force.

We had to consider the degree of confidentiality the government wished to maintain over our preparations. It is impossible to disguise urgent preparations for deployment of thousands of Navy, Army and Air Force men and women and their machines. Fortunately, the government was prepared to 'grit its teeth' and, if discovered, advise that preparations were prudent and in no way pre-empted an Indonesian invitation for international intervention, or a resolution by the UN Security Council authorising an international force.

Some may be surprised, because of my infantry origins, that I considered logistics first. Grandiose plans to deploy, employ and sustain thousands of personnel, as well as fleets of ships, vehicles, aircraft and major equipment of all types from the three services won't work without sufficient logistic support, both on the ground in East Timor and through a 'pipeline' back to the Australian mainland. This pipeline had to connect to an efficient distribution system from depots and warehouses located around the nation, backed up by commercial suppliers, transport operators and logistic and communication infrastructure. This Australian military and commercial supply chain would also have to sustain allies who would send combat forces, but expect the ADF to sustain them after arrival. Complicating logistic considerations was uncertainty — up to the point of total ignorance! — of when and what type of forces other countries would commit to the operation — especially if the initial deployment did not go well. My best guess and that of my superiors, Air Vice Marshal Bob Treloar and Major General John Hartley in Sydney, and Admiral Chris Barrie, the CDF in Canberra, was that contingents from other nations would deploy gradually over one to two months, when and if my initial lodgment was successful. Notwithstanding this prediction, logisticians from the three services would have to prepare for a logistic effort characterised by speed, flexibility, velocity and stamina.

The Defence Department had pared back organic ADF logistic capabilities during the 1990s. The ADF did not have significant capabilities or capacity for large-scale terminal operations, that is, the running of airfields and ports for movement of personnel and supplies. Terminal operations would either enable or cripple my intentions in East Timor. I didn't need to visit East Timor to know what we would be up against. A look at the map revealed that distribution of supplies around the island would be a major undertaking, given the parlous nature of the few roads and the limited number of airfields. Darwin would be the crucial logistic hub. Local logistic units would have to be reinforced and infrastructure upgraded to do the job. In other words, while logistic activity in Darwin was outside the area of operations in East Timor and units there would not be part of the deployed force, servicemen and women serving in Darwin would have to make it a vital 'gateway' for a supply chain into East Timor. In every way they would have to work as hard and successfully as every logistician serving in East Timor.

From the beginning, my staff and I knew that the ADF logistic system was structured and trained to support an infantry brigade of around 3000 men and women. It would have to stretch itself to support at least twice that number of Australian troops and sustain a large fleet of ships, vehicles, aircraft and equipment. Within a month or so after the beginning of the operation, this overstretched system would then have to stretch again to support an unknown number of coalition combat and support units from the region and around the globe.

Although my first concern was logistics, I knew what Australian combat and supporting forces would be available. Before we got down to the 'bean-counting' of what combat forces we would need to take, I felt I had to develop a philosophy of how we would act in East Timor. My assumption was that, in order to meet international, regional and Australian national expectations, my orders would most likely be something like, 'Restore law and order quickly and comprehensively throughout East Timor.'

I wanted combat elements of the force to be powerful, flexible and highly mobile. The terrain in East Timor meant that infantry, helicopters and light armoured vehicles would be at a premium. Engineers would be necessary to help the force make best use of very dodgy roads, bridges, airstrips and beach landing areas. Communications challenges in East Timor would be typical of what we'd come to expect in the mountainous, jungle clad, stormy environment of our region. Finally, on the combat side, I would need a sophisticated and responsive ground reconnaissance capability. Lieutenant Colonel Tim McOwan's Special Air Service Regiment would be suited perfectly for this work — a good foil for the marauding militia whose tactics would most likely be to operate clandestinely from safe havens to conduct surprise attacks on East Timorese and members of the international force, as well as UN staff and humanitarian aid workers.

The environment offered considerable similarities to that of Vietnam and Malaysia where I had worked in the past — I thus had a good idea of what the conditions would be like.

The army units that would go were obvious. Most combat force elements would come from Brigadier Mark Evans' Rapid Deployment Force based in Townsville with some mechanised infantry and wheeled light armoured vehicles coming from Brigadier David Hurley's brigade in Darwin. Brigadier Jeff Wilkinson's Logistic Support Force would have to provide the logistic troops and assets. His two force support battalions based in Townsville and Sydney would be vital to the success of the operation. I would also need Lieutenant Colonel Roger Joy's joint support unit based near my headquarters in Brisbane to provide communications both within East Timor and back to Australia — the 'glue' for the operation.

I envisaged the Navy having three roles and possibly a fourth. During the lodgment of land forces, our Navy — in company with coalition naval vessels — would create a maritime presence that would powerfully symbolise international resolve. Secondly, naval amphibious and logistic vessels would move troops, equipment and supplies to various parts of East Timor and sustain them from supply dumps set up at ports in Australia. Thirdly, naval vessels would operate close to shore and act as floating helipads, warehouses, hospitals and communication nodes for land forces ashore. Finally, I envisaged naval vessels possibly acting in a constabulary role in the event that hostile groups might try to move by sea to avoid land-based security forces.

The Royal Australian Air Force and other participating coalition aircraft would have a conventional role within the supply and distribution chain. The Air Force would operate a vital supply bridge from Darwin to East Timor and from other airfields in Australia to East Timor as necessary. Given the relatively short distances involved (a couple of hours by air), I didn't see a need to base Australian or allied aircraft, such as C130 Hercules transport aircraft, on the ground in East Timor. However, I did see shorter range transport aircraft, like Caribous, and certainly helicopters being based in East Timor. Plainly though, the Air Force would operate, sustain and protect airfields.

My headquarters would be the headquarters for the multinational force and would incorporate elements of Navy and Air Force, as well as a small Special Forces, headquarters. The question was, 'Who would command this international intervention?' Clearly, it would be an Australian officer and (my!) military judgement would suggest that it should be me because I had commanded my headquarters for almost two years as well as most of the land force elements that would be going to East Timor. I knew all of the commanders and key members of their staff very well. Since early in the year, Brigadier Mike Smith had been a UN force commander in waiting. Admiral Barrie had appointed him to assist the UN with planning a multinational force to provide security during a UN-supervised transition to independence, if the East Timorese voted to reject autonomy within Indonesia. Mike Smith, the government and Admiral Barrie expected his early involvement to position him to command the force when it deployed under the terms of the 5 May Agreement at the end of 1999. However, the outbreak of violence after the ballot disrupted this orderly plan and changed the circumstances of international involvement.

Unbeknown to me, there was some debate in Canberra about who should command the force — Smith or me. For a number of years, the Army had tended to post its 'best and brightest' to Canberra for extended tours of duty on the staff as soon as it decently could after they had commanded at brigadier level. These individuals might emerge from time to time for jobs in command, such as the one I was doing, but the general feeling was that the commander/operations sphere was a 'sleepy hollow'. The significant and 'real' battles would all be fought and won in Canberra. While the Army had been busy in a limited and spasmodic way employing contingents and expeditionary forces in places such as Somalia, Cambodia, Western Africa, Rwanda and Bougainville, it was pretty clear that there was no imminent need to employ a major general and his headquarters offshore. Mike was well known in Canberra and a fine, well-educated and capable officer. He felt entitled to command. He had done his homework on the situation in East Timor. He had developed relationships among departmental officials in Canberra and bureaucrats in UN headquarters in New York. He was far better known among higher government circles in Canberra than me.

Early one afternoon, another officer phoned me and told me with great excitement that he had been told he would command the force. Just that morning, I'd had a conversation with Admiral Barrie who had told me that I would be the force commander. Hoping there hadn't been a last-minute change, I kept my powder dry during our conversation, murmuring phrases of the support that he would receive from me and my headquarters. If there had been a late change of appointment, I assumed that I would step aside and he would take command of my staff. I hoped desperately that he was wrong! The next morning (the day after the UN Security Council passed its resolution authorising intervention) Prime Minister Howard announced that I would command the force. That other officer and I have never spoken about our conversation again.

I was a little surprised at the flurry of somewhat half-baked reporting that followed mention of my name. Some of it was factual — fair enough — but some of it came from the ubiquitous 'anonymous sources', 'defence sources', 'government sources', apparently, there are scores of experts out there who shape events and pass information anonymously through the media. I have been 'lucky' ever since to have the advice and commentary of those sources telling me what is going on, what I should do, or even what I have done — the invisible and unaccountable advisory staff!

The next few days passed in a professional and personal whirl as we increased the readiness of force elements to deploy and specified the desired 'order of march' for the Australian advance guard of the international force. In secret, we ordered some units to move north, put others on standby to move. We also pre-positioned other elements elsewhere for rapid deployment. Representatives from Canberra and from Australian embassies overseas began serious discussions with potential coalition partners, seeking information on what they might deploy to strengthen the operation.

Personally, Lynne and I started to review what we would need to do in preparation for what was likely to be our longest separation during our married life. The boys were old enough to handle the separation with equanimity. I knew, however, that depending on how long the deployment was to last, Lynne and the boys would have to handle the mechanics of moving from Brisbane to Sydney, my new posting, in the New Year while I was still away. There are no more traumatic interruptions for families during a military career than the uprooting process of moving from a home in one place to the next. We'd had plenty of moves. As I knew she would, Lynne said she would be fine. Indeed, she was looking forward to returning to Sydney — our hometown — even though we had enjoyed Brisbane immensely. She obviously did not want me to have one domestic care in the world — a wife and best friend beyond compare!

The day after my appointment (which, due to time differences, had been Thursday, 16 September), I travelled to Canberra to discuss the mission with Admiral Barrie and to participate in briefings and conferences. It was very important for me to understand the preoccupations, issues and moods in Canberra before deploying. By now the Defence media machine had got into full swing. There was considerable discussion about how much I would engage with the media while in the capital. Up until that time, I had stayed well away from the media spotlight in order to give my full attention to preparing Australian forces.

During that Friday, I spent most of my time with Major General Mick Keating, the senior staff officer for operations at Admiral Barrie's headquarters. In my view, he was the powerhouse of military professionalism in Canberra. Among the million and one details we covered, we had to name the force. We felt a bit guilty in doing this because this was the staple work of a Canberra committee. We had visions of staff officers and bureaucrats going into paroxysms of rage having been deprived of the chance to take such a weighty matter under consideration. Mick and I tried various combinations, agreeing that it had to roll off the tongue. He came up with the suggestion that the force be called 'International Force in East Timor' or 'INTERFET' for short. This suited the notion that, while the force was to be in East Timor under UN auspices, it was not a 'blue beret' force, and thus needed its own distinctive identity.

More significant for me than naming the force was the mood at Defence Headquarters. Apart from Mick Keating and one or two of the service chiefs, who I saw only very briefly, I was taken aback by the gloomy mood that pervaded a number of senior military officers and bureaucrats. They appeared to be despondent and gave me a sense that the whole operation was 'courting disaster'. Somehow the carefully managed Australian strategy in the region had gone wrong and had been overtaken by unforeseen and unhelpful events. I felt that their pessimism was both unjustified and undesirable. They were the strategic command group that was supposed to be watching my back, giving me directions and enabling the operation. One senior figure opined at a meeting in Defence that day, 'By Monday, we could be at war with Indonesia!' Mick Keating and I exchanged a hard look across the table. After the meeting, I said to him, 'Not if I can bloody well help it!' He wholeheartedly concurred.

In a way, this sense of gloom and despondency, while disappointing at the time, had a beneficial effect on me. I realised that I would need to have an iron grip on operations, goals and relationships from where I stood in East Timor until such time as this mood in Defence in Canberra dissipated. Mick and I resolved to remain in constant touch, both routinely and instantly, if any urgent issue required our attention. We committed ourselves to injecting decisiveness, energy and optimism into the chain of command so we could play our part in helping others return to the business of getting the job done rather than lament the unexpected circumstances that required Australia to do the job.

Defence media advisers recommended that I should appear on *The 7.30 Report*, for an interview with Kerry O'Brien. I duly reported to the ABC television studio in Parliament House for my first live networked and national media appearance. My preparation for this first opportunity to communicate with the Australian people and an international audience had been three separate short courses where media instructors interview military officers and critique their performance. The first of these had been in 1984, when I commanded 1 RAR in Townsville. I attended a second course before I took over as commander of 6th Brigade in Brisbane in the early 1990s. My last course was in 1998 after I had taken command of 1st Division. Each had been most useful in organising and simplifying what needed to be done and how to get messages across. I breathed a silent prayer of thanks as I put in an earpiece and prepared to speak to the unblinking eye of the camera. Kerry O'Brien was in the ABC's Sydney studio.

It was a long interview, conducted in a very sympathetic, professional and grave manner by O'Brien. I assessed that Australians wanted honest, not slick answers. Many of them were dotted with phrases such as, 'I don't know' or 'I can't be sure' — and that was the truth. The operation would have its risks and the Australian people knew it. At the end of the interview, Kerry O'Brien asked a question along the lines of, 'Tonight there are a very large number of mums and dads out there watching. Is there any final thing you wish to say to them?' While I hadn't anticipated that exact question, I had it in the back of my mind that there was one thought I would like to express to underscore my approach to the mission. So I looked as squarely as I could at the camera and said, 'I'll take care of them.' That was the end of the interview and I went straight back to Defence Headquarters.

When I arrived there the interview was a hot topic. One senior colleague, who was discussing the interview with me, gave me a measured look with his eyebrows arched in scepticism, and, referring to my last remark, said, 'Gutsy call, mate!' I didn't reply to this somewhat facetious comment. I reflected to myself that his attitude epitomised the age-old difference between commanders and staff officers: commanders accept responsibility; staff officers measure probabilities. I was really glad that Kerry O'Brien had given me the opportunity during the interview, especially with that one question, to 'set out my stall' so to speak. I wanted to tell Australia and every other participating nation or nations contemplating participation that I planned to get the job done quickly, correctly and sensitively, with a minimum of risk and suffering. I wanted this message to permeate not only all of the young Australians who would serve the nation with me in East Timor, but all their loved ones and interested Australian onlookers as well. That same message applied equally to the young men and women who would be sent to East Timor from other nations and their loved ones back in their home countries.

8

Lodgment

AFTER THIS SHORT BUT ESSENTIAL visit to Canberra, it was back to Brisbane to make final preparations for lodgment. My plan was to meet the Indonesian general in charge of stabilising the situation in East Timor, Major General Kiki Syahnakri, on 19 September in Dili to prepare the way for the arrival of INTERFET the next day. Indonesia's General Wiranto had sent him with Java-based *Kostrad* (Strategic Reserve) troops, the equivalent of the ADF's Rapid Deployment Force, to relieve and evacuate local commanders and their troops who had failed to quell post-ballot violence and destruction. En route we would refuel in Darwin and I would hold a media conference in order to reinforce messages that I wished to communicate nationally, regionally and internationally.

This media conference would be another 'first' in what had been a surreal week. As I strolled towards the old indoor basketball court building at the Air Force base in Darwin, a wide-eyed flight sergeant rushed up to me to tell me that media representatives had assembled and what the layout was like. I asked whether there were many there, to which he replied in awestruck tones, 'Sir, there are hundreds of them.' My purposeful stride became a rather nervous walk. Ian Martin accompanied me. As we entered the room, Ian muttered in my ear, in the way that some Brits can joyfully pass on worrisome news, 'You're on your own, mate!' As I looked at the densely packed media scrum — later described as the biggest assembly of media representatives seen to date in Australia at one time — I consoled myself with the thought that no matter how many questions came from the throng, I could only answer one at a time. Though it was historic and important, the conference was over quickly due to time constraints, and I was off to Dili.

Appearances, demeanour and first impressions would be important. I took Major General Songkitti of Thailand, who would be my deputy commander, Colonel Neo, commander of the Singaporean contingent, and Lieutenant Colonel Roger Joy, my chief signals officer from DJFHQ, who would site and establish my headquarters in Dili. Thus, I would meet General Syahnakri with representatives from the regional neighbourhood. The government had been kind enough to lend me a Falcon VIP jet. My staff had also organised a small Special Forces protective detail. It was bizarre, sitting in the whisper quiet environment of an executive jet, being served tea and biscuits while surrounded by colleagues in uniform and heavily armed SAS troopers, cruising above the Timor Sea towards a city so obviously devastated and in trouble.

During our final approach to land, I noticed the widespread destruction of dwellings and other buildings in the city. There was a blanket of smoke haze lying over the city and several centres of fire. After touchdown, I looked out through an aircraft window. A kaleidoscope of impressions hit me as we rolled towards the terminal. I noticed a large reception committee of people in uniform and an attendant media scrum of considerable size waiting. Next I noticed all the security. General Syahnakri had positioned hundreds of his troops in the vicinity of the strip, including on high ground overlooking the airfield. I tucked this observation away in the back of my mind as a factor to consider for the arrival of INTERFET troops the next day.

As our pilots brought us to the appointed parking spot with great panache, I made a spur of the moment decision. My colleagues and I had pistols strapped to our belts — common practice on operations. Members of my protection party were armed to the teeth and wearing sunglasses. Looking out the window, I noticed that General Syahnakri had a sidearm. There would be a good, if subtle and possibly unnoticed, message if I left my personal weapon and escort behind thereby emphatically and explicitly showing my confidence in his security arrangements. So in a flash, I told my party, 'Weapons off!', and ordered the SAS fellows, 'Stay on board' — much to their chagrin — and down the aircraft steps we went. I was very aware that even though the operation officially started the next day, in effect it was starting exactly at that moment. General Syahnakri and I could get off to a good, bad or indifferent start. It was up to us to create the right first impressions for attentive politicians in Canberra and Jakarta, as well as governments and millions of people around the world who were taking an interest in the fate of the East Timorese people. If I did not display the appropriate respectful, diplomatic but firm demeanour, the chances were that we would get off to a bad start and this would increase the risks of the operation.

Among the many faces at the foot of the aircraft steps was the very welcome sight of Colonel Ken Brownrigg, Australia's army attaché to Jakarta. Alongside him was General Syahnakri with some of his principal staff. After brief introductions, and with smiles replacing words due to the language barrier and the hubbub — all faithfully recorded by the posse of mostly regional media — General Syahnakri and I left the tarmac surrounded by media representatives and followed by our respective entourages. We entered the VIP terminal that was separate from the main terminal. It was in pretty good shape. I found out the next day that the main building complex had been looted, vandalised, and the floor covered in human excrement, whether as a deliberate act or the desperate recourse of people who had been denied access to lavatories because they had been destroyed. It was not a place for General Syahnakri and I to meet and have broadcast to the world. As we passed through the main doors of the VIP terminal before getting into cars, our progress was enlivened when a TV camera team in front of us, walking rapidly backwards, stepped back through the plate glass doors, luckily without injury. The remainder of the media group took this stumble by their colleagues in their stride and surged on.

The short ride of about 5 kilometres or so into Dili was instructive. Dwellings observable from the road were largely deserted. Burnt household possessions and roofing iron lay scattered and twisted throughout piles of ashes that had been family homes and businesses. Skinny dogs roamed about scavenging. There was no vehicle traffic apart from our convoy. The roadway into town was lined every few metres by stony-faced Indonesian soldiers in field dress, with weapons at the ready. At one point, near a roundabout close to the airport, I saw a group of twenty or thirty men in civilian dress wearing the red and white coloured bandannas favoured by militia groups. I think they must have known what was happening. They were not carrying weapons, but if looks could kill, I wouldn't be here today. Further on at the port, I saw thousands of people crammed on the wharf in miserable conditions, waiting to board ships that were alongside.

General Syahnakri was a pleasant, willing individual, who seemed to be very aware that between us we needed to ensure that our young men and women did not clash accidentally and possibly precipitate an unhelpful confrontation. This was the good start that I had been hoping for. A thought occurred to me as we were riding into town. In a very real sense I would be 'playing for my country' when we sat down to discuss what lay ahead and to negotiate arrangements for the lodgment. I hoped I would be on my game! At times like these when the stakes have been high, I have tried to step outside myself and consider how others might view or regard me. Plainly there is my physical presence, which I cannot do much about but can moderate with body language. Secondly, there is my physical demeanour about which I could do plenty. Lastly, there is what I would say and how I would say it — the most important ingredient in negotiations. I resolved to be amiable, forthright, confident and receptive to the degree I thought consistent with the INTERFET mission. My purpose at this conference would be to make the necessary coordinating arrangements with General Syahnakri and his staff for my forward elements to arrive in Dili efficiently and with a minimum of friction and misunderstanding. There were two competing pressures on me at the time. One was the need for transparency in order to avoid misunderstanding and the other was my instinctive reluctance to provide any evildoers with advance information that could be used against my troops.

When we arrived at General Syahnakri's headquarters, courteous staff officers ushered us into a meeting room on an upper floor. There were several rows of chairs set out facing each other across a long, low set of tables that were adorned with scribble pads, cold bottled water, and even some food — all of which I took as a good sign. We arranged ourselves in these rows of chairs like two football teams lining up across from each other before a big game. I had a team of no more than half a dozen or so; General Syahnakri had a few more. I assumed that they were his principal staff from Jakarta and some local senior commanders. There were no introductions. We left the media representatives downstairs milling about awaiting the results of our deliberations.

We got down to business after a short ritual of expressions of goodwill and earnest endeavour. I used these niceties to emphasise my very strong desire to work with Indonesian security forces to stop any more violence within East Timor in order to facilitate the speedy distribution of lifesaving humanitarian aid. This effort had to be followed by the provision of shelter and essential services, such as clean water, to thousands of displaced persons whose homes had been destroyed.

Back in Brisbane, I'd laid out an ambitious programme for the deployment of INTERFET. I directed that two infantry battalions of about 700 men each, supported by light armoured vehicles and helicopters, should arrive and secure key locations in Dili within 24 hours. I wanted to make a powerful and immediate impression on the militia whose rhetoric had contained bloodthirsty promises of stubborn resistance to INTERFET. This rapid build up of over a thousand heavily armed troops and scores of armoured vehicles and helicopters was also intended to give confidence to ordinary East Timorese, the millions of people watching on television and any governments considering supporting the intervention with follow-on forces. I also wanted immediate respect from local Indonesian security forces, many of whom I assessed would be pretty disenchanted with our presence.

As I explained this build up to General Syahnakri and his staff through Ken Brownrigg, who acted as my interpreter, I spoke of the need to land up to thirty C130 Hercules transport aircraft into the airfield in the first 24 hours. This created animated discussion among officers on his side of the table before one staff officer murmured in his ear. He paused and then said that this number of landings would not be possible because the airfield did not have the capacity to land and unload that many aircraft in so short a time. I said that we would be operating both day and night. He pointed out that his air traffic controllers would only work until 5 p.m. I replied that INTERFET air traffic controllers would both assist and then replace his people in the tower. This answer didn't stop murmuring on his side of the table. After conferring with his staff again, he offered that the airfield lacked the necessary landing lights and navigation aids for night-time operations. I pointed out that all of the pilots conducting these night landings and takeoffs would use night vision goggles. Notwithstanding this somewhat tit-for-tat debate, I gained the impression that General Syahnakri was keen to collaborate with the deployment of INTERFET and was not being an obstructionist. To me though, the most important factor in the success of the arrival would be his control over his troops, and their control over local Indonesian security elements that had been causing problems, as well as armed militia gangs.

After the conference, I returned to the airfield and directed Roger Joy to remain overnight with the small SAS group from my aircraft and select a site for INTERFET headquarters that we would occupy the next day. I left him with my close protection detail to assist and ensure his safety. I also left him in the care of Ken Brownrigg whose primary task was to monitor the way in which the Indonesians reacted to my visit and the plans I had outlined. He would be my eyes and ears on how the Indonesians were preparing for our arrival. Large, slow C130 transport aircraft full of troops would be prime targets for those wishing to oppose INTERFET and embarrass both the Australian and Indonesian Governments. If arriving aircraft were engaged, we'd be off to the worst possible start. I had directed Lieutenant Colonel Tim McOwan to fly in low and hard with a heliborne force of about ten Blackhawks in the gloom before dawn ahead of the first C130s to prevent anyone firing on them.

Within minutes of arriving back at the airport, we were roaring off in the Falcon jet heading south towards Darwin for the few hours left of Sunday, 19 September 1999 — a busy, eventful and unforgettable day. Arriving in Darwin late that afternoon, I drove out to Robertson Barracks deep in thought about the complexities of what we were planning to do and the obvious limitations at Comoro airfield and at the port. These limitations would put great pressure on pilots, ships' captains and specialist movements personnel. This was pressure and risk that I could not avoid because I was convinced that in the first 24 hours I had to demonstrate that a modern, powerful and highly technically developed force was arriving to save the East Timorese people from terror, displacement and the further destruction of their homeland. Any weakness or 'pussy-footing' at the start might embolden hostile groups to try their hand at more violence in defiance of INTERFET. Having reassured myself that this was the best course of action, I arrived at Robertson Barracks and was swept up again in obligations to brief my staff, confer with my superiors in Canberra and reassure the commanders of coalition contingents that all was well. Amid these activities, I also had to be available to my staff to resolve a myriad of issues that had been vexing them while I was away.

About 9 p.m., Ken Brownrigg rang from Dili with an urgent issue to discuss. He had spoken to Roger Joy and was concerned about my plan to send in the heliborne force. I had mentioned the early arrival of helicopters ahead of the C130s to General Syahnakri, but without technical detail. Brownrigg assessed after visiting groups of Indonesian soldiers guarding the airport and also positioned on the high ground overlooking the tarmac that there would be no overt hostility to INTERFET's arrival. However, he was convinced that because of the general air of tension and some apprehension, the sudden and dramatic arrival just before dawn of a large number of helicopters, flying at low level from the sea and disgorging Special Forces troops, might prompt what we were looking to avoid — an accidental armed clash. Ken put his case strongly. Such a major change to the plan at this late stage was no small thing. McOwan and his men were already into their final preparations and would leave in a few hours.

I guess this was one of the times that you earn your general's pay and accept the responsibilities of command. I decided to back

Ken's judgement and my own instinct following my meeting with General Syahnakri. There was some jaw dropping by my staff and among the helicopter and Special Forces fraternity when I announced that we would dispense with the dawn helicopter operation. Helicopters would arrive in a routine higher altitude manner later on the Monday or even the day after. The first troops on the ground would be those carried on Hercules aircraft, landing very soon after dawn. To the great credit of all concerned, this major change was absorbed and accomplished professionally. There was no discernible confusion. The first plan was too proactive. After second thoughts, I assessed that it might have precipitated an accidental clash. However, I wouldn't want to make a habit of such late notice changes.

Earlier that evening one of my staff called my attention to a television broadcast, showing the Prime Minister, John Howard, and Mrs Howard, visiting troops in Townsville. Two things were obvious. The troops and their families were very glad to see the PM and his wife at that moment of high drama and some trepidation. Secondly, the Howards were obviously concerned and apprehensive about what lay ahead. I looked forward to meeting the Prime Minister and other senior political and military leaders at the airport in Darwin the next day before I went to East Timor. I wanted to reassure them that all that could be done to make the operation successful had been done.

It was very late before my staff and I could contemplate grabbing a few hours sleep. Based on the mental churning I was experiencing, I'd be surprised if very many of them actually dozed off. Dawn in Darwin rushed at us all. I had a short but highly valued shower on the presumption that it might be the last proper cleaning that I could undergo for a while, a quick cup of coffee and then out to the airport. By this time, our first troops were arriving on the ground in Dili, and our troopships were on their way. Darwin airport was a maelstrom of activity, with very large military aircraft and chartered aircraft seemingly filling all available parking and taxi areas. All the RAAF personnel and movements staff seemed to have a sense of urgency and focus as they helped launch this air armada on the biggest military operation that had been seen for many years in our part of the world.

Around 9 a.m., the Prime Minister's jet arrived and I met him, Mrs Howard, Kim Beazley and the rest of the party at the aircraft steps and took them to a nearby RAAF building to give them a short briefing. I knew they were keenly interested in the briefing, but I also assumed they were sizing me up. I kept it low-key, short and free of military jargon. I told them that we had the wherewithal for the job and that I was very confident in the quality of the men and women from the three services and their leaders. After a quick cup of coffee, I left them to continue their visit to the military units in Darwin. It was now time for my personal staff and me to head off to whatever awaited us in East Timor.

I observed several changes as I approached Comoro airport for the second time in a VIP jet. There were a number of coalition and Indonesian warships close to Dili Harbour and further out to sea. The airfield itself could best be described as organised bedlam, with Hercules aircraft landing, taking off and jam-packed on the apron. Brigadier Mark Evans, Commander 3rd Brigade and overall commander of INTERFET land forces, was there to meet me. Mark had arrived direct from Townsville in a C130 aircraft not long before me. By this time, he had the best part of an infantry battalion on the ground at the airport and was getting ready to send troops to secure the port. Mark told me that the demeanour of Indonesian troops at the airport was quite benign. Syahnakri's *Kostrad* troops looked on with interest, but not malevolence. The major threat would possibly come from locally recruited and employed Indonesian territorial units. General Syahnakri had ordered them to leave East Timor and occupy new bases in West Timor. The arrival of INTERFET confirmed, once and for all, that they had to leave their homes and bases after years of service in East Timor.

The airport was bursting at the seams with the ceaseless arrival of aircraft full of troops and stores, and one aircraft full of media. The first-hand, live coverage testified to their determination and professionalism, as well as the immediacy of modern military operations to the world. I could only speak with Mark briefly because he had work to do commanding his troops and supervising their arrival and deployment. I also had work to do of a more politico–military nature. I needed to establish my headquarters and get cracking. Roger Joy had been hard at work and had found a temporary headquarters site at the heliport where Tim McOwan and his men had based themselves. Roger took me there and Colonel Mark Kelly, my chief of staff, brought me up to date with what was going on. Having found where I could leave my backpack, I had two important matters to attend to. First, I wanted to call on Ian Martin, who had flown in during the morning and was back in the UN compound, located a few kilometres from the heliport. This was an important symbolic meeting designed to reinforce the notion that INTERFET and the UN were at one in the effort to end violence and stabilise East Timor. Secondly, I had to see General Syahnakri as soon as possible to tell him how the deployment was going and to hear whether he had any concerns.

Ian Martin and his team were in good shape, although it would take them several days to set up and function again. Their compound had been thoroughly trashed. General Syahnakri was pleasant, but I surmised that he had his hands more than full getting many thousands of Indonesian troops out of East Timor. His job would become more difficult now that the media had arrived to broadcast to the world what had happened to the East Timorese people and their homeland. Naturally, the East Timorese would become increasingly angry about what had happened as they returned to their villages and towns. More practically, he had a myriad of logistics and movements challenges to meet in order to ensure that troops got away on time and in good order.

The first day rushed on with troops in the city apprehending some militia who were still foolishly parading around, oblivious that their circumstances had changed. Dealing with the militia was a complex business. We had to guarantee their human rights and judicial entitlements as well as recognise that the Indonesian Government still had jurisdiction in East Timor. INTERFET had to exemplify the shared values of the international community of nations, as embodied in the UN Charter, and comply with international law. In an operation that was being broadcast to the world, our moral and ethical ascendency was as important as our military superiority. Our policy in relation to apprehended militia depended on the circumstances of their capture. When INTERFET soldiers detained them for being armed, they turned them over to the Indonesian police after some limited questioning. When INTERFET soldiers discovered militia committing a crime, such as setting buildings alight, then commanders gathered eyewitness statements and turned them over to the Indonesian police with this *prima facie* evidence and recommendations on charging. After that it was up to the Indonesians. No doubt many militia with murky pasts from the previous months of mob violence and recent wrongdoing regained their freedom because we stuck to our legal obligations and complied with international law. However, their temporary detention and questioning, as well as the continuing presence of heavily armed INTERFET troops, persuaded them that it was time to end their rampage and leave town.

Late that afternoon, an amusing anecdote was doing the rounds about the method by which one militiaman was apprehended. He was riding as a pillion passenger on a motorbike driven by another militiaman and was armed with a home-made firearm. These fellows rode very close to an INTERFET foot patrol down near the port, giving appropriate epithets and dirty looks, when a very large Australian soldier plucked the pillion passenger clean off the back of the bike, holding him suspended as the rider proceeded oblivious to the sudden departure of his comrade. One less weapon on the streets!

I was up early next morning, keenly anticipating the arrival of the second of the Australian infantry battalions by sea. As I got to the port, the newest Navy ship was making a careful approach to the wharf. HMAS *Jervis Bay* was not only a sight for my sore eyes, but intrinsically most impressive. The INCAT Company in Tasmania had built it for the civil register as a fast catamaran ferry. The Navy had leased and commissioned it to act as a sort of wide-bodied jet on the water. It was capable of moving several hundred troops and a considerable number of cross-country vehicles and stocks in one lift from Darwin to Dili at a maximum speed of 45 knots — about a 12-hour run. Meeting this first INTERFET troopship as it docked was quite an experience. The main jetty at the port was a seething mass of humanity. Many hundreds of East Timorese men, women and children, carrying what possessions they could, were crammed onto the jetty, guarded by a contingent of Indonesian Marines. I assumed that these were East Timorese who wanted to leave to go to West Timor or elsewhere as a result of the national vote on independence. They looked totally miserable.

At the time, the challenge for me was how to get some priority for INTERFET to use wharf space. General Syahnakri needed the port as the major hub for withdrawing Indonesian military and civilian personnel and their belongings, as well as vehicles, equipment and stocks. He was also using the port to embark thousands of East Timorese who had worked for the Indonesian Government and assessed that the prospects of further employment under an indigenous administration were slim. Later I realised that these East Timorese were concerned about their pensions and needed to find employment in Indonesia to preserve their entitlements. I needed the port to bring in my troops and their vehicles and equipment as well as thousands of tonnes of supplies. Humanitarian aid agencies also needed the port to transfer urgently needed food and medical supplies from ships to vehicles for onward distribution.

I needed to carefully manage relations between INTERFET and the Indonesian military and civil authorities running the port and influence priorities for its use. When the *Jervis Bay* came alongside, I went aboard to greet the ship's captain and the battalion commander, Lieutenant Colonel Nick Welch. The Australian infantry soldiers were tense, but raring to go. They were trained to plan for the worst-case scenarios and to be ready to fight. I had a few quiet words with Nick so that he could pass on to his men that things were going pretty well but they needed to be alert and disciplined because there would be some provocation from the last of the militia groups still present in Dili.

The ship's captain was pretty chirpy and so were his crew — proud as punch of their new vessel and its capabilities. My Navy colleagues had told me that our Indonesian counterparts were very interested in — indeed suspicious of — *Jervis Bay* because of its radical, ultra-modern shape. There were rumours that it was some kind of very sophisticated intelligence ship. After I had returned to the jetty to watch the battalion disembark for a few more minutes, I noticed two young Indonesian military officers, one marine and one infantry lieutenant, standing together nearby, gazing in awe and suspicion at the sleek angles of the catamaran. On the spur of the moment, I invited these two youngsters to come aboard for a walk around the ship, from the bridge to the passenger and cargo spaces. The captain was agreeable, and our little 'show and tell' took place. I'd hoped it would do the trick!

We initiated one of INTERFET's most important rituals that day — regular media conferences at the same time and place each day. The media, like the military, thrives on coordination and routine so it was good to set a time and place for conferences. The first venue was the forecourt of a scruffy, beachfront hotel, much favoured by the media, called the Tourismo Hotel. A little later, I had another meeting with

General Syahnakri and his senior staff. This meeting was also an opportunity to set up more consultative rhythm and structure for the operation. We agreed to meet daily at the same time in a group that would be called the 'Joint Security Coordination Group'. This name symbolised partnership between INTERFET and Syahnakri's security forces to restore law and order in East Timor. His enthusiasm for this joint structure gave me a valuable inkling of a feature of the broader Indo–Australian military relationship that I would have to develop later. Our Indonesian counterparts appreciate and warm to initiatives that speak of partnership and sharing. This was a very important and valuable insight.

At this particular conference, I announced that I had several civilian persons, who had been arrested for carrying weapons, under escort outside. I now wished to hand them over to the Indonesian police. My intention was to send a clear message that INTERFET would not act arbitrarily and harshly against East Timorese who happened to favour the pro-integration cause, even when they offended by carrying weapons. I realised that this might mark my soldiers and me as a 'soft touch'. But the gamble was worth taking in the interests of maintaining and improving on the early goodwill shown by General Syahnakri and his staff. After this gesture, I returned to military business and announced that INTERFET would be projecting forces east to Baucau, East Timor's other large town, the next day. We were here, and soon we would be there, and then everywhere.

9

Some Close Calls

AS THE HECTIC SECOND DAY drew to a close, my staff informed me that they had received vague reports concerning an attack on journalists. While initial reports were imprecise, we ascertained that a group of armed men had bailed up and attacked a couple of journalists in a small car at about 5 p.m. at an unknown location. Later, a report came in that one of the journalists who had been attacked had been set free but was lost and in hiding in the undergrowth. He had called his editor in Fleet Street in London using his mobile phone, asking if the editor could arrange help because he feared for his life if he tried to get back to the Tourismo Hotel alone.

By this very roundabout method, we pieced together enough to know that we had one journalist hiding in fear of his life somewhere in the 'Badlands' of Dili's eastern suburbs. We also formed a view that another journalist, with whom the first journalist had been travelling, and his East Timorese driver and another East Timorese, who had been acting as an interpreter, had been last seen in the same area, but were now unaccounted for. This was a very unhelpful turn of events. Troops were scarce and extremely busy. We were flat out securing the airport, the road into town, the port and the inner business district and the residential suburbs of the capital.

These missing journalists had wandered well and truly outside our security umbrella. With night falling and having just enough information to go on, I directed Mark Evans to mount a search operation. One of the search parties found the journalists a little after midnight — a long day for cavalry troopers and infantrymen who had been awake since the early morning and had patrolled most of the day in blistering heat carrying heavy loads of ammunition and water. Apart from some superficial injuries suffered while being knocked about, the journalists were fine. The East Timorese driver and interpreter were still unaccounted for. Later the driver turned up with a terrible eye injury that had been sustained from a blow with a rifle butt. The interpreter may have met a worse fate and was never seen again. I was livid that these journalists had done their own 'expert' security assessment and decided it was fine to take themselves off, well outside INTERFET's well-communicated security cordon. They had been lucky.

During the evening of the same day, we started to receive reports of a Dutch journalist who had also gone missing after what was termed a 'motorcycle accident' caused by men dressed in Indonesian army uniforms firing their weapons. The next day in the late morning, I began my scheduled press conference with assembled media representatives. After I had delivered my briefing, we were all agog when one of the journalists present stated that the missing Dutch journalist was dead and that he had seen his body. I was unimpressed with him for not passing on this information to INTERFET troops in his vicinity once he had seen the body. I said so in a fairly rapid-fire exchange. He affirmed, in his defence, that he had passed the news and the location of the body to INTERFET troops in the area.

This was obviously a very important and tragic event, so I cut the press conference short and raced off to consult with Mark Evans and the battalion commander who had responsibility for the area where the body was located. I found that the latter had received a report some time earlier concerning the body of a journalist, but had not referred it on to Mark or to me, or followed it up at that stage. I was pretty cranky about it at the time and a bit terse with both of them. Privately, I made some allowance for the battalion commander, a fine officer but, like the vast majority of his colleagues, lacking in experience on operations. He had let this reporting requirement slip because of the absolute overload of information and tasking that he and his men were experiencing. It's a kind of 'battle shock'. It was understandable that well-trained but inexperienced officers and soldiers in the very early hours of a high tempo operation would be affected by this condition. The first 48 hours had been exhausting. Some soldiers were operating in a trance-like state, with their reactions slowed and a great weariness pressing them down. Commanders at every level, who were also under physical and mental pressure, had to dig deep and try to rest themselves and their men as much as possible in the testing circumstances that they found themselves in.

Anyway, I put a bit of a bomb under them and raced back to the Tourismo Hotel. When I got there, I collared the journalist, asking him if he could take me back to where he had seen the body. I wanted to intervene personally in this sensitive matter, save time and respond quickly now that the world would soon know that this journalist had not been as lucky as his colleagues the day before. I gathered up my small Special Forces close protection group and drove out, using the journalist as a guide.

He took us on the main road east out of town to the outer suburb of Becora. On the way there I passed a car coming the other way with General Syahnakri sitting in front, looking quite anxious and offering only a stifled wave of recognition. When we got to the incident site, I discovered Colonel Geerhan, commander of the Indonesian garrison force in Dili, standing on the roadway among a group of about ten of his soldiers. Fortunately, I had met him earlier in the year when I visited a company of our parachute battalion, 3 RAR, exercising with *Kostrad* units near Bandung in Java. I had been there representing the ADF at a ceremony and parade of Australian and Indonesian troops that marked the end of this combined activity. Colonel Geerhan had been the regimental commander of the troops that had exercised with our soldiers. He had hosted me during my visit in a most respectful and professional manner. We had got on well. Our last meeting was a lot more felicitous than this one was going to be.

My entourage had grown by one vehicle, a ratty old utility truck crammed with a small group of media that I had privately nicknamed 'the ferals'. The leader of this pack affected a red bandanna in the 'drive-on' style popular in gangster rap movies. I instructed my bodyguard to keep the ferals at bay, while I went to where the body lay. Geerhan and I, accompanied by one or two of our soldiers, walked in about 60 metres off the roadway to the backyard of a small house, an area shaded by trees and tropical growth, but quite clear underfoot. There lay the body of a tall, blond Caucasian male facedown, dressed in slacks and a short-sleeved shirt. While I was anxious not to disturb a crime scene, I looked closely at the nature of the injuries to the body. This poor fellow had been murdered and mutilated and had been dead for some time. I told the commander of my escort to guard the crime scene and to do his best to prevent unnecessary and unauthorised access into the general area. By this time, the 'ferals' were circling closer. I had given him a difficult job because this group would prove to be a handful.

It was time to get some messages across to Colonel Geerhan. I spoke quietly, but with heavy emphasis, that this appeared to be the body of Mr Sander Thoenes, a journalist working for the British *Financial Times*, who had been reported missing the previous day. I told him that, in my opinion, Thoenes had been murdered brutally and that I had received information that Indonesian troops had been responsible. Geerhan looked sick at this moment. I told him that I would leave my escort to guard the scene awaiting Indonesian police and INTERFET military police. I emphasised that I was relying on him personally to ensure the safety of the men I was leaving, and any other persons in the area.

I decided to bring media representatives into line for their own good. At the next media conference I spoke in strong terms, telling them to behave more responsibly for their own safety. While I understood their natural instincts to chase stories and compete among themselves for the most newsworthy ones, I cautioned them that East Timor was still a very dangerous place. We could only protect them where INTERFET soldiers could see and shoot. Beyond areas where INTERFET had established a deterrent presence, there were individuals and groups who were looking for defenceless targets for their murderous animosity.

I informed General Syahnakri in a subsequent meeting of my suspicions that Indonesian territorial troops withdrawing from the east had possibly attacked two journalists several days before and had also killed Sander Thoenes around the same time. I proposed a joint Indonesian and INTERFET investigation, monitored by the UN police in East Timor. I also told him that I had an eyewitness to the attack on Thoenes in protective custody. (During that day, we had secured the East Timorese who had been riding the motorbike on which Thoenes had ridden pillion.) He readily agreed to the notion of a joint investigation.

The story from the East Timorese man who we had in protective custody was chilling. He had agreed to take Thoenes on his motorbike to the east of Dili. The lead elements of an Indonesian territorial battalion, also riding on motorbikes and leading a convoy into Dili for a stop before continuing their road journey west out of East Timor, saw them and gave chase after Thoenes' driver turned the motorbike around and attempted to flee. Their pursuers shot Thoenes off the bike or fired shots close enough to force him off the bike. Soon after, the East Timorese rider and his bike went over and he fled. That was the last he saw of Thoenes. It appeared that these outriders shot Thoenes again and mutilated his body either where he fell or closer to where his body finally lay. All this happened around 5 p.m. on Tuesday, 21 September.

I found out later that this battalion of rogues had resumed their journey later that same night and encountered INTERFET troops further down the main road through Dili. Mark Evans had set up several vehicle control points on this east–west road as snares for truckloads of militia that had been barrelling around the streets at night brandishing weapons, firing shots and calling out threats against INTERFET troops. The first check point was commanded by a 22-year-old officer. In addition to his platoon of some thirty soldiers, he was assigned two pairs of snipers, a section of Assault Pioneers and a detachment of two light armoured vehicles — a small team, quickly assembled for a task, commanded by a junior leader.

At about 10 p.m., twenty or so armed outriders rode up to his control point on motorbikes at the head of the Indonesian convoy. This young commander did not expect such a large group of vehicles and armed men, estimated at sixty trucks loaded with about 500 soldiers, their personal belongings and loot. His orders were to stop, disarm and search anyone who was armed but not dressed in uniform and who did not have proper Indonesian military identification. The outriders were dressed in a mixture of military and civilian clothing. After they stopped, their leader made it clear that he was not going to show his identification and angrily declared that the convoy should be allowed to pass immediately.

Clearly outnumbered and facing an aggressive group, the young commander had very little time to decide what to do. Each one of his subordinates, including snipers hidden in the vicinity, had to assess the situation and keep calm. The territorials were angered by the outcome of the ballot as well as the orders they received from General Syahnakri to leave East Timor. Believing that they were cloaked in darkness, a number of territorials in the first trucks took aim at this young officer, his interpreter, a 23-year-old lieutenant from his unit, and his men.

Quietly and without the need for orders, the Australian infantrymen, who could see the territorials clearly through their night vision goggles, kept their weapons at their sides but, at the same time — guided by their laser designators — trained their muzzles up towards those who had raised their weapons. Green dots that only the Australians could see appeared on the chests of those who were taking aim at the two lieutenants. The snipers, also using laser designators, moved their point of aim onto those presenting immediate danger to the two lieutenants negotiating with the leader of the outriders. The cavalrymen turned the machine guns mounted on their vehicles onto the first trucks. A radio operator reported immediately to company headquarters about what was happening and sought direction.

The Australians were prepared to unleash volleys of aimed, automatic fire if the territorials looked like they were about to open fire. They were confident because they could see their opponents clearly through night vision goggles. They were also trained to maintain fire discipline. Above all, they overcame their personal fear because they trusted their mates to stand with them if there was a firefight. No one used the cover of darkness to move away. Every one of them came forward and formed a firing line behind their young commander.

Most importantly, they had not increased the tension by shouting orders to each other, aggressively raising their weapons or calling out to the territorials to drop theirs. For their part, the territorials decided not to fire because none of them appeared to want to take the chance of being hit first by return fire from the troops and two armoured vehicles that faced them.

The Australian company commander further down the road quickly realised that it was in everyone's interest to allow the convoy to proceed to Indonesian territory in West Timor without further delay. He directed the radio operator to tell the platoon commander to do so. Weapons were lowered. The convoy drove through the control point.

If this temporary stand-off had been handled any differently, the consequences could have been disastrous. Lesser-trained junior officers may not have withstood the pressure of the situation. Lesser-trained troops might have panicked and opened fire, or worse, fled into the night leaving their leaders to their fate. The territorials may have opened fire if the small contingent of troops facing them had presented an intimidated target rather than an immediate, aggressive response.

Australians should be grateful — I certainly was — that the Army invests substantial resources in training individuals, junior leaders and small teams for modern military operations. In my day as a junior leader on operations in Vietnam, my decisions had an immediate impact on my troops and the enemy, but not on the affairs of nations. In today's military operations the decisions of junior leaders still have those immediate impacts, but modern telecommunications and eager journalists can magnify every incident and send descriptions and images instantly around the world for scores of experts and commentators to interpret for millions of viewers and listeners. Thus, the decisions of junior leaders and the actions of their small teams can influence the course of international affairs. Arguably, the future of Australian–Indonesian relations may have been determined by the professionalism of that young officer and his small team at that control point in Dili on 21 September 1999.

What if there had been a clash in the dark that night and other

Australian and Indonesian forces had been drawn into an escalating confrontation? Was there a brooding, over-the-horizon presence of American forces ready to make the difference between success or failure on the ground in this early part of the INTERFET mission, when many thousands of Indonesian troops were rubbing shoulders with arriving INTERFET contingents? In later years a furphy or legend of the operation emerged that an American Marine expeditionary force and other forces were on hand from the beginning to 'back up' if anything went wrong. I have the utmost respect and a great deal of affection for my colleagues in the US armed forces, but the legend is simply not true. The American Government — with some relief — took Australia's word that the ADF could handle the operation. I can assure anyone who wants to know that I did not ever have any American force as an 'ace up my sleeve'. I was most grateful to have a US Army communications battalion as part of the force, but this non-combatant unit simply assisted us with our long-haul communications within the country. At no stage did I think that a major 'Big Brother' presence was necessary or appropriate.

A more deterrent American maritime presence came later, a week or so into the operation. I was grateful for the occasional visit by large US navy helicopter carriers. For brief periods, they multiplied our in-country air resupply capability significantly by effectively doubling the number of transport helicopters we had available. The US armed forces in the Pacific area were under very strict force protection protocols which meant their aggressive employment on combat operations was curtailed severely. Further, their personnel rest and rotation policies strongly militated against deployments ashore for protracted periods.

The attacks on the two journalists and the murder of Sander Thoenes, while typical of some of the earlier murderous violence meted out to many East Timorese, made a very deep impression on the media contingent in Dili and INTERFET soldiers. To a large extent, Australian and Indonesian relations were now in the hands of young Australian and Indonesian soldiers in Dili. This was a pressure-cooker environment. General Syahnakri and I had to manage this situation very carefully indeed. I know he was very conscious of the risks involved and was doing his best to evacuate troops as fast as trucks, buses and ships became available to take them away. He was also aware that he and his commanders had to keep their troops from roaming around because returning East Timorese, uplifted and emboldened by the INTERFET presence, were starting to assemble in mobs to taunt and throw stones at any Indonesians they found moving around Dili. Restoring law and order now had the added complication of dispersing crowds of aggrieved and angry East Timorese, and standing between them and armed and resentful Indonesian soldiers.

Just a few days before, Dili had been virtually deserted apart from Indonesian security forces and some rampaging groups of militia driving around in trucks setting buildings alight. At night, the brooding, immense hill mass that dominated and framed the capital to the south and east came alive with hundreds of twinkling fires. This phenomenon looked like the camp fires of a bivouacking army. They were the fires of many thousands of displaced East Timorese who had fled from their burning homes and marauding militia. After observing the arrival of INTERFET by air and by sea, many people returned almost immediately, hopeful that INTERFET would bring food and water. They camped in the ashes of their homes in their devastated city, profoundly saddened but hopeful, their resilience underscored by playful and happy children smiling and waving.

This was exemplified for me in one incident. Sometime in those first few days, while I was driving around, I glanced down an alleyway and saw a milling group of East Timorese kids. Believe it or not, they were playing cricket with great enthusiasm. I stopped the vehicle and continued to watch for a few more moments. I noticed that a large Australian infantry sergeant, with his rifle slung out of the way over his back, had initiated the game with a tennis ball and a straight piece of wood that was being used as a bat. Each time a kid slogged the ball, he would lead them in a chant of, 'Aussie! Aussie! Aussie! Oi! Oi! Oi!'. This was a memorable, uplifting moment for me, seeing the smiles on the faces of those kids. I was not surprised at the compassion and good humour of the Australian sergeant. Aussie troops all over the world have shown that they empathise with the circumstances of those who have been displaced, traumatised and impoverished by conflict. Australian troops believe in a fair go for all and, like their compatriots, have a special affinity and sympathy for the most innocent of victims — the children.

Around this time we moved into our new headquarters, the Dili public library. It was a three-storey building in a gated compound close to the heart of Dili, and on the edge of what one might call the government precinct — a cluster of official buildings virtually constituting an inner suburb of the capital. INTERFET could occupy damaged and gutted buildings in this area without displacing East Timorese or denying existing facilities and amenities to them. The drawback of using these buildings in general and the library in particular was that each had been systematically ransacked, trashed and burnt. While most were structurally sound, no amenity or fitting had escaped the attention of the mobs. During the clean-up, my staff found a live grenade under a sheet of roofing iron in the foyer — the clean-up crew, comprised mostly of officers and clerks, trod very carefully after that!

I liked the location and the building, but insisted that there be no elaborate repairs. I did this for a number of reasons. I wanted the headquarters working immediately, not distracted by tradesmen renovating work areas. I could have set up the headquarters in tents, as we had trained to do, but thought it sensible to choose a more advantageous environment for our many computer-reliant systems. Bricks and mortar are better than canvas, especially in the wet and humid climate. I also wanted, in all ways, to remind people — my own INTERFET troops, Indonesians, East Timorese, even senior visitors from Australia, and especially the UN — that we were in East Timor as an emergency force for a short stay, not settling back for the long-haul and making ourselves comfortable in the process. There was also one additional reason. Later, when visitors came to the headquarters after the situation in East Timor had become quite benign, it was useful for them to receive the unspoken reminder, as they walked around the building, of the damage done by rioters in September 1999. So, apart from a surface clean-up, and some sheets of corrugated iron and canvas over the roof to keep out the rain, the library became HQ INTERFET. I slept on a stretcher in my office, just as my staff initially did in their offices, and trudged down two flights of stairs to the Portaloos located in the grounds adjacent to the building as they did in the early days.

On 24 September, our fifth day in the country, a number of events coincided to give the operation a positive jolt. The previous day, General Syahnakri had suggested we hold a joint press conference at his headquarters. I agreed immediately. Images and words reiterating our common purpose to end the violence in East Timor would be beneficial. However, I thought it was a courageous initiative, given events over the last few months and the recent incidents with journalists and the murder of Sander Thoenes. I expected that he would get an absolute grilling. I was right. He struggled manfully to answer questions diplomatically, but the many keen and pointed questions put to him from a sixty-strong crush of journalists from all around the world were mainly about the conduct of Indonesian security forces. By chance, Syahnakri's media conference occurred at the same time as INTERFET troops and armoured vehicles swept through the city and helicopters flew low and hard over it. Mark Evans had proposed to me that the time had come to assert control of Dili. These sudden and intense activities were demonstrations of strength as well as resolve to clear the city of the last militia groups. He used his two Australian infantry battalions and all of his armoured vehicles in the sweep and a large number of our Blackhawk helicopters to observe and intimidate from the air. In a totally unpremeditated way, almost every time General Syahnakri went to speak, a Blackhawk would go by at window height drowning out his words for those few moments. When I spoke or the media asked me a question, the Blackhawks were elsewhere! I knew that if we had tried to orchestrate it, it would never have worked that precisely. Still, our troops had flushed out the last militia in Dili — another good thing.

Admiral Barrie, the Australian CDF as well as the military commander of the lead nation in INTERFET, visited that same day. I was happy with how the visit turned out. He saw INTERFET flexing its muscles and everyone getting on with the job of both protecting and helping East Timorese returning to the city. I was troubled, however, by the gloomy and pessimistic nature of the intelligence briefs at my headquarters and a briefing delivered by the intelligence officer on Mark Evans's headquarters. It was not that I did not think the hard work was behind us — far from it. Our troops still had many hazards and dangers in front of them. But I thought we had made a good start with a good plan and a sound formula for the future. While Indonesian security forces were culpable in the past, my profound impression of General Syahnakri was that he intended to get troops and police out of East Timor with as much speed and honour as he could manage. While this would still leave a tense situation on the East/West Timor border, I expected the militia would become weaker and weaker in most of East Timor having lost their sponsors. While I didn't contradict my intelligence officers, I did provide some comment to Admiral Barrie to balance their assessment. Intelligence is advisory. Commanders should not regard it as conclusive.

The continuing dangers of the operation were evident the next day. A small group of INTERFET military police and UN investigative staff, escorted by a Special Forces close protection detachment, drove out to Tibar, a medium-sized village of several thousand people, located about a 10 minute drive west of Dili on the coast road. Their task was to investigate reports of mass graves. While there, they encountered a car load of militia, whom they apprehended. A more senior Special Forces commander and several more of his troopers drove out to reinforce the group and to take the captured militia in for questioning. Soon after his arrival, a large number of heavily armed militia drove up in trucks, apparently alerted to the capture of their comrades. They raised and aimed their weapons at the commander and his group. He assessed immediately that he and his group were outnumbered and outgunned. He handed the detainees over to the militia commander and withdrew his men rapidly, giving the militia a win and leaving them in control of Tibar.

While I understood and endorsed the commander's decision — we might have had significant casualties and been defeated if a firefight had erupted — I was nonetheless quite angry that an INTERFET element had been forced to back off in front of the villagers of Tibar. We had gone to Tibar without sufficient strength, or a back-up plan for rapid reinforcement. I did not want to give the militia one inch. After he returned to Dili, I reminded the commander that his rules of engagement would have allowed him to open fire on the militia because they were threatening our troops directly by pointing their weapons at them. I emphasised that the moment was surely coming when our troops would have to do just that.

On 27 September, the eighth day since our arrival in Dili, General Syahnakri was ready to hand over security responsibility for East Timor to me. Most Indonesian forces had departed and he wanted to leave that day. In practical terms, INTERFET was already running security for the whole country. However, it was important to be diplomatic and observe the niceties. The Indonesian Parliament had not yet ceded control of East Timor to the UN. Officially, Indonesia remained responsible for the country until its parliament approved the transfer of control. General Syahnakri arranged a short handover ceremony attended by media representatives. We both got our points of view on the record with some verbal gymnastics. He left late that afternoon. I was grateful to him for his close attention to any issue that might have led to an accidental clash of INTERFET and Indonesian troops. He and his staff had put in a mighty effort to evacuate thousands of personnel and their belongings. He left a 1300-strong garrison force in Dili under command of an army colonel, although a police brigadier was the senior uniformed Indonesian remaining in East Timor. A group of diplomats, who I presume reported back to Jakarta, also remained. They lived in a small enclave of government residences west of the port on the seafront. The garrison and their diplomat guests didn't seem to do much but wait for the due date to leave for good.

Meanwhile, an emergency had arisen at the village of Com, located on the north coast in the far east of the country. An air reconnaissance revealed a large number of people gathered on the jetty. It looked like militia were herding them against their will in order to embark them on ships. All Indonesian authorities had left that part of East Timor so there could be no official reason for this embarkation. I decided to look into it. A young major, an INTERFET Special Forces squadron commander, assembled a force and flew by Blackhawk that night to investigate. He landed his men some distance away and patrolled forward in the darkness. After speaking with a few locals, the major and his men discovered that a group of well-armed militia were holding the people on the jetty under threat. Most of the militia had gone to bed in a nearby house, leaving a few to guard their captives. The major put a cordon around the house and called on the militia to surrender. After a half-baked and unsuccessful escape attempt, his troopers captured the group and had them lie on the ground with their hands behind their heads. Bahasa linguists among our soldiers told the people on the wharf that they could return to their homes. A group of thugs were disarmed in front of their compatriots, an INTERFET force had set several hundred people free and no shots had been fired. This was an excellent result that exemplified the initiative and courage of Australia's Special Forces and was a great bounce back from the unsatisfactory outcome at Tibar.

I had an obligation as part of my mandate to facilitate the delivery of humanitarian aid with whatever resources I could spare. Primarily, though, INTERFET was there to create a secure environment for aid to be delivered by others. At this stage of the operation, I did not have surplus means to deliver aid. However, during the first ten days there was a groundswell amongst aid agencies that people in more outlying regions of East Timor were starving and needed urgent food supplies. My information was that there was no starvation occurring in East Timor. However, I understood the reaction of those people charged with the responsibility of providing humanitarian assistance. As a result, some emergency air drops took place into areas assessed as being in need.

Air drops are risky if there aren't people on the ground to guide aircraft in, and to keep locals clear of drop zones. For these urgent drops, pilots did their best to aim at open areas that were free of people. On one drop, a food container landed on or bounced into the leg of a small child, Nelson Suares, who sustained severe injuries. East Timorese helpers rushed him to the INTERFET hospital in Dili. Our surgeons operated but could not save one of his legs, which had to be amputated. I visited Nelson not long after his surgery. I was quite moved by the sight of the poor little tyke, heavily sedated and lying there surrounded by his mother, father and sister. I did not know then, but help from Australia was on its way.

On the tenth day after our arrival, the first major coalition contingent arrived in Dili. It was fitting that it was an infantry battalion from our ANZAC ally across the Tasman Sea. There is a symbiotic and sibling relationship between Australia and New Zealand, personified in our sporting teams, but pervading both our societies and certainly our military forces. When the chips are down, we know that we will help each other. When you are working with Kiwis on operations you rely on them to the same degree as you rely on your fellow Australians — no greater expression of regard can be made about Kiwis in uniform. I had met Colonel Martyn Dunne, the shrewd, professional, hard-nosed and good-humoured New Zealand national commander, early in the operation. He had become one of my closest and most trusted colleagues. I considered him to be an outstanding leader with excellent diplomatic skills.

On 30 September I went to a compound that housed a vacant primary school. It would be some time before the children of Dili would be back at school. Martyn briefed me that I would meet and greet the first major contingent of Kiwi combat troops to arrive in East Timor there. I had worked closely with Kiwis in Vietnam and for me there was a delicious mix of anticipation and nostalgia in having these great infantrymen as part of INTERFET. New Zealand Special Forces had been in Dili from the outset, but this was a major and welcome reinforcement. Perhaps it was my heightened emotions, but I detected a dramatic atmosphere on that afternoon. There were hundreds of curious locals looking over the walls and crowding into the periphery of the schoolyard. They were excited, but strangely quiet. There were a number of journalists and television crews there to record the moment.

As I entered, I knew what had caused the excitement among the East Timorese. There, arrayed across the schoolyard in front of me, were over 150 male soldiers standing impassively in ranks, rifles set aside, bare-chested and bare-headed. At the side of this group, a young female Kiwi soldier started to sing a wild and lilting refrain in Maori. Then a very muscular Maori soldier began to weave in and out of the ranks of his comrades, calling upon them in the tongue of his race. When he reached a crescendo, with an enormous roar, the Kiwis started the Haka, their national warrior welcome and expression of fierce intent. The waves of noise rolled and rebounded through the courtyard. The rhythmic stamp of the soldiers' boots stirred up the dry, red clay dust of East Timor in a billowing cloud. As the Haka progressed, the soldiers started to advance on me until, as the mighty last phrase came forth, the front rank was only an arm's length away. That's the way to announce yourself! I made a short speech and departed — an uplifted man!

The arrival of the Kiwis three days after General Syahnakri's handover marked the end of the first phase of Operation *Stabilise*. I now had sufficient troops to hold Dili and to occupy the

East/West Timor border. In the first ten days INTERFET had achieved excellent results. Dili was safe for the UN and aid agencies to get to work and for East Timorese to not only begin to rebuild their country, but to begin their journey to independence. The airport and port were open and receiving hundreds of personnel and thousands of tonnes of supplies, scores of vehicles and many items of equipment each day. People and supplies were also flowing into Baucau to the east.

The next phase was about to begin. Mark Evans was poised with his brigade to deploy down to the border and seal off East Timor from outside interference. Infantry battalions and other military and humanitarian units from regional allies and from allies around the world were inbound. Also coming in were hundreds of representatives from a wide variety of organisations and governments that had business in East Timor. I looked back to Australia for the support I knew I would need to cope with this influx of well-meaning, but possibly high maintenance organisations, groups and individuals.

10

The Expanding Ink Spot

IT WAS NOW TIME TO EXPAND the operation. I favoured a conventional strategy of concentrating in one area, like an ink spot, and then expanding and consolidating to create other ink spots of security in important areas and eventually linking up all of the ink spots to provide a secure environment throughout East Timor, an area approaching the size of Tasmania. I did not favour going everywhere at once just to give an appearance of doing things boldly and quickly. When INTERFET troops arrived in an area, they would stay. Therefore, although INTERFET elements had been into the high country south of Dili, a considerable distance east towards Los Palos and had established a presence in Baucau, we had not appeared on the ground in the western regions bordered by West Timor.

I had asked Mark Evans to come up with a plan to deploy to the west with a well-supported infantry battalion — about a thousand strong. He advised that he would start by consolidating on the north coast at the village of Batugade, close to the West Timor border, and in Balibo, a town due south of Batugade in the hills overlooking the northern coast and across the border to Atambua, the first major town in the northern area of West Timor. Although I could see the logic of what he was proposing, inwardly I sighed at the mention of Balibo because of the very evocative cachet that town had in Australian attitudes to East Timor's history. The killing of four unarmed Australian journalists and a British camera crewman in Balibo in 1975 was seared into Australia's memory and had been the focus of controversy and ill-feeling ever since. I was hoping that people in Australia would not think that we were playing a game of symbols, rather than just doing a professional military job of going to the tactically important places first. Journalists would accompany early flights into Balibo. However, I quickly vetoed a suggestion by some media representatives that it would be nice if they could go there first — by themselves — to film the troops arriving later!

Mark's push to the border and occupation of Batugade and Balibo went like clockwork. There were no hostile groups awaiting his troops. I visited both towns on 3 October, soon after our troops had established themselves. Balibo is picturesque, offering spectacular views over the rugged and beautiful mountain and river flood plain landscape of that part of East Timor. The prominent hill in Balibo is crowned by an old Portuguese colonial era fort, complete with battlements. Following historical precedent, the Australian battalion commander, Lieutenant Colonel Mick Slater, set up his headquarters there and where previous military and civilian governors must have done so. While there, I visited the buildings in which the group of Australian journalists and a British colleague had been living during the days before they were murdered back in 1975. Needless to say, the people of Balibo and Batugade were delighted to see INTERFET setting up their towns as bases of operation.

About this time an imbroglio concerning the 'hot pursuit' of miscreants into West Timor raised its head in Canberra. Many media representatives love hypothetical scenarios, especially controversial ones. The Defence Minister, in reply to a question about a hypothetical situation of INTERFET troops chasing hostile groups near the East/West Timor border, suggested that INTERFET had a right of 'hot pursuit' from East Timor into West Timor under certain circumstances. As often can be the case in these situations, some journalists interpreted the Minister's mention of a possible 'right' as an 'intention' to pursue criminals into Indonesian sovereign territory. Australian, regional and, not least, Indonesian media erupted. It took no time at all for a member of the media contingent in East Timor to put the question to me. I replied that I had no intention of 'hot pursuit' because I would rely on the Indonesians to either prevent criminals from coming into East Timor in the first place, or to arrest them the moment they entered West Timor territory. The issue dropped off the radar screen quickly but demonstrated that musing about what might happen, even in passing, can set 'the rabbits running'.

A useful advisor when political and diplomatic issues were in the offing or a crisis had erupted in the media was James Batley, the Australian Consul General in East Timor. As part of my daily routine, I used to call on him for a chat. He had flown back to Dili on 1 October and had settled back into his consulate building not far from the heliport. This fortress-like building, designed for a handful of people to work in, had been used by a considerable number of people as a dormitory when the militia violence peaked in September. Ken Brownrigg had arranged for *Kostrad* troops to protect it from arsonists. INTERFET took over these duties on the first day of the lodgment. I found James's knowledge of East Timor politics, advice, and astute assessment of unfolding events to be invaluable. He was one of Australia's most experienced regional diplomats who had worked with the ADF in Bougainville and was now at the cutting edge of another new good neighbour operation. At our first meeting, he was relaxed and cheerful — in fact, the mood I always found him in!

Around this time an unusual incident occurred. After my regular evening briefing, a staff officer murmured in my ear that a boy had arrived at the headquarters with a message for me. I went down to the foyer and spoke with the lad through an interpreter. His name was Lafu. He looked no older than about ten, but was possibly about fourteen years old. Whatever age he was, when I first saw him he was having a tension-relieving smoke on the front verandah of the headquarters! He was from the Oecussi Enclave. He said that he represented the people there, especially those resisting the militia. He had travelled overland from the Enclave and had crossed the border from West to East Timor at Motaain, near Batugade. After he made himself known to our troops, they put him on military transport to Dili. He was carrying a note that he had folded and concealed in a slit in the side of his thong. The people of Oecussi implored our urgent assistance, both to stop militia depredations and to bring humanitarian assistance. I thought Lafu was a very brave young man and told him so. I told him that I was much moved by his plea. I would send troops to Oecussi as soon as I could. I put him in the care of Tim McOwan's headquarters staff and they arranged for him to go to one of the cantonments occupied by East Timorese guerrillas who had fought the Indonesian armed forces since their invasion in 1975.

This cry for help left me with a considerable dilemma. I was in serious danger of overstretch if I redeployed troops from Dili to the Enclave. Thinning out in Dili would risk a resurgence of militia activity in the city. I needed newly arriving and inbound regional battalions from Thailand, the Philippines and Korea to secure the expanses of the country's eastern regions. I had just committed all of my available Australian and New Zealand infantry to the crucial border districts. Nonetheless, I asked Mark Kelly to get the staff to work up a plan for securing the Enclave as soon as possible. I did not want to just visit, patrol and manoeuvre for a period of time and then leave. It was a principle of our operations in East Timor that INTERFET arrived in an area and stayed to protect the people — the ink spot concept. The Oecussi Enclave was remote and isolated. I had to send a garrison of tough troops who needed little handholding and could operate independently. We put our thinking caps on.

A couple of days after this move down into the border regions, we experienced the first major challenge mounted by the militia since INTERFET arrived on 20 September. We now had a presence in the northern part of the western regions, but I did not have sufficient troops just yet to occupy the southern districts around the major town of Suai, located on the south coast near the East/West Timor border. I'd already decided to conduct a reconnaissance-in-force using a group of Major Jim McMahon's men supported by light armoured vehicles. This type of force had proved to be most successful earlier in the operation, penetrating well ahead of infantry units, examining roads and ascertaining whether there were any remaining hostile groups.

On 6 October, McMahon's force had established a roadblock in Suai and had apprehended a number of men who appeared to have come from West Timor. Suddenly, another truck full of men approached the roadblock at high speed. As the vehicle zigzagged through a herringbone of chicanes, the driver failed to obey any of the signals to slow down and stop. The troopers assessed that he was running the roadblock deliberately and opened fire, aiming at the engine block and front tyres in an attempt to disable the vehicle. The vehicle ground to a stop under this hail of bullets. Ricochets and metal fragments had grazed a few passengers. This was the first time that INTERFET troops had been compelled by their rules of engagement to open fire. I was keenly interested in the circumstances of this incident and was satisfied subsequently that the troops had acted correctly and proportionately. They detained the driver and his passengers, treated the lightly injured and brought them all to Dili for further questioning because their actions suggested that they had something sinister to hide.

Throughout the day, more people appeared to be coming across from West Timor in suspicious circumstances and were surprised on the road by McMahon's troopers and detained. Late in the afternoon of 6 October, McMahon decided that the best thing to do was to return several truckloads of these people to West Timor. His men loaded them onto the trucks they had arrived in and formed a convoy for the 30 minute ride back to the border. Not very far out of Suai, with the vehicles laden with civilians leading and several military vehicles carrying soldiers bringing up the rear, a hostile group, hidden on both sides of the road, ambushed the convoy with heavy fire directed at the military vehicles. The Land Rovers braked heavily on the shoulder of the road and the troopers started to return fire as hard as they could go. The ambushers had wounded two SAS soldiers in the first burst of fire. While the others returned fire vigorously, several troopers bravely dragged their wounded mates to cover and a medic started to treat their wounds.

Back in Suai, McMahon gathered together troops on hand, including several light armoured vehicles, and raced to the sound of the guns. By now, the late afternoon was transitioning into a gloomy, tropical twilight. As soon as McMahon and his reinforcements arrived, they spread into a line, and with armoured vehicles in fire support, launched a ferocious assault to clear the ambush area. Ambushers fled under the weight of fire and in the face of the advancing troops, leaving two of their number dead. McMahon's radio operator had been keeping my headquarters informed and more details flowed in over the next hour or so. Of course, the electrifying news was that INTERFET had sustained its first casualties. Fortunately, McMahon was quick to inform me that based on the advice of his medics he did not think the wounds were life-threatening, although they were quite serious. I was most impressed with the initial and subsequent treatment of both casualties. They were attended to immediately under fire, stabilised for evacuation and flown by helicopter to the INTERFET hospital, which was ready for them, and surgeons operated on both men soon after arrival. McMahon and his men remained in Suai to ensure that the people did not think that INTERFET had been defeated or driven off by this ambush.

The story of the ambush and the firefight in Suai became a race to the truth. I had learned by now that where the media have wide access to information in an area of military operations, their reporting can help or hinder — clarify or confuse. Early pieces of information from a dramatic newsworthy event never contain all of the reality, but will shape initial perceptions and how it is reported. These perceptions will become the first versions of reality, or 'facts', before the full story is known. I figured that I had only a matter of hours before the media would be broadcasting elements of the story. In order to pre-empt the possibility of unhelpful and erroneous reporting, I decided to give an ad hoc press conference at the Tourismo Hotel, knowing that because of time zone differences, some of the press and electronic media representatives would be out of cycle. However, I was convinced that it was more important to provide as accurate a version of the incident as I knew it before some of the furphies could emerge.

I suppose it was somewhat dramatic, materialising at the Tourismo in the mid-evening, amid a bunch of journos who were kicking back after a hard day's reporting, but I got their attention. I gave an outline of the events of the day with special reference to the battle in the late afternoon and stressed three things. First, our troops had acted professionally and decisively in the face of an ambush. Second, our two casualties were expected to recover. And third, the ambush was folly that the militia should not repeat if they did not wish to be killed like their two comrades.

The other significant event of this day was the arrival of the senior Thai officer, Major General Songkitti, who was to be in command of the Thai contingent and would also be my deputy commander. His arrival symbolised the very welcome commitment that regional countries were about to make to the security of East Timor and the journey the East Timorese were about to take to independence under the auspices of the UN. Major General Songkitti was arriving for the second time after his all-important presence when I met General Syahnakri in Dili on 19 September. In the intervening period, he had been back in Thailand preparing the Thai infantry battalion for deployment. He had also spent time in Jakarta. I assumed that he had done good work ensuring that the Indonesian Government and the Indonesian armed forces understood and concurred with Thailand's motives for participating in INTERFET. I looked forward to working with him for the duration of the mission.

After Mark Evans had settled his headquarters into Suai with advance elements from the New Zealand infantry battalion, INTERFET became a garrison force. While there would be further incidents and many matters needing my attention, I was ready to embark on a comprehensive round of visits to all parts of the force, and to call on senior UN officials and prominent East Timorese leaders. Without doubt though, my special pleasure would be to see first-hand the men and women of INTERFET doing a magnificent job under demanding circumstances and in austere living conditions. I wanted to encourage and congratulate them in person.

I knew that INTERFET would accomplish its mission for two reasons. The first was the courage of ordinary East Timorese who had suffered and endured for twenty-five years, and were now sniffing the beautiful scent of independence. The other was the astonishing skill, cheerfulness and energy of all the people of INTERFET. Whether it was the men and women of the Philippines contingent running medical clinics or animal husbandry classes in their area of operations, or the Koreans treating the locals in the Los Palos district with exquisite courtesy — it didn't matter — it uplifted me no end.

Over the years I had had a lot to do with the Royal Australian Air Force, however, I was now finding out what a profoundly 'can-do' organisation it was. There were mind-boggling technical challenges associated with the provision of air support, which us mere soldiers thought would be showstoppers. For example, serious engine unserviceability that seemed set to ground an aircraft for days, but to my Air Force staff they were par-for-the-course issues, quickly resolved and 'here is your aircraft'.

It was also great fun visiting the ships of the various navies supporting the operation. There is a timeless protocol about visiting ships that involves visitors paying some important courtesies, such as saluting the bridge, as they first arrive on board. I was always punctilious about maritime etiquette. However, I have never been the most agile of creatures and scaling some of the ships' ladders when they were anchored out in Dili Harbour made a dignified boarding a somewhat tricky proposition. Privately, I used to rate the ships in our little fleet by the degree of difficulty involved in boarding, with crawling from ladder to deck like a drunken lizard scoring a 9.5.

On one unforgettable occasion, Commodore Brian Robertson, the INTERFET maritime component commander, and a great friend and a very fine naval officer, accompanied me as a member of a small entourage to visit a foreign ship anchored in Dili

Harbour. Members of the crew came to the Dili wharf to ferry us to the vessel in one of the ship's small 'rubber duckies'. The crew had tied their dinghy to a small floating pontoon that was tied to the wharf. Both of them had stepped to the bow and were fiddling with the line instead of at least one of them being there to help the old boy (me!) come aboard. It was just after dark as I stepped on to the slimy surface of the pontoon and began moving gingerly towards the bobbing dinghy. I did the full dipsy-doodle, ending up horizontal and falling nose first onto the metal deck of the dinghy. I just managed to draw up one knee to break my fall before impact. I lay flat out and facedown for a long moment thinking, 'I've broken my leg!', before telling myself not to be a sook and rolling over to relish the moment.

It was almost worth the pain to see the looks on the faces of members of my little entourage, notably Brian Robertson. I'm sure they thought I would be a stretcher case! In gazing about, I saw that the two ratbags at the front of the dinghy were studiously ignoring the situation and pretended to be oblivious to my pratfall. When we made our way out to go aboard the very large ship, I rated it at about 8 out of 10 for its ladder, which I had to negotiate with the added disadvantage of one very gammy leg. When I got aboard, the captain may have mistaken the tears on my cheeks as the joyful emotion of being with him and his ship's company. Still they were marvellously hospitable and the fluid eventually drained from my knee.

On another occasion several weeks later, when boarding an Australian Landing Craft Heavy (a flat-bottomed, square-nosed ship with a large open deck and a ramp at the front to allow vehicles to drive on and off, normally to and from a beach), I encountered another 'challenging' ladder. It wasn't so high, but good ladders have spreaders, longer horizontal boards attached, which help to prevent the ladder twisting during the climb up or down. This ladder had very short spreaders. As I climbed, I managed to twist on the ladder so that I was between the ladder and the ship's side. Brian, with great zeal, unexpected agility and concern for my safety, leapt from the boat below and grasped me in a rugby grip around the legs. The scene befitted a Laurel and Hardy movie. There was me, elephantine at the best of times, hanging from the ladder, holding it in a desperate and weakening death grip, with a large man hanging off my legs. Every man and woman in INTERFET would have paid thousands to watch this pantomime performance. The only saving grace was that my trousers did not fall down.

Frequently when visiting ships, especially ships of the Royal Australian Navy, I had wonderful opportunities to talk to the sailors individually and often to an assembly of the whole ship's company. I found them endlessly curious about operations ashore and implicitly interested in whether their presence was important. I took every opportunity, especially when talking to them collectively, to tell them how important it was that land forces had the support of our ships at sea. Their contribution was not just to move the many thousands of tonnes of supplies. The presence of warships emphasised that this powerful land force with a UN mandate had come ashore with the guarantee and the constant over-watch of INTERFET vessels from various navies. I spoke of their ceaseless vigil at sea. I praised the way in which they interacted with the troops and the East Timorese, with their working parties constantly ashore bringing skill and energy to the

Meeting with Major General Kiki Syahnakri on 19 September 1999 in Dili in order to prepare the way for the arrival of INTERFET the next day. Ken Brownrigg is between and behind us.

Aussie soldiers in a typically good-humoured encounter with FALINTIL warriors and supporters.

Me (in the headphones) and the INTERFET RSM, Dale Sales, flying over East Timor in a Blackhawk in October 1999.

Talking (mostly with my hands!) to the arriving Brazilian military police in late 1999.

The Remembrance Day service, 11 November 1999, in the hills outside Dili. Rufino Alves Correia, one of the original *Criados*, helps me lay the first wreath.

AAP Images/AP: Charles Dharapak

An ad hoc meeting at the border crossing between East and West Timor in Motaain. Falintil Vice Commander Taur Matan Ruak (TMR) (second from left), UNTAET Administrator Sergio Vieira de Mello (second from right) and US Ambassador Richard Holbrooke (far right).

Packed stands at the Dili Sports Stadium for a friendly soccer game between INTERFET and East Timor. José Ramos-Horta asked me to present the trophy to the winning East Timorese side.

Australian Government Department of Defence

As is customary, senior officers serve the diggers their meal at Christmas, and in 1999 it was a breakfast barbecue in Dili for the men of Delta Company, 5/7 RAR.

A review of the outgoing troops in Dili with Lieutenant General De Los Santos, Commander of the UN Forces in East Timor, in 2000.

AAP Images/AP: Ed Wray

Soldiers folding the INTERFET flag, which was lowered for the last time on Wednesday, 23 February 2000.

At the Governor's Palace for the formal transition from INTERFET to the PKF. From left to right: Xanana Gusmao, Lieutenant General De Los Santos, Sergio Vieira de Mello, me and Bishop Belo.

Australian Government Department of Defence

A day of great goodwill: Xanana Gusmao and a large crowd of East
Timorese had come to see us off at the dock before we boarded
HMAS *Jervis Bay* back to Darwin. Sergio Viera de Mello
is behind Gusmao, to his right.

The start of a 'ferocious hug'! A lovely big welcome home cuddle
from Lynne, right there on the tarmac at Sydney airport, after five
months away.

task of rebuilding. Air and sea power played a vital role in the INTERFET operation. I constantly referred to this fact, not just to our Air Force and Navy people, but also to the soldiers ashore.

One of the vital ingredients of peace and security in East Timor was the role and conduct of FALINTIL — Forças Armadas de Libertação Nacional de Timor-Leste (Armed Forces for the National Liberation of East Timor) — the pro-independence East Timorese guerrilla army. First as the armed wing of Fretilin — Frente Revolucionária de Timor-Leste Independente (Revolutionary Front for an Independent East Timor) — a pro-independence political party, and later as FALINTIL, some of these warriors had been fighting, hiding and surviving for twenty-five years. All of them were entitled to feel that they had a very large stake in the present security arrangements as well as the future safety and prosperity of the new nation of Timor Leste.

Yet therein lay a predicament. Many in Indonesia and a significant number of East Timorese pro-integrationists felt that FALINTIL carried its share of culpability for what had gone on since the Indonesian invasion in 1975. Be that as it may, during the period before the 3 August ballot, and even when violence erupted thereafter, FALINTIL units had remained in their cantonments away from heavily populated centres and refrained from military action. This must have been extraordinarily hard when they learnt of the dreadful atrocities perpetrated by pro-integration militia against their compatriots.

So, on two counts — their long struggle and their recent restraint — members of FALINTIL deserved consideration. Yet there was considerable commentary, especially in regional media, recommending that INTERFET should not just disarm the militia but should apply the same rules to FALINTIL. This seemed to ignore the fact that it was the militia who were wantonly killing people and burning houses while FALINTIL both maintained discipline and kept to their agreements to remain in their jungle camps. Now that INTERFET had ejected the main militia groups, the liaison officers that I kept with FALINTIL and other visitors to them reported a growing frustration on the part of the guerrillas and a need for acknowledgement and inclusion. I resolved to meet with their leader, the man who stepped up when Xanana Gusmao was arrested and who had been leading FALINTIL ever since, a legendary warrior figure within East Timor — Taur Matan Ruak, a *nom de guerre* meaning 'Seeing with both eyes open — always awake'. (Later, with his approval I and my staff called him 'TMR' for brevity's sake!)

Keeping tabs on indigenous guerrilla armies is a classic Special Forces job. I had a couple of very experienced officers who had initiated a close relationship with FALINTIL very early in the operation. These men now quickly set up a meeting in the remote mountain village of Uamori. On 8 October, I flew up there in a Blackhawk helicopter. The landing pad was a few hundred metres from the first dwellings of the village. The pathway from the landing zone to the village was divided by a shallow, but swiftly running mountain stream — about 20 metres wide. One of my Special Forces officers met me and we headed out on the path towards the village. As I got to the stream, I looked over and saw several armed FALINTIL soldiers on the far bank. All of them had quite long hair down to their shoulders — it was a FALINTIL tradition not to cut their hair until they had achieved victory. Among this group was a small, nimble, boyish figure who watched as I started across the creek. As soon as I entered, he bounded into the stream from his side and TMR and I had our first meeting ankle deep in water. It was a very symbolic start as we demonstrated that we could always meet at least halfway on issues.

We walked to the meeting house in relative silence and passed a number of fierce-looking FALINTIL fighters. They appeared to be torn between ogling me and my accompanying staff, and looking appropriately ferocious. TMR and I had a lengthy meeting. I told him that I had no intention of disarming FALINTIL. I proposed that members of FALINTIL transition into a new East Timorese security force or return to civilian employment. For his part, TMR wanted INTERFET to pay more attention to information FALINTIL was able to provide about militia or militia supporters and sympathisers. This was not as simple as it sounded. We had many more tip-offs than solid evidence to support action on our part. I was not prepared to order INTERFET soldiers to arrest individuals where there was a danger of grabbing people based on suspicion, neighbourhood squabbles or old resentments. TMR also asked us for help to relocate FALINTIL groups from some of the cantonments. I was happy to help. This decision was vindicated later because I found out that he wanted them concentrated in one place so that he could exercise tighter control over some who wanted to wander off as armed freedom fighters to enjoy the early fruits of liberation. It was crucial for INTERFET to be the only legitimate armed 'player' in the country.

One of the sidebar issues I discussed with TMR was young Lafu, the intrepid young boy from the Oecussi Enclave. TMR vouched for his sincerity and suggested that I send him back into the Enclave with some means of communication so that pro-independence citizens in the Enclave could tell us what was happening. I said, 'My only concern is for the boy.' To which TMR replied, 'If he dies, he dies for the motherland.' These few words spoke volumes for the attitude of the people who had suffered much and were prepared to keep suffering to achieve the prize of a free and independent future. As I walked away from our meeting, I felt I had met a soldier and a patriot of real substance. I hoped that I could gain and keep his friendship. On a number of future occasions with the media and other interlocutors, I was able to stress that I had a very good working relationship with FALINTIL in general, and with TMR in particular. This relationship not only defused critical external commentary to some degree but also assisted when the INTERFET/FALINTIL relationship hit a rocky patch from time to time.

So the next morning, 9 October, I was feeling entitled to a quiet sense of satisfaction at the way many of the jigsaw pieces of the operation were being put in place. The majority of Australia's regional allies had either deployed their forces or had committed them with a timetable for their arrival. We had survived a vexed period without a major incident when there were many thousands of Indonesian soldiers and young men and women from INTERFET rubbing shoulders in a tense environment. Aid agencies were starting to operate freely. I'd reached a good initial accommodation with FALINTIL. I now hoped that many of the people who had left East Timor either willingly or under duress would be able to return. I was starting to think about border arrangements for the passage of displaced people, their reception, screening, feeding, medical care and transport. On operations, you can always rely on the unpleasant present to disturb the rosy future! This was the day of what we came to call in INTERFET the Motaain Incident.

We had an infantry company of about a hundred soldiers plus some other support staff in a small garrison position at the village of Batugade within a few kilometres of Motaain, the site of an East/West Timor border post. Intelligence staff offered the officer commanding at Batugade a fairly hazy report that militia were threatening and beating up East Timorese somewhere near Motaain. He decided to move up there in strength to investigate. With virtually his entire company, he patrolled towards the border on both sides of the road, looking for any signs of militia activity. For this movement, he and his troops were using official Indonesian maps of the area that included border markings. Eventually, the leading elements of this long line of soldiers arrived at the border. Their maps showed that the border was a couple of metres in front of the first man. There they stopped.

At this stage a young Indonesian army lieutenant saw the first few of these soldiers and ran up to meet them. Off to the right, about 50 metres away and a little way in front of them, was a larger group of Indonesians, estimated at several dozen, some of whom were dressed in military uniform (either army or police) and some of whom were dressed in T-shirts and uniform trousers and boots. Suddenly, members of this group started firing automatic weapons at the few Australian soldiers they could see at the border. These lads took immediate cover with bullets flying in amongst them —

it was a minor miracle that none of them was hit. While this was occurring, the Indonesians had not noticed that they were outflanked by Australian soldiers moving further back in the column because of the winding shape of the road. The Australian soldiers acted to protect their mates and fired a short volley of shots which hit two Indonesian policemen shooting at our men. One of these policemen subsequently died. A full-blown border incident had now occurred.

Fortunately, the Indonesian group that had opened fire jumped aboard trucks and drove away. A young Indonesian lieutenant, who had been talking to the first group of troops, performed very creditably and bravely. When the shooting started, he remained close to the Australians being shot at, waving his arms and calling on his colleagues to cease firing. Finally, the discipline of the Australians held. Apart from the few shots fired for the immediate protection of those being fired upon, there was no further aggressive action, or undisciplined or frightened shooting.

The other piece of good fortune in what was a very unfortunate incident was the coincidental presence of Major David Kilcullen, who basically was along for the walk as he had another job in the battalion and had no particular responsibilities for this task. He was a fluent Bahasa speaker and proved to be very cool under pressure. At the incident site, he spoke with the small posse of senior Indonesian officers who had rushed to the scene and, in doing so, played a major role in defusing any further conflict. The Indonesian position was that the first few Australian soldiers had actually strolled across the border by several metres; according to an old concrete border marker set back a short distance off the road. Kilcullen, using the official Indonesian map, was able to point out that the border marked on the map was still several metres on from the leading soldier. He demonstrated that the Australians had not been acting in any aggressive way and had started a conversation with the young lieutenant when they had been fired on.

Thus, at the local level, the incident was being sorted out satisfactorily. However, the coincidental presence of several journalists and a camera crew began another race to the truth. I spoke to Mark Evans telling him I was relying on him to manage 'the race' downwards and to diffuse any residual tension. I knew I would have my hands full dealing with the tension upwards! When I had enough reliable facts, I passed them on to Australia and thought of how I would further manage the incident. I decided on three themes: first, the Australian troops had genuinely believed on the basis of the Indonesian map that they were standing in East Timor and were acting in an unprovocative way; secondly, our troops had received heavy fire and the few shots fired back were in self-protection; thirdly, this incident emphasised beyond doubt that there was a need for border control protocols between INTERFET/the UN/East Timor and Indonesia. These themes emerged in the initial reporting.

I proposed that INTERFET and Indonesian authorities instigate a joint investigation of the circumstances of the incident, especially to prevent any future recurrences. Like the Joint Security Coordination Group structure I had used as a mechanism for cooperating with General Syahnakri and his staff, this idea of setting up a joint investigation was a success. The Indonesian police brigadier and his staff in Dili, who were now the senior uniformed Indonesians in Dili, agreed immediately. While it took a few weeks to complete the investigation, I was very satisfied that both sides agreed on the bare bones of the incident. Sadly though, this tragic incident did not lead automatically to the drafting of the necessary border control protocols — that needed a bit more work. Some weeks later when I had the chance to visit the actual incident site, I was amazed, as an old infantryman who had been in combat, at the evidence of bullet strikes in the close vicinity to where young soldiers had been standing and then taking cover — again our luck had held.

The Motaain Incident pointed up an ongoing difficulty for INTERFET. After the departure of General Syahnakri, Major General Adam Damiri became the senior Indonesian officer responsible for Indonesian security operations in West Timor. He now had the authority to negotiate processes and protocols for sensible management of border security. He appeared not to be disposed to do so. He had been mentioned several times in 'dispatches' in relation to the violence that had occurred in East Timor, especially during the last few months before INTERFET intervened. (Some years later he was convicted in Indonesia for his involvement.) In late 1999, he proved to be remarkably elusive. He did not reply to my correspondence. I lost count of the number of times I made attempts to speak to him on the phone to arrange a meeting in order to set some work in motion to make the border safer and more controlled. In fact, if it was not so serious, it would have been a competitive game to track him down to his various phone numbers in order to have any sort of conversation with him at all.

Securing mutually-agreed border protocols was important unfinished business. I was worried that without agreed arrangements, there remained high potential for Indonesian security forces and INTERFET troops to have further misunderstandings in the border area. The border line itself was very long (about 150 kilometres), ill-defined, ran through rugged terrain and was totally permeable to the inhabitants of the border regions as well as criminals and hostile groups, such as the militia. Much of it needed to be patrolled and observed; very little of its length was practically impassable. We had frequent cases of unauthorised border crossings. Most of them were by East and West Timorese trading and visiting relatives. However, other informal crossings, such as armed Indonesian soldiers wandering around looking for game to shoot, were recipes for disaster. Over the period of weeks that I attempted to contact Damiri, I became more and more frustrated that an obvious and mutually beneficial initiative proved to be beyond his consideration.

II

Combat and the Coming

OUR NEXT CONFRONTATION WITH the militia occurred on 16 October down in the border regions, but this time further north of the last encounter at Suai. Once again the SAS were in the thick of it. A sergeant was leading a patrol that was following up on some vague intelligence about a militia group operating in the vicinity of a village called Aidabasala. This small group of about five SAS troopers were having a brief break in a creek bed early on that morning when the lead elements of a large militia group blundered into them. A ferocious firefight then ensued for over an hour before the small patrol was able to break contact and move to a safer area, and Tim McOwan was able to get reinforcements to them from Dili. The militia group were determined to kill the sergeant and his men and had the numbers to do so. They repeatedly probed and attacked the patrol. Each time they were bloodily repulsed. Each soldier of this tiny group held his nerve, covered his mates and shot with deadly accuracy. The Australians hit their marks several times and the militia group finally had enough and withdrew carrying their dead and wounded comrades.

It was a credit to their training and character that the patrol had survived unhurt — there were plenty of near misses. Their leader had performed admirably; moving around within the tight perimeter of his patrol, encouraging and backing up his soldiers when the various attacks occurred and doing what was expected of him — acting above and beyond the call of duty, leading his troops in combat. For his actions and example, he was subsequently awarded the Medal of Gallantry which I was privileged to witness Her Majesty the Queen pin on his chest at Government House in Canberra a few months later in 2000. Beyond the particular details of the action, I was content that a savage lesson had been taught to the militia groups who thought of bringing violence back into East Timor. At the press conference in Darwin on 19 September, I had said that the trained men and women of INTERFET would be a tougher proposition for the militia than defenceless East Timorese. This and the action at Suai had heavily underscored these remarks.

The next day, Sunday, 17 October, was the occasion of a celebratory Mass at Dili Cathedral. The people of East Timor are overwhelmingly Catholic and very devout — you could put up the 'house full' signs at every church on just about every Sunday. I thought I would slip in the back of the church and attend, given the celebratory nature of this service and the fact that Bishop Belo, a Nobel peace laureate and one of the two bishops in East Timor, would be the celebrant. I also sought both the upliftment and reflection that opportunities to worship provide, and wished to show a connected interest and support for Bishop Belo and his parishioners. A few of my staff were interested to accompany me in addition to my ubiquitous close personal protection soldiers, by now military police rather than Special Forces. I instructed the bodyguards not to carry firearms in the church. I'm sure they felt a little underdressed, but their weapons were handy. Dili Cathedral was already packed when we got there about 10 minutes before the service was due to start. I was able to squeeze into a rear pew with my offsiders while the bodyguard folks were in the choir loft and upper gallery of the cathedral.

Our presence caused a minor ripple of interest, but this attention elevated when Bishop Belo, still not robed for Mass, marched down the aisle, seized my hand and despite my murmured protestations led me and my small group up to the front pew, where fortunately we did not have to displace any occupants. Although the whole liturgy of the service was conducted in the indigenous language, Tetun, it was intriguing nonetheless. The only jarring note was when a Japanese journalist who had cottoned on to the fact that I was in the congregation wandered up with his tape recorder and sought to interview me during the consecration! I gave him short shrift. During Bishop Belo's sermon, also in Tetun, I couldn't understand a word, but 'INTERFET' kept popping up so I thought he was probably giving us a pat on the back. But the most remarkable part of the service — the vivid and indelible memory of that hour and a half — was the singing. The very large congregation crammed into the cathedral and the hundreds crowding around the entrances and windows outside sang wonderfully melodic, often haunting, hymns with such beautiful harmony, passion and full-throatedness that I had a lump in my own throat every time they raised their voices in song. As the final hymn drew the service to a close, I was much moved and thought to myself that the faith, forbearance and courage of these people were indomitable. As the Bishop brought up the rear of the procession of clergymen out of the cathedral, he again seized my hand to accompany him into the forecourt where we were both mobbed by the crowd.

I found it interesting that Bishop Belo was not seen in the same light as his colleague in Baucau, despite his very prominent international status as a Nobel laureate and close association with the independence movement. The Bishop of Baucau, Bishop Nascimento, was widely and warmly regarded, especially for his role in keeping the lid on violence in the Baucau region — both before and after the ballot. His sparring partner was a locally notorious militia leader called Juanico, a colourful and piratical figure who led a bloodthirsty band. Juanico was a native East Timorese and a former non-commissioned officer in the Indonesian armed forces. In his militia incarnation he had helped to orchestrate a fair degree of violence against pro-independence people in the Baucau district — the number of house burnings testified to his malevolence and criminality.

Remarkably, the destruction in Baucau was less than in most other places after the ballot. Many East Timorese attributed this to the benign influence of Bishop Nascimento. During the operation to evacuate UN and aid agency people and some East Timorese who had worked for them in the first half of September (Operation *Spitfire*), it was Juanico's men on the Baucau airfield who had blocked an Australian C130 full of people wanting to go to Darwin before an agreement was brokered for the flight to proceed. Bishop Belo was the most prominent of the evacuees on that aircraft while Bishop Nascimento remained throughout. The militia burned Belo's house to the ground in Dili and his life was likely to have been in considerable danger, so his evacuation made a lot of sense. Nonetheless, Nascimento seemed to have the edge over Belo in the people's minds for his role in the crisis. For his part, Juanico took his militia band to Atambua in West Timor and, from time to time, added his own bloodcurdling threats to those emanating from his militia mates. Interestingly, during the course of the INTERFET operation, I had a number of backdoor approaches from him about reconciliation with the pro-independence majority in East Timor. We'd cautiously followed up, but they never amounted to anything concrete. I must say, I never really held out much hope that some of these hard-core militia, all with a bevy of criminal cases to answer, would reconcile and return to East Timor in my time there.

I now turned my attention to events closer to the capital. Although most of the Indonesian troops had left, the repatriation of the Indonesian garrison and a fleet of vehicles and tonnes of equipment and supplies were continuing through the port. Every few days an Indonesian landing craft, acting as a troopship and freighter, would nudge into the shore and drop its bow ramp inside the port area. Indonesian terminal operators would then load military vehicles, other equipment and soldiers' personal possessions over the next day or so. Then the soldiers would come aboard and off the ship would go. East Timorese had become used to this routine. As time went by, crowds began to gather to vehemently demonstrate their anger against the embarking

Indonesian soldiers. In response, some soldiers cocked their weapons and pointed them at the mob.

On one notable day, I received word that a crowd had begun to throw stones at Indonesian soldiers. Alarm bells rang in my mind. I jumped into a vehicle and raced down to the wharf to see what INTERFET could do to prevent anything worse happening. I was relieved when I got there to find that the newly arrived Australian infantry battalion, 5th/7th Battalion, the Royal Australian Regiment (5/7 RAR), had the situation in hand. Not only had they established a cordon at some distance to put the stone throwers out of range, but they had put a hessian screen along the jetty's cyclone wire fence so that the stone throwers couldn't see any juicy targets! Among the soldiers was a great big fellow, with a peaches and cream complexion, sweating copiously, but with a big grin. He turned out to be a new British exchange officer with the battalion who said to me, 'With all this stone-throwing, it's just like Northern Ireland, only a bit hotter!' I suppose it helps to have a frame of reference.

I was impressed with these soldiers from one of the 'younger' Regular Army infantry battalions based out of Darwin's 1st Brigade and their commander, Lieutenant Colonel Simon Gould. The 5th/7th Battalion was equipped with tracked armoured personnel carriers, familiar to me from my year in Vietnam, but upgraded and very useful in East Timor. After the usual couple of days of disorientation, Gould and his men hit their straps. They'd arrived a few weeks after the start of the mission and were now helping to hold down Dili while their Townsville colleagues from 3rd Brigade were at the border.

The professionalism and initiative of this battalion had been exemplified in the use of the hessian screen as a crowd control measure. Later, I not only witnessed but also participated in another act of leadership and initiative by a junior NCO from this battalion that mightily impressed me. By this time, we had started to receive thousands and thousands of displaced people from West Timor and other parts of Indonesia. They came by bus and truck, by aircraft and on foot. On a number of occasions they returned by ship to the port of Dili before heading off along roads and pathways. INTERFET had taken a significant role in facilitating this return, as well as providing security screening before passing them on to the UN and aid agencies for assessment and material assistance. This security screening was somewhat rudimentary. The focus was on preventing contraband — specifically weapons, ammunition and other ordnance — from entering the country. In addition, INTERFET troops monitored all of the land and maritime entry points to manage crowds and ensure good behaviour in the general vicinity.

One particular day, I happened to be out in my vehicle heading along the waterfront in Dili near where displaced East Timorese were landing by ship. On the edge of the disembarkation area was a very large crowd of East Timorese gathered to see if any friends and loved ones were among those arriving. On this occasion, the gathering looked a little different: that unmistakable look of a crowd working up to a riot. All those on the outside were pushing and shoving towards the centre, craning their necks and waving their arms in the air. Those closer towards the centre seemed to be heaving and struggling as if they were in a brawl.

Right at the centre of this angry pushing and shoving crowd was an armoured personnel carrier. I could make out the heads and shoulders of four or five Australian soldiers. I was most concerned because they appeared to be grappling with the mob. Something ugly and dangerous was brewing. I told my driver to move up to the edge of the melee. Much to the consternation of my bodyguards, I started to walk into the mob muttering to my young escorts to be cool and just ease their way into the centre, basically in my wake. I was banking on the belief that most of the crowd would recognise me. It seemed to work, especially with those outside the 'epicentre' where all the trouble was occurring. The crowd began to calm. By the time I got to the centre where the soldiers were, some kind of truce was in place, although there was still much invective being thrown and hateful looks being shot at somebody in the middle.

In the small space just behind the armoured personnel carrier, I came on the reason for the crowd's agitation. Our soldiers were protecting an East Timorese man who was dishevelled, bloody, bruised and very frightened. He was the subject of the abuse and the murderous glances of the crowd; more was in prospect. I asked a young corporal in charge of the soldiers what was happening. Amidst the shouts and angry gestures of the crowd, he seemed very cool and spoke in that respectful but offhand way so beloved of diggers:

> Gedday, boss. We were just watching the crowd when they started to shout. They ran and surrounded this bloke here and started to give him an almighty floggin'. We jumped in and dragged him here, but they're still after him and I reckon they'd like to kill him.

Looking around, I agreed with him. It turned out that somebody in the crowd had called out that this individual was a militia. That was enough to set everybody off. Resolving this situation without further violence would be a real challenge. I asked the corporal what he thought ought to be done now. He said:

Boss, it might be time for a bit of a show. What about if you walk up to this bloke and look him up and down and give him a filthy look, so the mob can see you're not keen on him. Then come back to me and give me some arm-waving instructions to put him in the back of the carrier and drive off. The mob will get the message that you're ordering his arrest and for him to be taken off to gaol. That should do the trick. We'll take him to the Doc and then hand him over to the police to see if he's got any form. What do you reckon?

I thought it was a good plan and I played my part. The soldiers bundled the man under threat into the back of the carrier and it roared off up the road taking him to safety and medical treatment. The crowd, in that great Timorese characteristic of passionate moods, cheered me as I returned to my vehicle with chants of 'Viva INTERFET'. Corporal, take a bow.

At about this time, plans for going to the Oecussi Enclave started to take shape. We retrieved Lafu, the brave young emissary, from TMR's cantonment and spirited him back into the Enclave with a satellite phone. We had trained him in its use as TMR had given him a strong endorsement. Although we could have made his return overt, to do so would have tipped our hand about our intentions. The Special Forces managed his covert return very professionally. Provided that he didn't run immediately into evildoers, the risk to him wasn't too bad. In the meantime, my staff had been busy planning how to safely occupy this remote, large and difficult piece of territory and provide for its longer term security. The minimum force necessary was an entire infantry battalion, but I did not have one on hand and the next one was not due to arrive in East Timor for some weeks.

Instead, we came up with Ambino Force. Ambino was the old Portuguese colonial name of the Enclave. A small headquarters would command an entry force of my redoubtable Australian SAS and a Gurkha company from the British Army, who would follow-up with a beach landing and secure the main town of Oecussi. This 200-strong force would not be capable of offering security to all the inhabitants of the Enclave, but it was certainly capable of providing an obvious and strong presence around the town of Oecussi. Elements could then drive out and visit more outlying villages.

I planned to sustain Ambino Force as a patrolling and garrison force for several weeks until I could relieve it with an infantry battalion. The major challenge was to create a new sense of security and confidence within the Enclave without 'pulling on' a major confrontation with either the local home-grown militia or any of their dislocated mates who had been ejected from the main territory of East Timor and were now brooding in a couple of big encampments in West Timor, not all that far from Oecussi. I was taking a risk. If the militia in the Enclave decided to attack Ambino Force or renew attacks on the long-suffering civilians of the Oecussi Enclave as a response to the presence of INTERFET soldiers, I would have a dilemma. Even though I would have backed any

INTERFET soldiers who were engaged in a battle with equivalent or moderately superior numbers of militia, my resources to continue to do so if the militia persisted with further attacks were limited. The campaign would suffer a major setback if distance and other priorities meant that I could not support and reinforce our troops there and had to withdraw them for their own safety.

The key to all the success of Ambino Force would be the quality of its commander and fortunately I was able to put my hands on a beauty. When I had been a commanding officer in Townsville in the mid-1980s, Mick Crane had been a young lieutenant in the gunner regiment and he had impressed me then. Now somewhat more grizzled, he was about to get a chance to command an exotic mix of soldiers from the most elite regiment of the Australian Army and representatives of arguably the finest soldiers in the British Army — the Gurkhas. Both would need an iron bit and a short rein. I told Mick as much.

We quietly and secretly launched the operation to establish a presence in Oecussi on the night of 21/22 October. I had no obligation to inform Indonesian security forces because they were not present in the Enclave. I didn't broadcast outside INTERFET that the operation was about to launch. It was a discreet early morning amphibious activity during the darkest hours. In order to avoid a potentially hot and disastrous reception on the beach, some of our extremely professional Navy clearance divers swam in and checked out the beach and beyond before giving the go-ahead to the troops waiting in Navy landing craft. I had a restless night waiting for news of how the landing had gone. All went very smoothly. Within a few short hours Ambino Force was safe and secure ashore and had begun the business of exploring and reassuring inhabitants of the Enclave. The call from Lafu and those who sent him had been answered.

Crane and his troops were there for several weeks. Their presence created a secure environment for the delivery of humanitarian assistance much earlier than would have been the case if I had waited until I had a battalion to send there. Ambino Force put a considerable dampener on the activities of the militia. Their vigorous patrolling and obvious professionalism backed these criminals off for the time being. However, significant challenges remained ahead for INTERFET down in Oecussi. Sometime later, when I was visiting Oecussi, the parish priest ushered me to the steps of the church in the township where a delighted but dignified little boy presented me with the ubiquitous East Timorese scarf or stole. Lafu was in good form that day, but he did have to put out his cigarette before this mini-ceremony!

The dilemma I faced for the Oecussi Enclave exemplified how we had to juggle priorities in the early part of the operation before our force levels grew. Sometimes it was a matter of employing deception — 'smoke and mirrors' — to ensure that we never spread our forces so thinly. Our forces could not afford to be ineffective in any new place or, even worse, in any place that INTERFET had previously secured. In these early days, some of the aid agencies in particular seemed to feel that they ought to be able to wander far and wide and that INTERFET should continue to bifurcate itself for this purpose. We had been both agile and lucky. After establishing Ambino Force in the Enclave, we had reached the limit of our agility. I was reluctant to further test our luck.

*

In the years before 1999 one of the great inspirations of the independence movement in East Timor had been the iconic guerrilla leader, Xanana Gusmao. Xanana had been imprisoned in Jakarta for a considerable number of years. He was a sort of 'national leader in exile', even though that exile was internal. As a natural consequence of the plebiscite, the Indonesian Government released him and he moved to Darwin immediately. I had been waiting with interest for the propitious moment for his return — a keen judgement fundamentally for him and for his political apparatus, and secondly for the UN. For me, the issue was one of the consequent effects of his return on internal relationships and security — both his security and the implications of his return home for the overall security situation in East Timor. From all I knew of Xanana, he was considered to be a most charismatic and revered figure by the vast majority of East Timorese and his presence would add a whole new dimension to the operating environment within the country. There was a certain amount of international jockeying to see who would have the primary interest in advising and assisting Xanana's return, but inevitably INTERFET and I, as Commander INTERFET, were the gatekeepers for this important event.

As it transpired, Xanana's desired arrangements coincided strongly with what I would have preferred. He asked to be brought back into East Timor covertly so that he could make a planned, deliberate and safe first public appearance in his homeland. I sent a small group of Special Forces to Darwin a day or so ahead of his planned arrival to meet with him and to engender his confidence that he would be treated with utmost dignity and that his wishes would be met whenever possible. By his own request, we brought him by RAAF aircraft into Baucau after dark on 21 October and flew him in a Blackhawk helicopter to Dili. He arrived without public attention at an old seafront villa in the capital, which INTERFET personnel had sequestered and cleaned up for his temporary accommodation.

Overnight a Special Forces detachment guarded him as he slept. The next morning he met a number of callers who also arrived at the villa secretly. Understandably, I was one of these. It was both a thrill and a fascinating opportunity to meet this man, who had been at the core of East Timorese pro-independence armed resistance for twenty-five years. While I had seen photographs of him, these did not do him justice. When I arrived at the villa, I came into a very bare but clean front room where almost immediately Xanana joined me through an internal doorway. Dressed in a camouflage military uniform, he was a slim figure, although taller and bigger than most East Timorese men. The famous steel grey hair and beard completed the immediate picture — by any standards a handsome man. I made a short speech saying how delighted all my troops and I were that he had made such a happy return and how much we were looking forward to working with him as the undoubted popular hero of his people. I dwelt particularly on my intention that INTERFET would assist him to travel widely in East Timor to speak to his countrymen and women. For his part, Xanana was very warm about the efforts of INTERFET to restore law and order in his homeland and how he looked forward to working with INTERFET and the UN on the journey towards full independence. About the only feature of this relatively short initial discussion which took me a little by surprise was how softly spoken he was. I was leaning in closely to catch what he was saying and even given that this was our first meeting and his English may have been a little rusty for formal discussions, I was intrigued to think that a man so evidently reserved could be so avidly admired by his people. His political organisation had planned a very large public gathering down at the Governor's Palace — the political centre of East Timor — for a little later that morning. Xanana would make his first public appearance there. I hoped the PA system was a good one!

At the due time, I moved the short distance from my headquarters to the plaza in front of the Governor's Palace for my first ever political rally. I comforted myself with the thought that I was the senior security guard! I was amazed at the throng — the area in front of the dais was jam-packed. Perhaps as many as 10,000 East Timorese, mostly Dili residents, given the short notice of the rally, had crammed into the UN car park area and back towards the harbour. Martyn Dunne, my New Zealand mate commanding Dili Command, met me. He had troops all over the place to supplement the UN civilian police, and plenty of infantry including medics and radio operators. Xanana's Australian Special Forces bodyguards, reinforced for the occasion, were there, peering vigilantly through their dark glasses. After some preliminary remarks, Xanana stepped from out of sight to the podium. The effect was electric. A huge sigh arose from the crowd and then a stupendous cheer and cry of joy. The UN and the international community had urged freedom; the voters had demanded it; Indonesia had ceded it; INTERFET had assisted it, but Xanana represented it. There were many moments, technical and emotional, as well as important to history, in my time in East Timor and thereafter, but that moment was without parallel.

Although this first snapshot remains a vivid memory, the real revelation came in the next moment. Xanana, after taking a long moment to gaze out at the people and to let the cheering subside to some degree, raised his arms and in a booming, rhetorical and impassioned flourish started to address the crowd. His rolling sonorous phrases and his theatrical body language held the crowd spellbound. He was interrupted frequently by the crowd responding to his rhetoric by cheering, roaring both approval and sometimes condemnation, and even by crying and sobbing in mass grief. I didn't understand a word, nor did most of the troops, because he spoke in Tetun, but we all got the message: East Timor's leader had arrived home to lead his people and the people embraced him.

This marvellous performance continued on for some time until, with a deft sense of the moment, Xanana Gusmao brought to the crowd from the shadows behind him, and onto the dais alongside him, the legendary guerrilla leader who had stepped into his shoes after he was arrested all those years ago — Taur Matan Ruak, 'TMR'. Standing together, hands clasped and arms raised, the two men bathed in the rapturous adulation of the crowd. If you have to attend your first political rally, you may as well attend a remarkable one.

12

Steady to Unsteady State

RIGHT AT THE OUTSET OF THE mission, I thought that those who arrived in late September in the advance guard would probably either be able to get the job done in about six months, handing over to a UN force or, if the job still had legs, rotating out after a six-month tour of duty. Either way, I was riding our land forces pretty hard: working them for long hours in a demanding climate under austere living conditions that lacked amenities and comforts. Logistically, I had no room for amenities and camp stores, such as stretchers and tentage that would add some comfort. I had to concentrate on the basics — food, water and rations — because our supply chain could not handle much more. About this time, several journalists wrote pieces that complained that I was denying Australian troops alcohol. They advanced various reasons for this policy, including that I was a teetotaller! My attitude towards alcohol on operations is simple. A military operation in harm's way is no nine-to-five job where we could switch off our responsibilities when the sun went down. We carried our weapons everywhere, loaded with live ammunition. We were all responsible to act immediately and wisely and, if necessary, with lethal force, if the threat justified it. Also, I thought it was reasonable to oblige our men and women to observe wider Australian community standards relevant to drink-driving for the duration of their time in East Timor.

I had always had in mind that, if the security situation allowed it and there was enough space in the supply chain, then the Aussies could have alcohol, but in the form of a ration — not open slather: the old military adage 'two beers per day, per man, perhaps'. I also would not allow alcohol in base areas in and around Dili until I could offer the same privileges to the men and women serving in the border region and other remote localities. So, when it became logistically possible to supply alcohol to Australian troops, I asked Mark Evans, who commanded all Australian combat troops and was the present 'king' of the border regions, whether he wanted those troops to have a beer ration. Knowing my policy on alcohol, he decided — correctly in my view — that there would be no alcohol for troops serving on the border and in areas where there was a chance of militia violence: he wanted a 'dry' operation. He made this decision knowing that his men and women would have access to an alcohol ration when they were taking a break in a rest area that I was setting up in a building complex on the seafront of Dili Harbour for the ease of frontline troops. When his people were back there, not only could they have a slightly increased alcohol ration to the rest of INTERFET, but they could eat all those foods that soldiers crave when they are living on hard rations.

Thus, the Aussies, with an international reputation for a strong thirst, were among the most abstemious of contingents in

INTERFET. All I could reasonably require of the other contingents was that no act related to their alcohol policy should bring discredit on INTERFET. Some of the other contingents gave their people free rein. Indeed, some of them provided alcohol with two meals a day! For instance, the Italian Army contingent, a company of the renowned and tough Italian parachutists, the Folgore, had quite a liberal policy, but I hasten to add I was unaware of any adverse behaviour attributable to alcohol consumption.

There were no double standards at the Australian watering hole in Dili that we established for a large number of Australians working in the headquarters complex and military precinct. The headquarters personnel staff gave visitors the same little card entitling them to the same strictly policed daily beer or wine ration as the Aussies. One evening I was heartened to see a large group of Italians in the Australian bar mixing in happily. A staff officer with me commented that this had become a regular occurrence. I thought that it was a bit odd to have Italians in every night given that they could only get a maximum of two beers with us and presumably something more than this ration back in their own camp area. I must have been off the ball when I became perplexed by this phenomenon. After I commented to my staff officer, he gave me one of those looks you reserve for the bewildered and said, 'Sir, look where they're sitting!' I took another look and it all became clear — they were sidling up to our numerous servicewomen, some of whom were in uniform, some in T-shirts and shorts, all armed to the teeth. The Italian Army at that time still had not incorporated women into service — these young fellows were intrigued and were quite prepared to trade more alcohol for feminine company.

*

Management of coalitions requires close attention. By now INTERFET was starting to look like a miniature version of the UN General Assembly. Although we weren't quite at the 22-nation mark — the eventual INTERFET total — we were well over halfway there. My Chief of Staff, Mark Kelly, ensured that representatives from every nation attended morning conferences and we consulted with national commanders frequently on any matter that might impact on their national interests. Mark also organised visits for national commanders and their staff around East Timor so they could report back to their home countries and also, in some cases, give them something to do.

Tending to the coalition of nations comprising INTERFET wasn't all beer and skittles. Each of them had their sense of dignity and precedence. Some contingents seemed to always have a 'niggle', mostly over tasking on operations. There were occasional verbal spats between some staff officer and some senior man in one of the contingents. Disputes over the level of logistics support or the intricacies of financial reimbursement were not uncommon. My staff and I never trivialised or ignored these issues. Our policy was that no minor estrangement or cause of resentment would last beyond sundown. It was vital that every contingent felt valued and integrated as part of the INTERFET team.

I was always on the lookout for ways to bring other national contingents into prominence, not just through their military performance, but as proud representatives of their nation. In addition to conferences, consultations and visits, I hit on the notion of inviting national contingents of any size to nominate some national day or occasion that happened to occur during INTERFET's tenure to celebrate, and for them to invite representatives from other INTERFET contingents to celebrate with them.

When contingents eagerly seized upon the idea of celebrating national days, I was delighted. We had some most memorable and enjoyable events. Some were fascinating insights into rich cultures, some were simply exuberant and enjoyable interludes, all of them were great vehicles and catalysts of goodwill. I will never forget the celebration by the Thai contingent of His Majesty the King's seventy-second birthday — a most auspicious one within Thai culture. To add significance to these celebrations at the Thai headquarters in Dili, there was a direct television link to the major celebration by the people of Bangkok in the presence of the King. Thai TV crossed to our celebration at the appointed time. It was an absolute revelation to see how profoundly reverent and proud the Thai soldiers in our midst were to be under the gaze of their hugely respected monarch.

Australia's cultural contribution was both traditional and typical — the 1999 Melbourne Cup. Unfortunately, our direct TV broadcast link back to Australia was not yet available widely to Aussie troops. We had to videotape the race at a single point and then replay the tape a short time later — as if live — and even later in places like the wet canteen in Dili and at the INTERFET headquarters complex. For an hour or two, these locations and other Australian bases and units around Dili and throughout East Timor looked like the paddock at Flemington. Men and women dressed in a combination of uniform and fashion concoctions — set off elegantly with rifles and pistols! Silly hats abounded and sweeps and Calcuttas were at every hand, with appropriate precautions for urgers who had found out the results beforehand and were looking to make a killing.

These rituals and dress codes overwhelmed our international friends and visitors. The Aussies put niceties of discipline and dignified behaviour on hold as we prepared to let off steam for the race that stops the nation. One foreign officer asked me why a number of male soldiers were holding rolled up newspapers. 'Watch them during the race,' I replied. When the race was under way, he did as I instructed and started to shout with laughter when he saw them starting to 'go the whip' as the field entered the straight — one hand out holding the reins and urging on the nag while the other thrashed the newspaper along their own thighs. The same fellow asked me subsequently whether it was always like this, to which I replied that it was not normally this quiet! I think many of our visitors in 1999 would like to visit Australia for the Cup some day.

It was a big week for sporting events in Australia. In rugby union, Australia's campaign to win its second World Cup had been proceeding with great promise. The Wallabies had been the form team of the past year. Australia's likely opponent in the final always looked to be the All Blacks from New Zealand. In a stunning upset, the French, 'Les Bleux' had knocked the All Blacks off in a magnificent game the previous weekend. The outcome was a France vs. Australia final. While our Kiwi brethren in INTERFET were in deep mourning, the Aussie and French contingents were cock-a-hoop.

The French contingent was based on a very professional medical clinic, protected by some of the toughest looking French marines and soldiers you would ever want to meet. They were led by Jean Branstchen, a Special Forces colonel based in New Caledonia, whose company I greatly enjoyed and whose professionalism was admirable. Jean was both shrewd and most amiable, a very popular and effective commander of an important and highly respected contingent. He and I relished the prospect of the Rugby World Cup final. Privately, I was convinced that the French had played so outstandingly well to beat the All Blacks in the semi-final that they didn't have another game of this quality in them. Everywhere I went that week the Aussies that I encountered would rapidly bring the discussion around to our prospects for the final. In the light of this overwhelming interest and support, and as an old rugby tragic myself, I sent a fax to the captain, John Eales, and the team wishing them well on behalf of all of us.

By now we had a few more outlets able to receive satellite transmissions. Indeed, I now had a TV in my office, normally tuned 24 hours a day to regional or world news. I felt that I had to share this great viewing spot for the final with Branstchen and some of his cohorts. It turned out to be one of rugby's great international finals. With only a few minutes to go and Australia clearly the probable winners, one of the French officers stood up with a very gloomy face and wandered out of my office. I thought to myself 'poor loser' and got on with watching the death throes. As the ref blew full-time and cheers erupted all over Dili wherever Australians were able to watch, the Frenchman walked back in to my office with a tray full of glasses of fine French champagne. Gallant losers then toasted magnanimous winners. I gave our French contingent ten out of ten for style and good humour.

Remembrance Day, 11 November, was another opportunity to embrace both other members of the coalition and the East Timorese. There is a special bond between Australia and the East Timorese that originates in the early years of the Pacific War against Japan. The people of East Timor gave generous and courageous support to our soldiers in a harrowing and bloody guerrilla campaign. Australia sent the men of the 2nd AIF Independent Companies — equivalent to commandos today and an Australian forerunner to our Special Forces — to harass the Japanese in East Timor in 1942. For many months our soldiers fought grimly and very courageously to harass, attack and evade 20,000 Japanese troops, who hunted for them relentlessly. Hundreds of East Timorese either supported our men directly by accompanying them on their operations or by sheltering and feeding them over the months of the campaign. Many lost their lives and many others suffered hardship and brutality at the hands of the Japanese for their sympathy and support to our troops. The marvellous old soldiers of the Independent Companies who served in East Timor particularly remember and honour the loyal and courageous support of the group of East Timorese men, who acted as guides and bearers — nicknamed the *Criados* (Portuguese for servants).

For several months in 1942 Australian soldiers manned a clandestine observation post in the high ground south of Dili, coincidentally in the vicinity of where many East Timorese displaced from Dili camped out until INTERFET arrived in September 1999. Several years before, Australian veterans had established a small war memorial by the side of the road near the site of the observation post. This was the obvious spot, with its panoramic view of the city far below, for the Australian national Remembrance Day service. We invited representatives from all countries participating in INTERFET, from the UN staff and from FALINTIL. Indeed, anyone who wished to attend was welcome. The service was planned to follow the traditional format — prayers, hymns, an occasional speech, wreath laying, the Ode and bugle calls for the Last Post and Reveille. I was particularly pleased to welcome the head of FALINTIL, TMR, to the service that morning.

All the Aussies were most impressed and moved when we learnt, just as the service was about to start, that one of the original *Criados*, 82-year-old Rufino Alves Correia, was attending. As soon as I'd heard, I sought him out within the crowd and brought him to stand with me and invited him to help me lay the first wreath. Although stooped with age, he seemed quite spry and very alert, neatly dressed in shirt, slacks and a fedora hat. At the solemn moment of laying the wreath, we both stepped back and saluted — his salute was certainly just as crisp as mine. The solemnity of this auspicious moment was broken briefly on our return to our place on the roadway. As we walked back, I noticed a substantial pothole about a metre across and quite deep. When we got to the edge of it, I stopped to offer a steadying hand to Mr Correia. He, mistaking my concern, nimbly hopped across the pothole and extended his hand to help me over to the general merriment of those who observed his gesture. Nearly sixty years on, still helping Aussies!

UNAMET had played a major role in East Timorese affairs in 1999. Led by a dedicated and unflappable Brit, Ian Martin, the mission had done wonderful work until the ADF evacuated Martin, his staff and many locally employed East Timorese in the face of very high levels of violence and danger. Martin and some of his staff returned with INTERFET on 20 September and started preliminary work to re-establish a strong and capable UN presence. They were very busy facilitating the delivery of humanitarian aid, coordinating with the emerging political leadership of East Timor, constituting the civil arm of lawful authority in the country and preparing the way for the follow-on UN mission.

As an electoral mission, UNAMET was not structured for the nation building and governance tasks that a UN administration would need to perform. There was a need for a new leader and a new mission in East Timor. By late November, staff at the UN in New York had begun planning and deploying the United Nations Transitional Administration in East Timor (UNTAET). I had enjoyed working closely with Ian Martin for nearly two months but I keenly anticipated the arrival of his replacement, the Special Representative of the Secretary General and Transitional Administrator, Sergio Vieira de Mello. He would greatly influence the future of East Timor, but more particularly, he and I would make arrangements for the withdrawal of INTERFET and its replacement by a UN force. Vieira de Mello was a very prominent and highly regarded UN official with a strong operational background in the United Nations High Commission for Refugees (UNHCR). He was Secretary General Kofi Annan's 'Mr Fix It', having recently set up the mission in Kosovo, an area located in the former Yugoslavia. He seemed to be an inspired choice to oversee East Timor's pathway to full independence. He was a Brazilian who spoke fluent Portuguese, the *lingua franca* of many older East Timorese and their leaders. He was experienced in setting up difficult missions in post-conflict areas of the world, and he possessed undoubted diplomatic skills.

One of the biggest issues in setting up an organisation in a devastated country is 'real estate' — how will facilities and infrastructure be shared around? Martin had called several lower-level conferences to regulate and allocate real estate for both the inbound UNTAET and various other agencies and administrative organisations. There was some crinkling of lips among my staff, who became aggrieved that Martin was allocating buildings and compounds to the UN that had been cleaned and occupied by INTERFET — meaning the UN would benefit from the soldiers' hard work. I had to soothe some ruffled feathers, but also take a strong stand on behalf of the UN peacekeeping force (PKF), an important component of UNTAET, that would follow and replace INTERFET. This force would need decent offices and barracks accommodation in Dili and elsewhere. I think I saw off the worst of the 'claim jumpers'. Ian Martin and I remained good friends into the bargain. So, I was about to say farewell to one friend, and hopefully gain another in the person of Sergio Vieira de Mello.

On 17 November 1999, I met Sergio out at the airport and my initial impressions were entirely favourable. He was a slender man of average height. Most women who'd seen him remarked that he was splendidly handsome. He spoke very eloquent and educated English and had a most engaging and charming manner. During our time together I came to like him a great deal. From time to time we would disagree about particular matters, but we were always able to find a way ahead. Some of the usual jaded old cynics thought that he wouldn't stick it out for very long, preferring to be closer to the bright lights of New York or Geneva, but it didn't surprise me at all that he did a long tour of duty in East Timor.

At this early stage, we exchanged information on the situation in East Timor, clarified our respective jobs and mandates, and confirmed the significant interdependence of our activities. He had a clear and practical grasp of the strategic direction for UNTAET. He also had a skilled diplomat's appreciation of the subtleties, nuances and dynamics of the political terrain, both within East Timor society and among the international community. My mandate did not make me subordinate to either UNAMET or UNTAET. However, I considered it vital that I collaborate in every possible way to support Sergio and UNTAET, well beyond the simple boundary of convenience. It was timely for there to be a noticeable transition from military governance to a civilian model that included INTERFET in a prominent, but supporting role. I reserved the prerogative to have my way if the security situation demanded it, but Sergio and I understood that the circumstances would need to be dire before I would act contrary to his plans and wishes. We got off to a flying start and never looked back.

Sergio had a piquant and razor-sharp sense of humour. One time when we were having a cup of coffee, I was grousing on about an East Timorese politician's outburst vilifying and condemning INTERFET for some quite trivial issue. He listened politely for a while and then, with a wry smile, told me not to take such purple prose too seriously as it was a deeply ingrained practice in East Timorese politics. He recounted the advice he had received from a senior Portuguese politician in relation to political language in East Timor. He described it as having the chief characteristic of 'murderous vociferation'. He was right then, and I would see plenty of examples subsequently.

We developed a fraternal code of comfort when we had to endure unfair criticism or encountered some inevitable frustrations keeping everything on track. On one such occasion, Sergio and I were attending a conference and some drone revealed that an important action that I was urgently waiting on had not taken place. Sergio, possibly expecting a strong response, sought my reaction. Conscious of the other attendees and keeping a straight face and an even tone, I said that I was 'disappointed'. After the conference, over a cup of coffee, Sergio asked me about this response and I told him frankly that I was furious, apoplectic and had been ready to strangle the individual on the spot. We both had a laugh over my restrained use of diplomatic language and thereafter it became a personal code between us that when one or the other used the word 'disappointed', we knew that the speaker was ready to explode. A number of years later when Sergio, still posted to East Timor, attended a meeting I was also at Canberra, there was an issue which caused one of the senior Australians to go into a bit of a rant about UNTAET. This happened not once but three times, despite Sergio's soothing, diplomatic murmurings between rants. As we walked away from the room, I asked Sergio how he felt about the meeting. He said, 'Quite disappointed.' He needed to say no more!

Another person I liked from the outset was José Ramos-Horta, Bishop Belo's Nobel Peace Prize co-laureate and indefatigable spokesman for East Timorese independence. A shrewd, engaging and articulate man, his ceaseless globetrotting on behalf of his country's cause had given him extraordinary insight into international influences and relationships in the broad, well beyond his passionate advocacy. For obvious reasons, he had not visited his homeland for many years. He felt and cherished his eventual arrival home every bit as deeply as Xanana Gusmao, after so long in the wilderness of the skyscrapers of foreign capitals.

Our relationship was cemented after we first met when we co-sponsored an international-style soccer game between a team representing INTERFET and one representing East Timor. These low-key and casual arrangements always end up with a momentum and vibrancy of their own. Before I knew it, grave considerations about selection, coaching, training and staging the game were upon me. The vexed issues of proper soccer uniforms, footwear, field equipment and pitch preparation were all under the most serious study. We extended all of our considerations to the East Timorese team as well as our own to overcome any gaps in East Timorese soccer administration caused by recent disruptive events. All the instant experts around me soothed that with an INTERFET group that included many soccer playing nations — not least a platoon of Brazilians and a company of Italians — we should be able to put up a pretty good show.

On the appointed day I turned up at the Dili Sports Stadium, a place that had seen its fair share of misery and mayhem when tens of thousands of displaced East Timorese had returned there in the early weeks in search of missing loved ones. INTERFET had also used the area to accommodate, protect, feed and provide clean water and medical services to the returning populace. Our engineers had done a pretty good job producing a playable surface for the game. The stands and the outer were packed to overflowing by many thousands of East Timorese who had come to watch sporting combat in a game that the whole country loved.

On the sideline, away from the bulk of the crowd, organisers had set aside seats for Ramos-Horta and me. The game was exciting, but soon proved to be lopsided. A lithe, fit and talented East Timorese side, encouraged enthusiastically by thousands of shouting compatriots, easily played around and in front of a willing, honest, but outclassed, INTERFET team. As the game drew on, the hot and humid conditions took their toll on the international visitors. The East Timorese team won by several goals. The crowd was rapturous. Ramos-Horta was delighted and diplomatic. After the game I presented trophies to the winners and José presented mementos to the INTERFET team. He made a short speech, first in Tetun, to the obvious delight of the crowd, and then in English. I replied in English and prevailed upon him to translate my words into Tetun. I congratulated both teams, with emphasis on the victors, and declared to the crowd that this defeat was the only sort of defeat that I or any INTERFET member would accept in our time as guests in their country. That went down pretty well too!

In the way of things, the prospect of disaster can threaten after great moments of success and harmony. On 19 November, one of the most intriguing and challenging incidents during the whole INTERFET mission occurred suddenly and frighteningly. The crisis was precipitated by a tense situation in Dili. It was one of the very few times my junior leaders and small teams let me down. They faced an ambiguous situation. On 18 November, Australian troops on security duties in Dili responded to a call that a large number of armed men were congregating at a house nearby. On attending, the Australians found a group of heavily armed FALINTIL fighters loitering near the house. They apprehended them and disarmed them at gunpoint. In all of this, they complied with their orders that no arms were permitted apart from those carried by INTERFET and the UN police. The only exception to this rule applied to FALINTIL in their cantonments and these fellows certainly weren't in one at the time — the closest one was way up in the hills south of Dili, at a place called Aeliu.

This was one of those occasions when the 'strategic corporal' phenomenon applies. By that I mean, occasions when the actions of junior leaders and small teams at the tactical level can reverberate strongly at the strategic and political levels. On the face of it, this action only inconvenienced and embarrassed a group of FALINTIL fighters who were in the wrong place at the wrong time. However, Xanana Gusmao had extremely strong emotional ties to the men of FALINTIL. He had been their leader for many years of struggle for independence. He was extremely sensitive to their fair and dignified treatment. From the beginning, he had been a strong advocate for them and had sought to improve the living conditions of the fighters and their families living in the cantonments. Any perceived slight or indignity would spark his personal involvement. In this case, the FALINTIL fighters were nominally moving by truck from one cantonment to another — both outside Dili. It is likely that these men could not resist the temptation for a brief sojourn in the 'bright lights' and certainly weren't going to disarm while they took their detour. If they had done so, there would have been no problem.

Privately I cursed that our troops on the ground hadn't bumped the situation they found themselves in upstairs and then simply remained with the FALINTIL group in a sort of 'amicable, mutually agreeable detention' while more senior people sorted it out, either with TMR or Xanana himself. Either of them would have jumped on the errant fighters and dealt with them firmly.

Without their involvement, it took some hours to resolve the matter and tempers became frayed. Eventually, INTERFET troops negotiated an agreement: the FALINTIL group could continue their journey to the next cantonment with their weapons bundled up out of sight.

The word that whistled around the cantonments later that day and into the evening was that INTERFET soldiers had humiliated these warriors. Our Special Forces liaison officers at Aeliu, where Xanana was located, notified my headquarters by radio that he was furious and would bring a group of armed FALINTIL fighters into Dili the next day — in defiance of INTERFET — to protest the indignity to his men. This protest might also include asserting a continuing right and intention of FALINTIL to bear arms outside the cantonments now that East Timor was free. All of this information was extremely bad news for INTERFET, both politically and militarily. There were a number of possible negative consequences and scenarios — ranging from undesirable to disastrous.

After a flurry of phone calls both to and from our men at Aeliu, it was obvious that Xanana had a full head of steam up and was not interested in apologies or reasoning. He would neither speak to me personally, nor accept my apologies through my men. As it was getting dark, I dispatched Tim McOwan, whom Xanana knew and liked, up there by helicopter to convey apologies and my urgent counsel to Xanana not to go ahead with his protest. When he got there, Xanana refused to see him. What's more, he indicated that he no longer wanted INTERFET liaison officers around him and that they certainly could not accompany him into Dili the next day. It was starting to look like a Grecian tragedy unfolding. I could empathise with Xanana, who very much needed to be seen to uphold the honour and respect of his men in the face of the INTERFET monolith, but I could not allow him to flout our sensible policy about the bearing of arms in East Timor.

I had two choices. One course of action was to prevent Xanana and any armed group from entering Dili, by force if necessary. I had the troops to do the job, but I was most unattracted to this option for a variety of obvious reasons. Secondly, I could have another go at reasoning with him personally. I didn't think I would be able to get to Aeliu before he and his party left in the early hours of the morning, but maybe I could intercept him up in the high country before he entered the populated areas of Dili. I would wave him and his group down and have a roadside chat. Having decided on this course of action; I had quite a restless night.

Bright and early the next morning I rustled up my driver, a staff officer and my bodyguards. We drove out of Dili up to the first line of hills south of the city, near the village of Dare. There I took a couple of camp stools and some bottles of water off to a little lay-by and set up my temporary 'stall'. I kept my entourage and vehicles 100 metres away off the road sitting quietly, but no doubt a little nervously. After about a 30 minute wait, on the hairpin bends of the steep and winding road just starting to descend towards Dili, I heard the sound of a couple of four-wheel-drive vehicles roaring down through the gears and thought 'here's my man'.

Around the corner came a little convoy with Xanana in the front of the first vehicle and, to my surprise, his wife, Kirsty Gusmao, was sitting in the back of the same vehicle with both vehicles otherwise packed with armed FALINTIL fighters. I stood there like a traffic policeman waving them over with what I hoped was a friendly gesture — but to no avail because they roared past giving me a good collection of filthy looks. As they disappeared into the distance, I hurried down to my vehicle and waiting staff. I now had no option but to follow their little convoy into town. I was pretty despondent. All the months of hard work, careful diplomacy and relationship building seemed to be on the verge of being destroyed.

Much to my astonishment, only a kilometre or two further on, just on the outskirts of town, we came upon Xanana's two vehicles stopped on the roadway. Xanana and his men had just alighted and were marching off purposefully down the road towards town. With this further unexpected opportunity to patch things up, I jumped out of my vehicle with my close personal protection soldiers following and took off after Xanana. As I passed the first vehicle, I noticed Kirsty Gusmao was still inside so I briefly stuck my head in the window to speak to and reassure her. She told me that the vehicles had run out of petrol so Xanana had decided to walk into town. I told Kirsty in a few words that what was being done was a grave setback to the trust and amicability between INTERFET, Xanana and FALINTIL. The look on her face told me she comprehended this quite clearly. Then it was a bit of speed walking to catch up to Xanana. He was marching quickly, surrounded by gun-toting FALINTIL comrades as a human barrier. As I caught up, I thought that with his bodyguard and mine being in close proximity, this had the prospect of a bad recipe. As we walked along, I told my soldiers to hang back, took off my pistol, handing it to one of them and then moved ahead towards Xanana.

The FALINTIL fighters were very much on edge. They closed ranks and with body movements and motions with their weapons attempted to keep me outside their circle around Xanana. There is some advantage to being a somewhat elephantine ex-rugby union forward. I was able to insinuate myself into the group, notwithstanding their Trojan efforts, and to range up alongside Xanana. I spoke with him as we walked along for a short distance, but he made no reply. I was obviously getting nowhere. By now, a crowd was gathering and accompanying the group. I felt that in this setting I was wasting my time. At least, the growing crowd was cheering Xanana up and he acknowledged them.

I went back to my group. We jumped in our vehicles and took another route to Xanana's anticipated destination, the UN compound in the old government administration area of Dili, in order to bypass the crowd. By the time we got to the UN-occupied Governor's Palace where Sergio Vieira de Mello's office was located, the crowd had swelled and gathered outside. Xanana was inside. The crowd mood was ebullient and not hostile in any way to me or INTERFET. When I entered, I found that Xanana had gone to the upper floor office to meet Sergio. The narrow staircase leading up to this floor was completely blocked by his FALINTIL men. Again, I told my escort to hang back and I moved up the stairs, giving plenty of eye contact — filthy looks as good as I got. One chap moved to bar my way, but I tested his weight by lifting him by the elbows and found that I could easily move him gently to one side. Upstairs I found Sergio's office staff looking somewhat panic-stricken and one of Xanana's key FALINTIL lieutenants looking very edgy indeed. This was a young fellow I thought had tremendous promise — a fluent English speaker, very quick intellect and a bright future in East Timor's armed forces. I asked Sergio's secretary to get me in to see him and Xanana immediately. While I was being announced, I spoke briefly to the young fellow about the problems the action had caused. I'm sure he understood my point.

I was admitted to sit with Sergio who, for the only time I remember, looked a little nonplussed. Xanana appeared aggrieved, but less aggravated than when I had seen him last. For my part, I strove to be calm and reasonable but perhaps less affable than normal. I started with a genuine apology to Xanana concerning the events of the day before. I explained that my soldiers had acted in good faith in disarming his men because they were unsure of who they were and any armed group like them was not complying with INTERFET's mandate — they were acting outside the 'deal'. I paused after this point because I knew Xanana would want to get the matter off his chest, which he did. I then spoke about how committed INTERFET was to all the people of East Timor and how in particular we wished to work closely with him and to assist FALINTIL in any way possible. I pointed out that there were many interests, some domestic and some international, who would be delighted to see a break in the relationship between FALINTIL and INTERFET and who would be quick to crow 'I told you so' if there was a falling out between us. We were in danger of handing them a propaganda victory. I spoke about how the discipline and forbearance of FALINTIL had been magnificent, especially in the last few months, and I implored him to stick to the deal that there be no carriage of arms outside of the cantonments.

By now the temperature of the meeting had returned to a reasonable level. I informed Xanana that I was due to address a routine press conference at ten o'clock (in about 15 minutes!) and I wanted to be able to say in response to media interest that whatever had taken place was an aberration, that I had personally spoken to him and that the deal with FALINTIL about carriage of weapons was still in place. We agreed. He also agreed to order his accompanying FALINTIL fighters to secure and conceal their weapons forthwith, until they were back in the cantonment. We shook hands and I departed for my media conference a mightily relieved man. Predictably at the conference I got a question concerning the incident and I was able to make the reply I had rehearsed with Xanana. In news terms, the incident sank without trace. Our relationship with FALINTIL remained strong and the deal did hold. It took a gratifyingly short time for Xanana and I to return to amiable relations which continued to improve to a level I cherish today. But it was a close-run thing on 19 November 1999!

Perhaps in some ways this last incident was symptomatic of the success we had achieved. Possibly INTERFET had removed some of the major external stressors in the community. Without unifying adversity to face, internal politics, resentments and opportunism can emerge and start to become rampant. Around this time, prominent political figures below the level and stature of Xanana Gusmao and José Ramos-Horta started to become active. One leading member of a faction within FALINTIL suffered the indignity of having his home raided three times by INTERFET troops, each time on the basis of a hot tip-off that he had either weapons or militia secreted on the premises. Each time, the troops were different, but I suspect the tipster was the same!

People who are not under pressure and are returning to rebuilding their country can — especially in the hothouse environment of a place like Dili — become impatient with a substantial military presence. In fact, I knew it was okay to start drawing down the numbers of troops on the streets when I received a complaint that our armoured personnel carriers travelling up and down the road were noisy and dusty creatures, and would we kindly take them somewhere else. The staff officer who told me this was spluttering with outrage at the ingratitude of it all. He was surprised when I gave him a big grin, explaining that I took it more as a sign of confidence than of ingratitude. Nobody would like us driving armoured personnel carriers up and down Punt Road in Melbourne, if they perceived that they were not needed. Clearly, East Timorese citizens in Dili were feeling safe.

Safe or not, I was still earning my pay. I filled every day with a constant tending to the INTERFET machine and its smooth running and output. An average day was filled with endless visits, briefings, office calls, conferences and planning sessions — always ready to kick them all into touch if there was a crisis like the one concerning Xanana or indeed fitting crises in among scheduled meetings, or scheduling meetings in between crises. In this period where we had achieved a state of relative stability, I worked out that troops were facing challenges that were just as hard in many ways as when we first arrived. My philosophy was that we would allow no relaxation, no lack of concentration and no complacency that might embolden any adversary to try to set us back on their heels and attack the confidence of the East Timorese, the UN or the member countries of INTERFET.

I had many tough henchmen in this regard, particularly on my staff. But none of these astute and committed officers matched Mark Evans, who commanded the Aussies and Kiwis in the west.

Mark and his troops had been slaving away for months without a break and with no respite from me. Mark had enormous leadership and commonsense and kept his brigade right on their toes the whole time — and with their morale sky high. I told him how wonderfully he had performed a few months later, just before he left East Timor. Much to his surprise, I added that one of his most sterling qualities was his willingness to disagree with me and argue the toss on those occasions when he felt very strongly about things. Mind you, this didn't happen too often! My point is that it was especially difficult for Mark to have an Australian major general who knew him and his brigade very well, who was relying on the Aussies and the Kiwis to do the 'heavy lifting' and who, from time to time, undoubtedly dipped his grubby fingers into Mark's business. Mark showed himself to have a magnificent character for soldiering and higher command on operations. He was justifiably awarded the Distinguished Service Cross for his leadership during the INTERFET campaign — one of the stars of the show.

13

Support from Australia

TAKING INTO ACCOUNT THESE unexpected bumps in the road, the mission was proceeding smoothly and successfully by late November. The militia threat had passed and Mark Evans had positioned his troops to nip in the bud any infiltration across the border, though a lively cross-border trade in cigarettes and other commodities had returned and was growing as East Timorese sought to replace household products that had been destroyed during the violent aftermath of the ballot. Thousands of displaced East Timorese remained in West Timor. The militia fed them propaganda about conditions and dangers in East Timor to keep them frightened and under their control. I was pleased to see that the UN was engaged in setting up arrangements for these poor people to return under the auspices of UNHCR and other organisations who were experienced in returning displaced persons and refugees to their homes.

Our logisticians were doing a great job. The troops were eating fresh food, slept on stretchers under canvas rather than in their two-man tents on the ground. Showers and laundries were operating and the rest and recreation centre in Dili was in full swing. Amenities now included canteens with limited duty-free shopping, video hire and an Interflora service.

We could now look at downsizing some sections of the force. The US presence ashore was a signals battalion that had helped provide our long-haul internal communications within East Timor and international satellite connections. Now we were transitioning to higher reliance on commercial satellite communications using equipment and some magnificent workers from the Australian telecommunications giant, Telstra. As a direct result, we were able to release the American signallers quite quickly.

In addition, on 20 November I was able to farewell the first of the coalition's combat elements. It was time to say goodbye to most members of the British contingent who had been there from 'Day One' eight weeks before. I was most impressed with their commander and greatly appreciated their work in securing the UN compound in Dili and in the Oecussi Enclave. Later, I was delighted to see this fine battalion commander recognised with the award of the OBE for his service in East Timor. I recall watching him march proudly in front of his magnificent Gurkha soldiers on the day of their departure, led by their pipes and drums. All Gurkhas tend to be short and nuggetty and their marching pace is much quicker than normal. Their boss, however, was about 6 foot 5 inches tall and it was mildly hilarious to see him out the front with his long legs moving in a blur as quickly as they could to keep to the pace of the tiny steps of his troops.

The departure of these troops brought to mind one of the dilemmas of modern peace enforcement operations conducted in coalition. The coalition lead country will always strive to have as many 'flags' in the force as possible for political and military reasons. Contributing nations will monitor their broad interests as well as the daily doings of the coalition that might impact on them. Typically, they appoint officers of sufficient seniority to understand issues and to represent their countries interests direct to the force commander. Notwithstanding this imperative, generally, the seniority of the contingent leader will be relative to the size of the contingent. For example, the Brazilians were present in platoon strength and their senior man was a captain, who both looked after Brazil's interests and performed a job of work within our overall organisation. Colonel Martyn Dunne, the highly talented senior New Zealand officer, was the right rank to represent his country's interests, given that New Zealand supplied an infantry battalion, a helicopter squadron and some other elements to INTERFET. In fact, I lobbied for and obtained Martin's promotion to brigadier while we were there so that he could take over command of all the troops in the Dili region, an active and sensitive operational area requiring professionalism, energy and diplomacy. He did a magnificent job and continued to meet all New Zealand's expectations as the senior Kiwi officer.

The senior US officer was Brigadier General John Castellaw, who was a most impressive and good-humoured professional. While his country's strength on the ground was never more than a couple of hundred troops, large US naval vessels passing through the area would provide additional helicopter support from time to time and members of crews would come ashore to work on civil aid projects. Having John making these arrangements and coordinating American activities was a boon. He visited frequently, consulted regularly, and supported us consistently, but otherwise stayed out of our hair.

The British solution to this 'senior officer representing national interests' was more problematic. All up, the Brits had about 200 people on the ground in East Timor with the majority being a 120-strong company of Gurkhas from a British Army Gurkha Battalion serving in Brunei. The contingent commander was the CO of the Gurkha Battalion, a lieutenant colonel who would normally command the 700 or 800 men, but in East Timor he would be working 'down' to only 200 troops. In addition, Britain sent a brigadier from London to be their national commander. I first met this gentleman in Brisbane not long before we deployed. I had spent two postings in Britain, so I was positively disposed to working with British officers and troops. He asked me what principal staff job I would give him on my headquarters. My chief of staff was a colonel and having a brigadier asserting his presence would unbalance the team. At that time, I couldn't use him in addition to — and over the top of — my well-practised and cohesive staff team. Not only did he have too much rank but he also did not have enough familiarity with how we would do things, the best way to interact with regional forces, the situation on the ground in East Timor and our sensitive and key relationship with Indonesia. I politely declined, but privately thought he might find himself at somewhat of a loose end in East Timor where he would have three choices: micromanage downwards within his own contingent; become distracted by events naturally and upwards; or withdraw into his shell.

In the end it took a few months, but I think he and the British military hierarchy concluded that he was over-ranked and under-employed. They simply gave an 'honorary' colonel's rank to the young lieutenant colonel, who commanded the contingent, and that worked perfectly well — as it would have from the start. This observation about rank levels in coalition operations stayed with me. In later years, when the rank level of our senior man on the ground became a question, I would always tend towards the best man or woman at the minimum rank needed to be effective.

The unfinished business of the mission was securing an agreement on managing the East/West Timor border and the border of West Timor and the Oecussi Enclave. The Motaain incident had prompted some interest and promises of further consultation but nothing much was happening. Attempts to negotiate at various levels had met an Indonesian brick wall. In the third week of November, a prominent figure of the Clinton administration, Ambassador Richard Holbrooke, visited Jakarta and he and Ambassador Robert Gelbard, the US envoy to Indonesia, got their heads together and decided to give this issue a shake-up. On 21 November, I got a phone call from Ambassador Holbrooke asking me what I thought should be the principles and protocols for managing the borders. We discussed this briefly, but I said I had a working paper that I had been hoping to table with the Indonesians all ready to go. I faxed the document to him where he was staying with Ambassador Gelbard in Kupang, the provincial capital of West Timor. I welcomed Ambassador Holbrooke's interest, but thought that diplomatic processes would now take some weeks to unfold.

I was somewhat taken aback when Richard Holbrooke rang back a few hours later announcing that he had lobbied strongly and the Indonesians had agreed to attend a conference on border management at Motaain the next day. He and Ambassador Gelbard would attend. He expected a number of Indonesian senior officers including Major Generals Damiri and Syahnakri to also attend, and had also invited Sergio Vieira de Mello and TMR. I rang Mark Evans, my commander responsible for the whole border region and invited him to attend.

The next day I turned up at Motaain. The Indonesians had erected a large tent and set up tables and chairs for this ad hoc but momentous meeting. Unfortunately, bad weather prevented Mark Evans leaving his headquarters in Suai, but everyone else was there. From the outset, Richard Holbrooke, and to some extent Robert Gelbard, dominated proceedings with some early filibustering. I wondered where all of this was going. Then the Americans tabled a document that looked very similar to what I had sent to them the day before. They made it clear that they wanted an agreement that was based on the tabled paper before the meeting finished. Everyone appeared to be caught by surprise. It was a tour de force but did not endear them to the Indonesians present.

With copies of the document in front of us, everyone contributed some more rhetoric. For my part, I confined myself to expressions of earnest intent to work with the Indonesians to keep the border safe and to avoid and manage any misunderstandings. During all of this, the Ambassadors operated like a tag team, criticising the Indonesians on the subject of militia activities in West Timor. Warming to this topic, TMR jumped in with some supporting sentiments. From time to time we had breaks, ostensibly so that the experts on both sides could produce amended language within the document. I think the Indonesians appreciated some respite from being harangued. However, the Ambassadors built up their energy during breaks for renewed diatribes!

During one of these pauses in proceedings, Kiki Syahnakri and I wandered off to one side and had a very pleasant and frank chat. By now he was back in Jakarta, but would soon replace Damiri, whose headquarters were in Bali. I was glad that Syahnakri would retain responsibility for relationships with INTERFET and then the following UN peacekeeping force. He had done a good job under pressure in Dili and I suspect he was as aghast at some of the actions attributed to local Indonesian security forces as anybody else. Finally, the Ambassadors brought out the document with some minor amendment by both sides. General Damiri signed it and I signed it as a co-signatory. Then a number of other officials, including Vieira de Mello, Syahnakri and the Governor of West Timor, Piet Tallo, signed. I was delighted to have an agreement signed and sealed, but was still a little stunned by the 'cudgel diplomacy' used to get it. I reflected at the time that agreements help, but it would require much hard work, mutual understanding and relationship building on the borders to make it succeed. However, the outcome was that workable border protocols had been signed sealed and delivered.

Though I had hosted many visits before late November, the tempo picked up again as Christmas approached. The first of these would be most important. The Prime Minister, John Howard, was inbound. The itinerary of his visit on 28 November was busy, but would give him a good representative understanding of what was going on. I accompanied him throughout and also had plenty of opportunities to chat to Admiral Chris Barrie and the new Secretary for the Department of Defence, Dr Alan Hawke, who were also along.

The Prime Minister's stop off in Maliana typified his relationship with our men and women wherever he encountered them in East Timor — or elsewhere for that matter. Maliana is a town in the middle of the districts bordering West Timor. While Suai, because of its size, was the headquarters for all of our forces in the western part of East Timor, Maliana was an important hub for military activity. We chose it as the best place for John Howard to meet a large number of the troops doing the 'heavy lifting' in the harsh environment of these western regions. In discussing the proposed visit with Mark Evans and his commanders, I told them to brief their troops to not hold back and be shy of the Prime Minister. He wasn't coming all the way from Australia to admire a bunch of shrinking violets. Given the hard work that they had been doing, they were entitled to get a handshake from him. They took me at my word! We landed in Maliana by helicopter and John Howard moved across the soccer field where we had landed to a huge group of very tired and grubby diggers gathered at the far end around some armoured personnel carriers. One of his less experienced minders muttered to me that he hoped this part would go well. I had a feeling it would go better than just 'well' and told him so.

He was mobbed. John Howard approaches these things in a way that absolutely endears him to servicemen and women. When he comes up to a group of them, he won't tolerate them standing apart in some form of respectful semicircle. He dives in amongst them and starts talking to individuals with the result that the others all crowd round to listen to the exchange and to have a word themselves. Next thing you know, the troops are jostling each other politely for a chance to speak to him, to shake hands and to get him to sign their brassards, their flags, their shirts or some other memento. He is indefatigable in signing autographs and posing with people for photographs. I have watched this phenomenon for years now. I know that it is not contrived political artifice, but is his natural instinct and heartfelt pleasure when he is among the men and women of the ADF, the Australian Federal Police (AFP) or indeed any Australians he visits overseas who are working hard in demanding and challenging circumstances. For me, the comfort he gave to those desperately sad and bereaved Australians he met in Bali after the bombing in 2002 testified to his leadership and genuine compassion. On this day, I wrote in my official diary, 'the troops loved him'. The rest of his visit went well and paved the way for several other pre-Christmas visits by senior political leaders from INTERFET countries.

A couple of days later Mr Kim Beazley, the Leader of the Opposition, and a group of Labor Party members of Parliament visited and had a similar itinerary to the Prime Minister's, although Beazley and party substituted a visit to the Oecussi Enclave instead of the western regions of East Timor. The visit also went very well. Mr Beazley, in particular, was very popular with the soldiers. Hard on their heels came the Parliamentary Joint Standing Committee for Foreign Affairs, Defence and Trade led by Senator Alan Ferguson. I was a little bit 'visited out' by then, so I warmly greeted them and briefed them before sending them off on their visit. Besides, I had the then Portuguese

Minister for Foreign Affairs, Mr Gama, and his delegation only a short time later and needed to squeeze in a delegation from the European Union before him. Must have been winter in Europe.

The departure of traditional American and British partners and the arrival of contingents from nations such as the Republic of Korea, Kenya and Canada over the months of November to December began a period of transition towards the handover to a 'blue beret' peacekeeping force under UNTAET. In my mind's eye, I was aiming for the end of February 2000 to leave East Timor with the last INTERFET units. The border areas and everywhere else in East Timor were safe. Violent incidents would be an exception and not part of any renewal of a militia campaign to destabilise the journey to independence. There was still much work to do to rebuild infrastructure and to provide essential services to the people, but that was in the hands of international aid organisations. The UN force would be settling into a benign environment.

One of the features of Australia's military presence in East Timor as a major component of INTERFET was the huge public interest in the operation. The primary expression of this was through the media, but equally by the many hundreds of letters received every week, aid parcels, overtures from people wishing to in some way provide encouragement and support to our men and women. I clearly remember relatively early in the operation finding a group of stalwart Aussie seamen, part of the crew of a chartered civilian vessel, delivering stores to Dili and dispensing sausages and steaks to the hungry troops they met down at the

Dili port. They were members of the Maritime Workers Union and had brought a small portable barbecue and the meat, onions and eggs, etc, with them intending to share with their compatriots. The troops loved them!

One of the iconic Christmas moments in Australia is the 'Carols by Candlelight' television broadcast from the Myer Music Bowl in Melbourne a few days before Christmas Day. My public relations people told me of an approach from the Nine Network for INTERFET to provide a choir to sing the hymn 'Silent Night' for pre-recording in East Timor so the performance could be broadcast during the Carols concert a week or two later. It sounded like a great idea. I knew that in amongst the headquarters and support personnel in Dili, there would be no difficulty finding enough enthusiasts to form a substantial and enthusiastic amateur choir. To be even-handed about it, while the choir was dominated by Aussies, there were a number of our international friends incorporated into the group to add plurality and harmony.

Jon Stevens, a prominent lead singer with rock bands, led the team from Australia to record the hymn. His 'absolute heartthrob' status further encouraged many of the women who volunteered to sing in the choir. The technical people on the team decided that the best venue for the recording to take place was a small church at the southern end of Dili. I visited and stayed for the opening moments of the first rehearsal. All of these expectant and nervous INTERFET men and women were sitting in the pews. Jon Stevens, dressed in rock singer gear, gave them an introductory pep talk, finishing by saying that he would have them singing soon, but he would start off with a solo of the hymn. I'm sure everybody was amazed — as I was — by the wonderful tunefulness, power and emotion of this off-the-cuff and unaccompanied rendition. I know that from that point on, every man and woman in the choir gave it everything they had. The result shown at the Carols concert and viewed by us in East Timor was a wonderful, emotional bridge between the troops and their loved ones at home. It seemed to me that there were a few tear-stained cheeks in Melbourne — I know there were in Dili.

In the same vein as the 'Carols by Candlelight' project, John Farnham and his close friend and manager, Glenn Wheatley, an entrepreneur, visited during November. An old rocker and old soldier, Doc Neeson, former lead singer of the Angels, had conceived the idea of staging a major concert in support of the troops in Dili in the second half of December that would be broadcast live by major networks in Australia. He had shared it with Farnham and Wheatley, seeking their active support and participation to get it off the ground. I was conscious of the substantial effort this project would draw from INTERFET to help artists and technical crew mount a professional and significant occasion. However, given the wonderful outpouring of support we had received from Australia over the preceding months, I felt it was something we had to embrace in a wholehearted way. I was very proud of these three very patriotic Australians for proposing the project and offering their time and talent to make it work.

The day soon arrived for the concert and the cream of Australian show business talent was about to descend on us. Every Aussie I spoke to in INTERFET was jumping out of their skin at the thought that all these artists would come to boiling hot East Timor to entertain them. I was mindful of the troops on the border and elsewhere who would not be able to make it to Dili. Several artists, including Kylie Minogue, agreed to fly by helicopter to the border to give mini concerts, including the Enclave. After the mini concerts, these artists and others would congregate in Dili for the major concert on 21 December to be staged at the Dili Sports Stadium, where a huge stage, a mammoth sound system and television towers and gantries festooned the whole of the playing area. The talent arrayed for the event was a contemporary 'Who's Who' of the Australian music and comedy industries. John Farnham, Kylie Minogue, James Blundell, Gina Jeffries, Doc Neeson, The Living End, the Dili All-Stars and the inimitable Roy and HG were the major artists, and the Royal Military College band supported all the other musicians.

Roy and HG warmed up the crowd and did shorter pieces during the ad breaks on networks Nine and Seven. During their first piece, they invited every Aussie soldier to go to the border with West Timor and shout out in unison an uncomplimentary epithet to General Wiranto, the Commander in Chief of the Indonesian Armed Forces. I was in a small row of official seating and anxiously asked my staff officer, Major David Hay, whether we were 'on air' at this stage. He assured me we weren't. I thought we had got away with it but a few days later a kindly print journalist stuck it in his newspaper!

A flat area in front of the stage, back towards the grandstand, was jam-packed full of soldiers, sailors and air men and women, mostly from Australia but also from many other INTERFET nations. I was absolutely delighted to see how many East Timorese were in amongst the crowd. I noticed during the concert how many Aussies had hauled young East Timorese kids up on to their shoulders so that they could see the stage. With their rifles slung over their backs, kids on their shoulders, they still managed to sway, sing and dance to the music — both with rapturous looks on their faces. Thousands of Australians saw these images of the bond between Australians and East Timorese kids at home. After I returned, many people commented to me about how moved they were and acknowledged the subliminal message that the Aussies had made a true and deep connection with the East Timorese people.

Another moment which gave me a lump in the throat was when John Farnham sang 'You'll Never Walk Alone'. This was a very poignant choice of song for an audience of brave troops and grateful East Timorese mums and dads and kids. The gantry television camera roving over the crowd caught a close-up of a granite-faced Australian corporal staring straight ahead with tears rolling down his cheeks. I hope that, if he ever saw the concert on tape, he never felt a moment's embarrassment — he had plenty of tearful mates on that afternoon.

Kylie Minogue, a global sex symbol and very talented performer, got a huge cheer from the troops. They may not have known that earlier that day she had sung without accompaniment at Balibo, near the border. There had been a mix-up with loading helicopters and members of her band had been flown to the wrong town. I later found out that among the songs she performed, she had sung Eartha Kitt's 'Santa Baby' to an enthusiastic audience of troops and East Timorese. Though dressed in khaki pants, a T-shirt top and baseball cap, Kylie's rendition of this sensual Christmas song and modest sway of her hips 'brought the house down'.

After Kylie had 'brought the house down' a second time in Dili, John Farnham asked me onto the stage to make some brief remarks. Subsequently many soldiers who had been there, and others who wished they were, asked me if I'd met Kylie Minogue and if so, what she was like. As their boss, a general and a dear old boy, I confined my remarks to observing that she fitted just under my arm — even that innocent remark drew sighs of jealousy from the diggers. Perks of office!

The whole concert was hugely entertaining and an emotional rollercoaster for all attending. In my small official party, José Ramos-Horta and Bishop Belo both seemed to enjoy it immensely. As the telecast drew to a close, the whole ensemble gathered on the stage for the finale which was inevitably followed by a number of encores to the rapturous delight of the crowd. Doc Neeson led those on stage and the vast majority of the audience in a rousing version of the Angels hit, 'Will I Ever See Your Face Again?'. I was unaware that there was a more vulgar riposte to this song that was traditionally sung by audiences in the Angels' heyday. After the audience insisted that he sing the song again, presumably with this riposte in mind, he did it again, and the audience chimed in after the words, 'Will I ever see your face again?' with, 'No way, get f....., f... off!'. The crowd were delirious. Bishop Belo leant forward across Ramos-Horta and asked me, 'Mr General, what are they singing?' I weakly replied I wasn't sure, only to get a knowing look from José. In response to my second anxious inquiry of the night, my superb staff officer, David Hay, reassured me that the telecast had ceased before the magic words appeared. I was greatly relieved.

That night for a brief period before the artists and some of the support crew left East Timor on a RAAF Hercules aircraft, about a hundred young INTERFET troops from the three services had the opportunity to enjoy a barbecue and a beer ration with the performers. In fact, I suspect that some of the troops contrived to give the performers more than the ration! It was an exuberant and exhilarating celebration with much autograph signing and photograph taking. I think the artists enjoyed it every bit as much as the boys and girls in uniform. I for one will always remember and be grateful for the support and affection shown to INTERFET by these members of the Australian entertainment industry. Messrs Farnham and Wheatley have remained friends ever since.

In a postscript to this, I found out when I was Chief of Army that Doc Neeson, a nasho and a corporal in the Education Corps during his service, was entitled to the National Service Medal. I arranged to present it to Doc up in the Blue Mountains at a school fete. With due ceremony, we all gathered amid the kids and their parents and the lucky dip stalls and pony rides to give Doc his medal. A rocker through and through, Doc wore a scarlet bandsman's military jacket, which would not button up across the front, for the occasion. I didn't hesitate for a moment to pin the medal on the chest of this very generous Australian.

Christmas in East Timor was an especially emotional moment for all of us: for the East Timorese celebrating both the feast of Christ's birth and their new found freedom, and for the many thousands of 'outsiders' (the UN, the NGOs and INTERFET) because we were away from home and our loved ones. All over East Timor in barracks and bush camps, cooks sweated over stoves preparing a traditional repast. It is customary at a military

Christmas far from home for officers to serve the meals to the diggers and at Delta Company, 5/7 RAR (my old infantry company from 1975), I was a short order cook on the barbecue! (This was another Christmas away from Lynne and the boys — the first being in 1979 when I had been briefly in Rhodesia, now Zimbabwe, in the early days of the Commonwealth military operation to monitor the ceasefire there.) Back home, Christmas Day 1999 was a little more poignant for Lynne as our middle son Philip was undergoing Army recruit training near Wagga Wagga in New South Wales. Thank heavens for telephones!

14

Handover and Home

By EARLY JANUARY 2000, my staff and I were well advanced in planning our transition with the PKF, and INTERFET's departure from East Timor and return home. Before Christmas we had given a full set of planning documents to an American colonel who had been sent out from the UN headquarters in New York to plan the handover between INTERFET and the PKF. We hoped that our Christmas present to him and his early return to be with his family would help our cause. The question was whether the UN and contributing nations to the PKF would be ready to meet our self-declared end-of-February deadline. We were driving the transition process because we were reporting that it was time to move from the emergency phase to the reconstruction and nation-building phases. The Australian Government was supportive because it was looking for some financial relief and for other nations to share the 'heavy lifting' in East Timor.

Sometimes an eager new commander can push things along. In early January I was able to brief General Jaime De Los Santos, who had by now been confirmed as the first PKF commander. The Philippines Government promoted him to the rank of lieutenant general. Naturally, he was quite chuffed. He was affable and agreeable when I briefed him on our proposed transition arrangements, but in no way concentrated on the detail. He seemed to be in no particular hurry to take over in East Timor.

An unexpected visit gave the transition process a jolt forward. The Indonesian Peoples' Consultative Assembly had elected Abdurrahman Wahid, also known as Gus Dur, to replace President B.J. Habibie on 20 October 1999, and now President Wahid advised that he would like to visit East Timor on 24 February. This visit would be very important for the Indonesian/East Timorese relationship. Everybody in Dili, Canberra, New York and most likely Jakarta — and not least me — thought it would be a good idea if I wasn't in evidence on that day. I had been burnt in effigy twice to my knowledge in Jakarta and the Indonesian media had been quite critical of INTERFET, as well as the overall international intervention into Indonesian affairs. It was important politically and militarily for President Wahid to find Sergio Vieira de Mello in charge and Lieutenant General De Los Santos and his peacekeeping forces providing a secure environment in East Timor. President Wahid's visit would now act as a catalyst to hurry along the process of transition between INTERFET and the PKF. My staff and I had a new spring in our step. The staff at the Department of Peacekeeping Operation (DPKO) in New York might now give some more urgent attention to the plans we had given to the American colonel before Christmas.

Around this time another opportunity presented itself to give the Australians in INTERFET a morale boost. Australia had given our returning rugby heroes, John Eales's Wallabies, a magnificent welcome home for their feat in winning the 1999 Rugby World Cup. As part of that tremendous support from Australia to the team in Europe, we Aussies in INTERFET had sent a message of encouragement. I was extraordinarily thrilled when the Australian Rugby Union offered to send the World Cup, escorted by several Wallabies, for a quick visit to East Timor to show off the Cup to the Australian men and women of the force — an offer I accepted with alacrity. The Cup did the rounds down into the border areas and back to Dili, wherever there were large groupings of Australians. It must have been agony for the many Kiwis and fewer French men and women to watch the Cup triumphantly borne aloft, but everybody likes to exercise their boasting rights from time to time!

Years later when my own retirement from the Army was imminent, my good friend, Air Vice Marshal Bruce Ferguson, the New Zealand Chief of the Defence Force, sent me a videotaped message in which he said very warm and welcome things about the military-to-military relationship between Australia and New Zealand as well as our own friendship. I noticed that he was recorded standing next to the Bledisloe Cup, the ultimate prize in Australian and New Zealand rugby competition, and the Tri-Nations Cup. During an address of several minutes he never once referred to either of these trophies, but from time to time would pat one or the other like a favourite family pet. I got the message.

With security well under control, it was now time to 'thin out'. Indeed, it's axiomatic that no military force on operations is ever stable in structure and location for very long. Even during deployment, commanders and staff will have already begun to plan the rotations and departures of force elements in order to ensure that the force has fresh troops to maintain the desired tempo. The INTERFET operation was no exception. Often the units that are 'first in' become the 'first out'. On 10 January, I farewelled one of the Townsville-based infantry battalions from Mark Evans' 3rd Brigade, 2nd Battalion, the Royal Australian Regiment (2 RAR), and the Townsville-based armoured personnel carrier squadron, B Squadron 3rd/4th Cavalry Regiment. These men had been among the very first troops on the ground in September and had performed magnificently.

The boss of the battalion was Lieutenant Colonel Mick Slater, a very cool, tough and professional commanding officer who wielded his battalion to remarkable effect. In a highly symbolic moment on the eve of their departure, I spoke to the battalion en masse. It is always a thrill when you are in amongst happy, relieved and triumphant diggers who know they have done well and made a big difference. As part of this opportunity, I presented Slater with the Infantry Combat Badges (ICB) for his battalion. The Army instituted the ICB, a little bronze badge worn on the uniform by each entitled individual, during the Vietnam War as a special embellishment for infantry units that had been in combat. It was, and continues to be, highly prized. The Infantry Corps guards its entitlement and award jealously. Since Vietnam, apart from one or two Aussie infantrymen serving with non-Australian units, the only unit which had gained the ICB was the other Townsville-based infantry battalion, 1 RAR, for its tour of duty in Somalia in 1993. The men of 1 RAR thoroughly deserved the award for an arduous period of active service that was punctuated with short, sharp and nasty firefights with Somali bandits.

The award of the ICB to 1 RAR had been a cause of healthy jealousy from its Townsville neighbour, 2 RAR. Slater's men felt an additional sense of satisfaction because 1 RAR had missed being the battalion from Townsville to lead off on the East Timor operation by a matter of days. I had told Mark Evans that he could only take his 'on-line' infantry battalion to East Timor because I was assigning him the Sydney-based 3 RAR as his second battalion for the operation. Evans took this direction literally. He decided that if my warning orders for the operation had not arrived in his headquarters by the time 1 RAR was due to relinquish 'on-line' status to 2 RAR, the changeover would occur on schedule and Slater and his men would deploy with the brigade to East Timor. The changeover occurred at midnight on 12 September. My warning order arrived later that morning. These little jealousies and games of one-upmanship are quite good if they are kept in proportion. They contribute to keeping everyone sharp and competitive. I farewelled the troopers from the armoured personnel carrier squadron with the same sentiments as those I had expressed for the infantry. These blokes had performed outstandingly well. Their armoured personnel carriers took a real beating, but mechanically were kept in A1 condition. The squadron had played a crucial role in patrolling, troop movement and heavy firepower backup throughout the operation.

While the security situation certainly allowed for the repatriation of these powerful Australian combat units, I was left with less reserve capacity and fewer options for reacting to any unexpected threat or crisis. Although Australia had committed a

1200-strong infantry battalion group to the PKF, it was not yet on the ground. This meant that in the crucial border areas I had a New Zealand infantry battalion in the southern border regions, 5/7 RAR with their armoured personnel carriers in the northern border regions and the redoubtable 3 RAR down in Oecussi. All had their hands full maintaining a deterrent presence and patrolling over large expanses of sometimes very difficult terrain.

My next crisis was in Dili. On 15 January, UNTAET planned to hire several hundred East Timorese to begin work as support staff — drivers, cleaners, security guards and the like. This would be one of the first employment programmes designed to turn over East Timor's economic engine. United Nations staff selected the old indoor basketball stadium on the edge of the government precinct to register applicants for these jobs. We anticipated that thousands would turn up for a few hundred vacancies. Martyn Dunne assigned an Australian artillery battery of about eighty gunners to provide security for registration. This activity became an inauspicious start to the UN's transitional administration in East Timor.

The number of interview and registration positions was way too small to cater for the crowd. During the lengthy delay, those gathered became very restless and resentful. A rumour spread that those who were ahead in the queue were getting jobs before those following could even register. The senior UN official on the spot panicked as the crowd began calling out and shoving to get ahead in the queues. She decided to close the registration down with only a small number of lucky East Timorese having passed through. Well, the rest of the crowd went off like fireworks, launching a full-scale riot. They began throwing rocks at the gymnasium building and pulling fences down. The young Aussie soldiers formed a line to keep the mob from damaging or torching the building. The UN officials sensibly either stayed inside or moved off out of sight of the mob.

Suddenly, a sizeable rock hit a young gunner on the side of his head and he went down for the count with a broken jaw. When the crowd saw this unintended and deeply regretted injury to an Australian soldier, they stopped rioting. Sensible heads in the crowd prevailed over the firebrands. They dispersed without further incident, no doubt extremely disappointed that the vast majority of them had not been able to register for a job, let alone secure one: the 'unrequited aspirations' of a recently traumatised, but now broadly safe population, who looked forward to rebuilding their lives. I was concerned for the young gunner who would normally be sent straight back to Australia after sustaining this sort of injury. I didn't want him in years to come to have to reflect on the fact that he had been put out of the operation by the people he had come to help. I discussed his situation with the medicos, who then set up a medical management regime that allowed him to remain with his mates.

Around this time a crisis developed in the Oecussi Enclave, which in military parlance is 'terrible ground', or in the Australian vernacular, 'a bugger of a place'. It is very rugged, hilly, poorly served by roads and mostly jungle clad. The weather is changeable, with low cloud and rain descending suddenly and rapidly. Streams and rivers flood regularly, cutting off and isolating parts of the Enclave, sometimes for days at a time. Without doubt though, its greatest drawback is that it is a piece of East Timor widely separated from the main part of the country. West Timor borders all the landward sides of the Enclave. Like the East/West Timor border line, the border between the Enclave and West Timor travels through rough country and is not well marked. Local inhabitants move back and forward at will and hostile groups would have no difficulty sneaking in. It would take very significant numbers of troops to patrol and seal the border completely. Any commander who did not have thousands of troops at his disposal would have to manage considerable risk. Logistically, the Enclave was also a challenge. Its only airstrip was rudimentary and small. By helicopter it is an hour's flight and by Caribou transport aircraft somewhat more. By sea, it takes many hours to move and land significant stores or numbers of personnel. All in all, if you were contemplating having a fight you wouldn't want it to be there! Nonetheless, its inhabitants deserved and needed the protection of INTERFET, but it was a hard bargain.

As soon as I could after putting Mick Crane's Ambino Force down there in early November, I followed up by deploying 3 RAR to patrol and guard the place. For some time through December and January, there had been much posturing, sabre rattling and intimidation against the locals in the vicinity of the border, particularly in the south-east sector. From what we could ascertain from a variety of sources, all this trouble was instigated and orchestrated by one 'Moko' Soares, a militia leader who had allegedly done some grisly work in the Enclave, before and after the ballot, and was now simmering resentfully away in West Timor. There had been several sightings of Moko and members of his group near and over the border. Our eyes and ears were UN military observers and UN police. These unarmed and impartial observers from all around the world reported regularly on the activities along the border. We worked closely with them and shared our patrol reports and intelligence on Moko and his men. Their reports were helpful to us. Mark Evans and I passed on to our senior Indonesian counterparts as well as to the UN observer group that Moko and his men were destabilising the border region of the Enclave with provocative and threatening behaviour.

Moko and his cohorts further complicated the difficult issue of what nation would agree to have its troops occupy the Enclave after INTERFET left at the end of February. One of the more vexed issues for the transition between INTERFET and the PKF was the allocation of areas to international contingents. For example, the Portuguese, who had not been part of INTERFET, but would be a major player in the PKF as well as in the police component of UNTAET, were absolutely determined to operate close to Dili and thus be 'in the shop window'. The Thais and the Koreans were content to continue in the Baucau and far eastern regions respectively. The Kiwis and the Aussies were happy enough to remain in the western border regions. The Oecussi Enclave was a vacancy that was proving to be difficult to fill.

The Australian Government was not replacing 3 RAR with another Australian battalion and 5/7 RAR was destined to serve on the western border. The Enclave was not only remote — 'out of sight, out of mind' — but also a challenging place to secure and to sustain. No existing INTERFET contingent wanted to move there and none of the inbound PKF contingents appeared interested. Then along came the Jordanians. At my first meeting with the senior Jordanian officer heading up their reconnaissance team in late December, I asked him if his troops could be employed anywhere. He declared emphatically, 'They will serve anywhere!' I said, 'The UN will need a very good battalion for the

Oecussi Enclave.' And he replied, 'If you wish, the Jordanians will serve in Oecussi.' I nearly leapt for joy. I hoped that Moko and his henchmen would behave themselves or be deterred from continuing their campaign of aggressive posturing on the border and intimidating the locals. I was to be disappointed.

Again it is the way of things that, just when everything appears to be going smoothly, there is a horrible day that reminds commanders of the dangers of peacekeeping operations. That day for me was 17 January 2000, three days short of INTERFET's fourth month in East Timor. This memorable day began early when the trouble incubated by Moko and his thugs erupted in the south and south-eastern border area of the Enclave. In a coordinated series of incursions, armed militia groups came over the border at several points to intimidate, beat up and rob villagers in their homes and fields. Paratroopers from 3 RAR engaged them in firefights on a number of different occasions, wounding several and fundamentally chasing them back across the border. The commanding officer, Lieutenant Colonel Peter Singh, had manoeuvred his troops deftly and was on the job immediately protesting about these incursions. Both UN military observers and UN police backed his protests after Indonesian authorities in West Timor accused 3 RAR of shooting innocent farmers in the back. I spoke to Kiki Syahnakri in Bali by phone and wrote a letter to protest in the strongest terms. After a little bit of local posturing about 'who shot at whom first', the Indonesians accepted that Moko had to go as well as the local Indonesian military commander who appeared to have had difficulty controlling him and his men. So, General Syahnakri had Moko arrested and charged with a variety of offences, and told the Indonesian commander to pack his bags. Although the security situation in the Enclave remained tense, Kiki Syahnakri had brought the security situation to a much better level through his decisive actions.

While 3 RAR engaged intruders in the Enclave, 17 January also became memorable for another, sadder reason. We had had some close calls and bad injuries through both hostile action and in accidents. INTERFET had already lost a New Zealand warrant officer when he was killed in a motor vehicle accident and a Filipino soldier, who had succumbed to a heart attack. On 17 January we lost an Australian soldier to illness. Lance Corporal Russell Eisenhuth, a driver with a transport troop operating large military trucks around East Timor, had fallen ill a few days before with what appeared to be dengue fever. His condition seemed to follow the progression of dengue fever after he was admitted to INTERFET's military hospital in Dili. However, on the morning of 17 January his condition worsened rapidly and doctors planned to evacuate him to Darwin urgently. However, within a short time his health plummeted further until he was too sick to be moved. Sadly, despite the frantic efforts of an outstanding bunch of doctors and nurses, he died in the early afternoon. This sudden and totally unexpected turn of events devastated both the medical teams, who had tried so hard to save him, and his workmates.

I had met Russell on two previous occasions during visits. He was a quiet, mature and well-liked young man who was sorely missed. Whatever illness he contracted very fortunately did not afflict anybody else to such a devastating degree. When I thought of all the bullets that had been flying around over the past four months and the many confrontations, large and small, which could have led to shooting, it was poignant to think that we had lost a soldier to illness. Perhaps though, Russell's death underscored that there were significant hazards of a more general kind facing anybody living in the harsh tropical environment of East Timor.

The paratroopers of 3 RAR had done very well in a series of running encounters that required disciplined application of the rules of engagement and careful selection of targets, as the armed militiamen were often moving close to unarmed villagers and members of their families. Word of the actions that had sent Moko and his band scampering back over the border carrying their wounded got around the Enclave quickly. The people of Oecussi were mightily impressed. For the time being, the militia groups interested in causing mischief in the Enclave were leaderless and would not have been further emboldened by their experiences on 17 January. Privately, I was not only cursing the fact that the militia challenge had occurred within the overall framework of stability in East Timor, but also its location and timing. I was hoping that the shooting on 17 January would not cause the Jordanians to have second thoughts.

The men of 3 RAR were an exuberant and irrepressible lot, but also showed great compassion for the impoverished inhabitants of the Oecussi Enclave. This was epitomised during one of my visits there. I arrived one day at a far-flung outpost, the westernmost of 3 RAR's mini-garrisons that was occupied by a platoon — a great experience for the young platoon commander and his corporals. I was talking to a group of soldiers when one of them, a corporal, asked me if we could send a doctor to work in the area. I asked him whether his request was prompted by his soldiers being ill or ailing. He said, 'No', they were fine, but it was the locals who needed the doctor. I explained that I didn't have many military doctors. If it was the locals who needed a doctor, I would take it up with UNTAET headquarters in Dili. He thanked me and explained that a week beforehand he had been minding his own business when a panic-stricken East Timorese man had rushed up to him seeking immediate help because his wife was in the late stages of labour and all the other village women were elsewhere. The corporal had gone to this man's home and ended up delivering the baby. Looking at this rough-and-ready corporal, a machine gunner with muscles in his eyebrows, I marvelled at this latest demonstration of the Aussie 'have a go' spirit. I told him I understood why he needed the doctor — midwifery is outside the job description for machine gunners. He told me that he didn't ask for the doctor so much for routine births but his reputation had spread. He had attended a delivery a day or so before. This one was a breech birth and these were much more complicated! I took his point.

Fortunately, my fears about the Jordanians having second thoughts were not realised. A Jordanian battalion replaced 3 RAR in Oecussi. I was delighted to officiate at a handover on 5 February. This meant that the Jordanians were able to claim rightfully that they deployed to East Timor as a unit of INTERFET. They were very proud to have done so and this first Jordanian battalion distinguished itself for the few weeks they served under my command and, to my knowledge, continued to do so for the remainder of their tour under command of the PKF.

After substantial negotiation between INTERFET and the UN on the ground in East Timor as well as between officials in Canberra and UN staff in New York, the transition date between

INTERFET and PKF was set for 23 February. On this day responsibility for the security for East Timor would pass to the PKF and INTERFET's mandate would end and the organisation would be dissolved. Several thousand Australians and New Zealanders would transition from INTERFET to UNTAET, but others from Australia and elsewhere would go home. The emergency force sent to East Timor in September 1999 would pass into history.

One of the last battles my staff and I had to win in order to achieve a smooth handover was over the transition concept we had developed. Senior UN staff, including my friend Major General Mike Smith, the newly-appointed deputy commander of the PKF, wanted a comprehensive and instantaneous handover between INTERFET and the PKF. For a couple of reasons I preferred a progressive handover of parts of East Timor over several weeks leading up to 23 February. First, the eastern part of East Timor was by now very peaceful. The forces operating there would simply transition from being INTERFET units to being part of the PKF by putting on blue berets rather than their nation's headdress. There was no reason why that should not occur sooner rather than later. The PKF headquarters could take responsibility for the whole eastern part of the island comfortably. This preliminary transition would allow me to reduce the focus of INTERFET operations to Dili and west to the border progressively while the PKF managed the eastern half of East Timor. I could then reduce the number of troops supporting the units in the east and allow UN instituted contract support for some logistics functions to takeover and get used to their responsibilities.

Secondly, my concept gave HQ PKF time to 'shake out' before taking control of the whole of East Timor. My headquarters was an experienced and coherent organisation. The PKF headquarters would be, by its very nature, thrown together and unpractised — a novice entity. I thought it was a very good idea for De Los Santos and his recently assembled international staff to take on command and support responsibilities for forces in the east, such as the Koreans, the Thais and the Filipinos who had been in East Timor at a 'steady state' for some time. They were experienced units and had settled in their areas without being challenged. Their support arrangements were quite routine and mature.

Initially, Mike Smith was sceptical about whether the concept of a progressive handover was a good one. However, like the very professional officer that he was, he threw himself into making it work. Indeed, great credit for the subsequent smooth transition must go to him. He worked tirelessly and with great goodwill and good humour to negotiate all the arrangements, particularly the crucial questions of logistic support and communications. He sought the best possible deal for the PKF and was a tough negotiator. From time to time both our lips grew a little thin during negotiations in my office — that's what you get when you put a forthright Australian officer as the senior advocate for a group like the PKF. The UN got a consummate professional — totally loyal to his adopted cause and determined to get a satisfactory outcome; I got an earache!

During February Lieutenant General De Los Santos and I shared security responsibility for East Timor. The first transition occurred on 1 February when the units in the eastern portion of East Timor donned their blue berets and passed under De Los Santos' command. I was sorry to see these fine troops and good friends leaving our little tribe, but I considered that they would continue to perform in an outstanding manner under the UN flag. I kept harping on the need for continued focus on our major security tasks. There were plenty of distractions; visitors both technical and representational; discussions about appropriate welcomes in Australia for the troops; seemingly endless 'word smithing' of the transitional document; and a renewed burst of media interest. We had to accommodate these matters during each phase of the progressive transition and do a professional job of dismantling our own operation and returning to Australia and elsewhere.

Two of the more significant visits around this time were those by the President of Portugal, Mr Sampaio, on 13 February and four days later by the Secretary General of the UN, Mr Kofi Annan. I was very conscious that the Portuguese President was making an emotional as well as diplomatic visit, given the hundreds of years of shared history between Portugal and the people of East Timor. I had a meeting with the President in a reception room in the Governor's Palace. He was very well-informed, articulate and a charming conversationalist. Overall, his visit was very successful. I assessed that his manner and communications with the East Timorese leaders set the scene well for the Portuguese troops, supported by their police contingent, to assume security responsibilities for Dili and the central sector of East Timor.

The Secretary General's visit was also most interesting. It was fascinating to watch UN bureaucrats in Dili put everything on hold while they concentrated on their boss's visit. There was a strange sense of a royal visit, rather than a working visit by a very senior official to a mission area. Fortunately, this major activity did not affect INTERFET. Mr Annan did not visit my troops at all. However, we did have some of our troops as an additional security element lurking in the background in a sort of outer cordon to the UN police who provided his close personal protection. I did not want to lose, or have a Secretary General harmed in any way, on my watch! As it turned out, I was the only INTERFET person he spoke with at any length. My meeting with him was again quite strange. I found him either very shy or quite detached during our short time together, characterised more by the protocol to pass me through several layers of courtiers, before we actually got to sit down for a chat. He did say some kind words about INTERFET and Australia.

The few days left in the mission thankfully remained peaceful. I tripped around attending handover ceremonies in Oecussi and Suai. In Suai, as part of my farewell round of visits, I called on the Fijians who had been in INTERFET for only a month or so. They were a prominent regional contingent comprised of very professional and hugely popular soldiers who were going to continue in East Timor working for UNTAET. The farewell followed a familiar format. I delivered a short speech and handed over an INTERFET brassard, plaque and a framed 'order of the day' — a traditional form of 'illuminated address' with words pertinent to INTERFET having accomplished its mission. For their part, the Fijians made some warm remarks through their boss and I made to leave. Their commanding officer politely urged me to wait for a moment or two. I turned again to the assembled seventy or eighty men and they began to sing a beautiful hymn — a traditional Fijian folksong. These giant men, mostly older than their Australian counterparts, joined as brothers in that incredible communalism of South Sea Islanders, unselfconsciously and wholeheartedly raised their voices in the most tuneful and harmonious choir, warriors with the voices of angels. It is incumbent on generals at such times to maintain a proper air of benign gravitas. I was extraordinarily moved as I reflected on the richness of the polyglot culture of the soldiers' guild.

The next day, 21 February, I paid a farewell visit to TMR in his highland cantonment. This was another farewell pregnant with emotion, but leavened by my expectation that I would see this remarkable man again and again over the years, such was my conviction of his importance to the future development of his nation. Later the same day, the PKF assumed security responsibility for the western border regions of East Timor. From that moment the hard edge of the INTERFET mission ceased. Now we only retained a few operational support functions until the formal transition of responsibilities and the end of our mandate in two days' time. The next day passed without incident. I settled down for a few hours of sleep that last night, reflecting on the mission with a huge sense of relief and anticipation of a happy return, and just a hint of loss for the magnificent adventure and privilege that the whole thing had been.

At the outset, while I fully realised the direct risks and the ramifications of what we were setting out to do, I also had an abiding faith and confidence in the ability of the men and women who came from Australia and elsewhere to help the people of East Timor. I thought that we would overwhelm the militia quite quickly, as we did. I was also confident that we would be able to do so without falling into conflict through some dreadful accident with our neighbours in Indonesia. I thought that we could provide a very substantial helping hand to the necessary humanitarian effort to rehabilitate East Timor and also set up a conducive environment for the UN and aid agencies. I thought from the beginning that, if we Australians leading INTERFET worked very hard, we could create and maintain goodwill and excellent relationships within our coalition. This proved to be the case. I understood that the whole affair had injected a sour note into Australian–Indonesian relations, but I felt that we could do our job in a way that would limit the damage and provide opportunities for returning to closer relations in the future.

For a fellow who had been a little under two years before confidently but wistfully anticipating that he would finish his career as a brigadier commanding his old Alma Mater, the amazing good fortune which gave me the chance to 'play for Australia' in this way now allowed me to leave the field happily with an honourable result.

Wednesday, 23 February 2000 typified the wet season in East Timor: hot and sunny but with brooding cloud banks promising rain during the day. One advantage of living pretty rough with a minimum of amenities is that it doesn't take long to pack. Some of my staff were staying on a little longer to support the repatriation of the last few INTERFET elements that were packing stores, and cleaning and loading vehicles and equipment onto ships and aircraft. I said a very fond farewell to these men and women who had performed so wonderfully for the last 157 days. We hauled down the INTERFET flag for the last time — a flag which I squirreled away immediately as a memento — and I moved on down to the Governor's Palace for the transition ceremony — the signing of a memorandum formalising transition between INTERFET and the PKF. There were quite a few media folk present. The 'players' sat along 'the top table'; Lieutenant General De Los Santos and myself representing the two military forces, Brigadier Rezaqul Haider, a Bangladeshi who was the UN Senior Military Observer, Xanana Gusmao, Bishop Belo and Sergio Vieira de Mello. I can't remember if there were any speeches, but if there were, they were mercifully short and we got on with signing the documents. At this time Xanana Gusmao gave me a beautifully pressed and folded uniform which on examination I found to be his FALINTIL uniform from his time as chief of the resistance — a very significant and much appreciated gift. Then it was outside where a throng had gathered. After a few moments shaking hands, I drove off towards the dock in a little convoy with Gusmao and Vieira de Mello.

Arriving in East Timor had its own style — that of a sophisticated and purposeful military force arriving with all professional urgency. I came in on an RAAF Falcon jet. The air forces of the coalition had worked wonders during the operation, not least our own. But I felt that the formal INTERFET departure from East Timor needed to have style and a significance of its own. I did some plotting with Brian Robertson, commanding INTERFET's maritime component, and another great mate, Bruce Wood, commanding our air component, and arranged for a spectacular departure from Dili Harbour.

Down at the dock, HMAS *Jervis Bay* awaited. There was a large crowd of East Timorese, a posse of media, some troops in their UN berets and a few uniformed men and women still proudly wearing their INTERFET brassards. There was a good deal of emotion and after a few hugs all round, including me kneeling down to hug a couple of kids, I started for the gangway, pausing to take off my pistol and hand it to my driver who was remaining for a day or so with the muttered injunction, 'Don't lose it!' Probably typical of the symbiotic relationship the military necessarily has with the media in modern times, as I stepped to the gangway, a photographer I recognised whispered in my ear, 'Hey general, what about giving me THE shot!' I had to pay him. He and his mates never give in. I replied, 'Watch carefully as I get to the high point of the gangway.' When I got there, I did what I was planning to do anyway, turned around and gave everybody a big cheery wave, but I did give him the tip off.

The *Jervis Bay* was quickly under way and, after a little bit of cautious manoeuvring to get into the channel out of the port, it started to work up speed. In a very short time the catamaran was travelling like some giant speedboat with a huge twin rooster tail of water. As the figures on the dock got smaller, from my vantage point on top of the superstructure accompanied by Brian Robertson and Bruce Wood, we passed between twin columns of INTERFET naval vessels steaming along as a seagoing guard of honour to be joined within moments by a mini armada of INTERFET aircraft in a fly past. Soon, the harbour in the town of Dili sank below the horizon and it seemed that my only residual responsibility was to refrain from falling overboard. The hundreds of kilometres back to Darwin passed uneventfully although the weather roughened up during the evening.

As we slipped quietly into berth in Darwin at about 2 a.m., the heavy rain which had been falling for some time was now coming in almost horizontally. After farewelling the skipper and his crew,

I stepped down the gangway and was intrigued to see off to the side — 30 metres or more away — a small group of a dozen or so people holding banners. I thought to myself, 'A demonstration? At this time of night? In this weather?' I walked over to see what it was about. As I got closer I read the signs which said, 'Welcome home diggers! Welcome home INTERFET!' I was incredibly touched and asked what had brought them out in such foul weather. A man about my age accompanied by his wife and young adult kids said, 'I'm a member of the Vietnam Veterans Association here in Darwin and so are my mates. When we got home from Vietnam, nobody welcomed us and we've vowed that that will never happen again. So here we are. My wife and kids wanted to come as well.' When words fail you, sometimes a hug says it all.

After a couple of hours sleep, I took the keenly awaited opportunity to thank the men and women of the ADF and Australian public servants based in Darwin who had worked every bit as hard as our people in East Timor, albeit in different circumstances. Without their efforts INTERFET couldn't have succeeded. Then it was on to another Falcon jet for the long ride to Sydney — to my beloved, Lynne, and my sons, sorely missed these last months. Arriving in Sydney in the late afternoon, the jet rolled in to a side area near the Qantas terminal and when I looked out the window I could see a small reception party led by the Minister for Defence and a large media scrum led by nobody in particular. I didn't spot Lynne and wondered whether she had held back in the adjacent office building. After thanking the pilots and cabin staff for the ride, I clattered down the steps meaning to shake the Minister's and other dignitaries' hands, dance my way through the media and find my wife. As I launched off the bottom step, hand outstretched to the Minister, he said 'What about Lynne?', nodding back over my shoulder. I turned to see her just near the bottom of the steps. We had a lovely big kiss and cuddle right there in front of the mob. While I'd been away, in her usual calm and organised manner, Lynne had moved the whole family from Brisbane into the house that came with my next job, located in Victoria Barracks in Sydney. When I walked in the door of that house, one of many in our married life that she had made into our home, I felt truly happy — finally content that the mission was over and the job was done.

15

Army Command

AFTER JUST A FEW DAYS OFF relaxing at home, I started my new job as Land Commander. Still a major general's job — the same rank that I was before and during East Timor — but a more senior position with more formations to command: my old formation 1st Division (largely Regular Army), 2nd Division (an Army Reserve organisation), the Logistic Support Force (a mixture of regulars and reserves) and a few specialist organisations, such as the Special Forces and northern surveillance regiments. If we had a bigger Army, this would be considered a Corps command. It was a great job and, if East Timor had not come along, then I would have expected to do it for a couple of years and then retire. My priorities were to get stuck into preparing forces to serve in East Timor — our ongoing major operational commitment — and also to look after units that had not long returned from East Timor and needed to get back into shape. Overall, I had to keep an eye out on the preparedness of all of our deployable troops in case of an unexpected order from the government to take military action in response to a contingency — hopefully one we had trained for. Beyond these priorities, there were the responsibilities of everyday administration and training of the 30,000 or so troops in Land Command.

A few East Timor 'aftershocks' remained. There were a number of very generous invitations for INTERFET troops of the three services to take part in 'welcome home' parades around Australia. I attended some of these, and led the one in Sydney. I had marched on a number of occasions over the years with my old mob from Vietnam on Anzac Day in Sydney. That was always a thrill, especially in more recent years when the crowds attending the march have grown dramatically. On those occasions I was just another face in the ranks. In Sydney for the INTERFET march it was a bit different. I was out the front, like a circus elephant, and the crowd along George Street was vast. When you are leading like that, you wonder sometimes whether the diggers will play a trick on you by hanging back and letting you get ridiculously far in front. It would be a sign of weakness or lack of confidence to look back to check! It was a real buzz to mingle with so many INTERFET men and women from the Navy, Army and Air Force whom I had seen not long before. Generally, they had been very tired, quite grubby and working extremely hard in sweat-stained field uniforms. Now they all looked rested, spick and span in barracks uniforms and jumping out of their skins at the honour their fellow Australians were doing them. Thank you Australia, we loved it.

A major highlight of this fervent national embrace of INTERFET veterans was a 'welcome home' reception and lunch at the Great Hall of Parliament in Canberra. The Prime Minister and Leader of the Opposition made very kind speeches. I made one in reply and the presiding officers of the Senate and the House extended to the CDF, the Service Chiefs and me the rare privilege of sitting within each chamber for a short visit during the post-lunch session while each of them, on behalf of the members of their chamber, made very warm remarks about the men and women of the Australian Defence Force. This was an unforgettable day; the first of many visits to Parliament over the next five years.

In my speech in reply at the luncheon, I chronicled some aspects of the mission and offered my gratitude to the millions of supporters of our work, especially those within Defence working back in Australia, and my unqualified admiration for the men and women under my command. In an effort to encapsulate a fundamental idea into a short sentence, as I had done when I said 'I'll take care of them' to Kerry O'Brien in September, I invested my last two words with every ounce of the pride I felt in those young men and women by saying, 'Mission accomplished.'

While additional duties and wider community involvement prompted by the successful INTERFET campaign continued strongly for some time, the capstone to the previous incredible six months of my career came through the coincidence of her Majesty the Queen's visit to Australia in March 2000. I had exhorted all Australian commanders in INTERFET to be vigilant about meritorious performance and to 'write up' subordinates for later recognition. An important part of INTERFET's closure was to collate and prioritise many nominations for consideration in Canberra; first by the CDF and his Service Chiefs, then by the Defence Minister and, finally, by the Governor General. With the serendipity of Her Majesty's visit, it was possible for her to invest a handful of these extraordinary men and women with their awards in a ceremony at Yarralumla in late March.

I was there to get one as well having been appointed a Companion in the Military Division of the Order of Australia. I had been told to arrive a little early. I turned up with Lynne and the boys expecting a brief on some additional task, possibly a short speech. A senior member of the Governor General's staff greeted us and then told me that I was about to have a private audience with the Queen. At that moment I reflected on the journey from Underwood Street, Paddington, and wondered what the blokes in the SP bookies' shop would make of it all! Honouring the convention that you do not recount detail of conversations with the Queen, I found her to be relaxed, charming, informed and interested in what we had been doing for the last five months.

The investiture was a great honour. I was delighted that Lynne and the boys were there to see it all happen and to meet the Queen. Their wholehearted love and support were fundamental to my emotional wellbeing in East Timor and helped me to do my job more effectively. But the real thrill for me was watching the obvious pride and enjoyment on the faces of the men and women receiving awards and the beaming faces of their loved ones. After the investiture, the Queen moved around amongst the families with me making introductions. She was patient with me as I struggled manfully with wives and kids names!

Not long after I got back from East Timor, the New Zealand Consul General invited me to a luncheon at her home in Sydney. The function was in honour of the new Prime Minister of New Zealand, Helen Clark, who was making her first prime ministerial visit to Australia. I attended in uniform, the norm for these official functions. I got there at the appointed time as one of the early guests and, as the Kiwi Prime Minister was running a little late, there was quite a bit of mingling to be done. I noticed that great, eminent Australian and former Prime Minister Gough Whitlam had arrived as one of the guests. I had met him several times, but a number of years before. I decided to go over to him to pay my respects. I stood before him and said, 'Hello Mr Whitlam, my name is Peter Cosgrove, it's good to see you again.' Mr Whitlam looked me up and down for a moment and said, 'Are you one of theirs or one of ours?' Classic Whitlam — I meekly replied that I was an Australian and soon excused myself.

Life proceeded along ordained lines for the next few months. There were occasional instances of spontaneous recognition and congratulation from ordinary Australians going about their business as I went about mine. One of these was a most enjoyable moment on Anzac Day 2000 when I had been to a commemorative service for the Royal Australian Regiment at a little cul-de-sac called Regimental Place near Wynyard Station in George Street, Sydney. After the service I began a leisurely stroll up through town to where my old unit usually assembled among the Vietnam veterans. I was wandering along by myself, cutting through a few side streets where different veterans groups were assembling, when I came across a large group of veterans from a number of the wartime women's services of World War II. I was in civvies and thought I might sneak through, but I was spotted and it took me about 30 minutes to get to the next block.

*

In June 2000, the government announced my appointment as Chief of Army and promoted me to lieutenant general, effective in about four weeks' time. There had been speculation in the Army, and the media had tipped me for the job, so I was not hugely surprised. However, the announcement caused me to reflect on the enormous role that luck plays in such matters. Before East Timor, I would have been a rank outsider, if not a scratching in the field of contenders. Now only a few short months later, the self-styled pundits had me on a 'rails run' for the job.

I was thrilled with the prospect of commanding the Army that I had grown up in as a child, struggled through in my officer training and lived in with every fibre of my being for all of my life thereafter. I was so sad that neither of my parents nor my father-in-law were alive for the moment. I also felt for two magnificent army officers who had missed out, essentially because of my good luck — Major Generals Mick Keating, an unsung hero of the East Timor operation, and Peter Abigail, the Deputy Chief of Army, a fine leader and a powerful intellectual. The 'elimination rounds' for these sorts of jobs start years beforehand as people fall by the wayside through lack of aptitude or opportunity. The ones who are left for the 'final' feel devastated to miss out, especially if a 'bolter' gets up. I felt especially for Mick, whose stern, no-nonsense and forensic skill and indefatigable determination to get the best results for Australia's deployed troops did not endear him to some senior officials and ADF officers in Canberra. He and I spoke virtually every day of the operation. I was greatly comforted to have him looking over my shoulder, offering sage advice, and taking care of things in Canberra. He had a son serving in East Timor in a frontline position with the Special Forces, but at no stage would I have known that because of his focus on the job. Mick left the Army in the second half of 2000 after a most meritorious career. His talents and energy were a sore loss to the Commonwealth.

My 'ascension' to Chief of Army was pleasurable and memorable, occurring in a routine Army manner with a nice dinner. This occasion also marked the retirement of the outgoing Chief, a very well-liked, experienced and effective officer, Lieutenant General Frank Hickling. He and I shared the honours at the time as the two army officers with the most number of command appointments. On the personal side, this unexpected promotion and appointment meant another separation for Lynne and me. David, our youngest son, was in his final year of high school in Sydney at Waverley College. We had decided that he needed to have a parent on hand to support him for the remainder of the year. I got a little flat in Kingston in Canberra and commuted the short distance to and from Russell Offices — at least now I had running water, a hot shower and no pistol by my bedside! Lynne joined me quite often in Canberra and I would spend weekends in Sydney at every opportunity. Not ideal, but we figured we could handle it for six months.

As the Chief of Army, I was responsible for the conduct and good name of the whole Army. I was very conscious of this role and felt personally affronted by any acts of indiscipline or unfair, oppressive behaviour by any member of the Army towards anybody else. No 'ifs' or 'buts'. I insisted that all my subordinate commanders felt the same about anybody for whom they were responsible. In the third quarter of 2000, a major scandal erupted in the media and the Parliament over conduct of members of

3 RAR, one of the Army's most prestigious and, of recent times, one of the best combat units in East Timor. Aggrieved soldiers and their relatives made allegations that there was a climate of bullying and assault. The Commanding Officer, Nick Welch, had instituted some internal action against people involved, but the whole issue had erupted publicly in a welter of claims and counterclaims in the media.

The bullying and assault was confined to a particular clique of more junior soldiers and one or two others who condoned or turned a blind eye. However, individuals had made lurid claims concerning the extent of the problem within the unit. It made for nasty reading in the media. Members of Parliament took up the cause of several of the alleged victims. I was determined to find out exactly what happened, to fix the problem and to protect the reputations of all of those unfairly tarred with the same brush. It is a fact of life that some media representatives and politicians will seek persistently to imply that inappropriate behaviour and 'red neck' attitudes are institutionalised in and are part of the culture of the Defence Force. That is obviously not the case. Pockets of bad behaviour and prejudiced attitudes do exist in the Defence Force — as they do throughout society — but the evidence is plain in so many ways that the Defence Force is a tolerant, fair-minded and hugely empathetic organisation — ask the East Timorese.

Times have changed. The days are gone when a simple, low-level inquiry into bad personal conduct of a member or members of the Defence Force would be able to reach an early, absolute and unarguable conclusion that allows an issue to be resolved satisfactorily for all concerned — and closed. It is part of our newly litigious society that people will use every avenue of appeal and non-legal pressure, such as the media, and, where they can, the political process to make their case in order to achieve their objectives. In late 2000, individuals used these processes to elevate allegations of bullying within 3 RAR to the national level and they became the subject of parliamentary hearings.

My introduction to these investigative processes and this type of parliamentary forum occurred when members of the investigating committee invited me to appear in a closed session to answer questions. I brought briefing notes on actions that had been taken to investigate allegations, what we had concluded to date and what I was doing about it. I had nothing to hide. I was ready to discuss issues such as the possibility — which I would strongly refute — that such behaviour was entrenched and widespread. I expected to engage in intelligent discussions and deal with the facts.

My expectations were dashed when a parliamentarian asked me, 'General, who is paratrooper 6798434?' (This is not the real number because I didn't memorise what he said). I was well briefed, but I had neither memorised the six or seven digit Army numbers of every soldier in the Army nor the scores of soldiers that might have been involved in the matters before us. This melodramatic start preceded a series of widely drawn allegations and statements that were made in a questioning tone, but basically presented as facts and truths of a particular soldier's grievances. Another parliamentarian in a sort of 'tag team' manoeuvre took up the cudgels and made a wide and swingeing attack on the culture of the ADF. Echoing my code with Sergio Vieira de Mello, I was 'very disappointed'.

While I realised that it was my duty to be responsive, accurate and courteous to members of this committee, as I would be with any other organs of the Parliament, I delivered a sharp, concise reply, rejecting emphatically what this politician had said. He backed off with some conciliatory remarks. I stood up for my people on this first occasion and every occasion thereafter when they were being unfairly attacked for whatever reasons. This was an early glimpse of the rough-and-tumble of the political process. Later, someone in the room leaked to the media that some of the politicians in this closed — and supposedly confidential — session were disappointed with my performance. I took this as a compliment, given their behaviour over serious issues requiring mature attention and discussion.

This memory brings to mind the number of times over recent years that the cry has gone up that the military have become 'politicised'. Typically, the claim is that the ADF is acting in a way that is partial to a particular side of politics. I've got a view on this old chestnut, as a fellow at or near the top of the military tree for a number of years, especially in light of the fact that this salacious charge was thrown my way once or twice. For a start, the military must be absolutely obedient and attentive to the government of the day and its policies in all respects. If the government's directions to the military are legal, they must be obeyed without question. If a person in uniform objects on moral or ethical grounds, he or she should resign rather than disobey or subvert the orders they have received. Shrewd governments always canvass their important directions to the military before they are finalised to ensure that they are legal, workable and the best way of getting the job done. The higher up the tree I have climbed, the more I have become involved in high-level government consideration of defence matters and policy development.

Everything the ADF does is derived from government direction. At one end of the spectrum, private soldiers in the Solomon Islands are doing as they're told, obeying military orders derived from government direction. At the other end, the CDF and the Service Chiefs become involved in the formative stages of government policy — the framework of 'direction' to the ADF. They are privy to a wealth of considerations and options, many of them with political ramifications that lead to final policy decisions. The key issue is that they are privy to, but not active players in, the political dimensions of options. Every senior public servant in the Commonwealth works in a similar environment.

After the government of the day announces its policies and directions, the ADF, like all instruments of government, is obligated to help those policies and directions to succeed. It is also the duty of the CDF and the Service Chiefs to alert governments to problems along the way and recommend changes. Governments should expect both loyalty and fearless expert advice. It has ever been thus. So, the charge of politicisation should never rest on the proper exercise of these responsibilities.

What is improper is when anyone in the military acts within or beyond his or her duties for reasons of political benefit to themselves or anyone else. Paradoxically, and something which frequently escapes commentators, officers properly executing government policy are sometimes branded as 'politicised' whereas people who leak information about the execution of policies they don't like are actually the politicised ones — acting contrary to their loyal obligations for political reasons. Some journalists and politicians not in government won't see it this way. Journalists never change because they rely on these folks for stories. Members of Her Majesty's Opposition often have a Paulian moment when government comes their way!

The 3 RAR scandals took a while to resolve because it took time for several investigations, enquiries and some disciplinary trials to ramp up and run their courses, sometimes concurrently. In one of the sadder twists of the whole affair, Nick Welch became a casualty of the process. He had performed brilliantly in command in East Timor and had been decorated as a result. Furthermore, he had been making genuine efforts to weed out the few 'bad eggs' in his battalion. He had sent one non-commissioned officer for court-martial. However, it was alleged that he overstepped the mark in a brief, casual conversation with a brother officer, when he learnt that the officer would preside at the court martial. He remarked briefly, but unfavourably, on the defendant.

When this conversation emerged almost as a sidebar issue during investigation of the whole matter of problems in 3 RAR, Lieutenant Colonel Welch was charged with perverting the course of justice and tried before a Defence Force Magistrate. He was found guilty and received a harsh penalty. In light of this turn of events, he resigned from the life he loved and the professional family who held him in the highest regard, saddened and disillusioned. The ADF lost a brilliant officer destined for great things. I found it most ironic several years later when the view doing the rounds was that the military justice system was biased towards looking after senior ranks at the expense of a 'fair go' for junior ranks. Armed with short and selective memories, and another opportunity for 'a kick and a punch' at the military, these commentators overlooked this powerful example of an impartial and remorseless military judicial system.

*

For the Cosgrove family, 2000 had been another hectic and exciting year after my brief occupancy in a new job in Sydney, a government promotion and a move to Canberra. By December we looked forward to a quiet Christmas in Canberra, having finally consolidated the family, bringing us all together again in a married quarter in Duntroon after David completed his Year 12 exams. On one of those relaxing days in December, Lynne and I were sitting in our kitchen with the kids scattered around the house, when my old Army mate Bruce Osborn dropped in. Bruce was there to pick up an 'angel'. Bruce and his wife, Jan, were wonderful friends and we were godparents to each other's kids. My goddaughter, Cate Osborn, had lent me a little metal 'angel' stick pin, insisting that I wear it during my time in East Timor to keep me safe. Never one to tempt fate, I had complied and she had scrutinised my TV news appearances to see if she could spot it. Now it was needed for another traveller who was going to distant and dangerous places. The time had come to return the charm and keep someone else safe.

Early in our conversation with Bruce, the phone rang and I wandered out of the kitchen to answer it. It was a woman from the National Australia Day Council. She told me that the Council would be naming me as the Australian of the Year for 2001 on 26 January. I was overwhelmed but quickly pointed out that, as the Chief of Army, I had ongoing responsibilities and that I would from time to time be dealing with and become embroiled in controversies, as the ongoing 3 RAR saga was demonstrating. She told me that the Council had taken all that into account. Members were clear in their decision. I subsided into silence. She finished with her personal congratulations and remarked that the Prime Minister planned to call within the hour to pass on his congratulations. It was a somewhat befuddled general officer who rejoined Lynne and Bruce in the kitchen. Even though Bruce was a great friend, I thought it best that Lynne should be the first to know.

I waited until Bruce left and then started to think of some droll way of telling Lynne and then the boys. I should have got on with it because suddenly the phone rang. I realised, with the peptic shock that comes to the pit of the stomach when something important has been overlooked, that it was a fair bet that the caller was the PM. I dashed to the phone but Stephen beat me there. I stood there horrified at the thought that the PM would say, 'Hello, this is John Howard', at which point Stephen, with his quick eye for humour — his own and others — would burst into peels of irreverent laughter and say something like, 'Pull the other one, who is this really?' Fortunately, he answered the phone politely, listened momentarily and then said, 'Hold on Prime Minister. Dad, it's the Prime Minister for you.'

Most women, especially wives, have bat-like hearing. Lynne was in a distant corner of the house when these brief words passed between father and son. Instantly, like a wraith or a spirit, she materialised in front of me with that hypnotic look of inquisition that husbands find so difficult to withstand. As I accepted the Prime Minister's congratulations, she was mouthing, 'Wish them Merry Christmas from all of us.' I finished the phone call by thanking the Prime Minister again. Then, Lynne delivered a 'rocket' to the unannounced Australian of the Year for not passing on her recommended Christmas greeting. When I asked, 'Why was the absence of a Christmas greeting such a big deal?' she said, 'Well isn't that why he rang?' I explained the real purpose of his phone call. After a quiet, brief moment to absorb this news, much excitement erupted in the Cosgrove household.

Now all of us had to keep the secret until the eve of Australia Day! We did pretty well, but as is the way of these things, I started to get some 'knowing' glances as the day drew closer. In January 2001, the PM inaugurated a practice — that he has continued — of giving a major address to the Press Club on the day before Australia Day. The CDF, Admiral Chris Barrie, and I attended the address, along with many other senior officials and officers. As we left, Paul Bongiorno, a Channel 10 political reporter, buttonholed me at the entrance, producing a microphone from behind his back like a rabbit out of a hat and, with his camera team poised, popped the question of whether I was about to be announced as Australian of the Year. I'd tried hard in my dealing with the media to refrain from the hackneyed 'No comment', so, with no real other alternative, I just gave him a gormless look and kept walking.

By the afternoon, media interest in coming announcements became a little shark-like. A large number of people from all walks of life in Canberra and elsewhere had crowded into the public foyer of Parliament House outside of the Great Hall where announcements would be made about who would be Australian of the Year, Senior Australian, Young Australian and Australian Community of the Year. The presence of our boys accompanying Lynne and me on what was just another official occasion would give 'the game' away prematurely. Anticipating this, I had asked Stephen, Philip and David to stand a little separate from Lynne and me in the foyer where drinks were being served. I even directed them to sit in a separate section in the Great Hall (on reflection, this just shows a military man's obsession with keeping secrets!). The boys took their father's 'hush-hush' instructions in good spirit and even embellished it to a humorous degree. At one stage in the foyer, Lynne and I, who had been keeping our eyes out for them, eventually spotted them all when an arm belonging to one of them curled out from behind a pillar where they had concealed themselves and reached out, without revealing its owner, to pluck a beer off the tray carried by a passing waiter!

After the announcement, our lives were propelled again with a lurch into the celebrity fast lane, 2001 quickly becoming a frenetic balancing act between the wonderful opportunities and obligations of an Australian of the Year and the ongoing and increasing demands of commanding the Army in a time of considerable challenges to our national security. There was a palpable air of excitement in the Army in that year. Land forces had performed magnificently in East Timor and were continuing to do so. The 2000 Defence White Paper had provided very handsomely for all three services, although cost estimations arrived at by its authors turned out to be under the mark in many cases. However, the document encouraged the Army to commence a process of modernisation and development.

All of this was occurring in the Army's centenary year. We decided to celebrate officially on the first of March with a big ceremony in Canberra. The centenary celebrations provided important insights into the modern culture, heritage and continuing respect for traditions of the Australian Army. In a parade in the morning, the guidons, colours and banners of the whole Army were paraded by representatives of the unit or Corps from which they came. These 'flags' have great significance in the Army because all soldiers are imbued with the notion that all the unit's history, forebears, tradition and honour are represented in their piece of embroidered cloth attached to a wooden staff. To see them all together in a forest of colour gently stirring in the breeze was symbolic of the entire Army of today as well as that legion of ageing warriors and ghosts of soldiers past being present together on the great avenue leading to the War Memorial in Canberra.

That evening the Army put on a huge dinner in the Convention Centre in Canberra for about 1600 people. The Deputy Chief of Army, Major General Peter Leahy, was the fellow I'd put in charge of both the parade in the morning and the dinner that night. Peter had wanted to squeeze in 1901 diners (representing the first year of the Australian Army) but the venue simply wouldn't allow it. We had some of our venerated veterans, a wide range of officers and soldiers from the Army at large, officer cadets from both the Australian Defence Force Academy and Duntroon and, of course, a couple of non-military official guests, the principal among them the Prime Minister. It was run as far as was practical as a formal dinner with everybody in their military finery, with a band thrashing away and appropriate occasional speeches.

After everybody else had assembled at their tables, I had arranged for our most eminent and distinguished notables to enter the vast room last of all in particular groupings. The first of these groups was the general officers of the Army. They received a rousing and gratifying cheer from the exuberant crowd. Next group in were the two doyens of the Army, Lieutenant General Sir

Thomas Daly and General Sir Francis Hassett — our two most distinguished previous chiefs — who walked in and sat among many of their younger successors. The crowd roared for these wonderful warrior chiefs as they made their dignified way to their seats. Next came the Army's and Australia's three surviving Victoria Cross winners at that time, Sir Roden Cutler, Ted Kenna and Keith Payne. The noise, the cheering and the applause was stupendous. I hoped that this response underscored to these remarkable Australians that the Army cherished them dearly. Lastly, I brought in the Prime Minister, our guest of honour, to help the nation's Army to celebrate. Again, he received mighty and prolonged applause and cheering. I don't think that before this spontaneous outpouring that John Howard knew how popular he had become within the Defence Force — not because it was his government who sent us on operations and had recently promised us money to modernise, but because he so obviously liked and cared for — and worried about — the nation's men and women in uniform.

Wherever I went in 2001 as Chief of Army I sought to include 'Australian of the Year' activities. From time to time I made visits and attended functions and activities only in that capacity. In that way I was able to travel and visit extensively with community groups all over Australia. I lost count of the number of speeches I gave, but it would have been in the hundreds. When I became Aussie of the Year, media representatives bailed me up with the question, 'What will be your theme for your year in this role?' Some of my predecessors had chosen themes that were in the front of public consciousness and political debate at that time. I could not do this, even if I had wanted to, because of my military appointment. What I really wanted to do, however, was to be a ceaseless, enthusiastic and upbeat promoter of the talents and energy of Australian youth. My whole lifetime in the military had been spent in harnessing these qualities. I thought it was more than justifiable for somebody in my position to use the pulpit that I had been granted to persuade people of my generation of the wonderful qualities of youth and of their desires and worthiness for greater recognition and responsibility. As a consequence, I visited many schools and youth-oriented activities, one example being a Youth Leadership Forum for kids from many different schools. These were always fun and, whether or not the youngsters enjoyed my visit, I always did. Lynne accompanied me on a number of these visits, and she enjoyed them just as much as I did.

Over the years a number of people have asked me what was the highlight of my time as Australian of the Year. It's a tough question to answer because there were many. If I had to choose just one, it would be a visit I made to the School of the Air in Alice Springs. This is one of the most unusual forms of schooling that you will ever find. The pupils 'attend' over the radio, a scratchy high-frequency link connecting them from some remote place, a tiny settlement or a property hundreds of kilometres away from Alice Springs, to the school that is a cross between an ordinary primary school and a radio studio. Each kid has a curriculum, textbooks, a personal programme and a schedule of classes to be conducted over the radio link with their teachers who work in Alice Springs. All this was explained to me during the first part of my visit to the 'school room' and then I was brought to the main radio studio and sat with the principal at the microphone. Arrayed along a bench near us were the class teachers. This was going to be a radio version of an assembly by the whole school — dozens of kids on the radio simultaneously.

The real thrill and the realisation of what this School of the Air symbolises came to me a moment later when the principal kicked off proceedings by making a short speech saying who I was and why I was there and invited the kids to chime in with any questions. As he flicked the switch to receive, the airwaves erupted with a cacophony of youthful voices calling out for their question to be answered. I glanced over at the teachers sitting forward on the long bench. The looks of affection and delight on their faces spoke volumes as they identified their particular kids to the principal by the sound of their voices. I was profoundly impressed by this example of how mums and dads, teachers and kids were not prepared to allow the tyranny of distance to prevent them from getting an educational grounding. A little later the same day, I asked a large group of senior high school kids in Alice Springs how many of them were planning to go to university after they had finished high school — a large number of hands went in the air. Of that group, I asked how many had been pupils of the School of the Air. About half the hands stayed up. What a great message!

The last four months of 2001 was one of the most dramatic periods in Australia's recent history. In the second week of September, I was in Kuala Lumpur attending a conference of the Chiefs of Army of the Pacific region, co-chaired in 2001 by the

Chief of the Malaysian Army and the Chief of Staff of the United States Army, General Rick Shinseki. On the night of 12 September (the morning of the 11th on the east coast of the United States) the Chiefs and their wives were attending a reception hosted by the Malaysian Defence Minister in a Kuala Lumpur hotel. About 40 minutes into the reception, a rumour started to fly around the room that there had been an incident in New York in which a large jet had flown into a skyscraper (as we found out later, by this time both World Trade Center buildings had been hit). My instincts told me this was no accident so I grabbed Lynne and my ADC and said we would be leaving immediately to go back to our hotel and find out what was going on. On the way out, I encountered Rick Shinseki in the foyer outside the reception area. He looked shocked and grim. He told me that he had received word that the World Trade Center buildings had been struck by two large commercial jets. It was obvious to both of us that this was a terrorist attack. Just as he was telling me this, an aide handed him a piece of paper and when he read it, his grim face turned even paler. He told me, 'A large aircraft has just hit the Pentagon.'

Malaysian security stepped up amazingly. When Lynne and I had travelled to the reception, we came at a relaxed pace in a car that was one of a small convoy escorted by one police car out the front politely gaining the convoy priority in the traffic. Immediately after the terrible news, our hosts swiftly appreciated the gravity of what had transpired in the United States. When we made our unplanned departure from the reception, we jumped in the same car but this time we had our own police car with flashing lights and siren, and a couple of Special Branch plain clothes police on a motorbike with the pillion passenger brandishing a submachine gun to ensure nobody came close. Back in the hotel, like many thousands of other Australians, we were glued to the television for the rest of the night trying to work out what had happened, how it had happened and discussing what it meant for the future.

Dawn seemed to come very quickly. I had already resolved to return to Australia on the next available flight and had given those instructions to my ADC. I thought I should attend the breakfast session with the other Chiefs to mention what I intended to do and to find out any new information. The mood at breakfast was solemn to say the least. Rick Shinseki wasn't there when I arrived. However, there was a very touching moment when he finally joined us. Without premeditation or coordination, as he walked in, every Chief rose and applauded as a way of demonstrating our sympathy in the only collective way we knew how.

Back in Australia, I knew that my instinct had been right. While all of us were still absorbing the impact of this terrible act of globalised terrorism, the government was beginning to assess wider security implications and debating options for Australia. My job was to be available to participate in these discussions. One thing was for sure: many traditional theories of security structures and balances had just flown out the window. Soon we would join the West's first major response to these dreadful attacks.

In that momentous year of 2001, the great cycle of our democracy brought the nation once more to the point of a federal election. In the minds of the electorate, one catastrophic and unexpected occurrence, the attacks in the United States and one 'sleeper' issue — illegal immigration — would prove to be very influential. While terrible events, such as what became dubbed '9/11', tended to work in favour of the incumbent party at the ballot box, the question of illegal immigration was rather more vexed and complex. In the end, the voters clearly endorsed the government's policies on illegal immigration, reversed earlier opinion polls and disregarded the views of many pundits by returning John Howard's government with a solid majority.

During the election campaign, the ADF became embroiled in a controversy concerning what became known by the evocative title as the 'children overboard' scandal. By way of background, in 2001 the Defence Force was playing a strong law enforcement role in preventing illegal immigration via boats, sailing mostly from Indonesia to northern Australia. After Motor Vessel *Tampa* embarked a large number of destitute people off a foundering fishing boat in international waters north of Australia, the ship's master decided to land these people on Australian territory. This would have facilitated illegal immigration. The government directed the ADF to intervene. Members of the Special Air Service Regiment and some navy vessels collaborated to stop them from being landed and transported them, by agreement, to another country for processing. This created a furore amongst a very vocal lobby in Australia who felt Australia's policies in relation to illegal immigration were too harsh.

Around this time there was a flurry of vessels carrying people intent on illegal immigration. In one case, a navy frigate apprehended a vessel that was in bad shape. (Eventually it sank, leaving its occupants in the water, buoyed by life jackets given to them by the crew of the frigate.) An initial incorrect report arrived in Canberra suggesting that adults on the vessel had been holding children out over the side above the water to coerce the ship into taking everybody aboard and, presumably, then on to Australia. Pretty quickly after that initial report, it was obvious at lower levels of the chain of command that this particular act had not taken place. An ongoing problem was that the Minister for Defence was incorrectly using subsequent photographs of the vessel foundering and some of its passengers floating in the water in the media to substantiate the first proposition — that adult illegal immigrants had threatened their children's safety as a ploy to secure passage to Australia.

During the election campaign, the initial erroneous report was never publicly corrected, although the photograph conflation was corrected when the acting CDF, Air Marshal Angus Houston, told the Minister directly that there was no relationship between the photographs he was showing to the media and any issue to do with children being held overboard. After the election, a parliamentary inquiry took the majority view that this wrong and conflated information should have been corrected much earlier.

From where I sat as Chief of Army the whole issue came down to two questions. First, did the Navy act in any way other than with the most professional standards in their dealings with the vessel and its passengers? The answer is very emphatically that the Navy behaved and performed most professionally. The only possible criticism would be the initial reporting of the actions of some of those on the suspected illegal immigrant vessel. My next point is based on several decades of operational experience — the type of background not shared by members of Australia's commentariat. If commanders expect impeccable and factual initial reporting from people on the frontline of operations, they should not ask for impressions or facts. They should just get them to recite the dictionary. The golden rule is that early reporting always needs subsequent follow-up for confirmation.

The second issue of course is the way the information is passed up and down the chain of command and is treated at higher levels. I won't comment on what happened at the political level, but clearly it wasn't the ADF's finest hour at more senior levels. It is a fundamental principle for commanders to establish and pass on the truth. Early versions of operational information must never be treated as the 'be all and end all'. There were apparently enough doubts flying around about the initial report to trigger careful checking. Once careful checking reveals error or even that reasonable doubt exists, commanders must pass on this information to their boss. Angus Houston immediately spoke to the Minister as acting CDF after he was told by a subordinate that the Minister was continuing to refer wrongly to the photographs as showing the 'children overboard' situation. He was absolutely right to do so. I had been acting CDF the day beforehand. I would have done the same if the subordinate had brought the same assessment to me.

Well after the incidents, the election and the subsequent inquiry, Admiral Chris Barrie stated during a Senate Estimates hearing in 2002 that he had no reason to doubt the initial report that children had been held out as if to be thrown overboard from the vessel. A while later, he made a further statement saying that having spoken to the ship's captain, he now accepted that the original advice passed on to the Minister — that children had been threatened with being thrown overboard — was wrong. Chris was scarified for this in the media. It was a heavy blow to his standing and the reputation of the ADF.

Although there was great uproar concerning the 'children overboard' issue and the illegal immigration policy in general, I was more seized by the government's deliberations about our immediate contribution to the war on terror after 9/11. It was known that Bin Laden and Al Qaeda, the perpetrators of the attack, had very significant sanctuary and other support from the Taliban regime in Afghanistan. The United States went straight for the throat of this bellicose gang in a campaign that combined very sophisticated Western military technology and the skills, toughness and local knowledge of Afghan groups opposed to the Taliban. The Australian Government was willing to help. Our contribution was a significant number of our Special Air Service Regiment troops to operate in conjunction with the United States ground forces and other allies in Afghanistan. A little later on, Australia also provided Boeing 707 Air to Air Refueller aircraft working out of Kyrgyzstan to support air combat operations over Afghanistan.

My responsibility was to provide advice concerning what Army elements might be used. Our Special Forces were by far the best option — excellently trained and equipped and ready to go at short notice. Next, it was my job to ensure that their particular orientation, training and equipment for service in a wild and woolly place like Afghanistan was as good as it could be, given the urgent nature of their deployment. Finally, I would need to work with Admiral Barrie and his logistic commanders to ensure that Army-specific logistic support was delivered to the troops in the field when and where they needed it.

As our Special Forces got ready to go, I reflected on the serendipity of their training and development over the last year or so. The men who make up the Special Air Service Regiment are the very best soldiers, and sometimes sailors and airmen, in the whole of our Defence Force. The base level of skills in the regiment is incredibly high and diverse. In relation to their general-purpose equipment, no recent government has ever stinted in meeting their needs. The one thing any group would need before being sent to the extremely harsh environment of Afghanistan against very tough and skilful adversaries was experience. Like many other parts of the Defence Force, the Special Air Service Regiment had been endlessly training in traditional and new skills for decades since its last operational employment in the jungles of South Vietnam. After Vietnam, from time to time individuals might chance upon some operational experience while serving on exchange with an ally. However, this random sprinkling of experience would not have been good enough to prepare a large number of even elite troops for the demands of the operating environment and the shock of combat. In this respect, the invaluable experience was their service in East Timor. Fortuitously, a large part of the regiment received effective operational exposure in a harsh environment — possibly not as harsh as Afghanistan — with a potential adversary around every bush. In addition, I had a pretty shrewd idea that our fellows would measure up very well relative to other highly professional Special Forces alongside whom they were likely to serve. So off they went with the best preparations and equipment we could muster for them.

Deploying in late 2001, our Special Forces spent about a year in Afghanistan. They were involved in everything from long-range patrolling, liaison with tribal Afghans, participating in pitched battles and conducting intelligence-driven raids to capture operationally important materiel. During their time in Afghanistan, Sergeant Andrew Russell, one of the regiment's finest, was killed when the vehicle in which he was travelling hit a mine. Another young trooper in a separate mine incident received severe leg injuries. Again, given the number of times our fellows were in the firing line, it was amazing that more of them were not killed or wounded. As they probably got sick of hearing me say, it doesn't matter how good you are or how ill-trained and ill-equipped your enemy is — and many Afghans were neither — if he aims at you properly, you're in trouble.

I knew our boys were brave but I also wanted them to be eternally cautious. I visited them twice during that year, once to their base in Kandahar, and a few months later in 2002 at their new base in Bagram. In each case, I saw only those who were back in base because there were always a number out on long-range patrols. On each visit I was mightily impressed by their cheerful demeanour and the admiration in which they were held, as frequently expressed by their coalition colleagues. After each visit though, I did reflect that I could have taken a barber with me!

On my first visit to Afghanistan, because of the real danger of surface-to-air missile fire from Taliban remnants near the airfield at Kandahar, the drill was that aircraft, wherever possible, would fly in and out under cover of darkness. In order to achieve this timing, an Air Force Falcon jet flew my small party and me into Jacobabad, a US Air Force Base in western Pakistan. I was accompanied by that great Special Forces commander, (then) Brigadier Duncan Lewis. After arrival we transferred to a US C130 aircraft and commenced a high-altitude run of several hours into Afghanistan, spiralling down just after dark like a swooping hawk into the military airbase at Kandahar. At the end of my visit to the SAS, we reversed the process and started a long and somewhat boring flight back to Jacobabad. As the senior officer on the aircraft, I was invited to sit on the bench seat at the rear of the flight deck. The rest of my group sat in the cargo compartment. With nothing better to do, they were probably all asleep at the end of a long day.

The aircraft was from the Alabama Air National Guard. Based on hearing the accents of the flight deck crew through my headphones, I had no reason to doubt they were too. After we had re-entered Pakistani airspace and were no more than 10 minutes out from Jacobabad, we had an emergency. One engine erupted in flames and the crew shut it down immediately. Over the radio, I heard the pilot reject the indirect approach flight path to the airfield that he had just been offered and demand a straight-in approach. A moment or two later, one of the flight deck crew yelled out that there were significant (and very bad!) instrument readings on the other three engines. The flight engineer, who sits between and behind the two pilots, monitors some of their instruments and a whole bank of his own located just in front of and above his head. His hands seemed to move in a continuous blur over the panel. There was constant chatter on the intercom. The pilot silenced this banter by broadcasting a 'Pan' message — one level down from a 'May Day'. I could hear all this through my headset. There didn't seem to be anything useful for me to contribute over my microphone so I sat there trying to be the epitome of a laconic and cool Aussie officer.

Oddly, it did occur to me to go into the cargo compartment and tell my staff, but I figured that the crew operating in the cargo compartment would do that and probably would not want an amateur like me stumbling around during a mid-flight emergency. As you have no doubt deduced by the fact that I am now writing about it, we did not crash. The three remaining engines droned on and carried us safely back to earth. The pilots made an immaculate landing with the only unusual feature being the armada of fire engines and crash vehicles following us down the runway to where we took the first available turn off. As soon as the pilots had done this, they switched everything off and in the sudden deathly silence in the cockpit, the aircraft captain in a broad southern drawl announced, 'Gentlemen, welcome to Jacobabad, where the local time is 1.15 a.m. You may now remove your seat cushions from up your ass.' All I could think of to say to the pilots and crew on the flight deck was, 'You fellows sure know how to give an Aussie a good time!'

When I joined my colleagues in the cargo compartment, I was much annoyed to find that they had all of them (including Lewis) slept through the whole thing although one bloke had noticed the crew dashing around removing the internal Kevlar armour from the emergency exits. He thought they were just super-efficient getting ready for our routine landing. Sometimes sitting up the front with headphones on in a comfortable seat has its drawbacks!

16

Bali Bombings

ADMIRAL CHRIS BARRIE HAD become CDF in 1998. Usually a three-year term, the government extended his tenure for an additional year in 2001 and he was now coming to the end of his appointment period in mid-2002. There was the usual speculation about who would get the top job. While I was favourite, quite rightly Angus Houston, the Chief of Air Force, came into the mix as another very strong contender. Cynical sections of the media suggested that he was an outstanding candidate but had blotted his copybook by telling the truth over the photographs related to the 'children overboard' scandal. I thought that view was rubbish. Based on my conversations with government figures, he was held in high regard. And that should have been so. The pundits had to wait three years to be proven wrong about their assessment that telling the truth could disqualify a person from high public office in Australia. They were strangely silent then.

When I was selected as the new CDF, I thought the government was most likely taking into account my extensive experience as a commander on operations — of large forces, of a coalition, of joint Army/Navy/Air forces — in complex environments under strong international and domestic political pressures. Also, the CDF job was to be my twelfth in command. Possibly the government thought that this experience gave me some advantages in leading a large 'people-centric' organisation that was doing difficult things. I may be wrong in those self-serving assumptions, but I was thrilled to get the job! Once again, I reflected on how my good luck had propelled me to an unexpected senior appointment. It would have been the height of arrogance and self-delusion to have coveted this honour only three years before.

As usual, the media quoted anonymous sources, murmuring concerns that I was 'no intellectual' and would be out of my depth formulating high level Defence policy. In my view, when a person observes that someone else is, quote 'no intellectual' unquote, they are also making the unspoken further remark 'not like me'. It would be whimsical to ponder how things would play out if the journo's code allowed him or her to provide readers with the identities of the sources of this implied comparison. Only then could a fair assessment be made. I wonder how many qualified and experienced intellectuals would appear among the ranks of those who hide behind anonymity to opine that someone else is 'no intellectual'.

I came from a breed of commanders who tended neither to seek nor to be sought after for extended postings in esoteric and high-profile positions in Canberra. I dare say that some anonymous 'sources' felt I should remain solidly in their ranks.

More seriously, I felt I was smart enough to serve the nation as CDF. While policy formulation is most important, it was not as vital as the day-to-day command of the ADF, especially judgements about the use of the ADF on operations and Australian military force projection. Besides, I had plenty of 'policy wonks' around me in Russell Offices and at the Defence Headquarters in Canberra.

The position of CDF is not about a one-man band anyway. I was delighted to lead a strong team of very capable and professional senior officers. In my own service, Peter Leahy had taken over from me having previously been the Deputy Chief for a little over two years. He was seasoned in the ways of Canberra and, in all respects, ready to command the Army. In 2001 he had dealt with some quite significant issues, showing the government that he had plenty of mettle. Chris Ritchie took over the Navy — another excellent choice. Chris was tough, experienced and had a razor-sharp mind and a real strategic grasp. He helped me enormously by always having the ability to seize the heart of an issue and to spot the weakness in a course of action. Russ Shalders was promoted to vice admiral and took over as Vice Chief of the Defence Force. To some degree there was a sense of complementarity in his and my appointments. I would plead guilty to the charge of being outgoing and assertive. Russ is very professional, calm and measured — less demonstrative than me, but most effective in this senior appointment. While the Vice Chief has a range of ordinary duties, his principal task is to assume command of the ADF if the CDF is unavailable, for example, due to absence on travel or ill health. I had plans to revamp ADF higher command and control processes. Russ would feature strongly in this reform, so I was delighted to have a man of his worth as my deputy.

Last among the services' line up was the inestimable Angus Houston, who remained as Chief of Air Force. He was doing wonderfully well in command of his service. I had enjoyed his friendship and fellowship over many years, particularly in the last year since he'd taken over as Air Force chief. I knew I could rely on his total support and great talents to help me during my time as CDF. Angus is a class act as a man and as a professional. On the departmental side, I had got on very well with the Secretary, Dr Alan Hawke, ever since I started to work with him several years before. I knew instinctively that for Australia's defence effort to prosper, the Secretary and CDF must understand, respect and collaborate very closely with each other. Further, I wanted the relationship to be that of close friends. The extraordinary individuals who get to such senior rank in the Australian public service are — by any definition — great Australians. Friendship with them is not a task or a goal, but a privilege.

Relationships between military and civilian personnel in Defence have not always been as harmonious as I found them in 2002. The two groups had not worked hard to understand and collaborate with each other in the past. Legend within Defence is rich with tales of scheming, plotting, snubbing, blazing rows and mighty schisms: almost as if being the department responsible for combat needed to be practised and mastered internally as well as against the Commonwealth's enemies! Some retired bureaucrats thought that the military of today had way too much standing and influence with the government. Some were even worried that the

Secretary and the CDF might be too close professionally and not sufficiently adversarial.

I encountered one of these dear old boys at a reception for a retiring official from the intelligence community at Parliament House in Canberra. I recognised him and greeted him politely, introducing myself by name. Looking me over, he said, 'And what do you do?' I thought this was a bit rich. I would cop it from Mr Whitlam because, after all, he is 'Gough', but this fellow, a well-connected former bureaucrat, was simply being rude. I politely explained that I was the Chief of the Defence Force. He looked arch and observed, 'How are all of those Chiefs of yours, still in open rebellion?' I guess, from his point of view, this must have been the 'happy' state of affairs in his day when people of his ilk revelled in the unhealthy competition between the services for resources and primacy. Still remaining courteous, I explained that the service Chiefs were a very professional and collegiate group. I then drew his attention to one small point that he may not have comprehended during his career — not, after all, being a military man. I offered that I was a four-star general and they were three-star equivalents in their services. As a consequence, they did as I told them. I left him musing on that.

I took over from Chris Barrie on 4 July 2002. At the time, the ADF was projecting force nationally, regionally and internationally in quite different ways. In our territorial waters ADF maritime, land and air force elements were conducting law enforcement operations in order to seal Australian borders from illegal entry. Regionally, we were still conducting peace support operations in East Timor, maintaining a secure environment along the East/West Timor border. Internationally, we were participating in allied combat operations in Afghanistan. The ADF was busy and about to become much busier.

I have always opposed maintaining troops far from home out of habit or inattention. Our forces in Afghanistan were reaching the point where they were more of a 'presence' than units performing vital tasks on a day-to-day basis. By now, allied military pressure had scattered the Taliban to the four winds and forced Al Qaeda groups into deep hiding. In late 2002, the low operational tempo did not appear to justify the presence of our highly trained SAS soldiers. I was keen that they should return home, and they did so in November 2002, closing a most exciting and illustrious period in the history of this world-famous regiment. It was fortunate that circumstances allowed us to repatriate and regroup the SAS. We had new plans for them.

In Iraq, the Saddam Hussein regime continued to rule the roost, seemingly unweakened by the first Gulf War in the early 1990s or by the impact of UN sanctions. Allied aircraft had been conducting what had become known as 'no fly zone' operations for several years. They also did not appear to have had much impact, despite occasional retaliatory and punitive air strikes against Iraqi air defences. The vexed issue of weapons inspection was prominent within broad international attention being paid to Iraq. During his time in power, Saddam had used chemical weapons — now categorised as one of the so-called 'weapons of mass destruction' or WMD — not only in the long and bloody war with Iran but also more infamously against minority groups living in Iraq. These atrocities, allegedly executed on his order, marked him as a mass murderer and a wholly unscrupulous despot.

Over the years, weapons inspection teams had attempted to establish whether he had retained or had further developed and produced WMD as part of his military arsenal since his defeat in the Gulf War. Inspectors complained constantly of being thwarted. Consequently, they could never declare one way or the other on whether he had a WMD capability. So, with this international agency stymied, intelligence organisations around the world had the job of ascertaining whether the tyrant retained these lethal instruments.

Following the atrocious attacks of 9/11, many national intelligence agencies focussed intently on warnings and indicators that their people might be terrorist targets. Up until now, home-grown terrorist groups in the South-East Asian region had tended to direct their operations against their own governments or communities. The attacks in the United States acted as a rallying cry for these groups, who sought to emulate their murderous success. Jemiah Islamiah (JI), a South-East Asian organisation that had warped Islamic theology to justify killing innocent people, had registered on the intelligence 'radar screen'. However, there was no expectation that JI intended to expand its evil intent.

I have always been a 'news junkie' and my job required many late-night work sessions that occasionally extended into early morning. In the early hours of Sunday, 13 October 2002 — late Saturday night in Bali — I heard radio reports of bombs exploding in Bali's tourist area of Kuta Beach and near the American Consulate in the provincial capital, Denpasar. The reports were hazy about casualties but early estimates were that they would be considerable. My instinct told me that this could be pretty serious for Australia. Like many Aussies, Lynne, the boys and I had enjoyed holidays in Bali. I knew that the clubs and discos would have been packed with tourists, many of them Australians. I rang the duty officer at our command centre in Canberra. He sounded surprised to be hearing from the CDF at that hour of the morning. Surprise became a snap into action when I told him that, as a matter of prudence, I wanted him to get some of our planning staff moving into work straight away and to alert duty officers in some of our subordinate headquarters to do the same.

As night crept towards daylight, it became obvious that several terrorist bomb explosions had killed or injured many Australians, other international tourists and locals. This was Australia's first major terrorist bombing attack, though it occurred in Indonesian territory. The number of casualties quickly swamped local medical facilities that had been designed for a major traffic accident at the worst. I knew that Indonesian capabilities to provide sophisticated medical care, either in Bali or elsewhere in the archipelago were quite limited. Plainly, Australia needed to establish an air bridge into Bali, and to put doctors and nurses and their essential equipment on the ground as soon as possible.

In such cases, as we always do, the ADF turns to its medical units to get ready quickly and for the RAAF to deploy them as rapidly as possible. Being a Sunday, I thought that the longest delay would be notifying, recalling and assembling our aircrew and medical staff. I should not have worried. They flooded into work without needing to be recalled. They heard the terrible news in the media and shrewdly assessed that there would be a job for them. We quickly had C130 Hercules aircraft in the air heading north-west from bases on the east coast. At one stage, a worried staff officer advised me that we shouldn't dispatch aircraft immediately after they were loaded and ready because we didn't yet have diplomatic clearance for them to enter Indonesian airspace. I overruled him, telling him to 'Get on with it'. I was confident that, under the circumstances, even such an important requirement could be viewed as a nicety.

The very badly injured and traumatised Australians in Bali were hugely relieved when they heard our aircraft overhead and saw Australian men and women in uniform arriving to help them. The ADF joined many different agencies that were there to help in the tragic aftermath of the attacks. Ric Smith, the Ambassador to Indonesia and his consular officials in Bali, worked tirelessly with the Indonesian Government, the injured and the parents and loved ones of those killed and injured. They also coordinated the efforts of the hundreds of holidaying Australians who suddenly became a workforce to help their compatriots and others affected by the bombings, as well as the growing number of Australians arriving to help in an official capacity.

Members of our Australian Federal Police, supported by officers from some of the State police services, played a mighty role. Mick Keelty, the AFP Commissioner, demonstrated his leadership and competence by quickly dispatching a large contingent of police to help the Indonesians investigate the crime and to assist them with disaster victim identification. The Indonesians quickly agreed to our government's suggestion of a joint investigation. This initiative combined the undoubted investigative skill and profound local knowledge of the Indonesian National Police together with the deep technical expertise of the AFP in a rapid pursuit of the perpetrators. This willingness by the two governments to collaborate and Mick's astute judgement and drive were major factors in achieving early success in apprehending and then bringing a sound case against the terrorists. This success restored confidence. The Australian people were aghast that we had now become a prominent terrorist target. So many people displayed the most admirable courage, compassion and skill in the aftermath of this tragedy. I hoped that the terrorists had noted that Australians were not, and would not be, a meek target.

Although I was happy with the performance of the ADF after this attack, as always, I sent our planners back to the drawing board to consider and adapt to the lessons we had learned. While at this stage I had not brought forward my ideas on revamping our higher command and control arrangements, the response to the Bali bombings in October 2002 added weight to what I thought would be a worthwhile modification to our structure. In the aftermath, the government asked me to propose initiatives to increase the ADF's ability to adapt and respond to terrorist incidents directed towards us, especially in our region and at home.

I had been thinking about these matters since my arrival in Canberra. I was able to respond immediately with a principal recommendation that we create a Special Operations Command (SOC) to incorporate our Special Air Service Regiment, 1st Commando Regiment and 4th Battalion, the Royal Australian Regiment (4 RAR), a commando battalion. In addition to enhancing the existing headquarters of the Commander Special Forces to command these force elements, I also added a new small logistics component and our recently re-raised Incident Response Regiment. This regiment was responsible for bomb detection and disposal as well as detection and neutralisation of chemical, biological and radiological weapons. In addition, the regiment could assist in the aftermath of 'dirty' bomb explosions by quarantining casualties and conducting emergency decontamination. In short, SOC provided the government with a more coherent and integrated entity and an increased suite of options for participation in the world's response to terrorism. This command raised the profile and enhanced the capabilities of our Special Forces and allowed greater focus for development of their counter-terrorist capabilities. The government agreed immediately to these initiatives and allocated the funds to make it happen.

All over Australia, the Bali bombings galvanised governments and authorities that had hitherto been paying lip service to protective security to get their act together. In Defence, we started a major rolling programme to upgrade security of our bases, barracks and other facilities. Armed guards on many buildings and bodyguards for VIPs became par for the course. For a while there was a lobby within Defence trying to require our servicemen and women to commute to and from home in civilian clothes. I was dead against that restriction unless there was a specific threat in a particular area. The vast majority of Australians are proud of and uplifted by the presence of their men and women in uniform as they travel to and from work. If Australians perceived that the ADF was cringing from an invisible threat, we would be sending the wrong message. (Later, with some reluctance, I backed up a short term, expedient decision by a local commander when he became concerned about harassment of his people during the Iraq War in 2003.)

The ADF was now better poised to respond to both domestic and regional terrorist threats with prompt, strong and smart force projection, including emergency medical aid, if it was required. Having covered off on this emerging threat as a result of the Bali bombings, pressure was building internationally for a firm military response to the continuing defiance of Saddam Hussein, the President of Iraq, who was not complying with UN sanctions and weapons inspection regimes. The ADF had participated in the first Gulf War with distinction in 1991. It was now my responsibility to propose to the government options for participation in a re-run.

17

Back to the Gulf

In the second half of 2002, our contacts within the US military alerted us that a contingency — a 'what if' exercise — was in its early stages to force Iraq to comply with UN weapons inspection requirements. The government agreed that ADF liaison officers could monitor the development of these contingency plans in parallel with whatever diplomatic discussions were taking place. Much of the planning was taking place in Tampa, Florida, the home of the United States Central Command, a major military headquarters charged with American military operations in most of the Middle East and Africa. We sent a small team, headed by a brigadier, into Tampa to report back on what was being planned, what other friends and allies were saying and what the ADF might be asked to provide. I had enjoined the brigadier in the strongest terms that under no circumstances was he to foreshadow or comment on any Australian commitment. Concurrently, the international community elevated the level of rhetoric and condemnation. This action was no doubt designed to persuade Saddam that the United States and its friends were serious about establishing once and for all whether he had WMD by compelling his compliance with a comprehensive inspection regime.

Later in 2002, the government authorised me to take steps to prepare some elements of the ADF for operations in the Gulf region in case — at a later time — such operations should prove necessary. In thinking about what sort of forces Australia might contribute, my mind turned first to the Navy. For a number of years Australian warships had undertaken tours of duty as part of a multinational force protecting vital shipping trade and enforcing UN embargoes against Iraq in the Gulf. Plainly, our ships would be a powerful and welcome contribution if we joined the Americans and launched a new military campaign in that area. The Navy also had the high advantage of being well-prepared for just about any eventuality. Ships would be readily available, but not without some careful juggling of resources needed for border control operations and training commitments closer to home. Instead of deploying a single ship — the norm for an Australian contribution to the maritime security operation in the Gulf — the government might consider sending a naval task group of two warships and a logistics and general support ship.

Contributions from Air Force and Army were more problematic. In the case of the Army, any contribution had to be meaningful for reasons of national interest and reputation. We concluded that we could not deploy land forces of substantial size. The Army is quite small by international standards. We had our ongoing role in East Timor and the possibility of other contingencies in our region that would require rapid projection of high readiness units. Further, infantry operations in the Middle East would almost invariably involve infantry manoeuvres in light armoured vehicles. Our excellent armoured forces were best kept as a hedge against regional contingencies. Our single tank regiment, which might have been excused from a regional standby role, would have been vulnerable in the Middle East because it was operating old and technologically inferior German tanks. Simply, our tank regiment would have been an aging orphan among our allies. Consequently, Australian infantry and armour would stay at home and maintain readiness for national and regional deployment.

So, once again the best choice came down to recommending the deployment of a sizeable element of our Special Air Service Regiment. All of our potential coalition partners were in no doubt of the quality of our Special Forces. They could undertake long-range patrolling and deep surveillance and reconnaissance missions with as much proficiency as any other similar force in the world. So, while 'size' would not be a measure for our land force commitment, the commitment would be meaningful because of its 'significance' factor.

We had to think even more carefully about an Air Force contribution. Plainly, transport aircraft would be very useful, not only to support any other forces we might contribute but also as part of a coalition air transport element — you can never have too much air transport. The ADF also had sophisticated maritime patrol aircraft in the form of P3 Orion aircraft based out of Edinburgh, near Adelaide. This was a very good capability in the crowded waters of the Gulf where coalition naval units had been subject to attack in the past. The government might even consider that the time had come to commit combat aircraft, remembering that all military aircraft can be involved in combat: our C130s have been shot at more than once and our P3 aircraft can be armed with anti-submarine and anti-shipping weapons. Our choices were the highly capable F111, a bomber, or the dual-role F/A-18, a fighter capable of adaptation for bombing missions. The F111 had been a magnificent aircraft for many years. It had high speed, long range and a useful bomb load. This aircraft was also capable of precision high-altitude bombing using laser guidance. However, if enemy aircraft were hunting it, it would need fighter protection. Our F111s would also be orphans among our allies as Australia was the only country to still operate the F111. Also, given their venerable age, F111s were prone to serviceability problems beyond the skill and dedication of mechanics in the field. It would have been no good to send these aircraft only to find that our small fleet was grounded because of an 'aging aircraft' problem. While such serviceability issues can affect any type of aircraft, it was a safer bet for the ADF to nominate F/A-18 fighters. They could be used for laser guided precision bombing with a smaller bomb load and they could also protect themselves against enemy fighter attack. As a younger aeroplane, the F/A-18 had a better chance of a higher overall serviceability. Finally, within a likely coalition of the willing, there would be a large number of F/A-18s of various models. Therefore, I expected some compatibility in systems, interoperability and spare parts.

The government agreed to a proposed 'joint package' of a Navy task group, a Special Forces group as well as P3 Orions and F/A-18 Hornets. This was real Catch-22 stuff. Australia had not decided to commit forces to a coalition operation to compel

Saddam Hussein to comply with UN Security Council resolutions about weapons inspections. But in due course, if the Australian Government decided that it was in the national interest to make such a commitment, then prudent preparations had to be made now or force elements would risk deployment to a potential conflict under-prepared and under-equipped, or too late to be of any use. We were prepared and equipped quite well for contingencies in our region, but there was a different set of challenges for international force projection into a more modern threat environment that might include WMD.

The ADF had to procure a range of new capabilities and upgrade others. Ships needed additional state-of-the-art communications equipment. The SAS needed some new weaponry and better communications equipment. The F/A-18s needed additional bombs and missiles and software. All force elements needed upgrades in preventative measures against chemical or biological weapon attack. We procured a large number of additional protective chemical proof suits so that every man and woman could have one on hand at all times, with other suits in reserve. We bought a new range of tents for our aircraft squadron's base areas. These tents provided an 'overpressure' environment so that contaminated air would not drift in before people were able to put on their protective suits. We added technical experts from the Incident Response Regiment to the force in case our people found themselves in the vicinity of chemical weapon dumps. Finally, I insisted that all men and women who might deploy to the Gulf be vaccinated against the biological agent deemed most likely to be available to Saddam — anthrax. These preparations were expensive, but would not have been wasted had the government decided not to participate in military action in the Gulf. Much of the stuff we bought had great utility and relevance to a modern Defence Force in our region and would have been procured in the fullness of time — we just accelerated this capability development process.

During this busy period I had the opportunity to work very closely with Mr Ric Smith, the new Secretary who had replaced Dr Hawke. Ric was one of the most experienced and eminent diplomats of his era. He had been in Defence a number of years beforehand as a deputy secretary with an oversight of strategic policy. More recently, he had been our ambassador to Beijing. He was in the middle of a successful posting as our ambassador in Jakarta as I was taking over as CDF. He and his staff had been magnificent during the dreadful aftermath of the Bali bombings. Ric and I had hit it off immediately. Although Ric understands and can deal in the subtleties and nuances of diplomatic discourse, he is a worldly man and a plain speaker. Ric understands people extraordinarily well and is a great leader, especially when the pressure is on. Upgrading forces for contingencies in the Gulf at short notice required masterful coordination and drive. Ric displayed both qualities during this period. He also brought astute and measured judgement to all of the challenges we faced together. Time and again over subsequent years when I have been puce in the face over some difficult issue, Ric has not only provided the soundest and most useful advice, but unqualified friendship and frequent good humour to lighten the moment. He and his wife, Jan, are a magnificent couple and great friends to Lynne and me.

The great risk during all these preparations was leaks to the media that would create a public furore. Ric and I wanted to ensure that the ADF did not 'get out in front of' government's consideration of whether a commitment was warranted. I was most gratified that all in Defence and in wider government appreciated the sensitivity of these preparations. Unlike the commitment to INTERFET, the government was able to consider the evolving issues without a firestorm of speculation. As we entered 2003, I had growing confidence that the sort of capabilities the government might deploy would be up to the mark in terms of their competence to do an excellent job and to protect themselves in the unique environment of the Gulf.

In early 2003, the international community decided to 'up the ante' in order to ensure Saddam Hussein understood the very serious nature of the latest demand that Iraq comply with UN Security Council resolutions. A coalition of the willing, led by the Americans, decided that it was necessary for a credible military force to assemble in the region to demonstrate both an intention and a capability to take military action. Without this escalation, there is no doubt Saddam would simply have continued to behave as before.

It was at this point that the Australian Government decided to deploy forces as part of this international demonstration of resolve. Over several weeks, from ports and bases around Australia, men and women packed their kit bags and kissed their loved ones goodbye. Another Australian expeditionary force was headed to the Middle East. Following historical precedent that had begun in 1885, when a force from the colony of New South Wales embarked for the war in the Sudan, political leaders, senior military officers, loved ones and hordes of media gathered to farewell young Australians heading overseas into harm's way.

The government had been clear that these deployments did not automatically indicate a commitment to war. There would be no need for fighting if Saddam did as the international community required. Nonetheless, all the men and women in uniform knew that there was a significant possibility that they would end up in a war. I needed them to think that way because I'd rather have them ready in all respects for the worst thing that might happen than have them banking that it wouldn't, and then being surprised if and when it did. I had moved members of the small liaison team from *Tampa*, led by Brigadier Maurie McNarn, to one of the Gulf States and given him some extra people to run an Australian Joint Task Force Headquarters in charge of detailed national oversight of all our deployed Australian elements, even though they were logically under the senior coalition commanders, who would be responsible for separate maritime, air and special forces operations, on a day-by-day basis.

Our forces were permitted to train and integrate with their coalition counterparts, but were under strict embargo that they were to do nothing to impinge on the sovereignty of Iraq without specific orders. The government decision on 18 March 2003 to commit our forces was not the authority for them to act immediately against Iraq, much less enter Iraq without my specific further direction. Some commentators have breathlessly suggested that our Special Forces were sneaking around inside Iraq before formal hostilities commenced. That is incorrect. While they were among the first across the border after the expiry of President George W. Bush's ultimatum, they did not breach the embargo I had placed on them.

On 19 March, after a final meeting of the National Security Committee of Cabinet, I returned to Russell Offices and convened the strategic command group, comprising the Secretary, some senior officials and senior command and operational staff located in Canberra. I told them that the government had approved participation in a coalition offensive to compel Iraq's compliance with weapons inspections. I asked all my colleagues if any of them had any last-minute issues of concern or advice — there were none. I then signed orders authorising and directing our men and women in the Gulf to participate in offensive operations against Iraq in concert with coalition forces. These orders would take effect in the early hours of the following morning, Iraq time, after the expiration of the coalition ultimatum. It was a solemn moment. Though members of this command group were experienced men and women who had been involved in defence issues of great importance over their years of professional service, I doubt whether any of them had been present at a more significant moment than this.

These orders were transmitted with utmost speed to McNarn and his troops in the Middle East. For all of them it was a time of final preparations and no doubt for prayers and introspection. For us in Australia, all we could do now was reflect, and pray and hope that our men and women would be safe. I knew they would do their jobs with courage and professionalism.

In the early hours of 20 March 2003, our Special Forces crossed into Iraq. Combat came quickly in the form of brief skirmishes with border guards. Brushing them aside in short, sharp firefights, the Australians drove on to get as far inside Iraq's western desert as possible before dawn. Their mission was to hunt for any missiles that Iraqi armed forces might have pre-positioned and planned to fire into Israel in response to international intervention. At the fighter base in one of the Gulf States, our fighter pilots flew combat missions inside Iraqi airspace on that first day. At sea our warships adopted wartime rules of engagement and supported land forces ashore with naval gunfire. We were now in a real blue.

In my briefings to the government on the various hazards, threats and possibilities for a military campaign that was designed to overthrow Saddam Hussein's regime, I had been confident that, while there would be some fierce fighting and casualties — including some Australians — coalition forces would overwhelm Saddam's large but ill-motivated forces within a few weeks. Distances and keeping up logistic support would consume more time than stubborn resistance. The land invasion would need to cover a great distance to get to Baghdad, the psychological heart of the regime's will to fight. If even a modestly competent defence was encountered, this might take several weeks to overcome.

As expected, the key to success turned out to be the absolute domination of the air by the coalition. The Iraqi Air Force was a 'non-player'. Consequently, every Iraqi move on the ground became vulnerable to detection and attack from overhead. Also anticipated accurately was the fragmentation of forces defending the southern areas of Iraq. There was no love for Saddam Hussein in these regions. Much stronger resistance was encountered up the main highways towards Baghdad where National Guard troops and *fedayeen* — a form of politically motivated irregular troops — put up quite stiff resistance in towns and villages where coalition commanders were reluctant to use air strikes because of the danger of civilian casualties. Once or twice forward elements of coalition ground forces suffered temporary setbacks through over-confidence or speed, or both. Sometimes bypassing strong pockets of enemy caused considerable trouble for the following echelons of advancing coalition forces.·

Like the INTERFET campaign, journalists were reporting the action from the start. Though they accompanied units and were able to report first hand and broadcast 'live' to millions around the world, they did not always get it right. This was evident when the coalition advance slowed to a crawl during a very severe sandstorm. Journalists reporting the ground war, especially those located in units somewhere down the line of the advancing troops, started to report that the advance had bogged down. True enough, if they reported the correct cause and effect — the weather. However, they began reporting that troops were confused and didn't know what was going on, creating the impression around the world that the campaign had come unstuck — an instinctive preference to report newsworthy disaster rather than less interesting reports of slow progress and improvisation in difficult weather conditions. I reassured the government that the remarkable achievements to date would soon be resumed. The advance on Baghdad was still well within the planned timetable. Not long afterwards the weather cleared. Baghdad fell and the coalition occupied all of the key areas in Iraq. Saddam Hussein went into hiding and his regime collapsed.

As it turned out, the chemical protection suits were not needed. However, I for one was happy that we have a few more on the shelf than we did before — who would want to bet that terrorists will refrain from the use of such weapons in future? The anthrax inoculations were not put to the test, but in similar circumstances with the same degree of possibility of risk, I would advise and order an inoculation regime again.

The role of the media in this campaign caused me to reflect again on how just about every war or conflict these days has a significant media dimension. The first Gulf War in the early 1990s became a 'media' war. Countless viewers vicariously attended aspects of the war from the comfort and safety of their living rooms, sipping a cup of coffee while watching a smart bomb with a camera in the nose obliterate a poor Iraqi soldier driving a truck. As a soldier all my life, I sadly accept that the fate of this Iraqi soldier is what war is about: in order to win, killing is necessary. War has never been a gentle or nice business. However, in my opinion, it is obscene to broadcast it as part of the people's 'right to know' when in so many other ordinary ways those same people have eschewed the same 'right to know'. Examples are embargoes on broadcasting the graphic aftermath of road accidents, or executions or a range of other grisly accident or crime scenes. Civil societies have decided that they do not need to see every detail of death or injury on TV or in the newspapers.

There was some consternation during the war when I did not agree with media requests to release bomb camera footage from our F/A-18 air strikes. I also declined to provide 'body counts' as part of the day-to-day reporting. I confined my information on our Special Forces to broad descriptions of ground battles. One journalist thought I was being overly peremptory about my decision not to traffic in detailed descriptions and body counts — no doubt trenchant about the people's (led by his own!) 'right to know'. Others bristled with accusations of censorship. The dictionary reveals that a censor is one who examines books, plays, news reports, motion pictures, radio and television programmes, letters, cablegrams, etc, for the purpose of suppressing parts deemed objectionable on moral, political, military, or other grounds. I was not stopping media representatives from publishing something they already knew. I chose not to tell or show them something they thought they ought to know.

Apart from moral grounds, there were also some practical reasons for providing only selective information. There is an operational security dimension to releasing certain footage and statistics. Simply, an enemy can conceivably gain advantage from learning from us how many of his troops were lost in a particular action, or where a bombing strike took place. Secondly, if initial reports of enemy casualties are notified and then changed, the media will engage on the issue of false information. The next round of stories could be, 'What is the ADF covering up?' Lastly, the ADF could become open to the charge of deception if I decided to release graphic information on some occasions and then, for security reasons, chose not to do so at other times.

I also differed with journalists about the value of 'embedding' them with ground forces in general and with Special Forces units in particular. 'Embedding' is a modern term for what has been common practice in the past. For protracted periods, one or more journalists live, move, sleep and eat with a particular unit and report a sort of 'worm's eye view' of the war. There is nothing inherently wrong with this practice. Coverage of the Kokoda Campaign in New Guinea during World War II was an outstanding example of great journalism by journalists accompanying the troops and

Yarralumla, Canberra, March 2000. My investiture by Queen Elizabeth II as a Companion of the Order of Australia — Military Divison. I think you bend forward like this to be beheaded, as well!

The team at Government House for the investiture: Steve, Lynne, Phil and David (on my left).

Ticker tape on George Street. Leading the INTERFET troops at the 'welcome home' parade in Sydney was a great thrill.

Receiving the Australian of the Year award from Prime Minister John Howard at the Australia Day Awards at Parliament House in 2001.

A review of the Guard of Honour with Prime Minister John Howard at the Australian Army 100th birthday parade in Canberra.

Former Chief of the Defence Force Admiral Chris Barrie and me at the Change of Command ceremony in Canberra on 3 July 2002.

April 2003: talking to the SAS at Al Asaad Air Base in Iraq. I'm with the Minister for Defence, Senator Robert Hill (middle), and the Secretary of the Department of Defence, Ric Smith (right). Maurie McNarn, then a brigadier, is looking on.

Another visit to Baghdad: walking across the tarmac with our Ambassador to Iraq in 2004.

Australian Government Department of Defence

January 2005: back from a visit to Iraq, visiting the Asian tsunami relief operation in Aceh. With me is Lieutenant Colonel Ian Cumming, who commanded our marvellous Army engineers during the operation.

Air Marshal Angus Houston and me in Darwin in 2005 to see off a new contingent of Australian troops headed to Iraq. Angus was that day announced to succeed me as CDF and we were both delighted.

AAP Images/Len Menzies

Meeting Turkish veterans at the 90th anniversary ANZAC Day commemorations in Turkey in 2005.

The huge crowd at the Lone Pine service at Gallipoli in 2005.

Newspix/Ray Strange

Where it all started over forty years before. On the eve of my retirement, at the Royal Military College, Duntroon.

A lucky bloke, sitting alongside the very best of my luck, Lynne.

Here we go again! Queensland Premier Peter Beattie (centre), Innisfail Mayor Neil Clarke (right) and me reviewing the damage in Innisfail after Cyclone Larry struck on Monday, 20 March 2006.

sharing their privations and dangers. However, embedded journalists are looking at a vast canvas through a drinking straw. A lot of those reports from the Iraq War about loss of momentum and chaos during the sandstorm came from embedded journalists whose unit had been told to stop.

It is a fact of life that soldiers can never know moment by moment how the whole campaign is going because they generally don't know even what is happening just over the next hill. Under those circumstances, it is not unreasonable for a soldier to grumble that things must be crook otherwise, they may muse angrily, 'Why are we sitting here on our backsides?' So while embedding is much preferable to having journalists reporting from a five-star hotel hundreds of kilometres away, it needs to be balanced with a wider perspective. There is of course today a tendency for some journalists to become the main character, looking appropriately courageous and derring-do with troops dashing around in the background. In the case of Australia's part of the land war against Saddam Hussein, there is no journalist yet born whom I would have agreed could accompany our SAS into action. So, in terms of forthright post-war discussions I had with some journalists on the subject of them being embedded with the SAS, it was a strictly hypothetical argument!

It is an old soldier's tale that all battles are fought on the join of four maps. In the modern era you can add to that, 'Battles are fought a number of time zones away from Australia'. East Timor wasn't too bad in this regard, but Iraq was seven hours behind. I knew that this time difference would affect the schedule and tempo of operational reporting. Plainly, the daily wrap-up from our troops operating in the Middle East would come into Canberra in the early hours of the morning. We had to have many of our operations staff come in early to receive this reporting, to analyse it and extract from it the things we needed to do to support their ongoing staff support to the operation and the things we needed to tell the government and the public. Of course, life in Australia and in the seat of government continued to operate on Australian time so we couldn't just shut down later in the day because we felt tired since we had started early to deal with reporting from Iraq.

It was easy enough to allocate more staff officers and clerical staff to the Vice Chief to help with the requirement to operate in shifts, but I was a little concerned about our senior staff, for whom there were no obvious and easily available deputies. I fell into a routine of coming into the office about 4 a.m. when there was nobody else there. This made my personal staff a little uncomfortable, but I insisted that they keep to regular hours — it would be no use if we were all tired. From four until six I would read report after report filed overnight, making notes and generally trying to reach through the words to feel the pulse of the operation. From 6 a.m. onwards, visitors would come tramping in the door and the phone would start to ring. At 7 a.m. the staff would brief the whole strategic command group. As time went by, Maurie McNarn, commanding in the Gulf, was able to attend this meeting via a video link. This briefing and discussion would go for an hour or more. While it was on, other staff members monitoring the conference would be knocking together my brief to the Minister for Defence which soon became, with the Minister's agreement, a major classified daily bulletin to those other areas of government who needed to be right up to scratch on what was happening in the war.

At 9 a.m. the strategic command group and I would be at the Cabinet room in Parliament to brief the National Security Committee of Cabinet. I would inform the Prime Minister and ministers attending essentially what was in my brief to the Minister for Defence. Typically, I would add and discuss — according to their interest — any other aspects that they desired. From time to time there were sidebar discussions before or after these meetings on particular topics. For the remaining ordinary working hours we managed the day-to-day business of Defence, including those routine but important meetings related to resources and capability development affecting wider current and future Defence needs. By late afternoon, the first round of ad hoc operational reporting would be emerging yet again from our forces in Iraq and nearby, so the cycle would begin all over again. Given the bank-up of paperwork because of our focus on the war, I found myself often 'just hanging on a few more minutes to hear the midnight news'. Without doubt though, that period was so exhilarating and adrenaline charged that I don't recall ever feeling particularly weary or stale. Even if I had, I would have reminded myself that our people deployed would be feeling much wearier and were in infinitely more danger — that would have perked me up!

Those few weeks from March to April 2003 are now part of history and the conventional military campaign which so spectacularly ousted the Saddam Hussein regime is no doubt a textbook study of how a well-equipped, well-trained, well-led and technologically vastly superior force should operate. Equally, the desperately dangerous insurgent campaign which grew in the months after April 2003 shows how many of these technologically superior advantages can be circumvented by a determined and ruthless enemy. At that time, we were simply grateful that a murdering dictator had received his comeuppance and the Iraqi people could elect a representative government at some time in the future. We were also immensely thankful that Australia — lucky Australia — had again participated in dangerous military operations with no combat casualties.

The Royal Australian Navy had supported troops ashore with naval gunfire for the first time since Vietnam. Navy clearance divers had taken a leading role in clearing the port of Umm Qasr of deadly mines and other obstructions, thus allowing the delivery of urgently needed humanitarian supplies.

The Royal Australian Air Force had performed magnificently, with our men operating their aircraft as fighter-bombers over Iraq exercising extraordinarily mature judgement for young and till then inexperienced pilots in their engagement of targets. Our Hercules crews played a vital role late in the conflict when they delivered urgently needed medical supplies direct into Baghdad in the middle of the night with continuing combat operations happening all around them because an appeal had gone out for help to restock Baghdad's civilian hospitals. This was a separate operation, called *Baghdad Assist* and was mounted at very short notice as we stripped medical supplies from HMAS *Kanimbla*, our amphibious ship in the Gulf, and sent them into Baghdad. Our men and women flying surveillance missions over the Gulf helped protect the great naval armada and the priceless oil trade that continued during the war.

Our Special Forces had performed superbly — always my expectation. That they had done so without casualties was another stroke of amazing good fortune. They dominated a large area of the western desert regions of Iraq, areas from which Saddam had launched SCUD missiles at Israel in the first Gulf War. Iraqi Special Forces had attacked them and our men had defeated them every time. In turn, our Special Forces had sought them out and defeated them on several occasions. The SAS had shut down enemy military operations in their vast area and had even captured a major Iraqi Air Force base, Al Asad.

Not long after the dust had settled in Iraq, Robert Hill, the Minister for Defence who had replaced Peter Reith after the 2001 election, Ric Smith and I visited the troops of the three services in the Gulf. Of the many visits I made over the years to troops on operations, this was by far the most significant because of the circumstances. All troops on operations deserve accolades, especially from the bosses who have sent them there in the first place. I knew many of the men and women involved. As their military 'father' I felt particularly gratified to affirm the success of their efforts to them personally and to thank them on behalf of Australians in general and the ADF in particular for the acclaimed and professional manner that they had conducted themselves.

One of my more memorable experiences was sharing Anzac Day 2003 with the Royal Australian Navy on board HMAS *Kanimbla* at sea in the Gulf. There is something special for servicemen and women commemorating Anzac Day overseas on operations. They feel connected like at no other time to those original Anzacs of the three services who created the reputation in past conflicts, and to the standards and the ethos by which we live and serve. Before dawn the ship's company and we visitors all gathered on the flight deck at the stern of the vessel. In that faintly pearly hint of light that precedes dawn, I was deeply inspired by the scene of the dense grey ranks of sailors in their fireproof coveralls, gently swaying with the motion of the ship in the vast silence of those famous waters. As the sun thrust above the horizon for another day in the Middle East, it illuminated a memorable scene — our men and women, gathered around the white ensign at the stern, listening to the fading strains of the Last Post, as a flight of Australian F/A-18s, at masthead height, rocketed over our heads. No man or woman who was there will ever forget the significance and spectacle of that dawn service on Anzac Day 2003.

As part of the same trip, we visited the SAS, or the 'chicken stranglers' — a good-natured jealous jibe by other members of the ADF concerning their required capability to live off the land — at the Al Asad air base, about 100 kilometres west of Baghdad. In common with that part of Iraq, the place was barren and most inhospitable. The air base however was immense. The SAS were like slightly naughty children who had taken over an adult's fine weekender residence. It was de rigueur for them to conduct guided tours for visitors; showing off a number of Iraqi frontline combat aircraft that lay damaged or destroyed in conventional parking areas, as well as those in much better shape dispersed under trees and camouflage nets.

I had a few concerns around this time about a favourite Australian military practice of 'souveniring' (some wowsers might favour a more pejorative term — looting). Defence policy was quite strict and forbade sending or bringing warlike souvenirs, such as weapons, back to Australia willy-nilly. Nonetheless, I have a feeling that various cockpit instrumentation from some of these Russian-sourced aircraft may have found their way onto mantelpieces in Western Australia. During this visit I reflected on how the accidental good fortune of their lead-up to Iraq enabled the SAS to do such a great job. East Timor had been a good eye opener. Afghanistan had been a searching test. Iraq was where they confirmed their reputation as an equal to any other Special Forces group in the world.

Much has been said and written about the aftermath of the war leading to the present day perilous situation in Iraq. Without doubt, the victorious coalition made significant mistakes in those first few months after the regime was deposed and did not have mature plans for what to do next. Dismissing the Saddam's *Ba'ath* party apparatus holus-bolus was an error. Most members were not criminals. It was necessary, of course, to charge and bring to trial very senior *Ba'ath* party figures who had been implicated in crimes; it was also necessary to dismiss those other senior figures irredeemably identified with the odious ideology of the Saddam regime. But, in many other cases, membership of the *Ba'ath* party was a necessary precondition to employment in the public sector. These were the people who kept the railroads running and essential services operating.

In addition, it was a mistake to send Saddam's vast army home with a flea in its ear. This dismissal of Iraq's armed forces created not only a power vacuum incapable of being filled by the somewhat slender coalition resources, but it also sent back into the wider community a large number of militarily capable younger men disenchanted and jobless — a fertile breeding ground for an incipient insurgency. There were other errors, but in just these two areas I feel that we could have done it better. Why didn't we? Australia had set its contribution solely for the war phase. Our SAS, our Air Force fighters and our additional warships were very appropriate contributions for a campaign to oust Saddam but much less relevant for the situation that arose in the immediate aftermath. Our allies understood this and further understood that there would be some different, continuing Australian presence going into the future. Having done our bit to bring about the first-order, desired result, Australia was not in a position to direct the detailed decisions made on the ground afterwards and how the coalition might consider running the occupation.

The government determined that our ongoing commitment would primarily lean on a maintaining transport and surveillance aircraft in the area and a continuing maritime security presence by a warship. On land, apart from a protective element for our diplomats, we ran the air traffic control function at Baghdad International Airport and, at various times, sent training teams to assist with re-establishing a new Iraqi Army and Coast Guard as well as locate a surgical team in a military hospital near Baghdad. In more recent times, when the struggle for democracy in Iraq seemed to be at a tipping point, we contributed a sizeable combat element based on a light armoured cavalry regiment to protect Japanese military engineers in southern Iraq and dispatched another team to train troops to replace the task group that was protecting the Japanese in the south.

My parting memory of Australia's participation in the second Gulf War, and one that applied equally to my time in command of INTERFET, was about how to measure success. I learned a long time ago that the dumbest way to soldier was to calibrate professionalism and the seriousness of commitment by the high numbers of casualties. As CDF it was always my most profound principle to prepare, train, equip and operate in a way that accomplished missions, but also put into the hands of our men and women the very best chance to come home in one piece. If it ever comes to the day when our people have to die to save the nation or prove a point, they will do so — not gladly or willingly — but with the same courage and honour as their forebears ever did. In the meantime, I hope that a major part of my stewardship of these, my military 'children', was to inculcate the notion among their commanders of tomorrow that it was crucial to create the best possible opportunities for Australian forces to get the job done with minimum risk and, hopefully, without loss of life or serious injury.

18

Operations Close to Home and More Controversy

THERE IS AN OLD AUSTRALIAN saying, 'never a dull day'. It is used often in reply to the question, 'How's it goin', mate?' I was reflecting on some of the oft-voiced criticisms of our commitment into the Gulf that the dispatch of several of our powerful capabilities so far from Australia's shores would leave Australia exposed to the murky, unknown threat of regional terrorism. While the government offered public reassurances that we had taken all this into account, some of the commentariat still banged on about our vulnerability. By this time, most fighting had subsided in Iraq even though our forces were still in the theatre and on a war footing.

I was sitting in my office, feeling mildly weary when my phone rang to announce that a significant law and order issue had arisen in Victorian waters. A foreign cargo vessel of several thousand tonnes, the *Pong Su*, possibly owned — but certainly operated —

by North Koreans had been involved in a serious incident concerning drug smuggling into Victoria and possibly murder. It had fled the scene near to the Victorian coast at high speed with a police launch in hot pursuit, but now it was heading out to sea. The caller's concern was, given the size of the vessel and the dangers of an interception in open and rough waters, that the pursuing vessel would lose track of the ship and it would get away. Accordingly, the police had asked the Victorian Government to seek Commonwealth assistance.

After a quick couple of phone calls to establish whether the ADF had the right sorts of capabilities immediately available, I phoned Robert Hill and sought his permission to provide one of our highly capable maritime surveillance aircraft, a P3 Orion, to locate and maintain surveillance of the fleeing ship, while the police in their much smaller motor cruiser struggled gamely to keep up. A P3 Orion duly found the *Pong Su* and maintained surveillance for many hours before a C130 Hercules transport aircraft came on station when daylight made the task easier. Lawyers informed me that it was vital to legally maintain continuous surveillance on the *Pong Su* in order to substantiate the international legal principle of 'hot pursuit' in international waters. We did so. In the meantime, as this ship steamed further away from Australia, clearly determined to evade arrest, the government concluded that the police were neither equipped nor trained to conduct a 'noncompliant' arrest on the high seas.

This was a task for the ADF, another coercive tool for the government to use. The government agreed with my proposal to employ SAS troopers, who had been specially trained to conduct 'ship underway' opposed boardings. This group of specialists rendezvoused in Sydney with our newest warship, HMAS *Stuart*, an Anzac class frigate, that I had the thrill of seeing commissioned only a few months before. Orders were simple — sail immediately and, using the SAS group, arrest the *Pong Su*. In the meantime, the *Pong Su* started to angle back towards the Australian coastline but was still steaming like billyo away from the persistent and gallant police pursuit. The captain had made a strange change of course, but there was no doubt that he was never going to stop, and probably thought that the police would eventually drop off the chase.

This was going to be a tricky military operation, not a doddle. Our intelligence on these sorts of criminal enterprise ships revealed that on some previous occasions crew members on other ships had carried machine guns and surface-to-air missiles! Before long, the *Stuart* intercepted the *Pong Su* east of Port Stephens, located on the central coast of New South Wales. Commonwealth and Defence procedures about the use of military force in such circumstances are quite well developed, described and regulated. By this time, I was sitting with Major General Duncan Lewis, General Officer Commanding Special Operations Command, in my office in Canberra. Duncan had been briefing me continuously about the state of preparedness of his troops aboard the *Stuart*. The frigate had also taken aboard a policeman, who constituted the ongoing link between civilian law enforcement and the use of military force. In effect, the SAS were assisting him to investigate probable offences against Victorian law.

After manoeuvring close to the *Pong Su* in the accepted way and hailing her by radio and loudspeaker, calling on the ship to heave to and accept a boarding party, it became obvious that she would not comply. The *Stuart*'s captain now had options that included firing warning shots and then ultimately firing into the vessel. These courses of action were never contemplated seriously. There were no signs of armed crewmen or missiles bristling from the gunwales. Any firing would have been a last resort.

Following these warning procedures and no response from the *Pong Su*, the policeman asked the SAS commander to board the ship and arrest the crew. I was waiting for a call from the SAS commander requesting permission to do so. The SAS commander phoned me, described the situation, spoke about the readiness of his troops and recommended that he be given permission. I phoned the Defence Minister, briefed him and, at his direction, spoke to the Prime Minister. This is a good example of the way the military can be swung into action in such circumstances. The Prime Minister accepted my advice and gave me the go-ahead. All of this took about five minutes.

Moments after receiving my order, the SAS swung into action by helicopter and Zodiac-style rubber boat, often identified with Special Forces. A circling Coast Watch aircraft later provided dramatic video footage of troopers descending by rope from a helicopter and using climbing ladders off the Zodiacs and seizing the vessel, all while the *Pong Su* was steaming along as hard as it could go. Fortunately for all concerned, the North Korean crew did not resist. Police and a naval steaming party boarded the ship for its return in custody to Sydney Harbour. The *Pong Su* sat there into 2006, still in custody but as a reminder that Australia is no 'soft touch'. While this novelty was an unexpected operation for the ADF, I could not help but be glad that we had the chance to show that we could still project force in a prompt, strong and smart way at home, even when we were busy far away.

Participation in the Gulf War with a joint force triggered further reflections on the way the ADF was organised to command our deployed forces at the higher level. Some years earlier, two of my predecessors had instituted a careful and thoughtful reorganisation to create an intermediate layer of command between the CDF, the ultimate commander of the ADF who was accountable to the government of the day, and deployed headquarters and troops at the tactical level. After some wrangling about names, this extra layer was called Headquarters Australian Theatre. It was supposed to direct and support all elements deployed on operations, having been given the intentions of the government through the CDF and his headquarters staff. Thus, the CDF and the government would be able to focus on strategic and political/military issues and would refrain from delving into the minutiae of operations because Headquarters Australian Theatre would direct tactical operations.

There was some historical precedent for this additional layer of command in the way we had operated in World War II. However, there were two big differences. In World War II, we had almost half a million men and women in khaki alone with very sizeable numbers in the Air Force and Navy. Secondly, communications to and from the various battlefields and theatres of war were primitive then, compared with what we take as the norm today. When I headed off to East Timor, admittedly with a very large multinational force, the (then) CDF, Chris Barrie, cut out Headquarters Australian Theatre from the operational command loop, instructing me to deal directly with him and his staff in Canberra. I understood why he did it and I thought he was right. Simply, with the power of communications to discover and broadcast small but vital operational details almost instantaneously, another layer of command can actually impede the speed and span of information available to the government and their senior military adviser, the CDF.

If we ever got to a stage when the numbers of forces and the geographic span of their employment meant that the CDF was being drowned in information, then we would have to reinvent Headquarters Australian Theatre as a separate and distinct level of command. To keep the best of what was intended, but to acknowledge the immediacy and priority of the government's and the CDF's need for information, I appointed the Vice Chief of the Defence Force to be double-hatted as the Chief of Joint Operations Command. The two-star officer who used to command Headquarters Australian Theatre became known as the Deputy Chief of Joint Operations and with his headquarters responded moment by moment to the Chief of Joint Operations Command, who worked in an office about a 30-second walk from my office. By the time I left the CDF's job, I was satisfied that this new arrangement was working well. It had removed an unnecessary barrier to the speedy, comprehensive but discriminating provision of operational information to the CDF.

After the upheaval of late 2002 and early 2003, it seemed that we had reached a steady state in the span and scale of our operational commitments. At that time, recruiting and retention of our people in the three services was going great guns, and we had the promise of additional funds to modernise the future ADF. Australia's great joint policing effort with the Indonesians and other nations in the region was bearing fruit in hunting down JI terrorists and their sponsors. Was it finally time for a few dull days?

The next challenge for the ADF arose close to home in the South Pacific. Australian governments of either persuasion had wrestled for many years with the delicate relationship between large, predominantly white, rich and developed Australia and its numerous smaller Melanesian/Polynesian neighbours in the Pacific. Virtually all of these nations were poor, underdeveloped and likely to remain vulnerable micro-economies. Australian governments had for many years shied away instinctively from intervention — or even advice — that smacked of a new form of colonialism. Thus, Australia was a good regional neighbour when it came to providing financial aid to various countries, but exercised relatively light controls on how the money was administered as well as how and on what it was spent. To the degree possible, Australia monitored these island nations sensitively and offered advice and other non-financial assistance whenever it was welcomed. Unfortunately, more than once, recipient governments branded our assistance as paternalism amounting to colonialism. Despite aid and advice, several of these states endured partial implosions and seemed to be on a steady downward trajectory towards becoming failed states. No country in the Pacific wanted failed states in the region that could become havens or platforms for terrorism and international organised crime.

In mid-2003 an appeal for urgent assistance from one of these countries was to alter the landscape of Australia's relationship with the south-west Pacific region. The Solomon Islands had been a victim of significant inter-communal dispute and violence over a number of years. The economy was in decline and there was widespread corruption. Previous diplomatic regional peace missions had not been able to facilitate resolution of ethnic, economic and governance problems. The central government was moribund. In an example of the parlous state of the rule of law, a gang robbed the Prime Minister of the Solomon Islands in daylight on the main street of the capital city of Honiara. Sizeable groups of armed men roamed the city and had established enclaves where no honest policeman would dare to go to enforce the law.

By early 2003, the Solomon Islands Government was bankrupt, unable to pay for power generation or public service wages. The police force was heavily factionalised, some members, including senior officers, appeared to be corrupt and the morale of the force was shot. In April 2003, the then Prime Minister of the Solomon Islands, Sir Alan Kemakeza, appealed to Australia for help. He envisaged a comprehensive and protracted intervention into his country in order to re-establish law and order and to get representative government and sound public administration back in place. It was a brave call by a desperate man observing the flickering flame of meaningful nationhood about to extinguish.

In considering this request, the Australian Government was immediately mindful of the first-order problem — re-establishing law and order. There needed to be a secure environment in which to rebuild national institutions, effective governance, the economy and civil society. It was plain that Australia, New Zealand and willing and capable Pacific island countries had to become involved in order to provide expertise, manpower, energy, resources and impartiality. Inter-communal disputes fuelled lawlessness, but most of it was criminal rather than political or ideological in nature.

Resolving these problems and creating a secure environment was neither a conventional police task nor a straightforward military mission. The armed gangs in many cases had numerous and wide-ranging military style weapons including, in some cases, machine guns. For obvious reasons, most police forces in our region do not equip or train to combat this level of armed threat. Therefore, the criminality was a policing challenge, but the armed strength of the criminals suggested a military response would be necessary before transition to a policing solution.

My conclusion out of all of this was that, if Australia and others intervened, there would need to be a significant number of policemen and women backed up by a greater number — certainly initially — of heavily armed soldiers. I did not seek ADF control of the intervention. Police should lead and the military should support. This deterrent presence would give police the coercive power to arrest suspects and pursue their investigations in safety. I thought that this high-profile police presence and low-profile — but well-communicated — military back-up would be less traumatic for Solomon Islanders. It would also avoid a modern precedent of foreign troops exercising executive authority in fragile but sensitive Pacific island nations.

I was confident that the Australian Federal Police could lead an intervention successfully. I thought that Commissioner Mick Keelty and his leadership team, as well the sort of police men and women I had seen in action in East Timor, in Bougainville and in Bali, were a group who could take on this sort of deployment and make it work well. While deploying large numbers of people rapidly to remote places for protracted periods for complex missions was 'bread-and-butter' work for the military, the AFP had shown itself to be highly innovative and adaptable over the last several years. Besides, the ADF, and to some degree the New Zealand Defence Force, would be supporting and underwriting the 'expeditionary' aspects of the mission for all concerned.

While I think some AFP officers and officials were mildly surprised that the ADF opted to fill a secondary role, Mick immediately appreciated that it was the correct move. What I found uplifting was his decision, after consultation with his senior commanders, that the vast majority of police in the Solomon Islands would be unarmed during the performance of their duties. In Australia police officers are routinely armed. Even with armed military backup, it would take a lot of guts to stroll up to a known murderer, suspecting that he has a gun handy, equipped only with sunglasses and notebook.

In a remarkably short space of time, Australian and New Zealand diplomats facilitated the formation of a regional coalition and finalised a mandate. The Solomon Islands Parliament reciprocated by passing enabling legislation promptly. On 24 July 2003, the Regional Assistance Mission to the Solomon Islands (RAMSI) contingent deployed to this small, needy nation on Operation *Helpem Fren* — a fine example of neighbours helping another neighbour. A strong military presence provided by 2 RAR, the same battalion that had performed so well in East Timor, did the trick. The infantrymen returned to Australia a few weeks after arrival as a clear demonstration of their success. Hundreds of weapons had been handed in and destroyed. Criminals were in jail and prosecutions were proceeding. Once again the men and women of the ADF showed how they can be a force for good, gaining the goodwill, trust and support of the people in whose country they are operating. Several years later, RAMSI still continues to facilitate much needed stability, peace, confidence and rule of law for the people of the Solomons.

Meanwhile, Australia's ongoing military support to the occupation and rehabilitation of Iraq had achieved a mature form after the end of the war fighting phase. The ADF was still sustaining a joint task force comprising a headquarters, ships, units, and aircraft. In addition, the Australian Government was supporting coalition agencies and headquarters in Baghdad that were running the country with fifty or so men and women, mostly in uniform, but also some public servants.

The nation-building phase of the international intervention was about to receive a major setback. In the middle of 2003, with some trepidation, the UN established a sizeable presence in Baghdad. The senior man, the Special Representative of the Secretary General, was none other than my friend from East Timor, Sergio Vieira de Mello. When I learnt this, I was naturally very concerned. Sergio and his staff would be terrorist targets. In Iraq, and not least in Baghdad, the insurgents would treat the UN — like any other foreign 'interloper' — as a potential target for murder. I was comforted that Sergio's personal military assistant was a very fine Australian officer who knew Sergio well from East Timor days, Colonel Jeff Davie. I had worked with Jeff in Brisbane and had great confidence in him. I knew that he would apply all of his considerable skills and boundless energy to secure Sergio's safety.

Alas, there was nothing that Jeff could do to prevent what eventually happened. On Tuesday, 19 August, a large truck laden with explosives crashed its way in through the fortified gates of the UN compound and exploded against the wall of the main UN office building. That whole segment of the building disintegrated into rubble. Jeff Davie, who happened to be visiting a place a few kilometres away from the compound, returned immediately to the carnage and the chaos. He quickly established that Sergio was missing and was almost certainly in the rubble of the destroyed part of the building. He desperately searched among the twisted and broken metal and slabs of masonry. He and his fellow rescuers found Sergio trapped deep in the rubble, still alive but gravely injured. Despite their frantic efforts, this great servant of the international community died before he could be rescued. Not only had the UN lost one of its most talented and able representatives, but this attack and one other drove the UN presence out of Iraq — a real blow to the cause of peace.

While I was personally very sad that I had lost a friend and colleague for whom I had enormous respect, I thought of the people of East Timor and how they would be mourning this man who had guided, supported and nurtured them with such affection in those crucial early years leading to their independence in May 2002. For his actions on that day, in attempting to rescue his boss at considerable personal risk and, beyond that, his efforts to organise the overall rescue and subsequent recovery, Jeff Davie was awarded a thoroughly deserved Bravery Medal. I saw him in Iraq not very long after this tragedy and took him quietly aside to see how he was travelling and to tell him privately how proud we were of his efforts. I had received the Governor General's permission to tell him that he was to be decorated. With a look of anguish he told me he would give just about anything to have his boss Sergio still alive.

By now, with our Navy, Army and Air Force people spread in operations far and wide, it seemed like every week I was in perpetual motion — visiting, just back from a visit or just about to go to see our people somewhere on another visit. The government had directed the ADF to sustain simultaneous force projections; nationally, to support border control; regionally, to support capacity building in East Timor and in the Solomon Islands; and, internationally, to combat an insurgency in Iraq.

Amidst all of this, my paternal role in the ADF became more personal. I have felt like a military 'father' to the men and women of the Australian Defence Force. That figurative relationship with 71,000 or so people in uniform had become literal in relation to two young infantrymen in the Regular Army. Philip had joined the Army Reserve while I was away in East Timor — a surprise for Dad when he got home! A little later on he changed over to the Regular Army. David, our youngest son, followed the same pathway and was just emerging from his infantry training in late 2003. Philip was posted to 6 RAR, a battalion in Brisbane that was preparing to go to East Timor. David was slotted to go to 1 RAR, one of the high readiness battalions in Townsville that was always on standby for short notice deployment.

Being a private soldier in the infantry when your dad is the CDF is not all beer and skittles. But the boys handled it really well and would grit their teeth and get on with it on the rare occasions when some idiot would make an issue of the situation. Needless to say, I was enormously proud of them both for choosing to serve their country that way without the slightest bit of urging from me, and for the way they handled the novel situation shared by very few other people in the ADF. Throughout their time in uniform, while I remained extraordinarily proud of them I sought in public to either not mention or downplay their presence in the Army — I thought there was enough pressure being a young bloke making your way without the attention of the media.

Our eldest son, Stephen, had considered a career in the military at one stage. Indeed, he had been accepted for a place in the Australian Defence Force Academy in his final year at high school. After deep thought, he declined the position. I was overwhelmingly relieved because there would be nothing worse than sticking with the arduous training at the outset of military service if you weren't thoroughly committed to the life. Lynne, Steve and Matilda, the dog, think the conversation in our house can be pretty boring when you get three blokes rabbiting on about Army stuff!

I felt compelled, with apologies to my family, to join our men and women in Iraq and the Gulf region for Christmas in 2003. They were away from home and still in harm's way. Lynne and the boys were — as they always have been — most understanding. We vowed to have our family celebration a few days after Christmas when I got home. I had decided to be with the troops because at Christmas time the sense of separation from loved ones and those who care is never higher. Without getting maudlin, I told them all that their willingness to accept hardship and separation in the name of their country was, at once, what endeared them to the Australian community and set them on a pedestal. They were proud representatives of their nation and their armed forces and members of a special band of Australians who were doing their best to meet challenges in East Timor, the Solomon Islands, at sea in the Indian Ocean off the Australian mainland and, as members of small contingents or as individuals, at other places around the globe.

In a rather bizarre twist, I had lunch with our headquarters troops in Baghdad at one of Saddam's major palaces in a large reception room full of gilt and marble. As is the custom, the most senior officers serve lunch and then sit down to eat with the diggers. Taking advantage of my advanced age and rank, I put myself in charge of serving broccoli. As each young person came up to my serving point, I harangued any who looked like they wanted to pass me by and told them that their mums and dads especially wanted me to ensure that they ate their greens with their Christmas lunch. Very few left without a nice piece of broccoli adorning their plate. Thus, the first eighteen months of my tenure as CDF was marked in the way I wanted it to be — on operations with the troops serving broccoli! As I sat with them eating and chatting afterwards, I was conscious that after a long and wonderfully enjoyable career as a soldier I could see its final horizon in the distance.

It felt marvellous to be amongst these wonderful, confident and exuberant men and women. Equally as I shared their irrepressible good humour, a part of me felt the full weight of responsibility for their safety. My sense of this burden was alleviated only moments later when Santa arrived, whom as you would expect had a red cap with a white pom-pom and white trim and a flowing white beard and moustache. Santa had, as usual, a large bag full of presents over his shoulder, but there the resemblance to traditional Santa figures ended. This Santa was dressed in our desert pattern camouflage uniform, with military boots and his major fashion accessory was a

9 mm pistol in a shoulder holster. Still, he was a nice, kind Santa who had presents for just about everybody. Mine was a sort of a miniature camel which doubled as a key ring. I think my SAS bodyguards may have got something more practical like sharpening stones for their daggers.

On Thursday, 11 March 2004, there was a devastating act of terrorism in Madrid, the capital of Spain. Terrorist bombs set off in commuter trains killed and injured hundreds of people. Spain had been a prominent member of the coalition in Iraq and this attack appeared to have been timed to occur a few days before a Spanish national election. In the dramatic days after the bombing, the incumbent government made a claim that the bombings were the work of the Basque separatist movement, Euskadi Ta Askatasuna (ETA) — Basque Fatherland and Freedom. ETA had been a violent terrorist movement active in Spain for a number of years. However, this claim was debunked quickly and the government was exposed and its credibility weakened. Subsequently, the Spanish people booted the government out of office at the ballot box.

Back in Australia, overwhelming revulsion at the act and keen interest in the identity and motivation of the perpetrators dominated media coverage of the event. On Sunday, 14 March, Jana Wendt, a prominent journalist, interviewed Mick Keelty. The primary topic was the Madrid bombing and its aftermath and implications for Australia. In her preamble before beginning discussion with Mick, Ms Wendt canvassed that '... if the massacre in Madrid was revenge for Spain's part in the coalition against

Saddam Hussein's Iraq, then the implications for Australia could be very serious'. A little later, Mick volunteered the following: '... The reality is, if this turns out to be Islamic extremists responsible for this bombing in Spain, it's more likely to be linked to the position that Spain and other allies took on issues such as Iraq.' Mick went on to reinforce the fact that he believed that sooner or later a terrorist attack would occur in Australia. Watching this at home, I nearly fell off my chair. The juxtaposition of these two propositions was political dynamite. The Bali bombings had already demonstrated that Australians were a terrorist target. I agreed with Mick that we should expect to be a target within Australia and should take precautionary actions. But I did not agree that there was a conclusive link between the Islamic terrorists, who had perpetrated the attacks in Madrid, and Spain's position on Iraq — certainly on what we knew or didn't know at that time.

Predictably the media focus on this was intense over the next couple of days. This coverage, together with comments from those many Australians opposed to Australia's role in Iraq, created momentum for a notion along the lines of, 'If we hadn't gone to Iraq, we wouldn't be a target'. And more insidiously, 'If we moderate our behaviour and pull our heads in internationally, then the terrorists will leave us alone'. Had I been just another senior public servant within the government, all of this would have been good interesting stuff, but I would never have dreamed of entering the debate. Politicians were stepping up and filling the airwaves with comment. However, when a government spokesperson or politician advanced counter arguments to Mick's propositions, the reaction in the media was along the lines of, 'Well they would say that, wouldn't they?'

But here was the rub, I was not just any old senior official in wider government, I was the Chief of the Defence Force, a principal advisor to the government on matters of national security. I disagreed that a colleague in the business of national security, whom I liked and respected, could draw such an early and specific conclusion on such a vexed issue. I was also the fellow with many hundreds of our people in significant danger in Iraq and nearby. Finally, I had lived through the Vietnam era. I had watched the terrible divisiveness that Australia's participation in that conflict had on Australian society. I had witnessed and experienced the damage that can be caused by discordant and diminished public support to the morale and self-esteem of deployed troops.

So, I had a dilemma. Mick was and remains a magnificent leader of his police force and a loyal and trustworthy servant of the people of Australia — a quite extraordinary asset in the fight against terrorism. I felt sure he would be sick at the thought that the effects which I perceived occurring could be construed from his remarks. I wanted to comment but I had few options. I rejected either seeking out a media opportunity especially to air my view or to 'background' a journalist in private and become an anonymous source: I have never done that. Backgrounding can become a habit and, in its worst form, it is an insidious tool for cowards who fear going on the public record with their views.

As luck would have it, on Monday, 15 March, Robert Hill asked me to accompany him to a media conference to be conducted as a 'doorstop' outside one of our headquarters in Sydney. The subject of the conference was the relocation of that headquarters to Bungendore, near Canberra. With the extraordinarily sensitive atmosphere surrounding Mick's remarks, I figured the move to

Bungendore wouldn't get much of a run when it came time for questions. Standing with the Minister just inside the headquarters waiting for the appointed time for the 'doorstop' to start, I said to him that I thought the media would ask me about the issue surrounding Mick's remarks and, if they did, I would say something in disagreement. He didn't ask what I would say and I didn't tell him. At no stage did he or any other person ask me to say anything about the issue — they would have got a flea in their ear. This conundrum and my decision to comment to the media were mine alone.

Media representatives directed the first few questions to Senator Hill. The first one to me was, 'I'm wondering if you think we are at greater risk of a terrorist attack after Iraq?' In reply I said: 'I generally agree with Mick Keelty, he's doing a fantastic job, I see the same intelligence as he's seeing, and I disagree with him on this occasion …' A few words later on during the same brief monologue, I said: 'This is important stuff, and I believe that while Commissioner Keelty's point in a narrow sense — I can understand why he made it, I don't agree with it …' A short while later there was another question about Spain's decision to pull its troops out of Iraq; nothing in my reply became controversial.

I realised from the beginning that those who supported Mick Keelty's view would be unhappy with my contrary opinion. However, I was surprised by a storm of invective and abuse directed at me through the media. My remarks were widely labelled as an 'attack' on Mick Keeltey. Most descriptions of my actions alleged that the government had 'wheeled me out' to support their position. The whole controversy brought Mick very low. I was characterised as the particular villain who was responsible for this state of affairs.

Let me set the record straight. In relation to my remarks being an 'attack' on Mick Keelty, if I had said anything milder, then I would have said nothing at all. Some people took the view that as a senior official I had no place in commenting upon what another senior official had said. This is a double standard. If Mick had the right to comment publicly on the issue in the first place, then I also had the same right. Commentators also offered that Mick was a policeman and, therefore, entitled to draw a view on terrorist threats. I wasn't a policeman and, therefore, should have kept my mouth shut. This position was also untenable. I was the senior military officer in Australia. It would be both normal and expected for me to have an educated view on matters of terrorism and consequent threats to the nation. But, without a doubt, the charge that offended me the most — and that was completely false — was that I had been 'wheeled out'. People making this claim did not appear to even contemplate the thought that I might have acted reluctantly, but independently.

It was a dramatic episode at the time and certainly stood out during my period as CDF. There are aspects of it that I regret, such as the effect on Mick. I was disappointed by the overall feral and shallow nature of the debate after he made his remarks. Though by this time I was a seasoned veteran of public life, I also regretted the vilification of me. I recall one journalist writing some time after the event calling me a 'lickspittle'. It was only a short time later that he cruised up to me and wanted to have a chat about some other Defence issue.

I feared that there was the possibility of a schism between the leadership of the AFP and me. An article in a magazine that touched on the issue quoted an anonymous AFP source as saying,

'After the attack on Mick there was basically a corporate chunder within the AFP: there was enormous bitterness towards the government and the ADF. It was potentially a massive problem ...' I was pleased and relieved that this colourful assessment proved to be overblown. Our men and women were working side-by-side most effectively in the Solomon Islands and they have continued to work together in the closest possible way ever since. Mick and I sensibly re-established a cordial working relationship, but it may be that he still resents my comments. That is a pity, for he is an outstanding Australian. That said, I remain convinced I was right to make my remarks at the time and, if the same circumstances reoccurred, I would do it again.

19

Some Low Points, an Emergency and a Homecoming

THE ADF'S CLOSEST MILITARY and cultural affinities, aside from those shared with our ANZAC ally, New Zealand, are with Britain and the United States. In conflicts profound and occasional, we find ourselves working together comfortably and familiarly, time after time. We live in each other's countries, we attend each other's military schools, and we seek each other out at every professional international gathering. Setting aside the obvious wider social and cultural differences, in military terms, the armed forces of Australia, Britain and the United States are kith and kin. That presumption and deep understanding was never more sorely tested than over the Abu Ghraib scandal which occurred in 2003, but came to light in early 2004. Its initial ripples became waves that washed around the world and imperilled the reputation and the legitimacy of both the coalition in Iraq and the remaining global superpower, the United States of America. As these waves washed over Australia, it brought me to a very low period in my forty years of soldiering.

Abu Ghraib is a Saddam-era jail on the outskirts of Baghdad. A very large place, it housed many prisoners of the regime and, after Saddam was deposed, the coalition took over the jail in order to accommodate both criminals and detainees who were a threat to security. The United States Army operated the jail with specific responsibility for the security detainees. During 2003 several American army reserve personnel responsible for running the jail participated in the most disgusting and reprehensible mistreatment of Iraqi prisoners. This gross misconduct was brought to a head over time, originating with complaints from victims, and further exposed by whistleblowers and Red Cross reports. First, the US military and then American and international media started to dig deep. Inevitably, the detailed story of the mistreatment emerged. In Australia, we watched revelations in the media, accompanied by graphic photographs, with sadness and disgust. I was relieved that our forces had taken no prisoners in Iraq during fleeting contacts and we had nobody working at the jail.

As more details, led by more graphic photographs, emerged about these shocking events, Ric Smith and I thought — just for safety's sake — we had better canvass our own people who had been in Iraq and might have been remotely in a position to have been involved in any way or who might have known something about Abu Ghraib. We established a team for this task, led by a senior official. This team designed and distributed hundreds of questionnaires, essentially asking, 'Were you involved in or do you know anything about prisoner abuse, directly related to your time in Iraq?' We were relieved, as the responses flowed in, that — as I expected — no Australian had witnessed or participated in any mistreatment of prisoners. We knew that a middle ranking ADF lawyer had acted as a drafter of coalition responses to Red Cross complaints. This was a logical flow-on from his work as he was involved in arranging Red Cross visits to Abu Ghraib in the second half of 2003. It all looked pretty innocuous.

Around that time in mid-2004, there was some lurid media reporting, suggesting that Australians must be deeply implicated. Ric and I were comfortable that we had a pretty good handle on what our people who had served in Iraq knew because of the results of the questionnaires and the report from our investigative team. We wanted to pre-empt unhelpful speculation in the media and, in so doing, prevent ordinary Australians from thinking that the ADF had been involved in anything like the grotesque abuses at Abu Ghraib. This was reputation management, not cover-up. We put out a joint press statement on the Friday before a Senate Estimates session that was scheduled to begin on Monday, 31 May, and go through to Wednesday, 2 June. Hopefully, our press release would clarify our position in anticipation of the senators canvassing the issue during this session.

Immediately we encountered problems with the quality and comprehensiveness of the information we had to hand. This particularly related to the routine day-to-day activities of ADF lawyers working in Baghdad for various coalition departments and headquarters. Now that the issue had reached a head in Australia, some of them were volunteering additional information that had not come to light before. Even though at times I could have cheerfully strangled all of them for coming up with new recollections of discussions they had had, documents they had seen or written, and the detail of visits they had made, the crucial point — often overlooked in the ensuing controversy — was that none of them had ever gone to Abu Ghraib and conducted abuse, seen abuse, or condoned abuse. They did their jobs as professional lawyers and upright and moral men. I was deeply disturbed at the insinuation that they were somehow complicit in the evil acts that had so besmirched the Coalition, especially the US Armed Forces.

We did make significant errors in Defence though. We didn't appreciate early enough the detail that was contained in Red Cross reports of visits to Abu Ghraib. Our lawyers in Iraq had sent these reports to the Department in the first few months of 2004. If staff had realised their import — and if Ric and I had known — we would have expressed our concern both to the Australian Government and to our coalition partners. As it was, the abuses alleged were so grotesque and out of character for the US Armed Forces as a whole, that the initial media reports that included clear reference to high-level US military investigations of the issues gave us comfort, together with the knowledge that the ADF had nobody involved in the custody of any prisoners.

In any event, our press statement of Friday, 28 May, was a dud. We corrected it with a statement Ric made on our behalf about lunchtime on Tuesday, 1 June. We both received a hammering in the Senate Estimates hearings — justifiably so — about why we didn't correct it first thing on Monday morning when we knew over the weekend that some parts of our statement were questionable. I told the senators that on the Monday morning — and this is the really sad part — we didn't know what we didn't know. Every answer we gave in the estimates session was honest but we felt like those men in tartan shirts who run on the top of logs in Canadian rivers. I hated the fact that I couldn't give a comprehensive and straight answer to some of the more wide-ranging questions. It wasn't until Tuesday that we understood that the rest of our statement could stand. We now knew that the Department had received a collection of Red Cross reports, some detailing significant mistreatment of prisoners, rather than a single overarching, somewhat anodyne report, that the Red Cross had issued in October 2003. Although we had in 2004 received copies of those documents, no departmental or military officer understood that these piecemeal papers were actually all part of the October report. In this, we dropped the ball. Out of all this, I was glad to have the strength and integrity of Ric Smith by my side and the absolute conviction that no Australian serviceman or woman in Iraq would participate in or condone the maltreatment of defenceless people: no matter what the reason. Nonetheless, this was the low water mark of my time as CDF because we had been caught on the hop by a situation that I never thought could occur.

During 2004, Philip took the family name back to East Timor. He served as a digger in 6 RAR, a unit that completed one of the last operational tours of duty by the Australian Army in the world's newest independent nation. Like a hunter checking his traps, I made numerous visits to our operational areas over time. I had visited East Timor at least five or six times. Given my involvement in the initial emergency operation to restore peace and security and INTERFET, I was very circumspect about where I went and who I visited. I would always see TMR, by now formally installed as the Chief of the East Timorese Defence Force. I would always call on the head of the United Nations peacekeeping force. But I would never seek to see the UN head of mission or any of the political leadership of East Timor. I saw some of them in Australia from time to time, but it was a totally different matter to be dropping in to see them in Dili. This absence of protocol suited me down on the ground as it gave me maximum time with our troops. When I visited 6 RAR, Phil was stuck away up on a remote observation post on a hillside just below cloud level. It was great to see him and his mates, who managed to treat me with a fine blend of 'general-ogre' status and a kindly old duffer who was one of their mates' dads. We had photos taken all over the place and one of them sits on the fridge door, which is perhaps not the most dignified spot for such a historic photograph — at least by Cosgrove family standards.

All these years later, most Australians still regard the INTERFET mission as a high point in our broader international engagement and in our modern military accomplishments. One of the interesting aspects of that mission which came to life in 2004 was that of the 'switching off' of intelligence support to INTERFET for about 24 hours in December 1999. There has been much controversy and disagreement about the issue and much discussion about conspiracies, pro-Jakarta lobbies and untruthfulness. My impression of the whole issue will be somewhat low-key because in the end, during the operation in real terms, it caused barely a ripple.

Lieutenant Colonel Lance Collins was my senior intelligence officer, sent to me at short notice in early 1999. Lance was a very dedicated, hard-working and meticulous officer who would work incredible hours to produce the most detailed and exhaustive intelligence estimates. He had a significant bee in his bonnet about the Defence Intelligence Organisation, Australia's senior military intelligence agency in Canberra, and what he perceived to be their strong pro-Indonesian bias which he considered was shared by a number of other senior people in policy and leadership positions.

In the middle of 1999, he showed me a document he had written basically outlining his position on Indonesia and the significant criticisms he had of this 'lobby's' approach to the same data. It was explosive stuff and he had circulated the same paper to a number of other people in the intelligence community. I disagreed with him about the motives he ascribed to others and with his dire conclusions. I told him so and asked him to back off from what appeared to be a nugatory and damaging issue, for the sake of the need for my headquarters to have a working and mutually respectful relationship between my intelligence staff and the senior military intelligence organisation in the nation. He appeared to acquiesce, but I wasn't convinced that he would let the issue go. It was obvious that he had a real set against a perceived community of 'Indonesian apologists' (my term) in Canberra. I thought he was quite wrong. On the other hand, Lance had some excellent redeeming qualities so with my unmistakeable counsel for him to leave the hobbyhorse alone and to get on with the job I needed him to do, I thought we could press on. Things worked pretty well on the intelligence side due to the magnificent industry and professional nous of many people like Lance (including many of those he thought of as *bête noir!*). Some of the early intelligence briefs I received at various levels within the Australian part of

INTERFET tended to be somewhat gloomy and overblown but that was consistent with the settling-in period that all the troops in East Timor underwent.

Intelligence officers, though, are really in a cleft stick: some will be so narrowly forensic and methodical that they will tell you that the sky will fall on you by no later than 1400hrs tomorrow and when it does not occur assert that it has been postponed by 23 hours and 15 minutes. Others will be so bland as to never be wrong but to ultimately be quite useless. The best intelligence officers are those who bring you facts, their careful deductions, from time to time a courageous conclusion as the situation demands and always an open mind for alternative futures. This comes down to innate ability and experience, the latter usually with scars attached. Many of our intelligence officers had excellent ability — this was the winning of the experience 'with scars'.

Apparently one of our various intelligence links to Australia was not certified as being able to be used in the field without significant danger of being intercepted. It was not a link which served our immediate needs for troop safety and moment-by-moment operations. When it was cut off, Lance was highly exercised by the matter and complained to me that it had been deliberately cut off. When I enquired to Canberra about the shut down I was told that while the linkage itself was unauthorised, the cut in service was a technical problem. That was the end of that apart from a request from the head of the Defence Intelligence Organisation (DIO) that our intelligence staff confine themselves to the immediate operating environment for INTERFET rather than mulling over more widely drawn intelligence. I saw that as a routine reminder of turf ownership, probably exacerbated by the irritation between DIO and Lance Collins, and asked my Chief of Staff, the extraordinarily able Mark Kelly, to keep his eye on it. That's where the matter ended as far as I was concerned. The operational context was that by now INTERFET had reached a quite steady state of security and, although there remained challenges ahead, the danger of major hostilities was remote. While I would have preferred no imbroglio over the temporary loss of this one of several intelligence links, if I had known the furore to follow in years to come, I would have jumped on the issue and its antecedents very hard and much sooner.

We now know several years after the event and after two enquiries that somebody 'pulled the plug' on this particular link because they knew the link was technically unauthorised and, it seems, thinking they had approval to do so, before it was restored about a day later. Ultimately I would have preferred to know the real reason for the shutdown then and there — it would have been resolved in a matter of minutes.

Another blow to the Defence Force came later in 2004 in the form of an accumulating raft of complaints concerning what the media and some politicians decided should be called, 'the military justice system'. One or two extremely tragic cases where servicemen and women had taken their own lives had resulted in bereaved families being most concerned about practices or actions within the service environment. They believed that these practices contributed to or actually caused their loved ones to suicide. Some of them asserted that day-to-day behaviour by others in the ADF and unreasonable pressure on their loved ones caused these tragedies. Others felt that subsequent investigations and remediation by the ADF were inadequate, and that the chain of command was not learning from these tragic outcomes.

There is no doubt that in some of these cases, harsh, indiscriminate and insensitive practices or particular treatment brought vulnerable individuals to despair. And there is no doubt that some investigations and follow-ups were either shallow or shoddy — or both. What got me though was that virtually none of the suicides or matters related to them could be traced to the content of military law, accompanying legal policy or the application of judicial processes. The military justice system itself was characterised by sound policy and effective implementation and administration. To me, the undoubted concerns arising from some of these cases could be traced back to errant individuals and occasionally to small pockets of people — 'mini-cultures' — born and condoned in an environment of poor local leadership and management. These 'mini-cultures' occur in wider society, but should neither have evolved nor have been tolerated in the ADF. It was inevitable, given the attention paid to some of these very sad cases, that the government was moved to establish a parliamentary inquiry under the broad rubric of investigating 'military justice'.

Parliamentary inquiries normally begin with a degree of preparation and coordination prior to the conduct of hearings. Advertisements in newspapers invite people, who believe they have a matter of interest, to register their material, to correspond with the committee or appear in person before the committee. Following normal practice, Defence assembled a small team dedicated to preparing the Defence case, in consultation with appropriate experts within Defence. Their job was also to act as a link with the committee. Committees of this nature expect significant support from Defence. For example, the committee would expect this team to coordinate transportation and administrative support for witnesses. I thought we were off to a bad start when a leaked email from one member of the Defence team was taken to suggest that we would be 'fighting' the committee. That was an incorrect and possibly mischievous construction put on our actual position. The team's mission was to put the case that the 'military justice system' — a fairly broad term — was fundamentally sound.

Individuals, many of them ex-servicemen and women and some relatives of deceased members, brought cases to the committee. By definition, the vast majority of these witnesses had a grievance, some stretching back over many years. Many witnesses appeared before the committee in camera, so Defence could only guess at their identity, the nature of their grievance and what they said about Defence and individuals within it. Some harrowing evidence was taken in public. Bereaved parents, angry with the ADF about its actions leading up to the death of their loved one or a follow-up which they considered inadequate or self-exculpatory, put their cases in these hearings.

I had decided at the outset that the ADF would make no public rebuttal that amounted to questioning what these people said. They had already lost so much. I relied on the committee to ensure balance and to give Defence the opportunity to offer its view without having to rebut the evidence and concerns of others in an adversarial manner. The committee declined to hear any Defence evidence whatsoever in camera. That decision was very disappointing and left us making broad statements and assertions, bound tight by the strictures of privacy laws.

To me the 'justice system' was not 'on trial' at these hearings. The nature of the evidence that was given in public confirmed my observation. Witness after witness spoke of their grievances. Some complained that they had not been fairly treated by other people, not that the system did not provide a remedy. Some complained that the administrative system for providing redress for complaints, which were not automatically related to discipline, was convoluted, multi-layered and slow. I could agree with them, but I did note that all of them were people who had been knocked back at a lower level by a decision maker and thus were still aggrieved. It is a principle within our common worldwide complaint resolution process that all grievances ought to be decided at the lowest level possible. We have a lot of levels in the Defence Force. It is another principle that people should always have a right of appeal to the next level above. In relation to appeals, we still have a lot of levels and we are in an increasingly litigious age.

To my knowledge, because I did not have access to evidence given in camera, very few of the grievances aired in the inquiry cast doubt on ADF disciplinary/judicial arrangements. Fundamentally, the ADF exists to hurl cohesive and focussed teams day after day into battle with Australia's enemies, no matter where they are. Proponents of radical change to the so-called 'military justice system' obviously never understood this fact and that there were significant dangers with tinkering with this system. There was talk of comprehensively 'civilianising' the disciplinary/judicial system. This was a silly suggestion. Expert civilian investigators are co-opted and employed routinely whenever the requisite expertise does not reside within the ADF. Already many part-time military lawyers, both by need and choice, have significant experience within civil jurisdictions. The committee's broad definition of the 'military justice system' allowed for significant — but irrelevant — concerns to be raised under that banner during their inquiry.

I personally regretted every death whose tragic circumstances revealed shortcomings in behaviour and actions before and after they occurred. Where the committee found that we had not yet eradicated the last vestiges of bullying behaviour, I'll wear that on the chin — and so will everybody else in uniform. Where individuals with legitimate grievances have had to wait some inordinate amount of time before satisfaction, again I apologise. Revised arrangements for consideration of grievances should speed up the process while still trying to keep dispute resolution at the lowest possible level. On the matter of our disciplinary/judicial system, I strongly contend that the basics are right. While the ADF can always fine tune it, let no committee make this particular horse into a camel!

That year ended with an event of awesome dimensions never before seen in modern times. In a few moments, it is likely more people were killed than in any similar period of living history. On Boxing Day, 26 December 2004, a massive earthquake centred west of Sumatra threw up a giant tsunami which smashed ashore far and wide across the Indian Ocean. Early reports and increasingly graphic film footage, often shot by holidaymakers with video cameras, showed the shockingly violent eruption of nature as it wiped out coastal areas in Thailand and Sri Lanka. On that evening, as more and more reports came in, it was obvious that the loss of life was substantial. Given that the devastated Phuket resort area was a popular haunt for holidaying Australians, it became obvious that the ADF might once again be on its way to a disaster area.

On the evening of Boxing Day, I convened a meeting of the strategic command group for first thing the next morning. The staff, who had been monitoring government and media information overnight, briefed us and we received our first definitive advice of the location of the earthquake epicentre — the origin of the tsunami. As we looked at the map of the region, everybody realised that the damage to the west coast of Sumatra along the shoreline of the Indonesian province of Aceh must have been immense. We deduced this in part from the damage reports and images being shown from places much further away, such as Thailand and Sri Lanka.

Angus Houston had worked as a helicopter pilot in that area many years before. He told me about the layout of coastal settlements and the density of population along that coastline. We all concluded that the loss of life and damage could be staggering. The relative paucity of communications infrastructure in north-western Sumatra, and the probability that it had been wiped out by the waves, seemed to explain why there was virtually no news from that part of the world. I concluded that a major relief operation would be necessary in Sumatra and that the scale required would vastly exceed the capacity of the Indonesian Government to cope with in the short term. My feeling was that, as bad as the destruction looked in Thailand, the Thai Government and the

United States would play a major hand in disaster relief there. Similarly in Sri Lanka, I knew that the Indians and the Brits would rush to their aid. We focussed on helping Indonesia, as our close neighbour, and likely to be the worst hit.

I gave orders to start planning a major joint relief operation and to prepare force elements from the Navy, Army and Air Force to deploy with utmost speed. Fortunately, other relevant departments, and the Department of Foreign Affairs and Trade (DFAT) in particular, were also reacting quickly. There was to be an interdepartmental officials' meeting at the DFAT Crisis Centre in Canberra, chaired by one of their deputy secretaries and attended by one of our senior operational staff officers later that morning. I decided to 'up the ante' and attend in person. When Peter Shergold, Secretary of the Department of Prime Minister and Cabinet and head of the Public Service heard of the meeting, he also decided to attend.

I put the point strongly in the meeting, and Peter readily agreed, that Australia's relief effort should focus on Indonesia and that where we knew it was likely that some Australians had lost their lives in Thailand, we should offer some of our expert disaster victim identification people who had been so valuable after Bali. Even as we were having these discussions, the true picture started to emerge from Sumatra. Informed by new reports and graphic images, the government readily agreed to our recommendations on how we should go about the relief effort. Within hours, the most urgent and substantial international relief effort ever mounted by the ADF was underway.

As anticipated from our map reconnaissance, the worst hit part of Sumatra was Aceh, the location of an enduring secessionist rebellion. For many years the central government had directed a military campaign to round up insurgents belonging to Gerakin Aceh Merdeka (GAM) — Free Aceh Movement. The Indonesian Government and its security forces strictly controlled and ordinarily did not permit access by foreigners into Aceh. Even though the humanitarian need would be obvious and overwhelming, Indonesia could still be expected to be most sensitive about foreign visitors, especially foreign military contingents. There would also be some residual reserve about accepting ADF forces into the area after some of the controversy over Australia's leadership of INTERFET.

That day I rang my friend, the Panglima (or supreme commander), General Endriartono Sutarto, my equivalent in Jakarta. I expressed my sincere condolences on behalf of the ADF and all Australians for what we both assumed was a massive loss of life. I offered whatever help they could use and that we could muster at short notice. He thanked me and told me I was the first military leader to call. He accepted any help that we could send. I told him that help was already on the way. Our aircraft were in the air and would arrive in Sumatra in a matter of hours. I added that we were preparing more aircraft to fly in more men and women and humanitarian supplies. As soon as possible, we would dispatch a large naval amphibious ship full of supplies, engineer equipment, landing craft and helicopters. He seemed genuinely touched and most grateful.

An ADF air bridge reached out to Aceh. Aircraft after aircraft took off. All were full of doctors and nurses — mostly military but some civilian — medical stores, bottled water and water purification equipment, tentage and anything else we could think of that would be useful immediately. Meanwhile in Darwin our engineers were frantically preparing their equipment and stores ready to embark on HMAS *Kanimbla*, even then preparing to sail from Sydney. Australia's military relief effort started to pour into Sumatra. Once again our men and women returned to work without the need for orders in the middle of their annual leave. The redoubtable Ken Brownrigg, back in Indonesia as a brigadier and serving as our senior defence attaché in Jakarta, coordinated our efforts with the Indonesian military and civilian authorities. Once again I was leaning heavily on Ken's expertise. He went forward from Jakarta into Sumatra to ease the way for our arriving forces and to find out from the Indonesians where they wanted them and what they wanted them to do. Ken was one ADF officer who had had more excitement over a couple of years than many others experienced in a military lifetime. Ken's good offices once again made a significant impression on the Indonesian military hierarchy and underscored that our troops were there to help them and work under their broad direction. Some other relief contingents tended to treat the disaster area as a sort of a vacuum in which they could operate freely without consultation or direction. This prompted some resentment among the Indonesian security forces and authorities.

As the scale of the area devastated and the scope of the loss of life and injury became clearer, it was obvious that any urgent relief operation could only alleviate immediate suffering and help prevent the outbreak of epidemic disease. The Australian Government recognised the longer term requirement and must have boosted morale in Indonesia by announcing a major and unprecedented disaster relief financial package to be delivered over a number of years. Personally, I was very gratified that General Sutarto invited me to visit our troops involved in relief operations and then to visit him in Jakarta. This was a real breakthrough and an invitation I did not think would be forthcoming while I was in uniform. Simply, after East Timor, I was marked indelibly with the resentment that some in Indonesia would always feel about Australia's role in that event. Australia's immediate and wholehearted assistance after the tsunami was the catalyst for this invitation. I came direct from a visit to the troops on operations in the Gulf. I must have stood out a bit dressed in my desert pattern camouflage as I tramped around Banda Aceh, the capital of the province, and a city devastated by the giant waves.

During my visit I joined the Indonesian Chief of Army, General Ryamizard, just outside Banda Aceh where we sat for about an hour under a marquee talking about the disaster. At one stage in response to a question from me about the height of the wave at that particular spot, a narrow bay, he pointed to a quite visible mark on the cliff face behind us which I estimated to be about 25 to 30 metres from ground level. Obviously the headlands had compressed the waves in the bay, but it was an awful picture to carry away. While we were there, for a brief period we played that old collegiate game of 'Whatever happened to so-and-so?'. I asked after Colonel Geerhan, the fellow I had last seen in East Timor. Ryamizard replied enthusiastically, 'He's here!' and, turning to an aide, said 'Get Geerhan!' Moments later Geerhan came dashing up, wondering why his Big Boss wanted him and he blanched when he saw me. I didn't mention the exact circumstances of our last meeting for which I'm sure he was grateful, but I was intrigued to learn that he was posted to Aceh and had just returned to duty after recovering from knife wounds inflicted on him in a struggle with some GAM fighters. I murmured to him as I left that he should consider a less stressful line of work!

No account of the ADF's remarkable work in Sumatra after the tsunami would be complete without reference to the operation in the same general area immediately following and the tragedy that accompanied it. As the need for emergency military assistance in Aceh diminished, the government directed me to start dismantling and sending home the emergency military relief effort. Weary servicemen and women packed up stores, waved goodbye and left for home with the thoughts of a job well done and, in many cases, resumed their leave that had been interrupted by the disaster. Much of the heavy equipment of course had to be cleaned for re-entry into Australia and our amphibious ship HMAS *Kanimbla* stayed on station to load up this equipment and sail back to Australia. For many of the crew this extended absence must have seemed never-ending but eventually they turned for home, with just a keenly anticipated couple of days in Singapore before a fast run back to Sydney. They had just started to enjoy the bright lights, when a major earthquake, probably an aftershock to the Boxing Day earthquake and tsunami, occurred near the west coast of Sumatra.

This time we were concerned about the welfare of the people of Nias Island, located not far off the coast of Sumatra. I ordered *Kanimbla* back into action to mount an urgent relief effort. The ship steamed off as hard as it could go to the disaster area after quickly assembling the crew from their run ashore. On its first day conducting these new relief operations, a Sea King helicopter from *Kanimbla*, with eleven of our people — Navy and Air Force — crashed as it came in to land near the southern tip of the island. Nine aboard were killed in the crash and the two survivors were badly injured. This terrible tragedy, the worst loss of life in the ADF in many years, was especially poignant given the marvellous service which the ship's company and many aboard the helicopter had already provided in Sumatra and were again delivering in Nias Island. Those who died in the chopper crash were bringing a medical clinic to a remote village. Even though the captain of *Kanimbla* and his crew were devastated by this loss, they did extremely well in recovering and treating their injured mates and caring for the remains of those who had died. As well as coping with this tragedy — as I expected — the *Kanimbla* and embarked medical staff got on with the job of helping the people of Nias.

In what was certainly the saddest week of my time as CDF, we received home the bodies of these great young Australians in a moving ceremony at Sydney airport. President Susilo Bambang Yudhyono of Indonesia was visiting Australia during that time and attended the ceremony at the airport. He acted with great dignity and was obviously profoundly moved by the terrible sense of loss we felt and very impressed by the dignity and courage of all the loved ones present in their grief. It was perhaps that sacrifice on Nias Island and the moment of mourning at the airport as much as any other action by Australia that has drawn our two countries so much closer together. They were marvellous young people, some of whom I'd met and they remain sorely missed by all who knew them.

*

The chain of events that had started with the Boxing Day Tsunami was broken briefly for me on 29 December. Since April 2003, we had maintained a security detachment of infantry and light armoured vehicles in Baghdad in order to protect our diplomatic mission that was situated in modest and exposed premises in a suburb of the city. As time went by, the number of incidents challenging the security of our diplomats and soldiers started to rise. I recommended that we should move our diplomats into the heavily protected 'Green' or international zone in the centre of Baghdad where they would not be so exposed. The challenge was to continue to keep them safe in their original premises until contractors finished construction of a purpose-built Australian diplomatic compound inside the zone. We all had to grit our teeth and get on with it.

These security detachments (known as SECDET) did four-month tours of duty and comprised soldiers selected from the infantry and armoured units of the Regular Army, with a few individuals from other Corps. As my other duties allowed, every so often I would farewell these soldiers either just before they left or in some final stage of their training. Over time we developed a very intensive training programme for them and in many ways they must have been close to the best prepared soldiers we have ever sent anywhere. On 29 December, a Brisbane-based group was departing to become the latest SECDET. Lynne and I travelled to Brisbane to farewell them, not least because on this occasion Philip, our middle son, was among them. The group which had got them ready invited friends and relatives to assemble at the barracks located in the suburb of Enoggera in Brisbane.

On this day I wore civvies and we both attended as parents, without protocol or any other special consideration. We had about an hour with Philip and his mates before media representatives arrived to record the occasion and conduct on the spot interviews with soldiers and their loved ones. When this occurred, I went into a nearby building out of sight until the media left — there was no way I wanted Philip to have unnecessary public attention because of who his dad was, either then or while he was in Iraq. I was mildly amazed, but very gratified, that his identity remained private for the duration of his time in Iraq. Lynne and I were of course worried sick while he was away. I had both the advantage over other parents and the burden of knowing on a daily basis how SECDET were going, what they were up to and what dangers they were facing.

As it turned out, the SECDET of which Philip was a member had an extraordinarily challenging time with a number of incidents and attacks to cope with. In the worst of these attacks, a suicide bomber driving a large truck crammed with explosives attempted to smash his way through an earth-filled barricade to detonate his bomb flush up against the unfinished structure of the block of flats that the SECDET occupied. The barricade stopped his progress about 10 metres away from the shell of the building, so he blew himself and his truck up anyway.

An immense explosion engulfed the building. Thankfully, the barricade absorbed much of the blast. Fortuitously, the unfinished nature of the block of flats also helped occupants to survive — there was no window glass to be blown in and the concussion of the blast moved through and out of these open spaces rather than crushing and collapsing the building, which it probably would have done if the building had been finished. Philip and two other soldiers were on duty in one of these open spaces on an upper floor and were lucky to have not been seriously injured. One of Philip's mates recalled seeing him and another soldier enveloped in a giant orange flash and thinking, 'They're gone'. Although there were a number of minor injuries to other soldiers, including Philip, they all remained on duty. A warrant officer suffered an impact injury to his neck and needed to be evacuated back to Australia for treatment and recovery. To his enormous credit, as soon as he was fit, he returned immediately to Baghdad to finish his tour of duty.

The SECDET commander decided in the aftermath of this serious incident to let every one of his men and women phone Australia to reassure their loved ones that they were okay. Given the relatively few number of people this entailed, this was both a sensible and practical decision on his part. In due course, Philip phoned us at home in Canberra. The conversation went something like this: 'Dad, there's been a ...'; (me) 'I know, son!'; (Phil) 'and a big bomb ...'; (me) 'Yes, I know, son'; (Phil) 'and I've been slightly ...'; (me) 'I know, son'; (Phil) 'but I'm OK ...'; (me) 'I know, son'. This was the combat of Iraq. No trenches or dawn attacks, no steaming jungle or bunker systems, just a bunch of very determined and brave diggers interposing themselves between hidden and anonymous murderers and their helpless targets. A different war: all old soldiers ought to take their hat off to them.

I visited our people in the Gulf not very long after this incident. It was a special thrill when visiting the SECDET in Baghdad to see Philip in rude good health among this great cheery mob of infantry. That night in order for father and son to get about the only privacy available in the fort-like environment of the flats, he and I stood picket together on a machine-gun post overlooking a road going past. I hadn't done a machine-gun picket for many years, but I sort of remembered how, and I'm sure he was right up to scratch. My Special Forces bodyguard lurking not too far away was probably also quite good on the machine gun! Philip and his mates still had a while to go, but their morale was sky high and I had no doubts about them continuing to perform most professionally.

I remained keen for the diplomats to move into the Green Zone at the first available opportunity. I was relieved when they decided to move into temporary accommodation soon after, awaiting the completion of their purpose-built accommodation. The diplomats were now much safer, but we had to wait a little while longer to move our soldiers into military barracks in the Green Zone. The high danger of attacks on our diplomats and soldiers while they were outside the Green Zone, either moving or visiting some place, remained.

Once I was back in Australia, I rejoined Lynne in the ordinary role of all the other mums and dads and husbands and wives and kids and sweethearts, anxiously waiting until their loved one got home. For us, that day was 21 May 2005 in Brisbane. Although I'd taken pains to be as anonymous as possible when Philip left Australia, for his return I attended as part of the official reception group at Brisbane airport, in uniform as CDF. The local senior military officer asked me if I would like to be taken forward through the customs hall to meet the troops at the aircraft door. I declined because that would have been unfair on the other parents. Inevitably, some of the journalists attending to cover the return of these soldiers cottoned on to the fact that as well as a routine duty as CDF to welcome home some returning servicemen and women, on this occasion I had a special motive.

It was with relief and pride I watched Philip walking out of the customs hall. All I had to do initially was to keep myself from being bowled over by Philip's beautiful girlfriend, Lily, and Lynne, both of whom rushed forward to hug him to bits. After he disentangled himself from these deadly encounters, I gave him a bit of a hug myself and remembered back thirty-four years beforehand when my mother and my father, in uniform, met me at Sydney airport on my return from Vietnam. I seemed to recall a backbreaking hug from my dad on that occasion. Phil was actually in front, because in those days I didn't have a beautiful girlfriend!

20

Vale

IN LATE JANUARY 2005, an article appeared in a magazine based on an interview I had done with a journalist in late 2004. At one stage during a wide-ranging discussion, the journalist asked me about the future. I simply and directly stated that at the end of my three year contract as CDF — at midnight on the third of July 2005 — I would retire. When the article appeared, what amazed me most was that my intention to retire became the main and ongoing story! My decision to do so was simple and unequivocal, but the factors contributing to the decision were numerous.

In all of my time in the Australian Army, I had no master plan, no blueprint, no set piece career with discrete goals and timelines. Apart from the broad and continuous pleasure I had in serving, I had always kept my horizons quite short, only occasionally lifting my eyes a little more after Lynne and I married and we had kids. Even then, I had the air of a man who, having fallen from the top of the Empire State Building, exclaimed 'So far, so good!' as he passed each floor on the way down. I had progressed further up the ladder than I had ever dreamed. I had reached the top of my profession with only the possibility of more of the same. I had been in the Army for over thirty-seven years when I took over as CDF and my contract expiry would give me forty and a half years of service. I had never done anything else, never lived in the wider community as a private citizen with the freedoms, responsibilities and opportunities enjoyed by the vast majority of people outside the ADF. I was not 'pining' to be of that group, but curious about its lifestyle. Lynne and I had been very happily married for many years and she had been so marvellous in supporting me every step of the way, each day watching me sally forth like a kid with a new billy cart and patching me up when I got home. She had accepted so willingly and lovingly my absences, as well as the numerous commitments arising from my service that increased her burdens while bringing up the kids. They too had been fantastic — boisterous ratbags like most growing young men — but tremendously loving and obedient to their mum, and equally loving and forgiving of me. My family had done all of this unconditionally and with great good humour. I know that they would have supported me if I had wished to serve on, but I wanted to be on hand more as a husband and a father. As the boys entered adulthood, I was conscious that our time as father and sons in their exciting youth seemed to be flying past, so it seemed time to get on my parental bike!

I believe that, especially in the services, there is only one way to do any job and that is absolutely flat out with every atom of your skill, focus and energy. The platitude 'life is not a rehearsal' should also apply to jobs where you have responsibility and opportunity. Having been so lucky to become CDF, I wasn't about to sit back and admire the job. If I believed in the 'full on' approach as profoundly as I do, I must also concern myself that over time my energy and commitment might start to slip. I did not think that this would necessarily happen to me after three years, or even some undefined longer period, but I would probably not be the best judge of myself.

Next, I hoped to work with my fellow Chiefs in the most open and honest way in all respects, not least in informing their own natural aspirations and desire to peer into their own future. I wanted them keen, interested, positive and positively informed. For all of these reasons I made no secret of my intention to do three years in the job and retire. Specifically, I mentioned this intention to the Chiefs before I took over in July 2002, and from time to time as a reminder over the next three years. These reminders were never delivered in response to times of crisis when I might have been hot under the collar over some issue, but rather during our senior personnel planning conferences where we prepared succession options for the Minister for Defence. It may be that some of the Chiefs thought to themselves, 'I'll believe it when I see it!', but I suppose, in the end, seeing was believing.

In all of these reasons and the complexity of the relationships invoked by my staying or going, only one gave me pause for thought. My critics thought — among other shortcomings — that I was too close to the government. This was nonsense and misinterpreted my approach, which was not influenced by political preferences or personal ambition. I had a responsibility to be professionally close to any politician with whom I had a direct working relationship. The safety and the reputation of the men and women I commanded depended on the decisions of politicians and I had to do my best to shape those decisions for the common good of the ADF. Wouldn't it be terrible if men and women came to grief or were improperly supported because their CDF was running around preserving some self-conceived space between him and a political leader, to the detriment of trust and familiarity?

That aside, there is no doubt that I enjoyed the strong confidence of the government, as CDFs should if they are doing their job. For my part, I trusted them to take care of the ADF and to consider every use of the ADF with the welfare of our people in mind. I had affirmed several times that I would keep the Chiefs' contract dates lined up on mine so that when I left in the middle of 2005, the government would have all of the contenders at their fingertips. Despite my statements, there still seemed to be scepticism based on the notion that, as a favourite son of the government, I would stay for as long as I could. Nonetheless, I wanted to avoid the impression that I was bailing out or in some way leaving through discontent. A few fairly unsubtle references along those lines by me in the media took care of that possible perception and misinterpretation. So, there I was, finally entering my valedictory period.

Following this revelation of my approaching retirement, I was touched by how many people came up to me — many of whom that I hadn't met before — to express sadness that I was leaving and wishing me well in the future. They more than made up for the usual suspects who formed a small chorus line to give me a kick! Professionally, I was determined that my last five months or so would not turn into some form of 'extended lap of honour'. Together with my chief of staff, a brilliant officer, Colonel Angus Campbell, I plotted out the months ahead in a way which took into account the ordinary duties of the CDF and, near the end of my time, allowed me to capitalise on certain routine visits to say farewell to representative sections of the Navy, Army and Air Force.

One overseas visit that I was determined to make was to Gallipoli to commemorate the 90th anniversary of the landings at Anzac Cove. In acknowledging the growing significance of Anzac Day, a few years before, my predecessor, Chris Barrie, had negotiated with the Minister for Defence that wherever possible a three or four-star officer should be part of the Commonwealth delegation officiating at Anzac Day ceremonies at Gallipoli. I was the Chief of Army at the time; it would have been my turn to go next, so I thought it was a good rule! The Chief of Navy of the day, Vice Admiral David Shackleton — a good mate — realising that he would retire mid-year and that I would probably be CDF and therefore would have more opportunities to subsequently go to Gallipoli, asked if I would give him my 'spot'. I was happy to oblige. In the intervening years the demands of the CDF job had precluded me going and, as Anzac Day in 2005 approached, I kept my fingers crossed that no international event would pop up to prevent me from attending what for Australians in the services amounts to a moment of pilgrimage.

I had heard all the stories about how many thousands of Australians and New Zealanders congregated on the peninsula, but nothing really prepared me until I was there. Nothing can ready an Australian for the emotional impact of the atmosphere, the number of visitors and the ceremonies. On 24 April, Lynne and I, escorted by a Turkish army general and his wife, and with our little delegation trailing along, visited the battle sites where Australians and Kiwis and Turks fought so bravely and died in such numbers.

The terrain was incredibly difficult, especially for novice soldiers with crook maps as well as indifferent plans and senior leadership. This confirmation of all I'd read and studied offended my professional instincts. The 'muddling through' reaction to a poor plan with poor initial execution, has always been, and always will be, a 'soldier killer' tactic. It would make you weep to think of these wonderful young men, inexperienced, yet brave and resolute, clawing their way towards the deadly heights. In some ways their inexperience was both their downfall and the upliftment of the legend — more experienced troops would probably have balked.

If you closed your eyes on 24 and 25 April 2005, and just listened to the voices of what has in modern times become the annual 'new invasion' of Gallipoli, the rich accents and phrasing of our countrymen and women rolled around those deadly gullies and terrible spur lines in echo of our departed heroes. Turks too in their many thousands return on these days to honour the extraordinary courage of the Turkish soldiers in defending their homeland. In the camaraderie and easy respect between the visiting Aussies and Kiwis and these modern Turkish tourists is both balm and comfort to the memory of those who fought over the Gallipoli wilderness. As I travelled the battlefield, times without number, fellow Aussies spotted my slouch hat and then there would ensue the most exuberant and affectionate greetings, gossip and photo opportunities.

Of course in 2005 there was a fair degree of consternation about roadworks passing through the landing beaches. I've been to quite a few battlefields around the world, from Waterloo to Gettysburg, and in every case even the most reverent and attentive administrations have been compelled to improve the infrastructure, such as roads, to accommodate the explosion in tourism — a feature of affluent and literate societies. Simply, works of that scope were necessary to allow many thousands of people to properly experience the 'pilgrimage' to Gallipoli on the one day. I would rather have those works, which enabled a large crowd to assemble, than have people dissuading others from going because of the difficulties of gaining access for the various memorial services.

The Australian official party along with those of other nations stayed overnight at Cannakale, a town across the Dardanelles on the Asiatic side, or rather for the few hours of the night before starting the journey to Anzac Cove for the dawn service. After buses, a ferry and then more buses, we alighted just short of the Cove and walked through the darkness into the amphitheatre effect of many thousands of people crammed into every available piece of flat ground and tiered seating. Some intrepid souls had even scaled the first cliff-like slopes off the beach. The dawn service was most moving — a service deftly honouring all the combatants. Silently at sea, about where the troopships would have dispatched those first Anzacs, the presence of the Navy frigate HMAS *Anzac* represented all the men and women of the ADF.

After the dawn service, the official party moved off to a place a short bus ride away to wait for the several hours before the Australian commemorative service got underway at the Lone Pine War Cemetery. The Australian attacks on Lone Pine and our subsequent defence of the position were overall the most ferocious battles of the Australian campaign, a campaign where bloody battles and high casualties were commonplace. The actual ground over which these battles were fought is quite tiny; perhaps a couple of tennis courts in dimension. One end of this battlefield is now framed by a dignified and beautifully stark memorial with the names of the fallen inscribed. The flat space leading up to it is dotted with individual headstones. On Anzac Day, tiered seating is arranged around the remaining three open sides of the Lone Pine site. The service at Lone Pine is the main, exclusively Australian, service on Anzac Day. Consequently, the crowd was overwhelmingly Aussie.

Back at the waiting area one of the Prime Minister's minders sidled up to me and remarked that it was still some time before the PM and entourage (which included my little group) was due to arrive and then of course the ceremony would get under way immediately. She said that the PM had it in mind to sneak off early with minimum protocol and minders to say hello to the crowd at Lone Pine and did I want to go with him. I jumped at the chance to imbibe the atmosphere before the solemnity of the service, so before you could say 'Jack Robinson' I was sitting in a Turkish police car leading the PM's car up to Lone Pine.

I am so glad this happened; the experience there was unforgettable. The cold weather at the dawn service had warmed up a little, ushering in a bright, sunny day. When the PM and I arrived, we had to squeeze through the space between a couple of the tiered-seating stands, packed with Australians. As some in the mob turned their heads to see what was happening, a murmur growing to a roar greeted the instantly recognisable figure of John Howard. In those circumstances politics go out the window and the crowd was just thrilled to see their Prime Minister on this very special Australian occasion. I was in full uniform, crowned with the ubiquitous slouch hat, so I was recognised too.

The PM dived into the crowd in one direction and I went in the other. The whole place was absolutely teeming, every seat in the stands was full, the steps in the stands were full, and the flat space was full to overflowing. Most people, who had spent many hours outdoors, were rugged up and an Aussie theme predominated in their dress. There was a little bit of carping in the media later on about them standing or sitting on the graves — they had to, there was no other space. I'm sure the ghosts of the men in the graves would have cheered them on rather than have them miss this chance to commemorate the feats and sacrifices of their countrymen. The people were exuberant, high-spirited, irreverent and wonderfully affectionate to each other, to the day and to me. I felt in some ways they were channelling the admiration and affection Gallipoli invoked for our ancestors on to me, the nearest bloke they had in a uniform.

We engaged in a bit of chiacking backwards and forwards with one section of the crowd in one of the stands. In my usual booming voice (one or two journos have commented on this 'booming' so it must be true!), I told them that at the dawn service I thought the Kiwis had out-sung us on the national anthems — I had been surrounded by Kiwis that morning — and that we should really let it rip on *Advance Australia Fair* at the end of the service. They promised to sing the birds out of the trees. A beautiful service that was for Australians, conducted by Australians and in a place sacred to Australians was ended with an anthem, sent soaring into the Turkish sky, in a moment I will never forget.

The next couple of months were hectic — certainly never dull — but not dramatic. I made a final visit to the troops in the Gulf and found — as I always had — that they were in very good shape.

Every time I visited I came away uplifted, not least because they always made a point of telling me that, in their view, Australia was making a real contribution to the rehabilitation of Iraq. By now we had a contingent serving in southern Iraq protecting Japanese military engineers carrying out humanitarian work in Al Muthana Province. These men and women were based on a cavalry regiment and they had settled in very well. Sensibly they had established friendly relations with many of the influential Iraqi leaders in the vicinity. As I farewelled them, I knew that they would continue to do very well until eventually they could be replaced by Iraqi Army units that another contingent was in the process of training.

In late May I attended my last Senate Estimates, the routine mid-year session of the Senate Legislative Committee. These hearings go over several days and provide opportunities for senators, almost invariably non-government senators, to grill ministers and their bureaucrats on portfolio issues. The original intent of this committee process was to examine budgetary issues and those actions and plans impinging directly upon the Defence budget. Of more recent years, the focus of the sessions has shifted to encompass virtually any aspect of political or public interest in the portfolio. At times these sessions can become adversarial. On numerous occasions, members of the committee have ignored important issues related to such matters as Army training, Defence Science and Technology, or indeed the budget, in order to thrash away for days on a single issue, looking to wring every last drop of political and media advantage out of it. The Minister, the Secretary and CDF sitting permanently at the witness table, just had to 'wear it'.

This single-issue focus wasted the time of scores of senior officers and officials from Defence waiting very patiently in seats behind us for their programmed moment to speak about other quite significant matters. This form of political battle is now a fact of life, but not an attractive or comfortable one. Often while some senator had been thundering away on a pseudo-inquisition — my term for putting the boot in — they had drifted into unsubstantiated criticism of men and women serving in the ADF who were not in the room to defend themselves. At these times it was not unknown for me to murmur a few words of admonishment.

Finally, the clock ticked around to the programmed finish time for my last appearance before a Senate Estimates session. As the dust settled from the usual verbal fencing, Senator Mark Bishop, Opposition spokesman on Veterans Affairs, made very warm remarks about me, noting that it was my last appearance before the committee. He was followed in the same vein by the Chairman. I sought the opportunity for a brief reply quoted here from *Hansard*, which sums up this aspect of the way I saw my job:

Gen Cosgrove: Thank you. I wonder if I could make a very brief reply. I thank all members of the Legislative Committee for their generous thoughts on the eve of my retirement — 33 days to go today! I thank you for putting up with my occasional agitation, as I think it has been described, Senator Faulkner —

Senator Faulkner: I have never noticed it!

Gen Cosgrove: and my occasional intemperate language. If I do have a flaw, it is that I feel, and always have done, fiercely protective of the people I have the honour to command, albeit only for a few more days. I do very much respect the parliamentary process and would like to leave on the note that, even when from time to time I become a little churlish, I do at that moment also acknowledge the very important nature of parliamentary scrutiny of what we do. So thank you to the committee.

Committee adjourned at 9:03 p.m.

The main excitement of the month of June was the announcement of who would replace me and who would retire and who would get the other top jobs in the Defence Force. Of course I had given the government my 'two bob's worth' on this, but the government makes it own decision. I was delighted with the outcome. Angus Houston was a great choice to be CDF, in all respects. Popular, very smart and experienced both in the Canberra environment and in command and operational areas, genuine in his concern and care for people, and blessed with a marvellously involved and caring wife, Liz. I thought Angus was the right man for the job. Equally, I was delighted that my able and extremely hard-working Vice Chief, Russ Shalders, remained in harness as the Chief of Navy. At the senior level, the ADF has, both now and in the future, an embarrassment of riches — I won't mention any other names for fear of being accused of being an urger!

Late in June there was the usual round of farewell dinners and speeches and mass assemblies on ships and in bases and barracks. I think you could say that my attitude to all of these occasions was a goodly mixture of enjoyment and nostalgia as I said my farewells and then left these young men and women to their further careers. I also had feelings of unmatched enjoyment and satisfaction at the privilege of having been given the opportunity to serve Australia in this special way.

Every farewell was memorable but that from the Australian Army at Lavarack Barracks in Townsville was special because so many men and women I had worked with over the years somehow found their way there and the Army had brought my two soldier sons, Philip and David, up for the farewell. The Chief of Army, Lieutenant General Peter Leahy, showed the deft touch that characterises his whole command of the Army in providing a farewell that so honoured an old soldier. Their Excellencies the Governor General and Mrs Jeffery also gave Lynne and me a farewell dinner, which was a great honour coming from a deeply respected former colleague, now the Commander in Chief.

Another farewell which had special significance for Lynne and me was a dinner held in our honour by the Prime Minister and Mrs Howard at the Lodge. Attending the dinner were the Minister for Defence, Robert Hill, and his wife, Diana, Ric Smith, the Secretary, and his wife, Jan, and the service Chiefs and the Vice Chief and their wives. Around me there were the men who had been extraordinarily close and who had relied on each other profoundly over the last three years. All of us had had our ups and downs in that time, yet this was a strong and enormously successful team that had coped admirably with every security and humanitarian challenge — as well as the occasional scandal — that had come our way.

For my entire time as CDF, Robert Hill had been the Minister and two more unalike people you would struggle to find. And yet I have enormous regard for him. He was forensic, painstaking and wonderfully observant, with a memory like an elephant. He would occasionally drive me nearly to despair in his dogged pursuit of some detail of an issue, but this dedication to detail was a token of his drive for mastery of the matters that came before him. In this, he was not only right but he showed a tremendous capacity for work which would have floored a less capable politician. I remember on one occasion, a couple of years into our time together, when he remarked with a grin that he was starting to get the hang of all these acronyms and abbreviations and jargon we used in the Defence Force. Then he gave me a look when I grumped that now we'd have to change them all. I hope he knew I was joking! Hill was an extraordinarily powerful and effective voice for Defence in the corridors of the Parliament and in the Cabinet. I know that he was genuinely honoured to be the political leader of Defence and, like many of us who knew him, I liked and respected him a great deal.

The Prime Minister and I had a unique relationship. Unique certainly in that no other two people in the Commonwealth will look each other in the eye when a crucial question of national interest and the consequent actions and safety of the men and women of the ADF are in the balance. Of course, the Defence Minister shares these moments, but it's always the Prime Minister who carries the can. For nearly six years I had been the keenest participant in and student of the weight of these issues and the way in which John Howard has dealt with them. If history and those who write it are true to the facts, they will join me in the assessment that he has been a truly great leader in the face of adversity and challenge. He shows an extraordinary grasp of the import and the risks of the use of military power and he combines this with an unerring ability to connect at a personal level with the men and women of the Defence Force. Personally, Lynne and I have always got on very well with the Howards and I hope we always will.

For months I had been batting off various plans and schemes to have a formal farewell parade with troops, bands, fly pasts by aircraft and attendance by an array of dignitaries. My predecessors had set these precedents. I became quite grumpy and very vigilant in this regard. I am sure some of my staff wondered if this was the same man who was reputed by some of the more adoring journalists as always ready to 'attend the opening of an envelope'. In the end I told a couple of my staff that they just didn't get it. The public attention I had accepted — and sometimes sought when I had a message to pass — was to do with the job, not the man. To me it was somehow fitting that in these final moments of authority I should strive to act as the person I always felt I was — an ordinary soldier giving it a go. I just about got my way. I agreed that, on Friday, 1 July, my last day at the office, I would leave the main building of Russell Offices accompanied by Lynne at 11.30 a.m. sharp and pause on the veranda of the building to say farewell to my colleagues and speak briefly over a PA system to anybody from the office complex who wanted to come to say farewell. Then I would depart and the Royal Military College Band could play me out up the road with some rousing tunes.

It worked pretty much that way, except that — as I expected — some media representatives found out and lobbed up for the moment. At the microphone I said my thanks to all those who had gathered and a special word of thanks to my friend Ric Smith and expressed my delight in the new team led by Angus Houston. A final word of my love for the girl by my side and then it was, 'Wish me luck as you wave me goodbye'. Then came the top secret bit that was only known to my personal staff. I went to the War Memorial to lay a wreath on the tomb of the Unknown Soldier — a very private moment. Then it was a final, emotional farewell to my magnificent personal staff and then home for an early knock off! That night I had the enormous privilege at a formal dinner at Duntroon where I had started over forty years before, to promote Angus Houston, to Air Chief Marshal — four-star — the top rank in the military.

That was my last official act although I was still in harness until midnight on Sunday, 3 July. Nothing happened as the hours ticked by and I still don't know if I was relieved or disappointed. At a minute to midnight on Sunday, I called the duty officer at our Command Centre deep in the bowels of Russell Offices, probably much to his surprise, and asked if all was quiet? He said it was. I then said to him that I was signing off as CDF and wished him good luck. He returned the wish. I put down the phone, the clock ticked over and the great work of the Australian Defence Force went on.

Epilogue

BEFORE I RETIRED FROM the Army, all my respected predecessors counselled me to refrain from accepting overtures and offers of employment, paid or otherwise, for about six months. It sounded like very good advice — and I intended to take it — but there are offers and then there are offers! On Monday, 4 July 2005, at about 9 a.m., I was in the kitchen of our home in Canberra, a newly retired fifty-seven year old, contemplating both an empty bottle of champagne — the result of a midnight toast to the past by Lynne and me — and an uncertain future. The phone rang and it was Margaret Jackson, the Chairman of the Qantas Board of Directors, calling to offer me an appointment as a Director. I thought about it for a nano-second before saying, 'Yes!' (So much for all the advice.) Later that same week I accepted a consultancy with Deloitte to help with mentoring and developing leaders within the company. The uncertain future started to crystallise into the busy present.

Epilogue

Qantas is not only an iconic company, but an enormously vibrant and exciting corporate environment. The very nature of commercial aviation is highly contemporary, competitive and operational. Yet it is necessarily an enterprise where vision and strategy are vital because technology and market trends must be predicted and responses planned and acted upon with years of preparation. I have enjoyed enormously being a part of the company and being on the Board, surrounded by experienced Directors as the company deals effectively with a daunting array of challenges.

At Deloitte, I've mixed with younger executives either in, or contemplating, leadership positions. It's a lot of fun to 'de-mystify' the challenge of leading others by drawing on a very long career of getting it wrong and then getting it right. They are a great bunch in Deloitte — aggressive and ambitious — and the CEO, Giam Swiegers, is ardent about the difference that great teams led by committed leaders can make to competitive outcomes. To a fair degree, my involvement with these two companies replaces the void left by my departure from daily contact with the men and women of the ADF.

In addition to these early and ongoing commitments, I have taken on roles with the Sir John Monash Foundation, the Board of Qantas Superannuation Limited and an advisory role within the Fosters Group. I am Chairman of the Defence Industry Advisory Board in South Australia and recently became a Councillor of the Australian War Memorial. I am also involved one way and another with a number of charities. There's not as much spare time as I'd dreamed of!

Notwithstanding my new commitments, there is always time for my family. Both of the Cosgrove boys who were in the Army have ceased full-time service, although one remains in the Reserve. I admired greatly their time in uniform. It wasn't always easy for them to be diggers when their dad was senior and well known. They handled it very well, even when there was a brief flurry of nasty, inaccurate and personally directed reporting concerning one of them a number of months after my retirement, 'justified' on the basis that as I was public figure, so were they. Not all mums and dads would agree with this proposition. One of the great joys of this part of our lives is that Lynne and I can be more closely involved with our adult kids, without some of the pressures and concerns of the past few years.

Having settled into my new life, on the evening of Monday, 20 March 2006, I was sitting at home with Lynne, minding my own business, happy to think that the manuscript for my book (necessarily less this epilogue!) was in the hands of the publisher. The news of the day was full of reports of a severe cyclone, 'Larry', which had hit Far North Queensland around Innisfail in the early pre-dawn hours. While miraculously nobody was thought to have died, and even injuries were minimal, there had been tremendous damage to homes, infrastructure and the economy, especially crops. It was by any measure a major natural disaster and coming not long after Hurricane Katrina in the USA, government disaster relief and further responses were in the spotlight. The phone rang and it was Wayne Goss, former Premier of Queensland and now the Chairman of Deloitte, calling to say that the Premier of Queensland, Peter Beattie, had asked for my phone number and was going to call me very soon. Wayne and I speculated very briefly about what he might want, but it was obvious to both of us. Soon after, the Premier phoned and asked me to take charge of the recovery effort and, with an exchange of rueful glances and immediate acquiescence between Lynne and me, there was only one answer: 'Yes. When do you want me?'

Later that week I was in Innisfail, which was right in the cyclone's destructive path, at the start of a job, which continues today, of coordinating the recovery activities to help the community get back on its feet. For over three months I lived in the region, with occasional trips away for Board meetings and the like. Now I'm home, but I visit the Far North quite often to ensure the recovery remains on track. It's difficult to focus on positives when so many people's lives and livelihoods have been damaged, but the disaster brought to me, and to anybody who would look, a reminder of some of our most precious national characteristics: the stoicism and courage and good humour of Australians in adversity; their sense of community and cohesion and selflessness when the chips are down (they'll always tell you of someone doing it tougher when you are commiserating with them!); and their indomitable stamina and determination to put things right. Nothing was more indicative of this spirit than a sign I saw on the side of a collapsed house near Innisfail on the day I arrived — 'Just Larried'. It has been a privilege of the highest order to watch them triumph.

This story and the Cosgrove family story go on, even though the story of the soldier finished at midnight on 3 July 2005. There is still in life enough to occupy us all, challenges to be overcome, rights to be upheld, needs to be met, potential to be achieved, values to be lived. Like all of you, our future is full of mystery and promise. In all of this, I am that most fortunate of creatures — I have a loving family and I live in Australia.

Thank you for reading *My Story*.

Acknowledgements

There's generally only one book, if any, in an old soldier. Like a thank you speech at the Oscars, if behoves the warrior–author to be heartfelt, sensitive and pithy — more difficult than it appears! 'Oscars-like', I could thank anyone I've ever met; for me that would mean the men and women who are in *My Story*, especially those of the ADF across the decades and, of course, I do thank them, for there would a very different story without them.

While undoubtedly writing a book has a mechanical and technical quotient, it is essentially of the spirit. Authors are either manically preoccupied writing or, like charged atoms, virtually impossible to bring to the molecule of their computer keyboard. I was both, and grumpy and exhilarated and broadly inattentive to the rest of our family life during the time it took to get the words down, so my greatest and first acknowledgement is to Lynne, whose love, tolerance and unflagging support allowed me my Bohemian moments.

I would like to thank Robert Joske, who has been my friend and business adviser during the process, and HarperCollins for agreeing to publish *My Story*. It was a leap of faith for them to take on the project. When in August 2005, needing a manuscript by 1 March 2006, they learnt that I had not yet put pen to paper, but had set aside 'December, January and February' to write the book, they continued to smile and I was glad we were together on the project! In particular I would like to thank Shona Martyn, Alison Urquhart, my very calm, kind and able editor Lydia Papandrea, Christina Lee, and all of HarperCollins.

Acknowledgements

My researcher was an old friend and Army colleague, Colonel Bob Breen, himself an accomplished and widely known and read author. Bob was immensely helpful in not only keeping me straight on facts, sequencing and dates, but in offering most helpful editorial advice. If there are errors of time, place, event or identity, then of course they are mine! I am most grateful to Angus Houston, the CDF, and to Ric Smith, the Secretary of the Department, for their help in checking the manuscript for security faux pas and to the myriad of Defence photographers for their brilliant camerawork and for permission to use their photos.

My Story has my name on it, but like most things in my life, it is truly a team effort. Thanks, team.

Glossary

ADC Aide-de-camp. A junior officer who is a personal assistant to a senior military officer.

amphibious operation An operation in which land forces are landed and supported from the sea as a combat operation prepared to meet armed opposition. A landing from the sea by helicopter and/or landing craft to secure an area for the development of further operations.

armoured personnel carrier A tracked or wheeled armoured vehicle that is designed to carry troops tactically on operations with armoured protection and to provide some fire support and immediate logistic support.

batman (military) A valet to a military officer, normally an experienced private soldier or junior NCO, who in barracks and in the field will prepare an officer's uniforms, meals and accommodation, and carry out other tasks as directed.

battalion An approximately 800–1000 strong subdivision of a 1500–3000 brigade of soldiers, usually led by a lieutenant colonel consisting of three or more companies of 120–140 soldiers led by majors.

battery (artillery) The technical and administrative artillery unit or a sub-unit corresponding to a company or sub-unit in other corps of the army. Typically, it comprises a group of six or more guns or howitzers of the same calibre.

brassard Arm band showing a designation, logo or symbol.

brigade An approximately 1500–3000 strong military unit consisting of two or more combat battalions and/or regiments as well as associated support units.

cavalry regiment In times past, the term 'cavalry' was used to describe soldiers who moved and fought from horseback. Nowadays, the term is used for personnel who move and fight from light armoured vehicles. A cavalry regiment is comprised of several squadrons of armoured fighting vehicles and support vehicles. Modern conventional roles are to conduct reconnaissance and screening and transport operations, as well as skirmish with forward enemy elements and conduct raids.

CDF Chief of the Defence Force. A 4-star (Admiral, General, Air Chief Marshal) senior officer from the Navy, Army or Air Force who commands the Australian Defence Force.

CGS Chief of the General Staff. Title of a 3-star senior Army officer (Lieutenant General) who commanded the Army until the appointment title changed to Chief of Army in the mid-1990s.

chief of staff The senior or principal member or head of a staff, or the principal assistant in a staff capacity to a person in a command capacity; head or controlling member of a staff, for the purposes of the coordination of its work.

claymore (mine) An anti-personnel mine designed to be positioned low to the ground on pegs facing an expected enemy approach and exploded remotely through an electric cable.

coalition operation An operation conducted by forces from one or more nations, which may or may not be allies, acting together for the accomplishment of a single mission.

cantonment A large military training camp or temporary accommodation for troops, especially the winter quarters of an army.

combat forces Military forces designed, trained and equipped with weapons to apply combat power — the total means of destructive and/or disruptive force which military units/formations can apply against hostile forces at a given time. For land forces, they comprise force elements from armour, artillery, infantry and engineer corps.

command The authority which a commander in military service lawfully exercises over subordinates, by virtue of rank or assignment. Command includes the authority and responsibility for effectively using available resources, and planning and conducting military operations for the accomplishment of assigned missions. It also includes responsibility for health, welfare, morale and discipline of assigned personnel.

company An approximately 100–140 strong subdivision of an 800-plus battalion of soldiers, usually led by a major consisting of three or more platoons of 30–35 soldiers led by lieutenants or second lieutenants.

Corps (military) a. Military personnel who work together and are associated by their specialisation and function within armed forces. b. An approximately 30,000–40,000 strong tactical formation comprised of two or more divisions with additional supporting formations and units.

DJFHQ Deployable Joint Force Headquarters.

division (land forces) An approximately 10,000–15,000 strong self-contained military formation in an army that is capable of sustained operations, including a headquarters and two or more brigades.

exercise Military manoeuvre in a simulated wartime operation involving planning, preparation and execution. It is carried out for the purpose of training and evaluation. It may be a combined, a joint or single Service exercise depending on participating organisations. A field exercise is an activity conducted in the field under simulated war conditions in which troops and armaments on one side are actually present, and those on the other side may be imaginary or in outline.

FALINTIL Forças Armadas de Libertação Nacional de Timor-Leste (Armed Forces for the National Liberation of East Timor), the pro-independence East Timorese guerrilla army.

fatigue uniform Loose-fitting, strongly-woven clothing intended to be worn during hard manual labour and for prolonged periods in the field.

field artillery Ground-based artillery weapons (guns) designed primarily for the engagement of ground targets by indirect fire, classified by method of movement and calibre as follows: a. Pack, towed or self-propelled. b. Light — up to 120 mm. c. Medium — 121 mm to 160 mm d. Heavy — 161 mm to 210 mm. During the Vietnam War, the Royal Australian Artillery operated towed 105 mm field guns and 105 mm howitzers.

footprint (military) An informal military term to describe both the area occupied by and impact on the local situation of a deployed military force.

force elements The collective term for assembled and assigned military groupings of ships and vessels, sub-units and units, and aircraft that comprise a military force.

Fretelin Frente Revolucionária de Timor-Leste Independente (Revolutionary Front for an Independent East Timor), a pro-independence political party.

GAM Gerakin Aceh Merdeka (GAM) — Free Aceh Movement.

giggle hat Loose-fitting, strongly-woven head dress with a brim, designed for wearing during hard physical labour and in the field.

gunner A soldier who operates a large gun, typically a soldier in an artillery regiment, especially a private. Often used as an adjective or collective noun to describe military personnel from the artillery corps.

guidon A regimental flag or pennant, or the soldier who carries it.

Huey (helicopter) Slang for UHIB and UHIH utility helicopters commonly used by American and allied forces during the Vietnam War.

ICB Infantry Combat Badge.

INTERFET International Force East Timor.

joint support unit A grouping of communications personnel and equipment designed to manage and enable communication for a military formation on operations.

joint task force A grouping of assigned force elements from two or three Services (Navy, Army and Air Force) assigned to accomplish designated missions.

joint warfare Conduct of military operations involving force elements from two or three Services (Navy, Army and Air Force).

lodgment A small area of land that has been captured and held on the edge of enemy territory; establishing a foothold in enemy territory.

movements Military noun or adjective for tactical changes in the position or location of military units, as well as the act of changing location and position.

NBC (munitions) Nuclear, Biological and Chemical.

NCO Non-Commissioned Officer.

NGO Non-Government Organisation, typically an organisation that delivers humanitarian aid overseas.

NDC National Defence College.

node A terminal or other point in a computer network or deployed organisation where messages can be created, received or repeated.

NVA North Vietnamese Army.

ordnance Military weapon systems, including supplies for their use and equipment for their maintenance. Also, the army corps that has responsibility for managing weapons and supplies.

PKF Peacekeeping Force.

platoon An approximately 30–35 strong subdivision of a 100-plus company of soldiers, usually led by a lieutenant, consisting of three or more sections/squads of 8 or 10 soldiers led by corporals.

platoon lines The lines of tents or buildings that accommodate a platoon.

RAMSI Regional Assistance Mission Solomon Islands. An approximately 2500-strong regional peacekeeping force deployed to the Solomon Islands in 2003.

RAR Royal Australian Regiment.

regiment A battalion-sized unit about 800–1000 strong, normally commanded by a lieutenant colonel.

RPG Rocket Propelled Grenade.

rubber duckies Military nickname for dinghies with large inflatable tyre-like gunwales.

Rules of Engagement Directives issued by a competent military authority which specify the circumstances and limitations under which Australian forces will initiate and/or continue combat engagement with other forces encountered.

sapper A military engineer, typically a soldier serving in an engineer regiment, especially a private. Often used as an adjective or collective noun to describe military personnel from the engineer corps.

SAS Special Air Service.

screening (military) a. The temporary detention or stopping of persons, vehicles or vessels for the purpose of searching them for prohibited items such as weapons and ammunition. b. A force deployed forward, whether the covering force is out or not, for the immediate protection of the main defended position, to give warning and prevent enemy observations and reconnaissance of the forward edge of a battle area.

section A junior leader and small team of about 10 personnel. Typically, a section is a small group of infantry, led by a section commander with the rank of corporal. In the artillery, a section is a grouping of two guns and their crews.

Service Assisted Evacuation An evacuation of Australian nationals and other approved persons by the ADF in a permissive environment with the support of local authorities, who are in control of the situation.

Service Protected Evacuation An evacuation of Australian nationals and other approved persons by the ADF in a non-permissive environment opposed by hostile groups and possibly without the support of local authorities who may have lost control of the situation.

squadron a. A naval unit containing two or more divisions of a fleet. b. An element of a tactical air force belonging to a group and containing one or more flights. c. A tank or armoured cavalry unit belonging to a regiment and containing one or more troops.

Special Forces Specially selected military personnel, trained in a broad range of basic and specialised skills, organised, equipped and trained to conduct special operations. Special forces can be employed to achieve strategic, operational and tactical level objectives across the operational continuum.

special operations Measures and activities outside the scope of conventional forces conducted by specially trained, organised and equipped forces to achieve military, political, economic or psychological objectives. These operations may be conducted during peacetime, conflict and war, independently or in conjunction with conventional forces.

terminal operations Activities at a transportation facility used for the loading, unloading and in transit handling of cargo and personnel.

troop A small group of soldiers and vehicles/guns that forms a subdivision of a tank or cavalry squadron that is about the size of a platoon. Typically there are four tanks in a tank troop and four light armoured vehicles in a cavalry troop.

UNAMET United Nations Assistance Mission East Timor.

UNHCR United Nations High Commissioner for Refugees.

UNTAET United Nations Transitional Authority East Timor.

Index

Index

Index

Index

Index

Portugal, East Timor and, 218, 247, 265, 286–87, 293, 310
Power, Ash (Colonel), 153
prisoner mistreatment (Abu Ghraib), 403–7
public profile *see* media
Puckapunyal, Vic., 1–2
punishments, 38–39, 73, 94

Q
Qantas, 444, 445

R
RAAF *see* Air Force
racing, 12–14 *see also* Melbourne Cup
Ramos-Horta, José, 266–68, 275, 292
RAMSI (Regional Assistance Mission to the Solomon Islands), 391–92
RAN *see* Navy
ranks
  Cosgrove's progression
    lieutenant, 56, 106
    captain, 106, 110
    major, 115, 124
    lieutenant colonel, 128
    colonel, 135
    brigadier, 136–37, 143, 149, 313
    major general, 143, 146, 150, 277, 318
    lieutenant general, 323
    general, 352
  peace enforcement operations, 279–82
  staff & commands, 172–73
Rapid Deployment Force, 170, 179
Ready Reserve, 136–37
Red Cross (Abu Ghraib scandal), 404–7
refugees *see* displaced persons & refugees (East Timor); illegal immigration
Regional Assistance Mission to the Solomon Islands (RAMSI), 391–92
regional forces *see* multinational forces
regional role of Defence Force, 361–62, 364–65, 388–92, 394 *see also* East Timor; Pacific region
Reith, Peter (Minister for Defence, 2001), 341–42, 377
Remembrance Day ceremonies (East Timor), 260–62
reporting, military, 196–99, 341–42, 373–75
Reserve *see* Army Reserve; Ready Reserve
retirement of Peter Cosgrove, ix, 297, 428–32, 439–43
  later employment, 444–45
Rhodesia (Zimbabwe), 294
Ritchie, Chris, 350
Robertson, Brian (Commodore), 226–28, 314–15
Robertson Barracks *see* Darwin

Roy and HG, 290
Royal Australian Air Force *see* Air Force
Royal Australian Navy *see* Navy
Royal Australian Regiment
  1st Battalion (1 RAR), 46–47, 49–63, 92, 128–31, 177, 298–99, 394
  2nd/4th Battalion (2/4 RAR), 129
  2nd Battalion (2 RAR), 298–99, 391
  3rd Battalion (3 RAR), 51–52, 199, 299–300, 302–7, 325–26, 329–30
  4th Battalion (4 RAR), 357
  5th/7th Battalion (5/7 RAR), 243–46, 294, 300, 303
  5th Battalion (5 RAR), 70, 109–11, 124
  6th Battalion (6 RAR), 47, 70, 300, 394, 407–8
  8th Battalion (8 RAR), 92
  9th Battalion (9 RAR), 70–96
  commemorative service, 322
rugby
  Cosgrove's schooldays, 16, 21, 23–24, 43–44
  Cosgrove at Duntroon, 42–45
  Cosgrove's Army experience, 110, 118–23
  Cosgrove's sons, 137–39
  international, 138–39, 259–60, 297
Russell, Andrew (Sergeant), 345
Ryamizard (General), 420

S
Saddam Hussein *see* Iraq
Saleh (batman), 59
Salter, John, 56–57
Sampaio, Jorge (President of Portugal), 310
Sanderson, John, 148
SAS *see* Special Forces
school cadets *see* Cadet Corps
School of the Air, 336–37
schools *see* education
Sea King helicopter crash, 421–22
SECDET (security detachments, Baghdad), 423–25
security *see* law and order
Senate *see* Parliament
September 11, 2001 attacks & response, 338–40, 343, 345–47, 354 *see also* terrorism
Service Chiefs, 320, 430–32, 439–40
  government relations, 328
  retired, 335
Shackleton, David (Vice Admiral), 432
Shalders, Russ (Vice Admiral, Vice Chief of the Defence Force), 350–51, 374, 387, 439
Shergold, Peter, 417
Shinseki, Rick (General), 338–39

Index